Revolutionary Patriots

of

Harford County

Maryland

1775-1783

Henry C. Peden, Jr.

HERITAGE BOOKS
2008

HERITAGE BOOKS
AN IMPRINT OF HERITAGE BOOKS, INC.

Books, CDs, and more—Worldwide

For our listing of thousands of titles see our website
at
www.HeritageBooks.com

Published 2008 by
HERITAGE BOOKS, INC.
Publishing Division
100 Railroad Ave. #104
Westminster, Maryland 21157

Copyright © 1985, 1987 Henry C. Peden, Jr.

All rights reserved. No part of this book may be reproduced or transmitted in any form or by any means, electronic or mechanical, including photocopying, recording or by any information storage and retrieval system without written permission from the author, except for the inclusion of brief quotations in a review.

International Standard Book Numbers
Paperbound: 978-1-58549-208-4
Clothbound: 978-0-7884-7227-5

TABLE OF CONTENTS

Preface..iii

Introduction......................................v

Sources and Documentation Key...................vi

Revolutionary Patriots...........................1

Militia Company Captains, 1775-1776............245

The Bush Declaration, March 22, 1775...........246

The Association of Freemen, 1775-1776..........247

The Oath of Allegiance, 1777-1778..............248

Addendum: More Revolutionary Patriots..........249

Surname Index..................................254

PREFACE

This compilation has been made with great care, and it has been the ambition of the author that those who refer to this book may be able to locate a Revolutionary War ancestor in Harford County, Maryland, from whom they can subsequently join The Sons of the American Revolution, The Daughters of the American Revolution, and other patriotic and hereditary organizations.

The more than 3,600 men named in this book rendered active service in the cause of American independence between 1775 and 1783, either as an officer, soldier, seaman, marine, militiaman, or minuteman in the armed forces of the Continental Congress, or any of the several colonies or States; or, served patriotically on Committees of War, Safety and Correspondence; or, held a Civil Office, such as Judge, Juror, Legislator, Sheriff, Town Clerk, and Surveyor; or, as recognized patriots, performed overt acts of resistance to the authority of Great Britain, such as the Signers of the Association of Freemen, the Signers of the Bush Declaration, the Signers of the Oath of Allegiance and Fidelity to Maryland, and one, William Paca, who signed the Declaration of Independence; as well as gunsmiths who gave their services, citizens who gave material aid, ministers who gave patriotic sermons, men who served as militia substitutes, and others who unfailingly opposed Great Britain during the Revolutionary War.

Careful research has been made to obtain all the essential data that was available for each man, which makes this book far more than just a list of names. In the case of officers, in a large majority of instances, it has been possible to establish the dates of their commissions, when they took their oaths of allegiance, their promotions, resignations, their companies, pay certificates, bounty lands, dates of birth, death and marriage, and names of their wives and children. Similar data is also included for privates, but all too frequently the only information available is the name of the soldier on a muster roll or pay roll. Likewise, the same holds true for those who signed the Oath of Allegiance and the Association of Freemen, and many signers were also soldiers.

The matter of variations in the spelling of names is always puzzling in all works of this kind. To assist the reader, a separate entry has been made for each name in the index. In the text itself, variations are included in parenthesis after the surname. As might be expected with common names, like John Smith, for example, it is difficult to determine just how many different men had the same name. Rest assured that every effort has been made to present an accurate accounting. Nonetheless, errors do creep in. Hopefully, they have been minimized. And while the facts in the lives of many of these patriots are quite meager, it should not be difficult to identify ancestors, even where little more than their names appear. The reader should bear in mind that Harford County was created from Baltimore County in 1773, just two years before the flames of revolution were ignited. Thus, many patriots have ties with both counties and this should be kept in mind when performing subsequent research.

The key to sources and documentation at the front of the alphabetical listing of the patriots will show where the information was located and extracted. All entries in this book are documented. Users of this book now have the names of the Revolutionary patriots of Harford County before them in a single volume.

Gratitude is extended to all those persons who have performed, and continue to perform, genealogical and historical research, and, more importantly, publish and disseminate that information. Thanks to Ella Rowe, Joseph Carroll Hopkins, Robert W. Barnes, Renna Ambrose, Jon Harlan Livezey, Esther Hannon, Edward J. Goodman, Jr., and countless others for their untiring endeavours and research prowess which, in fact, have made this book possible. A special thanks to my wife, Veronica Ann Peden, and my son, Henry Clint Peden, III, for allowing me the time and giving me the encouragement to do this book.

It is sincerely hoped that this work may prove of lasting value to the descendants of Harford County's Revolutionary War patriots.

HENRY C. PEDEN, JR.

May 8, 1985

NOTES ON REVISED EDITION

Susbequent research has led to some changes and additions to the original book which resulted in this revised edition in 1987 and 1991.

Thanks to Margaret Smith Keigler of Monkton, Maryland for information on the Baker, Baldwin, Bussey, Garrison, Guyon, Hitchcock, Howard, Holland, Miles and Tolley families; to Michael J. Neill of Carthage, Illinois for information on the Rampley and Demoss families; to Joan Hobbs Burge of Ventura, California for information on the McClelland and Montgomery families; and, to Shirley L. Reightler of Bel Air, Maryland for information from the Minutes of the Harford County Court (1778-1780) pertaining to the families of Coaleman, Crosby, Evans and Hendersides.

Also, subsequent research by this compiler for Elizabeth N. Grizzell of Paris, Tennessee on the Wheelers of Harford County, Maryland, led to the proof that Ignatius Wheeler, Jr. was the Colonel during the Revolutionary War and not his father, Ignatius Wheeler, Sr. The record has been changed accordingly. Other contributors have been cited within the text.

HENRY C. PEDEN, JR.

February 10, 1987 and October 1, 1991

INTRODUCTION

In a society that is growing and advancing as quickly as the one in which we live, it becomes very easy to forget to take the time to look back and see where we have come from and recognize the deeds and contributions of those who came before us. This is especially true in a community such as Harford County where the growth in population has been so phenomenal.

Very few people today know the active role that Harford County played in the American War for Independence.

In this volume, Henry Peden has taken a giant step toward correcting this problem. Anyone who uses this work for any purpose will be impressed by the magnitude of the project that Mr. Peden undertook and the outstanding quality of the final product. Through countless hours of research, he has produced a work that will be an invaluable contribution to our understanding of our county's revolutionary heritage and will serve as an essential basic reference for the historian and genealogist. Most importantly, this work at long last provides recognition for the efforts and accomplishments, both great and small, of the Harford County patriots who played such a vital role in securing for us our independence and liberties. To them we should be forever grateful.

William O. Carr
Bel Air, Maryland

June, 1985

SOURCES AND DOCUMENTATION

All information in this book is documented. Parenthetical inserts will be found after each patriot's name to enable the reader to locate the source document or reference where that information was obtained. A letter, followed by a number, indicates the source and the page within that source. For example, "F-661" refers to the Archives of Maryland, Vol. XVIII, page 661. The only two exceptions are "HR-50" and "O-1" through "O-25." HR-50 refers to Card File 50, not page 50, at the Hall of Records in Annapolis. O-1 through O-25 refers to Volume 1 through Volume 25, not pages 1 through 25, of the SAR (Sons of the American Revolution) papers on microfilm at the Maryland Historical Society Library in Baltimore. A list of codes and sources follows.

A   -   Carothers, Bettie Stirling. 9000 Men Who Signed the Oath of Allegiance and Fidelity to Maryland During the Revolution. Vol. I. Baltimore: Privately printed, 1974.

B   -   Hodges, Margaret Roberts. Unpublished Revolutionary Records of Maryland. Vol. III. Baltimore: Privately printed, 1939.

C   -   Hodges, Margaret Roberts. Unpublished Revolutionary Records of Maryland, Vol. I. Baltimore: Privately printed, 1938.

D   -   Wright, C. Milton. Our Harford Heritage: A History of Harford County, Maryland. Glen Burnie, MD: French-Bray Printing Company, 1967.

E   -   Preston, Walter W. History of Harford County, Maryland. Baltimore: Press of Sun Book Office, 1901.

F   -   Archives of Maryland, Vol. XVIII. "Muster Rolls and Other Records of Service of Maryland Troops in the American Revolution, 1775-1783." Baltimore: Genealogical Publishing Co., Inc., 1972. (Originally published, 1900)

G   -   Directory of Maryland State Society DAR and Their Revolutionary Ancestors, 1892-1965. Published by the Maryland State Society, Daughters of the American Revolution, 1966.

H   -   Steuart, Rieman. A History of the Maryland Line in the Revolutionary War, 1775-1783. Published by the Society of the Cincinnati of Maryland, 1969.

HR   -   Hall of Records, Annapolis, Maryland. Gleanings from Card File 50, Revolutionary Records Index.

I - Rowe, Ella, and Hopkins, Joseph Carroll. "Men of '76," Maryland Genealogical Society Bulletin, Vol. 25, No. 3, (Summer, 1984), pp. 312-329.

J - Brumbaugh, Gaius Marcus. Maryland Records: Colonial, Revolutionary, County and Church from Original Sources. Vol. II. Baltimore: Genealogical Publishing Co., Inc., 1967.

K - Archives of Maryland, Vol. XII. "Journal and Correspondence of the Maryland Council of Safety, July 7-December 31, 1776." Baltimore: Maryland Historical Society, 1893.

L - Heitman, Francis B. Historical Register of Officers of the Continental Army During the War of the Revolution, April, 1775, to December, 1783. Baltimore: Genealogical Publishing Co., Inc., 1982. (Originally published, 1914)

M - Barnes, Robert W. Maryland Marriages, 1634-1777. Baltimore: Genealogical Publishing Co., Inc., 1975.

N - Newman, Harry Wright. Maryland Revolutionary Records. Baltimore: Genealogical Publishing Co., Inc., 1980.

O - Goodman, Edward J. Jr. Maryland Society SAR Index of Members and Patriots, 1889-1983. Baltimore: Privately printed, 1984.

P - Pierce's Register. (Register of the Certificates Issued by John Pierce, Esq., Paymaster General and Commissioner of Army Accounts for the United States, to Officers and Soldiers of the Continental Army Under Act of July 4, 1783) Baltimore: Genealogical Publishing Co., Inc., 1984. (Originally published by the DAR, 1914)

Q - Myers, Thomas M. The Norris Family of Maryland. New York: William M. Clemens, publisher, 1916.

R - Records in the Maryland Historical Society Library, in Baltimore, MD. (Gleanings of documented information found in Filing Case A and other records in the library.)

S - Sutherland, Hunter C. "A Brief History of the Bush River Friends Meeting of Harford County, Maryland," Maryland Historical Magazine, Vol. 77, No. 4 (December, 1982), pp. 365-369.

T - Kilbourne, John D. "The Society of the Cincinnati of Maryland: Its First One Hundred Years, 1783-1883," Maryland Historical Magazine, Vol. 78, No. 3 (Fall, 1983), pp. 169-185.

U - Briggs, Edna E. Gilbert Genealogical Data. Casper, Wyo.: Privately printed, 1954. (Supplemented with subsequent research by Joseph Hughes, Renna Ambrose and Esther Hannon)

V   -   Hughes, Joseph L. *Genealogy of the Hughes Family*. Perryman, MD: Privately printed, 1953.

W   -   Whitaker, Beaumont W. "The Whitaker Family of Baltimore County, 1677-1767," *Maryland Historical Magazine*, Vol. 79, No. 2 (Summer, 1984), pp. 165-182.

X   -   *DAR Patriot Index*, Vol. I. Washington, D.C.: National Society, Daughters of the American Revolution, 1966.

Y   -   *DAR Patriot Index*, Vol. II. Washington, D.C.: National Society, Daughters of the American Revolution, 1979.

Z   -   *DAR Patriot Index*, Vol. III. Washington, D.C.: National Society, Daughters of the American Revolution, 1982.

AA - *Maryland Pension Roll of 1835*: Report from the Secretary of War in Relation to the Pension Establishment of the United States (Baltimore: Genealogical Publishing Company, 1968; reprint of the original 1835 report).

BB - Peden, Henry C. Jr. *Abstracts of the Orphans Court Proceedings of Harford County, Maryland, 1778-1800* (Westminster, MD: Family Line Publications, 1990).

CC - Peden, Henry C. Jr. *Marylanders to Kentucky, 1775-1825* (Westminster, MD: Family Line Publications, 1991).

DD - *Archives of Maryland*, Volume XLIII. "Journal and Correspondence of the State Council of Maryland, 1779-1780"(Baltimore: Maryland Hist. Society, 1924).

A

ABLE, THOMAS.
    Private, Capt. John Love's Company No. 10, September 14, 1775.
    Private, Capt. Bennett Bussey's Company, July 20, 1776.
    Signer, Association of Freemen, 1776, Spesutie Upper Hundred.
    (E-116, E-127, F-60, I-318)

ADAMS, JACOB.
    Signer, Association of Freemen, 1776, Harford Upper. (I-325)

ADAMS, JAMES.
    Private, Capt. Rumsey's Company No. 6, September 16, 1775.
    Signer, Association of Freemen, 1775, Gunpowder Neck Hundred.
    (E-112, I-327)

ADAMS, JOHN.
    Private, Capt. Aquila Hall's Co. No. 4, September 9, 1775.
    Signer, Association of Freemen, 1776, Harford Lower Hundred.
    (E-109, I-324)

ADMISTON, ALEXANDER.
    Private, Capt. Aquila Paca's Co., July 24, 1776 (E-126, F-59)

ADY, JAMES.
    Signer, Association of Freemen, 1776, Gunpowder Upper. (I-326)

ADY, JONATHAN.
    Born c.1722, Baltimore County. Died 1800, Harford County.
    Married: Rebecca Yorke, 1743. Children: Rachel and William.
    Private, Capt. John Taylor's Co. No. 7, September 9, 1775.
    Private, Capt. Robert Harris' Harford Rifles; Private, Pa.
    Signer, Association of Freemen, 1776, Gunpowder Upper Hundred.
    (E-113, I-326, G-114, M-2, X-6)

ADY, WILLIAM.
    Son of Jonathan Ady and Rebecca Yorke.
    Born 1745. Died c.1780. Married: Chloe Staniford.
    Private, Capt. John Taylor's Co. No. 7, September 9, 1775.
    Signer, Association of Freemen, 1776, Gunpowder Upper Hundred.
    Signer, Oath of Fidelity and Allegiance to Maryland, 1778.
    (A-31, B-12, E-113, I-326, X-6)

AFFURLY, JAMES.
    Signer, Association of Freemen, 1776, Harford Lower. (I-324)

AIKENS, JOSEPH.
    Drafted, Militia, 1781; "Never taken up." (E-133, F-400)

AKERIGHT (AKSRIGHT, AKERITE), ISAAC.
    Private, Capt. Bennett Bussey's Company, July 20, 1776.
    Signer, Association of Freemen, 1776, Spesutie Lower Hundred.
    (E-127, F-60, I-319)

AKINS, CORNELIUS.
    Private, Capt. Paca's Company, July 24, 1776 (E-126, F-59).

ALBERT, PHILIP.
    Private, Capt. William Webb's Company No. 16, October 14, 1775.
    Signer, Association of Freemen, 1776, Deer Creek Upper.
    (E-121, I-323)

ALEXANDER, JAMES.
    Private, Capt. William Webb's Company No. 16, October 14, 1775.
    Signer, Association of Freemen, 1776, Deer Creek Upper.
    Signer, Oath of Fidelity and Allegiance to Maryland, 1778.
    (A-31, B-14, E-122, I-323, J-236)

ALEXANDER, MATTHEW.
    Ensign, Capt. John Rodgers' Company No. 5, September 15, 1775.
    Sergeant, 1st Company of Maryland Riflemen under Colonel Moses
      Rawlings, 1776, and 4th Maryland Continental Line through
      October 7, 1777.
    Fought in Battle of Fort Washington, November 16, 1776.
    (D-361, E-110, E-129, E-136, F-301)

ALEXANDER, ROBERT.
    Attorney at Law of the first Harford County Court in 1774-1775.
    (E-63)

ALLEN, HUGH.
    Signer, Association of Freemen, 1776, Gunpowder Upper (I-326).

ALLEN, JAMES.
    Private, Capt. John Love's Company No. 10, September 14, 1775.
    Private, Capt. William Webb's Company No. 16, October 14, 1775.
    Private, Capt. Aquila Paca's Company, July 24, 1776.
    (E-116, E-122, E-126, F-59)

ALLEN, JOHN.
    Private, Capt. John Taylor's Company No. 7, September 9, 1775.
    Signer, Association of Freemen, 1776, Bush River Upper.
    Signer, Association of Freemen, 1776, Gunpowder Upper.
    Signer, Oath of Fidelity and Allegiance to Maryland, 1778.
    2nd Lieutenant, 8th Battalion, Harford County Militia, 1778.
    (A-31, B-12, C-46, E-113, I-320, I-326, J-234)

ALLEN, WILLIAM.
    Signer, Association of Freemen, 1776, Harford Lower (I-324).

ALLENDER (ALLINDER), JOHN.
    Signer, Association of Freemen, 1775, Gunpowder Neck.
    Cadet, Flying Camp, enlisted by Lt. James Bond, July 5, 1776,
      Age 19, born in America (5'6½", light-colored hair), part of
      Col. Thomas Ewing's Battalion.
    Signer, Oath of Fidelity and Allegiance to Maryland, 1778.
    (A-31, B-14, E-125, F-54, I-327, J-236)

ALLENDER, JOHN JR.
    Private, Capt. Rumsey's Company No. 6, September 16, 1775. (E-112)
    Signer, Association of Freemen, 1775, Gunpowder Neck. (I-327)

ALLENDER, NICHOLAS.
    Furnished a gun to Harford County Committee, 1776. (E-330)

ALLENDER, THOMAS.
    Signer, Association of Freemen, 1776, Deer Creek Upper. (A-31, B-14)
    Signer, Oath of Allegiance to Maryland, 1778. (I-323, J-236)

ALLENDER, WILLIAM.
    Signer, Association of Freemen, 1775, Gunpowder Neck.
    Signer, Association of Freemen, 1776, Deer Creek Upper.
    Private, Capt. Rumsey's Company No. 6, September 16, 1775.
    Commissioned by Harford County Committee to collect the fines
        imposed on non-associators on the north side of Deer Creek, 1777.
    Signer, Oath of Fidelity and Allegiance to Maryland, 1778.
    Agent's Ledger No. 1, f. 1; Army Ledger No. 2, f. 167 (1780).
    (A-31, B-14, E-112, E-338, I-323, I-327, J-236, HR-50, O-3, O-14)

ALLIN, JOHN.
    Signer, Oath of Allegiance to Maryland, 1778. (A-31, B-30, J-247)

ALLISON (ALLESON), ALEXANDER.
    Signer, Oath of Allegiance to Maryland, 1778. (A-31, B-29, J-246)

ALLISON, JAMES.
    Born 1741. Died 1841. Married: Nancy_____.
    2nd Lieutenant, Capt. Archer's Company No. 2, 1775-1776.
    (D-359, E-107, X-12)

ALMONY, JOHN.
    Signer, Oath of Fidelity and Allegiance to Maryland, 1778.
    (A-31, B-23, J-241)

ALTON, JOHN.
    Signer, Oath of Fidelity and Allegiance to Maryland, 1778.
    (A-31, B-19, J-238)

AMBY, JOHN.
    Signer, Association of Freemen, 1775, Bush River Upper. (I-316)

AMES, WILLIAM.
    1st Lieutenant, Deer Creek Battalion, Militia, 1779. (C-43)

AMMOTT (ARMOTT), WILLIAM.
    Private, Capt. Patrick's Company No. 17, April 1, 1776. (E-122)

AMOS (AMOSS), AQUILA.
    Signer, Association of Freemen, 1775/1776, Bush River Upper.
    Ensign, Capt. Bennett Bussey's Company, July-December, 1776.
    Fought in Battle of White Plains, N.Y., October 28, 1776.
    Signer, Oath of Fidelity and Allegiance to Maryland, 1778.
    (A-31, B-19, E-126, E-137, F-59, I-316, I-320, H-50, J-238,
    K-170, L-70)

AMOS (AMOSS), BENJAMIN.
   Signer, Association of Freemen, 1776, Eden Hundred.
   Signer, Oath of Fidelity and Allegiance to Maryland, 1778.
   (A-31, B-19, I-323, J-238)

AMOS (AMOSS), BENJAMIN, CAPTAIN.
   Elected Captain at Upper Cross Roads, November 30, 1776.
   Captain, 8th Battalion, Harford County Militia, 1778.
   Signer, Oath of Fidelity and Allegiance to Maryland, 1778.
   (A-31, B-23, C-47, J-241, K-496)

AMOS (AMOSS), BENJAMIN JR.
   Signer, Association of Freemen, 1776, Gunpowder Upper (I-326).

AMOS (AMOSS), GEORGE.
   Signer, Association of Freemen, 1775, Bush River Upper.
   Signer, Oath of Fidelity and Allegiance to Maryland, 1778.
   (A-31, B-19, I-317, J-238)

AMOS (AMOSS), HENRY.
   Two signers by this name took the Oath of Fidelity and Allegiance
     to Maryland, 1778. (A-31, B-24, J-242)

AMOS (AMOSS), JAMES SR.
   Signer, Association of Freemen, 1776, Bush River Upper.
   Signer, Association of Freemen, 1776, Gunpowder Upper.
   Signer, Oath of Fidelity and Allegiance to Maryland, 1778.
   (A-31, B-23, I-320, I-326, J-241)

AMOS (AMOSS), JAMES JR.
   Signer, Oath of Fidelity and Allegiance to Maryland, 1778.
   (A-31, B-23, J-241)

AMOS (AMOSS), JAMES, of James.
   Private, Capt. Jacob Bond's Company No. 11, December 9, 1775.
   (E-117)

AMOS (AMOSS), JOSEPH.
   Private, Capt. John Patrick's Company No. 17, April 1, 1776.
   (E-122)

AMOS (AMOSS), JOSHUA, of James.
   Signer, Association of Freemen, 1775/1776, Bush River Upper.
   Private, Capt. Bennett Bussey's Company, July 25, 1776.
   Ensign, 8th Battalion, Harford County Militia, Appointed 1776.
   Elected Lieutenant at Upper Cross Roads, November 30, 1776.
   1st Lieutenant, 8th Battalion, 1778.
   Signer, Oath of Fidelity and Allegiance to Maryland, 1778.
   (A-31, B-23, C-47, E-128, E-267, F-60, I-316, I-320, J-241, K-496)

AMOS (AMOSS), JOSHUA.
   Signer, Association of Freemen: Bush River Upper, 1775; Eden, 1776;
     Gunpowder Upper, 1776.
   Signer, Oath of Fidelity and Allegiance to Maryland, 1778.
   (A-31, B-19, I-317, I-323, I-326, J-238)

AMOS (AMOSS), MAULDEN.
    Born 1747. Died 1845. Married: Rachel Bull.
    Son of William Amos and _____ Maulden.
    Private, Capt. John Taylor's Company No. 7, September 9, 1775.
    Signer, Oath of Fidelity and Allegiance to Maryland, 1778.
    (A-31, B-10, E-113, J-233, J-234, X-13, Y-5)

AMOS (AMOSS), MORDECAI.
    Signer, Association of Freemen, 1775, Bush River Upper.
    War Committee of Harford County, 1775.
    Signer, Association of Freemen, 1776, Gunpowder Upper.
    Sergeant, Jarrettsville Militia, Company No. 15, January 27, 1776.
    Private, Capt. Bennett Bussey's Company, July 25, 1776.
    Signer, Oath of Fidelity and Allegiance to Maryland, 1778.
    Administered the Oaths ("Worshipfull Mordecai Amoss"), 1778.
    (A-31, B-19, D-358, E-120, E-128, F-60, I-316, 320, 325, J-238)
    (O-23)

AMOS (AMOSS), MORDECAI JR.
    Signer, Association of Freemen, 1775/1776, Bush River Upper.
    Signer, Oath of Fidelity and Allegiance to Maryland, 1778.
    (A-31, B-19, I-317, I-320, J-238)

AMOS (AMOSS), MORDECAI, of James.
    Born 1753. Died 1842. Married: Margaret _____.
    Lieutenant, 8th Battalion, 1778, Militia of Harford County.
    (C-47, N-8, X-13)

AMOS (AMOSS), NICHOLAS.
    Born 1742. Died 1799. "Nicholas Day Amoss" married Christiana
      Ditto in 1761. One source spelled name "Nicklos Amos."
    Signer, Association of Freemen, 1776, Bush River Upper and Eden.
    Ensign, Capt. Charles Baker's Company No. 15, January 27, 1776.
    Ensign, 8th Battalion, 1778, Militia of Harford County.
    Signer, Oath of Fidelity and Allegiance to Maryland, 1778.
    (A-31, B-23, C-46, E-120, I-320, I-324, J-241, M-4, X-13)

AMOS (AMOSS), ROBERT.
    Born 1741. Died 1818. Married: Martha McComas in 1765.
    Signer, Association of Freemen, 1776, Bush River Upper.
    Administered the Oaths ("Worshipfull Robert Amoss"), 1778.
    Signer, Oath of Fidelity and Allegiance to Maryland, 1778.
    Court Justice, 1780, Harford County.
    (A-31, B-23, B-24, E-76, I-320, J-241, J-242, M-4, Y-5)

AMOS (AMOSS), WILLIAM.
    Born 1717, Died 1814. Married: _____ Maulden.
    Signer, Association of Freemen, 1775/1776, Bush River Upper.
    Signer, Oath of Fidelity and Allegiance to Maryland, 1778.
    (A-31, B-19, I-316, I-328, J-238, X-13)

AMOS (AMOSS, AMASS), WILLIAM, of Joshua.
    Signer, Association of Freemen, 1775/1776, Bush River Upper.
    Signer, Oath of Fidelity and Allegiance to Maryland, 1778.
    (A-31, B-29, I-316, I-320, J-246)

    One William Amos was a Captain, Deer Creek Batt., 1779. (G-299)

AMOS (AMOSS), WILLIAM, of James.
> Signer, Association of Freemen, 1775, Bush River Upper.
> Signer, Oath of Fidelity and Allegiance to Maryland, 1778.
> (A-31, B-19, I-317, J-238)

ANDERSON, CHARLES.
> War Committee of Harford County, 1775.
> Signer, Bush Declaration, March 22, 1775.
> Captain of Company No. 3, September 23, 1775.
> (D-355, D-358, D-359, E-108)

ANDERSON, CHARLES.
> Private, Capt. Robert Harris' Harford Rifles, 1776.
> Paid subsistence for four weeks, two days, October 2, 1776.
> (E-123, K-436)

ANDERSON, DANIEL.
> Private, Capt. Charles Anderson's Company No. 3, September 23, 1775 (E-108)

ANDERSON, JAMES.
> Private, Capt. William Webb's Company No. 16, October 14, 1775.
> Signer, Association of Freemen, 1776, Deer Creek Upper.
> Signer, Oath of Fidelity and Allegiance to Maryland, 1778.
> (A-31, B-19, E-121, I-323, J-238)

ANDERSON, JOHN.
> Signer, Association of Freemen, 1776, Eden Hundred (I-323).

ANDERSON, MATTHEW.
> Signer, Association of Freemen, 1776, Bush River Upper (I-328).

ANDERSON, WILLIAM.
> Private, Capt. Jacob Bond's Company No. 11, December 9, 1775.
> Private, Capt. Harris' Company Payroll ("Deserted")
> Signer, Association of Freemen, 1776, Bush River Lower.
> (E-117, E-130, F-304, I-319)

ANDREWS, ABRAHAM.
> Private, Capt. William Bradford's Company No. 13, Sept. 30, 1775.
> Waggoneer; delivered 166 blankets to Col. Hall at Head of Elk, 1776.
> Signer, Association of Freemen, 1776, Harford Upper Hundred.
> Signer, Oath of Fidelity and Allegiance to Maryland, 1778.
> (A-31, B-21, E-119, I-325, J-239, E-335)

ANDREWS, THOMAS.
> (Doctor) War Committee of Harford County, 1775.
> Signer, Oath of Fidelity and Allegiance to Maryland, 1778.
> (A-31, B-26, D-358, J-243)

ANDREWS, WILLIAM.
> Private, 4th Maryland Continental Line, 1776-1777.
> Corporal, July 1, 1777. Battle of Fort Washington, 1776.
> "At Hospital" June-July, 1777; with Gen. Scott, September, 1778.
> (E-129, F-301, E-136)

ANNIN, WILLIAM.
    Private, Capt. Josias Hall's Company No. 1, 1775. (E-106)
    Signer, Association of Freemen, 1776, Harford Lower. (I-324)

ANTILL, JOHN.
    Signer, Association of Freemen, 1776, Susquehanna Hundred. (I-321)

AOOISTOCK, PETER. See "Overstock, Peter."

APPLETON, EDWARD.
    Signer, Oath of Fidelity and Allegiance to Maryland, 1778.
    Militia Substitute, 1781, 3 years.
    (A-31, B-24, E-133, F-401, J-242)

ARCHER, JOHN, M.B.
    Son of Thomas Archer. Born 1741. Died 1810.
    Married Catherine Harris in 1766, daughter of Thomas Harris.
    Children: Thomas, Mary, Jude Stevenson, Elizabeth, Robert Harris,
        John Jr., and James.
    Graduated from Princeton College in 1760; received medical degree
        from University of Pennsylvania, Medical School in 1768.
    Came from a long line of physicians; lived at "Medical Hall."
    Organized a militia company at Lower Cross Roads, 1774-1775.
    Signer, Bush Declaration, March 22, 1775.
    Captain, Company No. 2, Harford County Militia, 1775.
    Committee of Correspondence, War Committee, June 11, 1775.
    Commissioned a Major of one of the battalions, January, 1776.
    Signer, Association of Freemen, 1776, Spesutie Upper Hundred.
    Represented Harford County at the State Convention in 1776.
    Established a linen factory in Harford County with James Harris
        in 1776 following a $300 cash advance from the Maryland Council.
        Linen for the Revolution was purchased in November, 1776, even
        though the record states "they ask more than the council allows."
    Signer, Oath of Fidelity and Allegiance to Maryland, 1778.
    Administered the Oath ("Worshipfull John Archer"), 1778.
    Pay Account No. 1, pp. 19, 29, 40, 63. Army Ledger No. 4, f. 9.
    Intendants Orders No. 2, f. 6. Intendants Day Book No. 2, p. 54.
    Agent's Ledger No. 1, f. 47. (Payments made between 1775-1794)
    Court Justice, Harford County, 1780.
    Presidential Elector, 1796.
    Served in U. S. Congress, 1801-1807.
    (A-31, B-14, B-25, B-27, D-355, D-358, D-359, E-76, E-96, E-107,
        G-124, H-50, HR-50, I-319, J-242, J-244, K-350, K-460, L-73,
        O-3, O-8, O-14, O-17, O-23, X-17)

ARKWRIGHT, ISAAC.
    Private, Capt. John Love's Company No. 10, September 14, 1775.
    (E-116)

ARMOTT (AMMOTT), THOMAS.
    Private, Capt. John Patrick's Company No. 17, April 1, 1776.
    (E-122)

ARMSTRONG, DAVID.
    Private, Capt. John Patrick's Company No. 17, April 1, 1776.
    Private, Capt. Robert Harris' Harford Rifles, 1776.
    Paid subsistence for two weeks, October 16, 1776.
    Signer, Association of Freemen, 1776, Deer Creek Lower.
    (E-122, E-123, I-322, K-436)

ARMSTRONG, JAMES.
    Signer, Association of Freemen, 1776, Harford Hundred.
    Signer, Oath of Fidelity and Allegiance to Maryland, 1778.
    Petit Juror, Harford County, 1783.
    (A-31, B-25, I-325, E-77, J-242)

ARMSTRONG, JOHN.
    Private, Capt. John Taylor's Company No. 7, September 9, 1775.
    Private, Capt. Robert Harris' Harford Rifles, 1776.
    Paid subsistence for five weeks, four days, September 25, 1776.
    Signer, Association of Freemen, 1776, Harford Lower.
    Signer, Association of Freemen, 1776, Gunpowder Upper.
    Signer, Oath of Fidelity and Allegiance to Maryland, 1778.
      Records indicate there were two signers with this name.
    (A-31, B-12, B-22, E-113, E-123, I-324, I-326, J-234, J-240, K-436)

ARMSTRONG, JOHNSTON.
    Signer, Association of Freemen, 1776, Deer Creek Lower (I-322).

ARMSTRONG, JOSH.
    Signer, Association of Freemen, 1776, Susquehanna Hundred (I-321).

ARMSTRONG, NATHANIEL SHEPHERD.
    Private, Capt. John Taylor's Company No. 7, September 9, 1775.
    Signer, Association of Freemen, 1776, Gunpowder Upper.
    (E-113, I-326)

ARMSTRONG, ROBERT.
    Private, Capt. Robert Harris' Harford Rifles, 1776.
    Signer, Association of Freemen, 1776, Deer Creek Lower.
      Records indicate there were two signers with this name.
    Paid subsistence for four weeks, three days, October 4, 1776.
    (E-123, I-322, K-435)

ARMSTRONG, SHEPERD.
    Signer, Oath of Fidelity and Allegiance to Maryland, 1778.
    (A-31, B-12, J-234)

ARNOLD, JAMES.
    Private, Capt. Benjamin Rumsey's Company No. 6, September 16, 1775.
    Signer, Association of Freemen, 1775, Gunpowder Neck.
    (E-112, I-327)

ARNOLD, WILLIAM.
    Signer, Association of Freemen, 1776, Susquehanna Hundred.
    Signer, Association of Freemen, 1776, Deer Creek Lower.
      Records indicate there were two signers with this name.
    (I-321, I-322)

ASHLEY, THOMAS.
  Signer, Oath of Allegiance to Md., 1778. (A-31, B-22, J-240)

ASHMAN, CHARLES.
  Private, Capt. Robert Harris' Payroll, 1776. (E-130, F-304)

ASHMEAD, JOHN.
  Born 1757. Died c.1794. Married: Elizabeth _____.
  Signer, Association of Freemen, 1776, Bush River Upper Hundred.
  Signer, Oath of Fidelity and Allegiance to Maryland, 1778.
  Source X-20 indicates he was a Captain. (A-31, B-30, I-320, J-247)

ASHMEAD, SAMUEL.
  War Committee, Harford County, 1775-1776. (D-358, K-281)
  Signer, Association of Freemen, 1776, Bush River Upper. (I-320)
  Signer, Oath of Allegiance to Md., 1778. (A-31, B-30, J-247)
  Captain, Deer Creek Battalion, Militia, 1778. (C-43)

ASHMORE, JOHN.
  Wife, Margaret. Daughter, Susanna, married Nathan Bemis.
  Owned Mill Green Mill on Broad Creek, which was used as a voting
  center for the Deer Creek Upper Hundred during Rev. War. (D-177)

ASHMORE, WILLIAM.
  Signer and Solicitor, Association of Freemen, 1775 and 1776,
  Deer Creek Upper Hundred. (I-315, I-323)

ASHTON (ASHTEN), JOSEPH.
  Signer, Oath of Fidelity and Allegiance to Maryland, 1778.
  Grand Juror, Harford County, 1779. (A-31, B-23, E-75, J-241)

ASK, THOMAS.
  Signer, Oath of Allegiance to Md., 1778. (A-31, B-30, J-247)

ATKINSON, JOHN.
  Signer, Association of Freemen, 1775, Spesutie Lower. (I-317)

ATKINSON, JOHN JR.
  Private, Capt. Dorsey's Company No. 8, Oct. 31, 1775. (E-115)

AYERS, STEPHEN.
  Signer, Oath of Fidelity and Allegiance to Md., 1778. (A-31)

AYERS, THOMAS.
  Signer, Oath of Fidelity and Allegiance to Maryland, 1778.
  Records indicate there were two signers with this same name.
  (A-31, B-23, B-29, J-241, J-246)

AYRES, THOMAS.
  Corporal, Capt. Greenberry Dorsey's Company No. 8, 1775.
  Born 1755. Died 1833. Married: Elizabeth Almony.
  Signer, Association of Freemen, 1776, Spesutie Lower Hundred.
  Signer, Oath of Fidelity and Allegiance to Maryland, 1778.
  Pay Account No. 1, p.16; Army Account No. 2, f.1 (1780-1784).
  (A-31, B-17, E-114, HR-50, I-318, J-237, Y-8)

B

BAGGOT, WILLIAM.
    Private, Capt. John Love's Company No. 10, September 14, 1775.
    (E-116)

BAILEY (BALEY), ARCHIBALD.
    2nd Lieutenant, Capt. John Rodgers' Company, 23rd Battalion,
      Harford County Militia, April 9, 1778. (C-6, C-44)

BAILEY (BALEY), CHARLES.
    Signer, Association of Freemen, 1775/1776, Susquehanna Hundred.
    Private, Capt. Charles Anderson's Company No. 3, Sept. 23, 1775.
    (D-357, E-109, I-321)

BAILEY, FRANCIS JAMES.
    Signer, Oath of Fidelity and Allegiance to Maryland, 1778.
    (A-31, B-14, J-235, J-236)

BAILEY, GREENBURY.
    Signer, Association of Freemen, 1775, Gunpowder Neck Hundred.
    (I-327)

BAILEY, GROOMBRIGHT.
    Signer, Oath of Fidelity and Allegiance to Maryland, 1778.
    (A-31, B014, J-235, J-236)

BAILEY, JAMES.
    Private, Capt. Benjamin Rumsey's Company No. 6, Sept. 16, 1775.
    (E-112)

BAILEY (BAYLY), NEHEMIAH.
    Signer, Association of Freemen, 1775, Spesutie Lower Hundred.
    (I-317)

BAILEY (BALEY), QUILLA.
    Signer, Association of Freemen, 1776, Susquehanna Hundred. (I-321)

BAILEY, SAMUEL.
    Signer and solicitor, Association of Freemen, 1775, Susquehanna.
    Captain, Deer Creek Battalion, 1779. (C-44, I-315)

BAKER, CHARLES CAPT.
    Born c.1738. Died 1796. Married: Elizabeth Wheeler in 1762.
    Signer and solicitor, Association of Freemen, 1775, Eden Hundred.
    Captain, Company No. 15, January 27, 1776.
    Captain, 8th Battalion, 1778.
    Signer, Oath of Fidelity and Allegiance to Maryland, 1778.
    Company Election Judge at Upper Cross Roads, November 30, 1776.
    Captain, Army Account No..1, p. 52, June 17, 1778.
    Depreciation Pay No. 2, p. 10; Depreciation Pay No. 3, p. 190;
    Army Account No. 1, p. 19, 1783-1787.
    (A-31, B-23, C-46, D-359, E-119, HR-50, I-315, J-241, K-496,
     M-7, Z-4)

BAKER, CHARLES
    Son of Morris (Maurice) Baker. Married Elizabeth Ditto in 1764
      (St. John's Parish). Daughter, Sarah, md. Asael Hitchcock, Jr.
    Signer, Association of Freemen, 1776, Bush River Upper Hundred.
    Signer and solicitor, Association of Freemen, 1776, Eden.
    Private, 4th Maryland Continental Line, 1776-1779.
    Rifleman at Battle of Fort Washington, November 16, 1776.
    "On furlough" March, 1778; detached to Col. Pope, April, 1778.
    Signer, Oath of Fidelity and Allegiance to Maryland, 1778.
    (A-31, B-10, E-129, E-136, F-302, I-320, I-323, J-233)

BAKER, GEDION.
    Signer, Oath of Fidelity and Allegiance to Maryland, 1778.
    (A-31, B-10, J-234)

BAKER, GRAFTON.
    Signer, Association of Freemen, 1776, Bush River Upper. (I-328)

BAKER, JOHN.
    Private, Capt. Robert Harris' Harford Rifles, 1776.
    Paid subsistence for five weeks, September 29, 1776.
    Signer, Association of Freemen, 1776, Gunpowder Upper.
    Signer, Oath of Fidelity and Allegiance to Maryland, 1778.
    (A-31, B-14, E-123, I-326, J-235, K-436)

BAKER, JOHN, of Theophilas.
    Signer, Oath of Fidelity and Allegiance to Maryland, 1778.
    (A-31, B-14, J-235)

BAKER, MAURICE.
    Signer, Association of Freemen, 1775, Gunpowder Neck Hundred.
    Signer, Oath of Fidelity and Allegiance to Maryland, 1778.
    (A-31, B-14, I-327, J-236)

BAKER, MORRIS, of Lawrence.
    Private, Capt. Charles Baker's Company No. 15, January 27, 1776.
    Signer, Association of Freemen, 1776, Bush River Lower Hundred.
    (E-120, I-319)

BAKER, THEOPHELUS.
    Signer, Association of Freemen, 1776, Gunpowder Upper Hundred.
    Signer, Oath of Fidelity and Allegiance to Maryland, 1778.
    (A-31, B-10, I-326, J-233)

BAKER, WILLIAM.
    Signer, Association of Freemen, 1775, Gunpowder Neck Hundred.
    Signer, Oath of Fidelity and Allegiance to Maryland, 1778.
    Records indicate there were two signers with this name.
    (A-31, B-14, I-327, J-236)

BALDWIN, WILLIAM.
    Signer, Association of Freemen, 1776, Gunpowder Upper Hundred.
    Private, Capt. Charles Baker's Company No. 15, Jan. 27, 1776.
    Signer, Oath of Fidelity and Allegiance to Maryland, 1778.
    Married Hannah Garrison, daughter of John, of Bucks Co., Pa.
    (A-31, B-24, E-120, I-326, J-242)

BALF, EDWARD.
    Maryland Line, last date May 7, 1781.   (F-414)

BANKHEAD, HUGH.
    Signer, Association of Freemen, 1776, Bush River Upper.
    Signer, Oath of Fidelity and Allegiance to Maryland, 1778.
    (A-31, B-29, I-328, J-246)

BANKHEAD, WILLIAM.
    Signer, Association of Freemen, 1776, Bush River Upper.
    Signer, Oath of Fidelity and Allegiance to Maryland, 1778.
    (A-31, B-30, I-328, J-247)

BANKS, ANDREW.
    Signer, Association of Freemen, 1776, Gunpowder Upper.
    Signer, Oath of Fidelity and Allegiance to Maryland, 1778.
    (A-31, B-10, I-326, J-233)

BARCLAY, GEORGE.
    Private, Capt. John Archer's Company No. 2, September 16, 1775.
    (E-107)

BARCLAY, JOHN.
    Signer, Oath of Fidelity and Allegiance to Maryland, 1778.
    Petit Juror, Harford County, 1783.
    (A-31, B-14, E-77, J-236)

BARCLAY, SAMUEL.
    2nd Lieutenant, Capt. Patrick's Company, October 1, 1776.
    (E-265)

BARNARD, RICHARD.
    Signer, Association of Freemen, 1775, Gunpowder Upper. (I-327)

BARNES, BENJAMIN.
    Private, Capt. Francis Holland's Harford Rifles, 1776. (E-124)

BARNES, BENNETT.
    Ensign, 23rd Battalion, April 9, 1778.   (C-44, C-7)

BARNES, EZEKIEL.
    Signer, Association of Freemen, 1776, Deer Creek Lower.
    Private, Capt. Patrick's Company No. 17, April 1, 1776.
    (E-122, I-321)

BARNES (BARNS), JAMES.
    Private, Capt. Anderson's Company No. 3, September 23, 1775.
    (E-108)

BARNES, JOAB JR.
    Signer, Association of Freemen, 1776, Deer Creek Lower.
    (I-321)

BARNES, JOB.
    Private, Capt. Patrick's Company No. 17, April 1, 1776. (E-122)

BARNES, JOHN.
    Private, Capt. Dorsey's Company No. 8, October 31, 1775.
    Private, Capt. Bond's Company No. 11, December 9, 1775.
    Private, Capt. Francis Holland's Harford Rifles, 1776.
      Records indicate there were two, possibly three, men with this name.
    Signer, Association of Freemen, 1776, Spesutie Upper Hundred.
    (E-115, E-117, E-124, I-319)

BARNES (BARNS), JOSEPH.
    Private, Capt. Bond's Company No. 11, December 9, 1775.
    Signer, Association of Freemen, 1776, Spesutie Upper.
    Deposition taken as a Soldier in a suit pending, Sept., 1778.
    (E-117, F-661, I-319)

BARNES, NEHEMIAH.
    Private, Capt. Aquila Hall's Company No. 4, September 9, 1775.
    Signer, Association of Freemen, 1776, Harford Lower Hundred.
    (E-109, I-324)

BARNES (BARNS), WILLIAM.
    Association of Freemen Committeeman, 1775.
    2nd Lieutenant, Capt. Dorsey's Company No. 8, October 31, 1775.
    Private, Capt. Bond's Company No. 11, December 9, 1775.
      Records indicate there were two men with this name.
    Signer, Association of Freemen, 1776, Spesutie Upper.
    Signer, Oath of Fidelity and Allegiance to Maryland, 1778.
    (A-31, B-26, D-357, D-359, E-114, E-117, I-319, J-243)

BARNETT (BARNET), JAMES.
    Born 1757. Died 1824. Married: Martha Finney.
    Private, Capt. Webb's Company No. 16, October 14, 1775.
    Solicitor, Association of Freemen, 1775, Deer Creek Upper.
    Signer, Association of Freemen, 1776, Deer Creek Upper.
    Signer, Oath of Fidelity and Allegiance to Maryland, 1778.
    (A-31, B-14, E-122, I-315, I-323, J-236, X-37)

BARNETT, JOHN.
    Signer, Association of Freemen, 1775, Bush River Upper.
    Signer, Oath of Fidelity and Allegiance to Maryland, 1778.
    (A-31, B-20, I-317, J-239)

BARNHILL, JOHN.
    Signer, Association of Freemen, 1776, Spesutie Upper.
    Signer, Oath of Fidelity and Allegiance to Maryland, 1778.
    (One source spelled his name "John Bamhill")
    (A-31, B-15, I-319, J-236)

BARNHOUSE, JOHN.
    Private, Capt. Webb's Company No. 16, October 14, 1775.
    Signer, Association of Freemen, 1776, Deer Creek Upper.
    (E-121, I-323)

BARRETT, JOSEPH.
    Signer, Association of Freemen, 1776, Bush River Upper. (I-328)

BARRETT, THOMAS.
    Private, Capt. Aquila Hall's Company No. 4, September 9, 1775.
    (E-109)

BARRY, MICHAEL.
    Private, Capt. Paca's Company, July 24, 1776. (E-126, F-59)

BARTLY, JOHN.
    War Committee, Harford County, 1775. (D-358)

BARTON, JOHN SR.
    Signer, Association of Freemen, 1776, Bush River Upper and Eden.
    Signer, Oath of Fidelity and Allegiance to Maryland, 1778.
    (A-31, B-23, I-320, I-323, I-324, J-241)

BARTON, JOHN JR.
    Signer, Association of Freemen, 1776, Gunpowder Upper and Eden.
    (I-324, I-326)

BARTON, WILLIAM.
    Private, Capt. Baker's Company No. 15, January 27, 1776. (E-120)

BASE, JOS.
    Signer, Association of Freemen, 1776, Bush River Lower. (I-320)

BASSETT, JOHN.
    Signer, Oath of Fidelity and Allegiance to Maryland, 1778.
    (A-31, B-19, J-238)

BAXLEY, SAMUEL.
    Private, Capt. Bussey's Company, July 25, 1776.
    Signer, Association of Freemen, 1776, Deer Creek Upper.
    (E-128, F-60, I-322)

BAY, ANDREW.
    Private, Capt. Taylor's Company No. 7, September 9, 1775. (E-113)

BAY, HUGH.
    Private, Capt. Taylor's Company No. 7, September 9, 1775.
    Signer, Association of Freemen, 1775, Bush River Lower.
    Signer, Association of Freemen, 1776, Gunpowder Upper.
    Signer, Oath of Fidelity and Allegiance to Maryland, 1778.
     Records indicate there were two signers with this name.
    Grand Juror, Harford County, 1779.
    (A-31, B-12, B-30, E-113, E-75, I-326, I-328, J-234, J-247)

BAY, WILLIAM.
    Signer, Association of Freemen, 1775/1776, Bush River Upper.
    Signer, Oath of Fidelity and Allegiance to Maryland, 1778.
    (A-31, B-30, I-316, I-320, J-247)

BAYD, WILLIAM.
    Private, Capt. Taylor's Company No. 7, September 9, 1775.
    (E-113)

BAYLIS (BAYLES, BALYS), BENJAMIN.
    Born 1734. Died 1782. Married: Deborah Austin.
    War Committee, 1775.
    Private, Capt. Anderson's Company No. 3, September 23, 1775.
    Signer, Association of Freemen, 1776, Susquehanna Hundred.
    Signer, Oath of Fidelity and Allegiance to Maryland, 1778.
    (A-31, B-25, D-358, E-108, I-321, J-242, X-45)

BAYLIS (BAYLES, BAILESS), DANIEL.
    Private, Capt. Anderson's Company No. 3, September 23, 1775.
    Private, Capt. Francis Holland's Harford Rifles, 1776.
    Signer, Oath of Fidelity and Allegiance to Maryland, 1778.
    Grand Juror, Harford County, 1780.
    (A-31, B-25, E-108, E-124, E-76, J-242)

BAYLIS, ELIAS.
    Signer, Oath of Fidelity and Allegiance to Maryland, 1778.
    (A-31, B-26, J-243)

BAYLIS (BAYLES), JAMES.
    Signer, Association of Freemen, 1775, Susquehanna. (D-357)

BAYLIS (BAYLES, BAILESS), JONAS.
    Private, Capt. Anderson's Company No. 3, September 23, 1775.
    Private, Capt. Francis Holland's Harford Rifles, 1776.
    Signer, Association of Freemen, 1776, Susquehanna.
    (E-109, E-124, I-321)

BAYLIS (BALYS), JOSIAS.
    Signer, Association of Freemen, 1775/1776, Susquehanna.
    (D-357, I-321)

BAYLIS, NACHE.
    Signer, Oath of Fidelity and Allegiance to Maryland, 1778.
    (A-31, B-26, J-243)

BAYLIS (BAYLES, BAILESS), NATHAN.
    Born 1748. Died c.1790. Married: Sarah _____.
    2nd Lieutenant, Capt. Anderson's Company No. 3, Sept. 23, 1775.
    (D-359, E-108, X-45)

BAYLIS, NATHANIEL.
    Signer, Association of Freemen, 1776, Susquehanna.
    Private, Capt. Holland's Harford Rifles, 1776.
    (E-124, I-321, O-5, O-8)

BAYLIS (BALYS), ROBERT.
    Signer, Association of Freemen, 1775/1776, Susquehanna.
    Signer, Oath of Fidelity and Allegiance to Maryland, 1778.
    (A-31, B-26, D-357, I-321, J-243)

BAYLIS (BAYLESS, BAYLES), SAMUEL.
    Born 1736. Died 1808. Married: Elizabeth Bayless in 1757.
    Children: Jemima, Elias, Platt, John, Phoebe, Mary, Mehitable,
       Sarah, Samuel, Zephaniah, Elizabeth.
    2nd Lieutenant, Capt. Patrick's Company No. 17, April 1, 1776.
    Signer and solicitor, Association of Freemen, 1776, Susquehanna.
    2nd Lieutenant, Deer Creek Battalion, 1778, under Col. Wheeler.
    Private, Capt. Anderson's Company No. 3, September 23, 1775.
       Records indicate there may have been two men with this name.
    Signer, Oath of Fidelity and Allegiance to Maryland, 1778. (O-6)
    (A-31, B-25, C-44, D-359, E-122, E-108, E-263, G-140, J-242, X-45)

BEACH, SAMUEL.
    Private, Capt. Rodgers' Company No. 5, Sept. 15, 1775. (E-110)

BEALL, JOHN.
    1st Lieutenant, Deer Creek Battalion, 1778. (C-43)

BEARD, THOMAS.
    Signer, Oath of Fidelity and Allegiance to Maryland, 1778.
    (A-31, B-24, J-242)

BEATTY (BEATY), ARCHIBALD.
    Sergeant, Capt. Rodgers' Company No. 5, September 15, 1775.
    Signer, Oath of Fidelity and Allegiance to Maryland, 1778.
    Grand Juror, Harford County, 1780.
    (A-31, B-22, E-110, E-76, J-240)

BEATY, WILLIAM.
    Signer, Association of Freemen, 1775, Bush River Upper Hundred.
    Signer, Oath of Fidelity and Allegiance to Maryland, 1778.
    (A-31, B-30, I-316, J-247)

BEAVEN, JOHN.
    Private, Capt. Webb's Company No. 16, October 14, 1775.
    Signer, Oath of Fidelity and Allegiance to Maryland, 1778.
    (A-31, E-121)

BEAVEN, JOHN I.
    Signer, Oath of Fidelity and Allegiance to Maryland, 1778.
    (B-23, J-241)

BEAVER, CHARLES.
    Private, Capt. Webb's Company No. 16, October 14, 1775. (E-121)

BEAVER, JOHN.
    Private, Capt. Webb's Company No. 16, October 14, 1774.
    Signer, Association of Freemen, 1776, Deer Creek Upper.
    (E-121, I-323)

BEAVER, THOMAS.
    Private, Capt. Webb's Company No. 16, October 14, 1775.
    Signer, Association of Freemen, 1776, Deer Creek Upper.
    Recruit, New Regiment, 1780. (E-121, E-131, I-323, F-343)

BECK, CALEB.
    Private, Capt. Aquila Hall's Company No. 4, September 9, 1775.
    Signer, Association of Freemen, 1776, Harford Lower Hundred.
    Signer, Oath of Fidelity and Allegiance to Maryland, 1778.
    (A-31, B-21, E-109, I-324, J-239)

BECK, JOHN.
    Private, Capt. Aquila Hall's Company No. 4, September 9, 1775.
    Signer, Oath of Fidelity and Allegiance to Maryland, 1778.
    (A-31, B-17, E-109, J-237)

BECK, MATTHEW.
    Signer, Association of Freemen, 1775, Gunpowder Neck. (I-327)

BECK, PETER.
    Signer, Oath of Fidelity and Allegiance to Maryland, 1778.
    (A-31, B-10, J-234)

BEK, JOHN.
    Signer, Oath of Fidelity and Allegiance to Maryland, 1778.
    (A-31, B-30, J-247)

BELL, DAVID.
    Signer, Association of Freemen, 1775/1776, Bush River Upper.
    Signer, Oath of Fidelity and Allegiance to Maryland, 1778.
    (A-31, B-29, I-316, I-320, J-246)

BELL, JOHN.
    Born 1738, Ireland. Died 1824, Harford County, Maryland.
    Married: (1)_____(2) Mary Kerr in 1773.
    Children: John,William,Mary,Elizabeth,Rebecca,Ephraim.
    2nd Lieutenant under Col. Wheeler, January 3, 1776.
    1st Lieutenant, Deer Creek Battalion, Capt. Anderson's Co.
    Signer, Association of Freemen, 1775/1776, Bush River Upper.
    Signer, Oath of Fidelity and Allegiance to Maryland, 1778.
    (A-31, B-19, G-148, I-316, I-328, J-238, X-51)

BELL, R.
    Signer, Association of Freemen, 1775/1776, Bush River Upper.
    (I-317, I-320)

BENFIELD, DAVID.
    Signer, Oath of Fidelity and Allegiance to Maryland, 1778.
    (A-31, B-19, J-238)

BENNETT, ABRAHAM.
    Private, Capt. Aquila Hall's Company No. 4, September 9, 1775.
    Signer, Association of Freemen, 1776, Harford Lower Hundred.
    (E-109, I-324)

BENNETT, BENJAMIN.
    Private, Capt. Aquila Hall's Company No. 4, September 9, 1775.
    Signer, Association of Freemen, 1776, Harford Lower Hundred.
    Signer, Oath of Fidelity and Allegiance to Maryland, 1778.
    (A-31, B-22, E-110, I-324, J-240)

BENNETT (BENNET), JACOB.
    Signer, Association of Freemen, 1776, Spesutie Lower. (I-318)

BENNETT, LEVIN.
    Signer, Oath of Fidelity and Allegiance to Maryland, 1778.
    (A-31, B-22, J-240)

BENNETT, PETER.
    Signer, Oath of Fidelity and Allegiance to Maryland, 1778.
    Signer, Association of Freemen, 1776, Harford Lower Hundred.
    (A-31, B-21, I-324, J-239)

BENNETT, ZEBEDEE.
    Private, Capt. Aquila Hall's Company No. 4, September 9, 1775.
    Signer, Association of Freemen, 1776, Harford Lower Hundred.
    (E-109, I-324)

BENNINGTON, JOB.
    Born 1758. Died 1823.
    Private, Capt. Paca's Company, July 24, 1776.
    Private, Matross, Maryland pensioner.
    (E-126, F-59, Y-16)

BENNINGTON, NEHEMIAH.
    Signer, Oath of Fidelity and Allegiance to Maryland, 1778.
    (A-31, B-14, J-236)

BENNINGTON (BENINTON), WILLIAM.
    Signer, Association of Freemen, 1776, Bush River Lower. (I-319)

BENSON, JAMES.
    Private, Capt. Alexander Rigdon's Company No. 12, December 2,
        1775. (E-118)

BENTLY, JOSHUA.
    Signer, Oath of Fidelity and Allegiance to Maryland, 1778.
    (A-31, B-23, J-241)

BENTLY, WILLIAM.
    Militia substitute, 1781. (E-132, F-400)

BENTON, HENRY.
    Signer, Oath of Fidelity and Allegiance to Maryland, 1778.
    (A-31, B-14, J-236)

BERRY, RICHARD.
    Private, Capt. Dorsey's Company No. 8, October 31, 1775. (E-114)

BESHANG, JOHN.
    Private, Capt. Webb's Company No. 16, October 14, 1775.
    Signer, Association of Freemen, 1776, Deer Creek Upper.
    Signer, Oath of Fidelity and Allegiance to Maryland, 1778.
    (A-31, B-14, E-121, I-323, J-235)

BETTS (BETS), WILLIAM.
    Private, Capt. Rigdon's Company No. 12, December 2, 1775.
    Signer, Association of Freemen, 1776, Deer Creek Upper.
    (E-118, I-322)

BEVARD, CHARLES.
    Private, Capt. Patrick's Company No. 17, April 1, 1776.
    Signer, Association of Freemen, 1776, Deer Creek Lower.
    Signer, Oath of fidelity and Allegiance to Maryland, 1778.
    (A-31, B-21, E-122, I-322, J-239)

BEVARD, JAMES.
    Born 1762. Died c.1809. Married: Mary Shidle.
    Drafted in militia; "never taken up," 1781.
    (E-132, F-400, X-57)

BEVARD, JAMES.
    Private, Capt. Patrick's Company No. 17, April 1, 1776.
    Signer, Association of Freemen, 1776, Deer Creek Lower.
    (E-122, I-322)

BIBB, JAMES.
    Signer, Oath of Fidelity and Allegiance to Maryland, 1778.
    (A-31, B-13, J-235)

BIDDLE, BENJAMIN.
    Signer, Association of Freemen, 1776, Bush River Upper.
    Signer, Oath of Fidelity and Allegiance to Maryland, 1778.
    (A-31, B-23, I-320, J-241)

BIGGS, JOHN.
    Born 1758. Died 1823. Married: Priscilla Wilson.
    Private, Capt. Aquila Hall's Company No. 4, September 9, 1775.
    (E-110, X-59)

BIGGS, NATHANIEL.
    Signer, Association of Freemen, 1775, Gunpowder Neck. (I-327)

BILLINGSLEY (BILLINGSLEA), FRANCIS.
    Born 1734/5. Died c.1800. Married: Asenath Howell.
    Signer, Association of Freemen, 1776, Bush River Lower.
    Signer, Oath of Fidelity and Allegiance to Maryland, 1778.
    Grand Juror, Harford County, 1780 and 1783.
    (A-31, B-10, E-76, E-77, I-320, J-233, X-59)

BILLINGSLEY (BILLINGSLEA), SILAS or SIAS.
    Born 1737/8. Died 1819. Married: Hannah Webster.
    War Committee, 1775.
    Signer, Association of Freemen, 1776, Deer Creek Upper.
    Petit Juror, Harford County, 1783.
    (D-359, E-77, I-322, X-59)

BILLINGSLEY (BILLINGSLEA), WALTER.
   Married Sarah Love in 1742.
   Signer, Association of Freemen, 1776, Spesutie Upper.
   Signer, Oath of Fidelity and Allegiance to Maryland, 1778.
   (A-31, B-28, I-319, J-245, M-15)

BILLINGSLEY (BILLINGSLEA), WALTER JR.
   Born 1744. Died c.1805. Married Ruth Clarke in 1772.
   1st Corporal, Capt. Love's Company No. 10, September 14, 1775.
   Signer, Association of Freemen, 1776, Spesutie Upper Hundred.
   Signer, Oath of Fidelity and Allegiance to Maryland, 1778.
   (A-31, B-28, E-115, I-318, J-245, M-15, X-59)

BIRCKHEAD, SAMUEL.
   Signer, Oath of Fidelity and Allegiance to Maryland, 1778.
   (A-31, B-17, J-237)

BISHOP, THOMAS.
   Signer, Association of Freemen, 1775, Gunpowder Neck. (I-327)

BLACK, JOHN.
   Signer, Association of Freemen, 1776, Bush River Upper. (I-328)

BLACK, ROBERT.
   Signer, Association of Freemen, 1775/1776, Bush River Upper.
   (I-316, I-328)

BLACKBURN, JOHN.
   Signer, Association of Freemen, 1776, Harford Upper. (I-325)

BLACKBURN, JOHN JR.
   Private, Capt. Archer's Co. No. 2, September 16, 1775. (E-107)

BLACKBURN, ROBERT.
   Signer, Oath of Fidelity and Allegiance to Maryland, 1778.
   (A-31, B-26, J-243)

BLACKLEAR, JOHN.
   Signer, Oath of Fidelity and Allegiance to Maryland, 1778.
   (A-31, B-28, J-245)

BLACKSTON (BLACKISTON), ELIJAH.
   Signer, Association of Freemen, 1775, Gunpowder Neck. (I-327)

BLACKSTON (BLACKISTON), THOMAS.
   Private, Capt. Aquila Hall's Company No. 4, September 9, 1775.
   Signer, Association of Freemen, 1776, Harford Lower Hundred.
   (E-110, I-324)

BLANEY, JAMES.
   Private, Capt. Robert Harris' Harford Rifles, 1776.
   Paid subsistence for five weeks, September 28, 1776.
   (E-123, K-436)

BLANEY, JOHN.
    Signer, Association of Freemen, 1776, Gunpowder Upper. (I-326)

BLANEY (BLEANY), THOMAS.
    Signer, Association of Freemen, 1775/1776, Bush River Upper.
    Signer, Oath of Fidelity and Allegiance to Maryland, 1778.
    (A-31, B-29, I-317, I-320, J-246)

BLUNDER, THOMAS.
    Recruit, New Regiment, July 17, 1780. (E-130, F-343)

BOARDSMAN (BOADSMAN), WILLIAM.
    Private, Capt. John Archer's Company No. 2, September 16, 1775.
    Signer, Association of Freemen, 1776, Harford Upper Hundred.
    Signer, Oath of Fidelity and Allegiance to Maryland, 1778.
    (A-31, B-25, E-107, I-325, J-242)

BOLTON (BOTTON), JAMES.
    Signer, Association of Freemen, 1776, Harford Upper. (I-325)

BOLTON, JOHN.
    Signer, Oath of Fidelity and Allegiance to Maryland, 1778.
    (A-31, B-14, J-236)

BONAR, WILLIAM.
    Signer and solicitor, Association of Freemen, 1775, Susquehanna.
    Signer, Oath of Fidelity and Allegiance to Maryland, 1778.
    (A-31, B-25, I-315, J-242)

BOND, BUCKLER.
    Private, Capt. Jacob Bond's Company No. 11, December 9, 1775.
    Signer, Association of Freemen, 1776, Bush River Lower.
    Signer, Oath of Fidelity and Allegiance to Maryland, 1778.
    (A-31, B-15, E-117, I-319, J-236)

BOND, DANIEL.
    Signer, Oath of Fidelity and Allegiance to Maryland, 1778.
    (A-31, B-19, J-238)

BOND, DENNIS.
    Petit Juror, Harford County, 1783. (E-77)

BOND, JACOB.
    Born 1726. Died 1780. Married: (1) Fanny Partridge in 1747;
    (2) _____ (3) Elizabeth _____. Children named
    in will: Jacob, Jr., Sarah, Martha, Charlotte, Ralph, Dennis,
    Ann, Priscilla. (E-206, 207, 208, 209, 210, 211)
    War Committee, Correspondence, June 11, 1775.
    Captain of Company No. 11, Militia, December 9, 1775.
    Signer, Association of Freemen, 1776, Bush River Lower.
    (D-358, D-359, E-95, E-116, I-319, M-16, Y-21, O-3, O-6, O-7)

BOND, JACOB JR.
    Private, Capt. Jacob Bond's Company No. 11, December 9, 1775.
    Signer, Association of Freemen, 1776, Bush River Lower Hundred.
    (E-117, I-319)

BOND, JAMES, of Joseph.
    Private, Capt. Jacob Bond's Company No. 11, December 9, 1775.
    Signer, Association of Freemen, 1775/1776, Bush River Lower.
    2nd Lieutenant, 8th Battalion, 1778.
    Signer, Oath of Fidelity and Allegiance to Maryland, 1778.
    (A-31, B-15, C-46, D-357, E-117, I-319, J-236)

BOND, JAMES.
    Signer, Association of Freemen, 1775, Gunpowder Neck. (I-327)
    Militia Substitute, 1781. (E-132, F-400)

BOND, JOHN.
    Member of Bush River Company. Married Aliceanna Webster. (E-232)

BOND, PETER.
    Private, Capt. Taylor's Company No. 7, September 9, 1775.
    Signer, Association of Freemen, 1776, Gunpowder Upper Hundred.
    Signer, Oath of Fidelity and Allegiance to Maryland, 1778.
    (A-31, B-12, E-113, I-326, J-234)

BOND, THOMAS, of John.
    Born c.1739. Died c.1791. Married Rebecca Stansbury in 1771.
    War Committee of Harford County, 1775.
    Representative to Maryland Convention, June 26, 1775.
    Agent's Ledger No. 1, f. 2, 1777.
    Intendant's Day Book No. 1, p. 31, 1786.
    (D-358, E-97, HR-50, K-496, O-14, O-15, O-22)

BOND, THOMAS, of Thomas.
    Court Justice, Harford County, 1774-1775. (E-61)

BOND, THOMAS JR.
    War Committee, Correspondence, June 11, 1775. (D-358, E-95)

BOND, WILLIAM.
    Signer and Solicitor, Association of Freemen of Maryland, 1776,
      Bush River Lower Hundred.
    Signer, Oath of Fidelity and Allegiance to Maryland, 1778.
    Administered the oath ("Worshipfull William Bond"), 1778.
    Lord Justice, Harford County Court, 1783.
    (A-31, B-15, E-263, E-77, J-236)

BOND, WILLIAM, of Joshua.
    Private, Capt. Jacob Bond's Company No. 11, December 9, 1775.
    Committee of Correspondence, War Committee, June 11, 1775.
    Signer, Association of Freemen, 1776, Bush River Lower Hundred.
    (E-117, I-328, E-96)

BONER, JAMES, of Barney.
    Private, Capt. Anderson's Company No. 3, September 23, 1775.
    (E-109)

BONER, JOSEPH.
    Signer, Association of Freemen, 1776, Susquehanna. (I-321)

BONER, WILLIAM.
    Private, Capt. Anderson's Company No. 3, September 23, 1775.
    Signer and solicitor, Association of Freemen, 1776, Susquehanna.
    (E-108, I-321)

BOOTH, RICHARD.
    Signer, Oath of Fidelity and Allegiance to Maryland, 1778.
    (A-31, B-10, J-233)

BORK, EDWARD.
    Signer, Association of Freemen, 1775, Bush River Upper. (I-316)

BOSE, WILLIAM.
    Signer, Association of Freemen, 1776, Deer Creek Upper. (I-322)

BOSLEY, WALTER.
    1st Lieutenant of Capt. Richard Cromwell's Company of the
      Gunpowder Upper Battalion of Militia, October 31, 1780.
    Intendant's Day Book No. 2, p. 72, November 3, 1785.
    (C-4, HR-50)

BOSLEY, WILLIAM.
    Private, Capt. Baker's Company No. 15, January 27, 1776.
    Signer, Oath of Fidelity and Allegiance to Maryland, 1778.
    Grand Juror, Harford County, 1783.
    (A-31, B-30, E-120, E-77, J-247)

BOTTS, GEORGE.
    Signer, Association of Freemen, 1776, Susquehanna. (I-321)

BOTTS, JNO.
    Signer, Association of Freemen, 1776, Susquehanna. (I-321)

BOTTS, JOSEPH.
    Pensioner (maimed soldier), 1778. (F-661)

BOWDEN, WILLIAM.
    Recruit, New Regiment, August 1, 1780. (E-131, F-343)

BOYCE, ROGER.
    Signer, Association of Freemen, 1775, Gunpowder Neck.
    Private, Capt. Rumsey's Company No. 6, September 16, 1775.
    Signer, Oath of Fidelity and Allegiance to Maryland, 1778.
    1st Lieutenant, 8th Battalion, 1778. "Gone to sea."
    (A-31, B-20, C-47, E-112, I-327, J-239)

BOYER, WILLIAM.
    Private, Capt. Bradford's Company No. 13, September 30, 1775.
    Signer, Association of Freemen, 1776, Harford Lower Hundred.
    (E-119, I-324)

BOYLE, JAMES.
　　Private, Capt. Harris' Payroll, 1776. (E-130, F-304)

BOYLE, THOMAS.
　　Private, Capt. Rodgers' Co. No. 5, Sept. 15, 1775. (E-111)
　　Signer, Oath of Allegiance to Md., 1778. (A-31, B-26, J-243)

BRADFORD, JOHN GEORGE.
　　Born 1721. Died 1808. Married: Margaret Bonfield, 1764. (M-19, Z-6)
　　War Committee, County Correspondence, June 11, 1775. (D-358, E-96)
　　Signer, Association of Freemen, 1776, Harford Upper Hundred. (I-325)
　　Signer, Oath of Allegiance to Md., 1778. (A-31, B-21, J-239)
　　Second Register of Wills of Harford County, 1780. (E-359)

BRADFORD, WILLIAM SR.
　　Born 1739, Baltimore County. Died 1794, Harford County. Source G-172
　　states wife Elizabeth Lightbody and son William Jr. Source X-79
　　states wife Sarah McComas, married 1764; and Source E-216 agrees,
　　adding 11 children, one of whom, Samuel, was father of Augustus W.
　　Bradford, Governor of Maryland during the Civil War.
　　Signer, Bush Declaration, March 22, 1775. (D-355)
　　War Committee, Harford County, 1775. (D-358)
　　Captain, Company No. 13, Harford Militia, 1775. (D-359, E-119)
　　Signer, Association of Freemen, 1776, Bush River Lower. (I-320)
　　Captain, 23rd Battalion, Harford County Militia, 1778. (C-45)
　　Grand Juror, Harford County, 1780. (E-76)

BRADFORD, WILLIAM JR.
　　Private, Capt. Hall's Co. No. 1, September 12, 1775. (E-106)
　　Signer and Solicitor, Association of Freemen, 1775 and 1776,
　　　Harford Upper Hundred. (I-315, I-325)

BRADFORD, WILLIAM.
　　Nephew of William Bradford, Sr.
　　Lieutenant under Colonel Alexander Lawson Smith. (E-214)
　　Lieutenant under Col. Rawlings 1st Co. of Md. Riflemen. (D-361)
　　Lieutenant in 4th Maryland Continental Line, 1776-77. (E-129, F-301)
　　Fought at Battle of Fort Washington, N.Y., Nov. 16, 1776. (E-136)
　　Furlough, Jan.-Feb., 1778. Resigned April 3, 1778. (F-301)
　　Source X-79 indicates a Lt. William Bradford married Margaret Hill
　　　Richardson, and died circa 1783.

BRADY, NICHOLAS.
　　Private, Capt. Paca's Company, August 5, 1776. (E-127, F-59)
　　Signer, Association of Freemen, 1775, Spesutie Lower. (I-317)

BRAGER, ROBERT.
　　Signer, Association of Freemen, 1776, Harford Upper. (I-325)

BRAKENRIDGE (BRECKENRIDGE), JOHN.
　　Private, Capt. Rigdon's Company No. 12, December 2, 1775.
　　Private, Capt. Paca's Company, August 5, 1776.
　　Signer, Association of Freemen, 1776, Deer Creek Upper.
　　(E-118, E-127, F-59, I-322)

BRAKENRIDGE (BRECKENRIDGE), WILLIAM.
    Private, Capt. Rigdon's Company No. 12, December 2, 1775.
    Signer, Association of Freemen, 1776, Deer Creek Upper.
    (E-118, I-322)

BRANAN, WILLIAM.
    Private, Capt. Rumsey's Company No. 6, September 16, 1775.
    (E-112)

BRANDRICK, WILLIAM.
    Signer, Oath of Fidelity and Allegiance to Maryland, 1778.
    (A-31, B-12, J-234)

BRANNON, TIMOTHY.
    Private, Capt. Harris' Company payroll. (E-130, F-340)

BRANNON, WILLIAM.
    Private, Capt. Anderson's Company No. 3, September 23, 1775.
    Private, Capt. Patrick's Company No. 17, April 1, 1776.
    Signer, Association of Freemen, 1776, Deer Creek Lower.
    (E-109, E-122, I-322)

BRASHER (BRASER), ROBERT.
    Private, Capt. Bradford's Company No. 13, September 30, 1775.
    Signer, Oath of Fidelity and Allegiance to Maryland, 1778.
    (A-31, B-21, E-119, J-239)

BREDEN, ROBERT.
    Signer, Oath of Fidelity and Allegiance to Maryland, 1778.
    (A-31, B-26, J-243)

BREWER, JAMES.
    Pensioner (maimed soldier), 1778.
    Signer, Association of Freemen, 1776, Susquehanna Hundred.
    (F-661, I-321)

BRICE, THOMAS.
    Signer, Bush Declaration, March 22, 1775.
    War Committee, Harford County, 1775.
    (D-355, D-359)

BRIDGE, JAMES.
    Private, Capt. Bond's Company No. 11, December 9, 1775.
    Signer, Association of Freemen, 1776, Bush River Lower.
    Signer, Oath of Fidelity and Allegiance to Maryland, 1778.
    (A-31, B-10, E-117, I-319, J-233)

BRIERLEY (BRYERLY), GEORGE.
    Born 1757.
    Private, Militia. Widow applied for pension.
    Signer, Oath of Fidelity and Allegiance to Maryland, 1778.
    (A-31, B-19, J-238, N-12)

BRIERLEY (BRYERLY), HENRY.
    Signer, Association of Freemen, 1775/1776, Bush River Upper.
    Signer, Oath of Fidelity and Allegiance to Maryland, 1778.
    (A-31, B-19, I-317, I-328, J-238)

BRIERLEY (BRYERLY), HUGH.
    Signer, Oath of Fidelity and Allegiance to Maryland, 1778.
    (A-31, B-31, J-248)

BRIERLEY (BRYERLY), HUGH JR.
    Signer, Oath of Fidelity and Allegiance to Maryland, 1778.
    One source misspelled his name "Hugh Bezerly, Jr."
    (A-31, B-28, J-245)

BRIERLEY (BRYERLY), ROBERT.
    Born 1749. Died c.1837. Married: Elizabeth Bell.
    Signer, Association of Freemen, 1776, Spesutie Upper.
    Signer, Oath of Fidelity and Allegiance to Maryland, 1778.
    (A-31, B-19, I-319, J-238, Z-7)

BRITCHARD, JOHN.
    Signer, Oath of Fidelity and Allegiance to Maryland, 1778.
    (A-31, B-26, J-243)

BRITTON (BRITTEN, BRITTAIN), WILLIAM.
    Sergeant, Company No. 15, Jarrettsville Militia, Jan. 27, 1776.
    Signer, Association of Freemen, 1776, Eden Hundred.
    Signer, Oath of Fidelity and Allegiance to Maryland, 1778.
    (A-31, B-23, E-120, I-324, J-241)

BROMLEY, JOSEPH.
    Signer, Oath of Fidelity and Allegiance to Maryland, 1778.
    (A-31, J-248)

BRONNLEY, ARTHUR.
    Signer, Oath of Fidelity and Allegiance to Maryland, 1778.
    (A-31, B-10, J-233)

BRONNWOOD, JOHN.
    Signer, Oath of Fidelity and Allegiance to Maryland, 1778.
    (A-31, B-10, J-233)

BROOK, THOMAS.
    Signer, Association of Freemen, 1776, Deer Creek Upper. (I-322)

BROOKS, JOHN.
    Private, Capt. Bradford's Company No. 13, September 30, 1775.
    Signer, Association of Freemen, 1776, Harford Upper Hundred.
    Signer, Oath of Fidelity and Allegiance to Maryland, 1778.
    (A-31, B-10, E-119, I-325, J-234)

BROWN, DAVID.
    Signer, Oath of Fidelity and Allegiance to Maryland, 1778.
    (A-31, B-30, J-247)

BROWN, EDWARD.
Signer, Oath of Fidelity and Allegiance to Maryland, 1778.
(A-31, B-17, J-237)

BROWN, FREEBORN.
Private, Capt. Josias Hall's Company No. 1, September 12, 1775.
War Committee, Harford County, 1775.
Grand Juror, 1783. (D-358, E-105, E-77, O-17)

BROWN, GARRETT.
Signer, Oath of Fidelity and Allegiance to Maryland, 1778.
(A-31, B-21, J-239)

BROWN, JAMES.
Signer, Association of Freemen, 1775, Spesutie Lower Hundred.
Private, Capt. Francis Holland's Harford Rifles, 1776.
Sold a gun to the Committee of Harford, August 24, 1776.
Signer, Oath of Fidelity and Allegiance to Maryland, 1778.
Born 1753. Died 1781. Married: Catherine McCormick.
(A-31, B-10, E-124, I-317, J-234, K-230)

BROWN, JAS. B.B.
Signer, Association of Freemen, 1775, Bush River Upper. (I-316)

BROWN, JOHN.
Private, Capt. Aquila Hall's Company No. 4, September 9, 1775.
Signer, Association of Freemen, 1776, Bush River Upper.
Signer, Oath of Fidelity and Allegiance to Maryland, 1778.
(A-31, B-22, E-109, I-328, J-240)

BROWN, JOHN, of James.
Private, Capt. Taylor's Company No. 7, September 9, 1775.
Signer, Association of Freemen, 1776, Harford Lower.
Signer, Oath of Fidelity and Allegiance to Maryland, 1778.
(B-23, E-114, I-324, J-241)

BROWN, JOHN.
Signer, Association of Freemen, 1776, Harford Hundred. (I-325)

BROWN, JOHN (Wheelright).
Signer, Association of Freemen, 1776, Gunpowder Upper.
Signer, Oath of Fidelity and Allegiance to Maryland, 1778.
(A-31, B-14, J-235)

BROWN, JOSHUA.
Born 1754. Died 1820. Married: Margaret Mansel.
Signer, Association of Freemen, 1775, Gunpowder Neck.
Cadet, Lt. James Bond's Flying Camp, July 9, 1776, under
  Col. Thomas Ewing's Battalion.
Born in America. (5'9¼", light-colored hair)
Grand Juror, Harford County, 1780.
(E-76, E-125, F-54, I-327, X-93)

BROWN, PEREGRINE.
   Signer, Association of Freemen, 1775, Gunpowder Neck. (I-327)

BROWN, ROBERT.
   Born 1757. Died 1833. Married: Dinah Bowen.
   Private, Capt. Aquila Hall's Company No. 4, September 9, 1775.
   Signer, Association of Freemen, 1776, Harford Lower.
   Signer, Oath of Fidelity and Allegiance to Maryland, 1778.
   (A-31, B017, E-109, I-324, J-237, X-93)

BROWN, SAMUEL.
   Private, Capt. Taylor's Company No. 7, Sept. 9, 1775. (E-113)

BROWN, SOLOMON.
   Signer, Association of Freemen, 1775, Bush River Upper. (I-317)

BROWN, THOMAS.
   Private, Capt. Aquila Hall's Company No. 4, September 9, 1775.
   Signer, Association of Freemen, 1776, Harford Lower Hundred.
   (E-110, I-324)

   Private, Capt. Webb's Company No. 16, October 14, 1775.
   Signer, Association of Freemen, 1776, Deer Creek Upper.
   (E-121, I-323)

BROWN, WILLIAM.
   Private, Capt. Bond's Company No. 11, December 9, 1775.
   Signer, Association of Freemen, 1776, Bush River Lower.
   Signer, Oath of Fidelity and Allegiance to Maryland, 1778.
   (A-31, B-10, E-117, I-319, J-233)

BROWNE, JOSHUA.
   Born 1751. Died 1819. Married: Hannah Hamilton.
   Private, Capt. Josias Hall's Company No. 1, September 12, 1775.
   Signer, Oath of Fidelity and Allegiance to Maryland, 1778.
   (A-31, B-14, E-106, J-235, X-93)

BROWNE, THOMAS.
   Signer, Oath of Fidelity and Allegiance to Maryland, 1778.
   (A-31, B-26, J-243)

BROWNING, THOMAS.
   Private, Capt. Aquila Hall's Company No. 4, September 9, 1775.
   Signer, Association of Freemen, 1775, Spesutie Lower Hundred.
   (E-110, I-317)

BROWNLY (BROWNLEY), JOSEPH.
   Private, Capt. Archer's Company No. 2, September 16, 1775.
   Signer, Association of Freemen, 1776, Spesutie Upper.
   Signer, Oath of Fidelity and Allegiance to Maryland, 1778.
   Grand Jury Foreman, 1779.
   Grand Jury Member, 1783.
   (B-25, E-75, E-76, E-108, I-319, J-242)

BROWNLY (BROWLEY), NATHAN.
Draft, Militia, 1781; "never taken up." (E-132, F-400)

BRUCE, JOHN.
Private, Capt. Dorsey's Co. No. 8, October 31, 1775. (E-115)

BRUCEBANKS (BRUSEBANKS), EDWARD HORTON.
Private, Capt. Aquila Hall's Company No. 4, September 9, 1775.
Signer, Association of Freemen, 1775, Spesutie Lower.
(E-109, I-317)

BRUCEBANKS (BRUSEBANKS), WILLIAM.
Private, Capt. Paca's Company, July 24, 1776.
Signer, Association of Freemen, 1775, Spesutie Lower.
(E-126, F-59, I-317)

BUCHANAN, ROBERT.
Attorney at Law of Harford County Court, 1774-1775. (E-63)

BUCK, JOHN.
Signer, Association of Freemen, 1775, Spesutie Lower. (I-317)

BUCKLEY, JOHN.
Private, Capt. Taylor's Company No. 7, September 9, 1775.
Signer, Oath of Fidelity and Allegiance to Maryland, 1778.
Signer, Association of Freemen, 1776. Records indicate there
were two men with this name: one in Harford Lower Hundred
and one in Gunpowder Upper Hundred.
"Ordered that Western shore Treasurer pay to John Buckley
6 lbs. for one month's adjutantcy to Col. Rumsey's
Battalion, of Militia, October 10, 1776." (K-330)
(A-31, B-22, E-114, I-324, I-326, J-240)

BUCKMAN, JOHN.
Signer, Oath of Fidelity and Allegiance to Maryland, 1778.
(A-31, B-28, J-245)

BUDD, GEORGE.
Signer, Oath of Fidelity and Allegiance to Maryland, 1778.
(A-31, B-22, J-240)

BULL, CACOB.
Signer, Oath of Fidelity and Allegiance to Maryland, 1778.
(A-31, B-19, J-238)

BULL, EDMUND.
Born 1729/1730. Died 1776. Married: Susana Lyon in 1752.
Children: Rachel, Esther, Mary, Jacob, John.
Private, Capt. John Love's Company No. 10, September 14, 1775.
War Committee, Harford County, 1775.
Signer and solicitor, Association of Freemen, 1775/1776,
Spesutie Upper Hundred.
(D-358, E-116, I-315, I-318, M-25, X-99, G-186)

BULL, EDWARD, of Jacob.
    Private, Capt. Bond's Company No. 11, December 9, 1775.
    Signer, Association of Freemen, 1776, Bush River Lower.
    Signer, Oath of Fidelity and Allegiance to Maryland, 1778.
    (A-31, B-28, E-117, I-328, J-245)

BULL, ISAAC, of John.
    Signer, Association of Freemen, 1776, Spesutie Upper. (I-318)

BULL, JACOB.
    Private, Capt. Bond's Company No. 11, December 9, 1775.
    Signer, Association of Freemen, 1776, Bush River Lower.
    Signer, Oath of Fidelity and Allegiance to Maryland, 1778.
    (A-31, B-25, E-117, I-319, I-328, J-242)

BULL, JACOB, of Edmund.
    Born c.1733. Died c.1776. Married: Rennis (or Ranrice) Bussey in 1752.
    Private, Capt. John Love's Company No. 10, September 14, 1775.
    Signer, Association of Freemen, 1776, Spesutie Upper Hundred.
    (I-318, E-116, M-25, X-99)

BULL, JACOB, of Jacob.
    Private, Capt. Bond's Company No. 11, December 9, 1775.
    Signer, Association of Freemen, 1776, Gunpowder Upper.
    Signer, Oath of Fidelity and Allegiance to Maryland, 1778.
    (A-31, B-28, E-117, I-326, J-245)

BULL, JACOB, of John.
    Signer, Association of Freemen, 1776, Eden Hundred.
    Signer, Oath of Fidelity and Allegiance to Maryland, 1778.
    (A-31, B-30, I-323, J-247)

BULL, JAMES.
    Private, Capt. Robert Harris' Harford Rifles, 1776.
    Paid subsistence for five weeks, September 21, 1776.
    (E-123, K-435)

BULL, JOHN.
    Private, Capt. Bradford's Company No. 13, September 30, 1775.
    Private, Capt. Francis Holland's Harford Rifles, 1776.
    Signer, Association of Freemen, 1776, Harford Hundred.
    Signer, Oath of Fidelity and Allegiance to Maryland, 1778.
    (A-31, B-21, E-119, E-124, I-325, J-239)

BULL, RICHARD.
    Private, Capt. Bradford's Company No. 13, September 30, 1775.
    Signer, Association of Freemen, 1776, Harford Upper Hundred.
    (E-119, I-325)

BULL, WILLIAM.
    Signer, Oath of Fidelity and Allegiance to Maryland, 1778.
    (A-31, B-12, J-234)

BULL, WILLIAM JR.
   Signer, Association of Freemen, 1776, Gunpowder Upper. (I-326)

BULLING, THOMAS.
   Maryland Line, last date, October 2, 1780. (F-414)

BULLOCK, JOHN.
   Private, Capt. Rigdon's Company No. 12, December 2, 1775.
   Signer, Association of Freemen, 1776, Deer Creek Upper.
   (E-118, I-322)

BUNTING, WILLIAM.
   Born 1742, England. Died 1786, Harford County, Maryland.
   Married: Billy Drew Andrew. Son: John.
   Cadet, Flying Camp, Lt. James Bond enlisted July 7, 1776,
      under Col. Thomas Ewing's Battalion (5'6$\frac{1}{4}$", short black hair)
   (E-125, F-54, G-187, X-100)

BURGESS, EDWARD.
   Recruit, 1st Md. Regt., July 13, 1780. (E-130, F-343)

BURK, JAMES.
   Pensioner (maimed soldier), 1778. (F-661)

BURK, RICHARD.
   Signer, Association of Freemen, 1776, Deer Creek Upper. (I-322)

BURKE, THOMAS.
   Private, Capt. Rigdon's Company No. 12, December 2, 1775.(E-118)

BURNS, ALEXANDER.
   Corporal, Capt. Rodgers' Company No. 5, Sept. 15, 1775. (E-110)

BURR, John.
   Signer, Oath of Fidelity and Allegiance to Maryland, 1778.
   (A-31, B-14, J-236)

BURTON, RICHARD.
   Signer, Association of Freemen, 1776, Gunpowder Upper Hundred.
   Signer, Oath of Fidelity and Allegiance to Maryland, 1778.
   (A-31, B-23, I-326, J-241)

BUSH, JOHN.
   Private, Capt. Robert Harris' Harford Rifles, 1776.
   Paid subsistence for two weeks, October 16, 1776.
   Signer, Oath of Fidelity and Allegiance to Maryland, 1778.
   (A-31, B-29, E-123, J-246, K-436)

BUSSEY, BENNETT.
   Born 1745. Died 1827. Married: (1) Anne Green in 1774;
   (2) Elizabeth Standbury Slade in 1806.
   Children: Martha, Elizabeth, Edward, Henry.
   Signer, Association of Freemen, 1775, Gunpowder Upper.
   Solicitor, Association of Freemen, 1776, as Capt. Bussey.
      (continued)

BUSSEY, BENNETT (continued)
    Captain, 8th Battalion, Flying Camp, February 20, 1776.
    Captain, 2nd Battalion, under Col. Josias Carvil Hall,
        July 20, 1776 to December, 1776.
    Fought in Battle of White Plains, N.Y., October 28, 1776.
    Army Account No. 1, page 49 (Captain). Major, 1777.
    Intendants Orders No. 2, f. 13, November 14, 1785.
    (E-126, E-137, E-266, F-59, G-191, HR-50, I-315, I-325,
      K-170, L-137, X-106, O-3, O-4, O-6)

BUSSEY, EDWARD.
    Born 1718. Died 1782.
    Private, Capt. John Love's Company No. 10, Sept. 14, 1775.
    Signer, Association of Freemen, 1776, Spesutie Upper Hundred.
    2nd Lieutenant, Deer Creek Battalion, 1778.
    Captain, June 17, 1778, Army Account No. 1, p. 52.
    Signer, Oath of Fidelity and Allegiance to Maryland, 1778.
    (A-31, B-28, C-43, E-116, HR-50, I-318, J-245, L-137, X-106, Z-8)

BUTCHER, JOHN.
    Pensioner (maimed soldier), 1778. (F-661)

BUTERSBO, JOHN.
    Signer, Oath of Allegiance to Md., 1778. (A-31, B-23, J-241)

BUTLER, GEORGE.
    Private, Capt. Archer's Co. No. 2, Sept. 16, 1775. (E-108)
    Signer, Oath of Allegiance to Maryland, 1778. (A-31, B-25, J-242)

BUTLER, JOHN.
    Recruit, 8th Maryland Regiment, 1780. (E-131, F-343)

BUTLER, JOSEPH.
    Born c. 1750. Died c. 1794. Married: Mary Ogle.
    Private, Capt. Josias Hall's Company No. 1, Sept. 12, 1775.
    Clerk, Committee of Correspondence, June 11, 1775.
    (E-96, E-106, X-106)

BUTLER, WILLIAM.
    Militia substitute, 1781. (E-132, F-400)

BUTTERS, JAMES.
    Furnished a gun to the Harford County Committee, June, 1776.
    (E-330)

BYARD, EPHRAIM.
    Signer, Association of Freemen, 1775, Susquehanna Hundred.
    Private, Capt. Anderson's Company No. 3, September 23, 1775.
    (D-357, E-108)

BYARD, JAMES.
    Private, Capt. Anderson's Company No. 3, September 23, 1775.
    Signer, Association of Freemen, 1776, Susquehanna Hundred.
    Signer, Oath of Fidelity and Allegiance to Maryland, 1778.
    Furnished a gun to the Harford County Committee, June, 1776.
    (A-32, B-27, E-108, E-336, I-321, J-244)

BYFOOT, MOSES.
Signer, Association of Freemen, 1776, Harford Upper.
Signer, Oath of Fidelity and Allegiance to Maryland, 1778.
(A-32, B-17, I-325, J-237)

BYFOOT, TAYMAN.
Private, Capt. Bradford's Company No. 13, September 30, 1775.
Signer, Association of Freemen, 1776, Harford Upper.
(E-119, I-325)

BYFOOT, WILLIAM.
Private, Capt. Taylor's Company No. 7, September 9, 1775.
(E-113)

CAHILL, JAMES.
Born 1749. Died 1851. Married: Ellender_____.
Private, Militia.
Signer, Association of Freemen, 1776, Gunpowder Upper.
(I-326, N-13, X-109)

CAIN (CAINE), EDWARD.
Born 1753. Died 1832. Married: Mary_____.
Signer, Association of Freemen, 1776, Eden Hundred.
Pensioner (maimed soldier), 1778.
Private, Maryland Line (Invalid "Edward Kain").
Signer, Oath of Fidelity and Allegiance to Maryland, 1778.
(A-32, B-22, F-661, I-323, J-240, N-31, X-109)

CAIN, JAMES.
Private, Capt. Archer's Company No. 2, September 16, 1775.
Signer, Association of Freemen, 1776, Spesutie Upper.
Signer, Oath of Fidelity and Allegiance to Maryland, 1778.
(A-32, B-10, E-108, I-319, J-234)

CAIN, PATRICK.
Recommended as Lieutenant by County Lieutenant R. Dallam
in Deer Creek Battalion in place of John Long, April 9, 1778.
(C-24)

CAIN, WILLIAM.
Signer, Association of Freemen, 1775, Bush River Upper. (I-317)

CAIRNS, ARCHIBALD.
Signer, Association of Freemen, 1776, Deer Creek Upper. (I-323)

CAIRNS (CAIRNES), JOHN.
Signer, Association of Freemen, 1776, Deer Creek Upper. (I-322)

CALDER, JOHN.
Signer, Oath of Fidelity and Allegiance to Maryland, 1778.
(A-32, B-15, J-236)

CALDWELL, JOHN.
Signer, Association of Freemen, Harford Upper, 1776.
Signer, Oath of Fidelity and Allegiance to Maryland, 1778.
(A-32, B-25, I-325, J-242)

CALDWELL, SAMUEL. See Calwell, Samuel.

CALGROVE, JOHN.
Private, Capt. Roger's Co. No. 5, September 15, 1775. (E-110)

CALLAHAN, EDMUND.
Private, Capt. Webb's Company No. 16, October 14, 1775.
Private, Capt. Francis Holland's Harford Rifles, 1776.
Signer, Association of Freemen, 1776, Spesutie Upper.
(E-121, E-124, I-319)

CALLENDAR (CALLINDAR, CALLENDER), JOHN.
Born 1750.
Private, Capt. John Love's Company No. 10, September 14, 1775.
Signer, Association of Freemen, 1776, Bush River Lower.
Private, 4th Maryland Continental Line, 1776-1779. Prisoner.
(E-116, E-129, F-301, I-320, N-13)

CALLENDAR, ROBERT.
Signer, Association of Freemen, 1776, Bush River Lower.
Signer, Oath of Fidelity and Allegiance to Maryland, 1778.
(A-32, B-10, I-320, J-233)

CALLENDAR, ROBERT JR.
Signer, Oath of Fidelity and Allegiance to Maryland, 1778.
(A-32, B-10, J-233)

CALMER, CHARLES.
Signer, Association of Freemen, 1776, Bush River Lower. (I-319)

CALWELL, DAVID.
Private, Capt. Taylor's Company No. 7, September 9, 1775.
Signer, Association of Freemen, 1776, Gunpowder Upper.
(E-113, I-326)

CALWELL (CALDWELL), SAMUEL.
Signer, Bush Declaration, March 22, 1775.
Signer, Association of Freemen, 1775, Gunpowder Upper.
War Committee, Harford County, 1775.
1st Lieutenant, Capt. Taylor's Co. No. 7, September 9, 1775.
Captain, 8th Battalion, Appointed April 25, 1776.
Solicitor, Association of Freemen, 1776, Gunpowder Upper.
Major, 8th Battalion, 1778.
Signer, Oath of Fidelity and Allegiance to Maryland, 1778.
(A-32, B-12, C-46, D-355, D-358, D-359, E-113, E-266, C-7,
I-315, I-326, J-234, K-310)
Wife: Ann Richardson. Sons: James, William, Thomas. (E-230)

CAMERON, JAMES.
  Signer, Association of Freemen, 1776, Gunpowder Upper. (I-326)

CAMP, JAMES.
  Private, Capt. Taylor's Co. No. 7, September 9, 1775. (E-113)

CAMPBELL (CAMMEL), DANIEL.
  Private, Capt. Dorsey's Company No. 8, October 31, 1775.
  Signer, Association of Freemen, 1775, Spesutie Lower Hundred.
  Signer, Oath of Fidelity and Allegiance to Maryland, 1778.
  (A-32, B-26, E-115, I-317, J-243)

CAMPBELL, DANIEL SR.
  Signer, Association of Freemen, 1776, Bush River Upper. (I-320)

CAMPBELL, DAVID.
  Private, Capt. Robert Harris' Harford Rifles, 1776.
  Paid subsistence for four weeks, one day, October 3, 1776.
  (E-123, K-436)

CAMPBELL (CAMBELL), JAMES.
  Private, Capt. Charles Baker's Co. No. 15, January 27, 1776.
  Signer, Oath of Fidelity and Allegiance to Maryland, 1778.
  (A-32, B-19, E-120, J-238)

CAMPBELL, JOHN SR.
  Signer, Association of Freemen, 1776, Bush River Upper.
  Signer, Oath of Fidelity and Allegiance to Maryland, 1778.
  (A-32, B-23, I-320, J-241)

CAMPBELL, JOHN JR.
  Signer, Association of Freemen, 1775, Bush River Upper. (I-316)

CAMPBELL, PATRICK.
  Private, Capt. John Love's Company No. 10, September 14, 1775.
  Private, Capt. Jacob Bond's Company No. 11, December 9, 1775.
    Records indicate there were two men with this name.
  (E-116, E-117)

CANDEAN or CANCLEAR, JOHN.
  Signer, Association of Freemen, 1776, Spesutie Upper. (I-319)

CANTLER, WILLIAM.
  Private, Capt. Rodgers' Co. No. 5, September 15, 1775. (E-111)

CANTLIN (CATLIN), WILLIAM.
  Drafted, Militia, 1781; "lame and unfit for duty." (E-133, F-401)

CAPBELL, JOHN.
  Signer, Oath of Fidelity and Allegiance to Maryland, 1778.
  (A-32, B-29, J-246)

CAPEN, THOMAS.
    Private, Capt. Robert Harris' Harford Rifles, 1776.
    Paid subsistence for two weeks, two days, October 20, 1776.
    (E-123, K-436)

CAPLE, JAMES.
    Substitute, Militia, 1781, 3 years.   (E-133, F-401)

CAREY, JOHN.
    Signer, Oath of Fidelity and Allegiance to Maryland, 1778.
    (A-32, B-26, J-243)

CAREY, MICHAEL.
    Private, Capt. Dorsey's Co. No. 8, October 31, 1775.   (E-115)

CARLAN (CARLEN), GEORGE.
    Signer, Association of Freemen, 1776, Deer Creek Lower.
    Signer, Oath of Fidelity and Allegiance to Maryland, 1778.
    (A-32, B-14, I-322, J-235)

CARLEN, WILLIAM.
    Drafted, Militia, 1781; "lame and unfit for duty." (E-133, F-401)

CARLILE (CARLISLE), JOHN.
    Solicitor, Association of Freemen, 1775/1776, Spesutie Lower.
    Private, Capt. Josias Hall's Co. No. 1, September 12, 1775.
    1st Lieutenant, Company No.2, Flying Camp. Harford Rifles,
        under Captain Francis Holland, October 15, 1776.
    Captain, 2nd Canadian (Hazen's) Regiment, November 3, 1776.
    Taken prisoner at Staten Island, August 22, 1777.
    Retired July 1, 1783.
    Depreciation Pay No. 2, p. 21; Depreciation Pay No. 3, p. 211.
    Army Ledger No. 2, f. 35; Agent's Letter Book No. 1, p. 217.
    (D-359, E-106, E-124, HR-50, I-315, I-318, K-350, L-144)

CARLILE (CARLISLE), LANCELOT.
    Signer, Association of Freemen, 1776, Gunpowder Upper.
    Signer, Oath of Fidelity and Allegiance to Maryland, 1778.
    (A-32, B-20, I-326, J-239)

CARLILE (CARLISLE), ROBERT.
    Private, Capt. Bennett Bussey's Company, July 20, 1776.
    Signer, Association of Freemen, 1776, Bush River Upper.
    Signer, Association of Freemen, 1776, Gunpowder Upper.
        Records indicate there were two signers with this name.
    Signer, Oath of Fidelity and Allegiance to Maryland, 1778.
    (A-32, B-23, E-127, F-60, I-320, I-325, J-241)

CARNAN (CARMAN), ALEXANDER.
    Signer, Association of Freemen, 1776, Deer Creek Upper. (I-322)

CARNAN (CARMAN), ANDREW.
    Signer, Oath of Fidelity and Allegiance to Maryland, 1778.
    (A-32, B-24, J-242)

CARNAN (CARMAN), JOHN.
    Signer, Association of Freemen, 1776, Deer Creek Lower. (I-322)

CARR, JOHN.
    Private, Capt. John Love's Company No. 10, September 14, 1775.
    Married Margarett Brownly in 1779, Harford County.
    (E-116, N-13, N-111)

CARR, MICHAEL.
    Private, Capt. Jacob Bond's Company No. 11, December 9, 1775.
    Private, Capt. Bennett Bussey's Company, July 20, 1776.
    Signer, Association of Freemen, 1776, Bush River Lower. His
      name was spelled "Mycal Car."
    (E-117, E-127, F-60, I-319)

CARROLL, GEORGE.
    Private, Capt. Patrick's Co. No. 17, April 1, 1776. (E-122)

CARROLL, JAMES SR.
    Private, Capt. Bradford's Company No. 13, September 30, 1775.
    Signer, Association of Freemen, 1776, Gunpowder Upper Hundred.
    Signer, Oath of Fidelity and Allegiance to Maryland, 1778.
    Petit Juror, Harford County, 1783.
    (A-32, B-17, E-119, E-77, I-326, J-237)

CARROLL, JAMES JR.
    Signer, Association of Freemen, 1776, Bush River Lower.
    Signer, Oath of Fidelity and Allegiance to Maryland, 1778.
    (A-32, B-10, I-319, J-233)

CARROLL (CARRELL), JOHN.
    Private, Capt. Anderson's Company No. 3, September 23, 1775.
    Signer, Association of Freemen, 1776, Susquehanna.
    Signer, Association of Freemen, 1776, Gunpowder Upper.
      Records indicate two signers spelling their names as shown.
    (E-108, I-321, I-326)

CARROLL, PETER.
    Private, Capt. Baker's Company No. 15, January 27, 1776.
    Signer, Association of Freemen, 1776, Bush River Upper.
    Signer, Oath of Fidelity and Allegiance to Maryland, 1778.
    (A-32, B-24, E-120, I-320, J-242)

CARSON, JOHN.
    Private, Capt. Taylor's Company No. 7, September 9, 1775.
    Signer, Association of Freemen, 1776, Gunpowder Upper.
    Signer, Oath of Fidelity and Allegiance to Maryland, 1778.
    (A-32, B-24, E-113, I-326, J-242)

CARSWELL, ROBERT.
    Private, Capt. Anderson's Co. No. 3, Sept. 23, 1775. (E-109)

CARTER, BENJAMIN.
　　Signer, Association of Freemen, 1776, Eden Hundred.
　　Signer, Oath of Fidelity and Allegiance to Maryland, 1778.
　　(A-32, B-23, I-323, J-241)

CARTER, DANIEL.
　　1st Lieutenant, Capt. Rigdon's Co. No. 12, December 2, 1775.
　　Signer, Association of Freemen, 1776, Deer Creek Upper.
　　(D-359, E-118, I-322)

CARTIN, JOHN.
　　Signer, Oath of Fidelity and Allegiance to Maryland, 1778.
　　(A-32, B-17, J-237)

CASEDY, ALLEN.
　　Signer, Oath of Fidelity and Allegiance to Maryland, 1778.
　　(A-32, B-28, J-245)

CASSELDINE, JOHN.
　　Private, Capt. Aquila Hall's Co. No. 4, September 9, 1775.
　　Signer, Association of Freemen, 1775, Spesutie Lower.
　　(E-109, I-317)

CASWELL, ROBERT.
　　2nd Lt. in the Deer Creek Battalion, 1779.　(C-44)

CATHERWOOD (CARTHERWOOD), JOHN.
　　Private, Capt. Rigdon's Company No. 12, December 2, 1775.
　　Private, Capt. Bennett Bussey's Company, July 25, 1776.
　　Signer, Association of Freemen, 1776, Deer Creek Upper.
　　(E-118, E-128, F-60, I-322)

CATMAN, JOHN.
　　Signer, Association of Freemen, 1776, Bush River Lower.(I-319)

CATTRILL (CATTRELL), WILLIAM.
　　Private, 4th Maryland Continental Line, 1776-1779.
　　Rifleman, Battle of Fort Washington, November 16, 1776.
　　(E-129, E-136, F-302)

CAVENAUGH, PATRICK.
　　Signer, Association of Freemen, 1776, Spesutie Upper. (I-318)

CHALK, JOHN.
　　Private, Capt. Baker's Co. No. 15, January 27, 1776.　(E-120)

CHALK, GEORGE.
　　Private, Capt. Baker's Co. No. 15, January 27, 1776.
　　Signer, Oath of Fidelity and Allegiance to Maryland, 1778.
　　(A-32, B-10, E-120, J-234)

CHALK, JOSHUA.
　　Signer, Association of Freemen, 1776, Gunpowder Upper. (I-326)

39

CHALMERS, GEORGE.
    Attorney at Law of Harford County Court, 1774-1775. (E-63)

CHALMERS, THOMAS.
    Deputy Clerk of Harford County, 1774-1775. (E-63)

CHAMBERS, WILLIAM.
    Signer, Association of Freemen, 1776, Gunpowder Neck.
    Private, Capt. Robert Harris' Harford Rifles, 1776.
    Paid subsistence for five weeks, September 21, 1776.
    (E-123, I-327, K-435)

CHANCE, JOHN.
    Signer, Association of Freemen, 1776, Bush River Upper.
    Private, Capt. Robert Harris' Harford Rifles, 1776.
    Paid subsistence for six weeks, two days, September 16, 1776.
    (E-123, I-320, K-435)

CHANEY (CHANCEY, CHAUNCEY), BENJAMIN.
    Private, Capt. Aquila Hall's Co. No. 4, September 9, 1775.
    Signer, Association of Freemen, 1776, Harford Lower.
    Signer, Oath of Fidelity and Allegiance to Maryland, 1778.
    (A-32, B-21, E-109, I-324, J-239)

CHANEY (CHANCEY, CHAUNCEY), GEORGE.
    Born 1738. Died 1801. Buried on Aberdeen Proving Grounds, Md.
    Private, Capt. Aquila Hall's Company No. 4, September 9, 1775.
    Signer, Association of Freemen, 1776, Harford Lower.
    Signer, Oath of Fidelity and Allegiance to Maryland, 1778.
    (A-32, B-21, E-109, I-324, J-239)

CHANEY (CHANCEY), GEORGE JR.
    Signer, Association of Freemen, 1776, Harford Lower.
    (Signer, Oath of Fidelity and Allegiance to Maryland, 1778.)
    (A-32, B-21, I-324, J-239)

CHANEY (CHANCEY), GREENBURY.
    Son of "Greenbury and Elizabeth Cheney" who married in 1725.
    Private, Capt. John Taylor's Compnay No. 7, September 9, 1775.
    (E-113, M-32)

CHANEY (CHANCEY), JAMES.
    Private, Capt. Aquila Hall's Co. No. 4, September 9, 1775.
    Signer, Association of Freemen, 1775, Susquehanna.
    (D-357, E-109)

CHANEY (CHANCEY, CHAUNCY), JOHN.
    Ensign, Capt. Anderson's Company No. 3, September 9, 1775.
    Signer, Association of Freemen, 1776, Harford Lower.
    2nd Lieutenant, 23rd Battalion, 1778.
    Signer, Oath of Fidelity and Allegiance to Maryland, 1778.
    Grand Juror, Harford County, 1780.
    (A-32, B-21, C-45, E-76, E-109, I-324, J-239)

CHANDLEY, JAMES.
   Signer, Association of Freemen, 1776, Susquehanna. (I-321)

CHANDLEY, WILLIAM.
   Signer, Association of Freemen, 1776, Spesutie Lower. (I-318)

CHAPMAN, WILLIAM.
   Recruit, New Regiment, July 17, 1780. (E-130, F-243)

CHASE, JEREMIAH TOWNLY.
   Attorney at Law of Harford County Court, 1774-1775. (E-63)

CHESNY, ADAM SHIPLEY.
   Signer, Association of Freemen, 1776, Gunpowder upper. (I-326)

CHEW, JOB M.
   Signer, Oath of Fidelity and Allegiance to Maryland, 1778.
   (A-32, B-19, J-238)

CHEW, RICHARD.
   Signer, Oath of Fidelity and Allegiance to Maryland, 1778.
   (A-32, B-20, J-239)

CHILDS, GEORGE.
   Private, Capt. Dorsey's Co. No. 8, October 31, 1775. (E-114)

CHINNETH (CHINETH, CHENOWETH), ARTHUR.
   Born 1752. Died c.1793. Married: Elspa Lawrence.
   Corporal, 4th Maryland Continental line, 1777.
   "At Hospital" January-March, 1778.
   On detachment with Capt. Lynch, April, 1778.
   Listed in one source as "Arthur Chenoweth, Jr."
   (E-129, F-301, X-128)

CHINNETH (CHINETH, CHENOWETH), JOHN.
   Born 1751. Died 1820. Married: (1) Rachel Kerr (2) Mary
      Buskirk.
   Sergeant, 4th Maryland Continental Line, 1777.
   "At Hospital" January-March 15, 1778.
   "At Hospital Peeks Kill" June-July 18, 1778.
   (E-129, F-301, X-128)

CHISWELL, ROBERT.
   Signer, Oath of Fidelity and Allegiance to Maryland, 1778.
   (A-32, B-25, J-242)

CHOCKE, GEORGE.
   Signer, Association of Freemen, 1776, Eden Hundred. (I-324)

CHOCKE (CHOCK), JOHN.
   Signer, Association of Freemen, 1776, Eden Hundred.
   Signer, Oath of Fidelity and Allegiance to Maryland, 1778.
   (A-32, B-23, I-324, J-241)

CHRISHOLM, THOMAS.
    Private, Capt. Dorsey's Company No. 8, October 31, 1775.
    Signer, Oath of Fidelity and Allegiance to Maryland, 1778.
    (A-32, B-17, E-115, J-237)

CHRISITE, ALEX.
    Militia Substitute, 1781. (E-132, F-400)

CHRISTIE, GABRIEL, Esq.
    Born 1755/1756, Havre de Grace, Md. Died 1808, Baltimore, Md.
    Married: Priscilla Hall.
    Children: Delia, Charles, Martha, Nathan, Eliza.
    Buried in Old Spesutie Churchyard, Harford County, Md.
    Private, Capt. Josias Hall's Company No. 1, Sept. 12, 1775.
    Signer, Association of Freemen, 1776, Spesutie Lower Hundred.
    Presented a gun for use by the militia, August 24, 1776.
    Signer, Oath of Fidelity and Allegiance to Maryland, 1778.
    Intendant's Day Book No. 1, p. 45, October 14, 1786.
    Served in U. S. Congress, 1793-1797, 1799-1801.
    Served in Maryland Senate, 1801-1806.
    Collector of the Port of Baltimore, 1806-1808.
    Mentioned in pamphlet, "A Walking Tour of Spesutia Cemetery."
    (A-32, B-17, E-106, I-318, HR-50, G-211, J-237, K-230, X-130)

CHRISTIE, JOHN.
    Private, Capt. Rumsey's Company No. 6, September 16, 1775.
    Signer, Association of Freemen, 1775, Gunpowder Neck Hundred.
    (E-112, I-327)

CLANCEY, DENIS.
    Private, Capt. Bennett Bussey's Company, July 20, 1776.
    (E-127, E-128, F-60)

CLAR, THOMAS JR.
    Signer, Oath of Fidelity and Allegiance to Maryland, 1778.
    (A-32, B-30, J-247)

CLARK, AQUILA.
    Married Mary Bull in 1760.
    Private, Capt. Baker's Company No. 15, January 27, 1776.
    Signer, Association of Freemen, 1776, Eden Hundred.
    Signer, Oath of Fidelity and Allegiance to Maryland, 1778.
    (A-32, B-23, E-120, I-324, J-241, M-34)

CLARK, DAVID.
    Married Salley Lewes in 1767.
    Private, Capt. Love's Company No. 10, September 14, 1775.
    Signer and Solicitor, Association of Freemen, 1775/1776,
      Spesutie Upper Hundred.
    Signer, Oath of Fidelity and Allegiance to Maryland, 1778.
      Records indicate there were two signers with this name.
    (A-32, B-13, E-116, E-262, I-318, J-235, M-34)

CLARK, JAMES.
    Private, Capt. Webb's Company No. 16, October 14, 1775.
    Signer, Association of Freemen, 1776: Records indicate there
    were two signers with this name--one from Spesutie Upper,
    and one from Deer Creek Upper.
    Signer, Oath of Fidelity and Allegiance to Maryland, 1778.
    (A-32, B-14, E-121, I-319, I-323, J-236)

CLARK, JOHN.
    Married Elizabeth Grates in 1764.
    Private, Capt. Rumsey's Company No. 6, September 16, 1775.
    Signer, Association of Freemen, 1775, Gunpowder Neck.
    Signer, Oath of Fidelity and Allegiance to Maryland, 1778.
    Grand Juror, Harford County, 1780.
    (A-32, B-25, J-242, E-76, E-112, I-317, M-34)

CLARK, JOHN.
    Married Sophia Lester in 1769.
    Private, Capt. Dorsey's Company No. 8, October 31, 1775.
    Signer, Association of Freemen, 1775, Spesutie Lower.
    Signer, Oath of Fidelity and Allegiance to Maryland, 1778.
    (A-32, B-30, E-114, I-327, J-247, M-34)

CLARK, JOHN REV.
    War Committee, Harford County, 1775.
    Signer, Oath of Fidelity and Allegiance to Maryland, 1778.
    (A-32, B-29, D-358, J-246)

CLARK, LAWRENCE.
    Signer, Oath of Fidelity and Allegiance to Maryland, 1778.
    (A-32, B-26, J-243)

CLARK, ROBERT.
    Private, Capt. Baker's Company No. 15, January 27, 1776.
    Signer, Association of Freemen, 1776, Eden Hundred.
    Signer, Oath of Fidelity and Allegiance to Maryland, 1778.
    (A-32, B-13, E-120, I-324, J-235)

CLARK, ROBERT SR.
    Corporal, Capt. Love's Company No. 10, September 14, 1775.
    Signer, Association of Freemen, 1776, Deer Creek Upper.
    Signer, Oath of Fidelity and Allegiance to Maryland, 1778.
    (A-32, B-13, E-115, I-323, J-235)

CLARK, ROBERT JR.
    Married Keziah Barton in 1750.
    Private, Capt. Rigdon's Company No. 12, December 2, 1775.
    Signer, Association of Freemen, 1776, Deer Creek Upper.
    (Signer, Oath of Fidelity and Allegiance to Maryland, 1778.)
    (A-32, B-14, E-118, I-322, J-235, M-34)

CLARK, SAMUEL.
    Signer, Association of Freemen, 1776, Deer Creek Upper. (I-322)

CLARK, WILLIAM of Robert.
    Private, Capt. Rigdon's Company No. 12, December 2, 1775.
    Signer, Oath of Fidelity and Allegiance to Maryland, 1778.
    (A-32, B-28, E-118, J-245)

CLARK, WILLIAM.
    Private, Capt. Love's Company No. 10, September 14, 1775.
    Signer, Association of Freemen, 1776, Spesutie Upper.
    (E-116, I-319)

CLARK, WILLIAM JR.
    Signer, Association of Freemen, 1776, Spesutie Upper.
    Signer, Oath of Fidelity and Allegiance to Maryland, 1778.
    (A-32, B-28, I-318, J-245)

CLARKE, DANIEL.
    Private, Capt. Archer's Co. No. 2, September 16, 1775. (E-107)

CLARKE, JOHN.
    Signer, Association of Freemen, 1775, Spesutie Lower.
    Private, Capt. Aquila Hall's Co. No. 4, September 9, 1775.
    Private, Capt. Paca's Company, July 24, 1776.
    Signer, Oath of Fidelity and Allegiance to Maryland, 1778.
    (A-32, B-20, E-109, E-126, F-59, I-317, J-239)

CLARKE, LARRENCE.
    Signer, Association of Freemen, 1776, Spesutie Upper. (I-319)

CLARKE, THOMAS.
    Signer, Association of Freemen, 1776, Spesutie Upper. (I-319)

CLARKE, WILLIAM.
    2nd Lieutenant, 23rd Battalion, 1778. (C-46)

CLAYTON (CLYTON), JOHN.
    Private, Capt. Bussey's Company, July 20, 1776. (E-127, F-60)

CLEMENTS, JOHN.
    Signer, Association of Freemen, Bush River Upper, 1775. (I-317)

CLEMMONS (CLEMENS), CHRISTOPHER.
    Private, Capt. Bond's Company No. 11, December 9, 1775.
    Signer, Oath of Fidelity and Allegiance to Maryland, 1778.
    (A-32, B-15, E-117, J-236)

CLEMMONS, PATRICK.
    Signer, Oath of Fidelity and Allegiance to Maryland, 1778.
    (A-32, B-29, J-246)

CLENDENIN (CLENDENEN), JAMES.
    Born 1737. Died 1795. Married Mary Fullerton.
    War Committee, Harford County, 1775.
    Signer and solicitor, Association of Freemen, 1776, Spesutie Upper.
    Captain, Militia, November 17, 1779.
    (C-43, D-358, E-262, I-319, X-137)

CLUVER, BENJAMIN.
    Private, Capt. Francis Holland's Harford Rifles, 1776. (E-124)

COALE, THOMAS.
    Signer, Association of Freemen, 1775, Gunpowder Neck. (I-327)

COALE, WILLIAM.
    Son of Skipwith Coale (Cole).
    Born 1740, Baltimore County. Died 1829, Harford County.
    Married: Sarah Webster, daughter of Isaac Webster and Margaret
      Lee, in 1761, Deer Creek Society of Friends (Bush River).
    Children: Isaac, Elizabeth, Sarah, William.
    Signer, Association of Freemen, 1776, Spesutie Upper Hundred.
    1st Lieutenant, Capt. Robert Harris' Harford Rifles, Co. No. 1,
      Flying Camp, Sept., 1776.
    1st Lieutenant, 8th Battalion, Harford Militia, April, 1776.
    Captain, 8th Battalion, 1778.
    Listed on the Muster Roll of the 6th Maryland Regiment, 2nd
      Battaltion, "serving in the Southern Army." Joined for 3
      years in October, 1780.
    Signer, Oath of Fidelity and Allegiance to Maryland, 1778.
    Petit Juror, Harford County, 1783.
    (A-32, B-30, C-47, D-359, E-77, E-123, E-267, I-319, J-247,
      G-219, M-36, S-369, X-144)

COALEMAN, MICHAEL.
    Continental Army, 1777-1780 (Family Support Allowance).(F-661)
                        (Wife, Catherine, and child, 1779)

COCHRAN (COCHEAN), ISAAC.
    Signer, Association of Freemen, 1776, Gunpowder Upper.
    Signer, Oath of Fidelity and Allegiance to Maryland, 1778.
    (A-32, B-12, I-326, J-234)

COCKERTON, JOHN.
    Signer, Association of Freemen, 1775, Gunpowder Neck. (I-327)

COE, WILLIAM.
    Militia Substitute, 1781, 3 years. (E-133, F-401)

COEN, EDWARD.
    Signer, Association of Freemen, 1775/1776, Susquehanna.
    (D-357, I-321)

COEN, THOMAS.
    Signer, Association of Freemen, 1775/1776, Susquehanna.
    (D-357, I-321)

COEN, WILLIAM JR.
    Private, Capt. Rodgers' Co. No. 5, September 15, 1775. (E-111)

COLE, EPHRAIM.
    Born 1750. Died 1822. Married: Sophia Ada Mitchell.
    Private, Capt. Anderson's Company No. 3, September 23, 1775.
    Signer, Association of Freemen, 1776, Susquehanna Hundred.
    (E-108, I-321, X-143)

COLE, JAMES.
    Born 1751. Died c.1776. Married: Sophia Hanson.
    Children: John, James, Samilia, Sophia, Sarah, Benjamin, Thomas.
    Private, Capt. Anderson's Company No. 3, September 23, 1775.
    Signer, Association of Freemen, 1776, Susquehanna Hundred.
    (E-109, I-321, G-223, X-143)

COLE (COALE), SKIPWORTH.
    Married Elizabeth Gilbert (widow) in 1797 in Harford County.
    Marriage proven through Maryland pension application, but source
      gave no details on his service or that of his father "Skipwith
      Coale." (M-35, N-112)

COLE, THOMAS.
    Private, Capt. Rumsey's Company No. 6, September 16, 1775.
    Drummer, Capt. James Young enlisted July 7, 1776, Flying Camp
      under Col. Thomas Ewing's Battalion.
    Born 1751, England. (5'2" tall with short black hair).
    (E-112, E-125, F-54)

COLE, WILLIAM.
    1st Lieutenant, 2nd Battalion, Flying Camp, October 19, 1776.
    Army Accounts No. 1,p. 83; Intendant's Ledger B, f. 150;
    Intendant's Orders No. 1, f. 76. (HR-50, H-68)

COLEMAN, GEORGE.
    Signer, Oath of Fidelity and Allegiance to Maryland, 1778.
    (A-32, B-23, J-241)

COLEMAN, JOHN REV. ("Parson" Coleman)
    Born 1758, Dinwiddie County, Virginia.
    Died 1816, Harford County, Maryland.
    Married: Pleasance Goodwin in 1783.
    Children: Rebecca (plus 5 who died in infancy).
    Sergeant Major in Virginia during Revolution.
    (G-224, X-144, E-213)

COLLINGS, ROBERT.
    Signer, Oath of Fidelity and Allegiance to Maryland, 1778.
    (A-32, B-30, J-247)

COLLINS, EPHRAIM.
    Private, Capt. Paca's Company, July 24, 1776.
    Signer, Association of Freemen, 1776, Spesutie Lower.
    (E-126, F-59, I-318)

COLLINS, ISAAC.
    Private, Capt. Dorsey's Co. No. 8, October 31, 1775. (E-114)

COLLINS, JACOB.
    Private, Capt. Dorsey's Co. No. 8, October 31, 1775. (E-115)

COLLINS, JOHN.
>Private, Capt. Dorsey's Company No. 8, October 31, 1775.
>Private, Capt. Paca's Company, July 24, 1776.
>Private, 4th Maryland Line, enlisted August 25, 1777.
>Hospital, January, 1778.
>Signer, Association of Freemen, 1776, Spesutie Lower.
>(E-114, E-126, E-129, F-59, F-302, I-318)

COLLINS, MOSES.
>Private, Capt. Dorsey's Company No. 8, October 31, 1775.
>Signer, Association of Freemen, 1776, Spesutie Lower.
>(E-115, I-318)

COLLINS, ROBERT.
>Signer, Association of Freemen, 1776, Bush River Lower.(I-328)

COLLINS, SAMUEL.
>Private, Capt. Dorsey's Co. No. 8, October 31, 1775. (E-114)

COLLINS, WILLIAM.
>Private, Capt. Dorsey's Co. No. 8, October 31, 1775.
>Signer, Association of Freemen, 1776, Spesutie Lower.
>(E-115, I-318)

COLTER, WILLIAM.
>Private, Capt. Harris' Harford Rifles, 1776. (E-124)

COMBEST (CAMBESS), ISRAEL.
>Private, Capt. Dorsey's Company No. 8, October 31, 1775.
>Private, Capt. Paca's Company, August 5, 1776.
>(E-114, E-127, F-59)

COMBEST (COMBESS, CAMBESS), JACOB.
>Private, Capt. Aquila Hall's Co. No. 4, September 9, 1775.
>Private, Capt. Dorsey's Company No. 8, October 31, 1775.
>Signer, Association of Freemen, 1775, Spesutie Lower.
>Signer, Oath of Fidelity and Allegiance to Maryland, 1778.
>(A-32, B-21, E-109, E-114, I-317, J-239)

COMBEST (COMBESS, CAMBESS), UTEY.
>Private, Capt. Dorsey's Company No. 8, October 31, 1775.
>Signer, Association of Freemen, 1776, Spesutie Lower.
>Signer, Oath of Fidelity and Allegiance to Maryland, 1778.
>(A-32, B-21, E-114, I-318, J-239)

COMEVE (COMENE),JOSEPH.
>Signer, Oath of Fidelity and Allegiance to Maryland, 1778.
>(A-32, B-29, J-246)

CONCKING, MATTHEW.
>Signer, Association of Freemen, 1776, Deer Creek Lower.(I-322)

CONDRON, JAMES.
    Militia Substitute, 1781. (E-132, F-400)

CONDRON, JOHN.
    Private, Capt. Bussey's Company, July 27, 1776.
    Signer, Association of Freemen, 1776, Gunpowder Upper.
    (E-128, F-60, I-325)

CONDRON, WILLIAM.
    Private, Capt. Bussey's Company, July 25, 1776.
    Signer, Association of Freemen, 1776, Eden Hundred.
    Drafted, Militia, 1781.
    (E-128, E-132, F-60, F-400, I-324)

CONHOWAY. MICHAEL.
    Signer, Oath of Fidelity and Allegiance to Maryland, 1778.
    (A-32, B-21, J-239)

CONLEY, THOMAS.
    Signer, Association of Freemen, 1775, Spesutie Lower. (I-317)

CONN, JOHN.
    Private, Capt. John Taylor's Company No. 7, September 9, 1775.
    Signer, Association of Freemen, 1776, Gunpowder Upper Hundred.
    (E-114, I-326)

CONN, ROBERT.
    Married: Elizabeth Cain.   Died 1798.
    Private, Capt. Taylor's Company No. 7, September 9, 1775.
    Private. Capt. Francis Holland's Harford Rifles, 1776.
    Signer, Oath of Fidelity and Allegiance to Maryland, 1778.
    (A-32, B-12, E-113, E-124, J-234, X-149)

CONNAWAY (CONNOWAY), LAWRENCE.
    Born 1756, Ireland.
    Private, Lt. John Smith enlisted July 15, 1776, in Col. Ewing's
      Battalion, Flying Camp. (5'3 3/4" tall with black hair)
    Signer, Oath of Fidelity and Allegiance to Maryland, 1778.
    (A-32, B-10, E-125, F-56, J-234)

CONNAWAY (CONNOWAY), MICHAEL.
    Private, Capt. Aquila Hall's Co. No. 4, September 9, 1775.
    Signer, Association of Freemen, 1776, Harford Lower Hundred.
    (E-110, I-324)

CONNELLY, MICHAEL.
    Sergeant, Capt. Harris' Company Payroll. (E-130, F-304)

CONNER (CONOR), ROBERT.
    Signer, Association of Freemen, 1776, Gunpowder Upper. (I-326)

CONNER (CONNOR), THOMAS.
    Private, Capt. Baker's Company No. 15, January 27, 1776.
    Signer, Association of Freemen, 1776, Eden Hundred.
    (E-120, I-324)

CONNEY, MORGAN.
   Drummer, Capt. Francis Holland's Harford Rifles, 1776. (E-124)

CONNIS, JOHN.
   Signer, Association of Freemen, 1775, Gunpowder Upper. (I-327)

CONNOLLY, JOHN.
   Private, Capt. Dorsey's Company No. 8, October 31, 1775.
   Signer, Oath of Fidelity and Allegiance to Maryland, 1778.
   (A-32, B-19, E-115, J-238)

CONNOLLY, JOHN JR.
   Private, Capt. Dorsey's Co. No. 8, October 31, 1775. (E-114)

COOK, JOHN.
   Private, Capt. Robert Harris' Harford Rifles, 1776.
   Paid subsistence for two weeks, October 16, 1776.
   Signer, Association of Freemen, 1776, Bush River Upper.
   Signer, Oath of Fidelity and Allegiance to Maryland, 1778.
   (A-32, B-29, E-123, I-328, J-246, K-436)

COOK, JOHN JR.
   Signer, Association of Freemen, 1775, Bush River Upper. (I-316)

COOK, WILLIAM.
   Private, Capt. Robert Harris' Harford Rifles, 1776.
   Paid subsistence for two weeks, October 17, 1776.
   Signer, Association of Freemen, 1776, Bush River Upper.
   (E-123, I-328, K-436)

COOLEY, JOHN.
   Born c.1757. Died 1809. Married: Sarah Gilbert.
   Private, Capt. Anderson's Company No. 3, September 23, 1775.
   Signer, Association of Freemen, 1776, Susquehanna Hundred.
   Private, Capt. Francis Holland's Harford Rifles, 1776.
   Signer, Oath of Fidelity and Allegiance to Maryland, 1778.
   Recruit, 8th Maryland Regiment, 1780.
   Grand Juror, Harford County, 1780.
   (A-32, B-26, E-76, E-108, E-124, E-131, F-343, I-321, J-243, Y-43)

COOLEY (COOLY), RICHARD.
   Signer, Oath of Fidelity and Allegiance to Maryland, 1778.
   (A-32, B-30, J-247)

COOLEY (COOLY), RICHARD JR.
   Born 1756. Married: Rachel Lewis in 1788.
   Private, Militia (wife applied for pension).
   Signer, Oath of Fidelity and Allegiance to Maryland, 1778.
   Marriage proven through Maryland pension appliction.
   (A-32, B-30, N-16, N-112, J-247)

COOLEY (COOLY), WILLIAM.
   Signer, Association of Freemen, 1776, Spesutie Upper.
   Signer, Oath of Fidelity and Allegiance to Maryland, 1778.
   (A-32, B-30, I-319, J-247)

COOP, BARACHIUS.
    Born 1760.
    "Barachias Cope" served as Private in Revolutionary War, and
        also served in War of 1812.
    "Borachich Coop" served as Militia Substitute in 1781.
    Army Accounts No. 1, p. 2.
    (E-132, F-400, HR-50, N-16)

COOP, HORATIO.
    Born 1758. Died 1843.
    Private and Wagoneer, Militia.
    Private, Capt. Harris' Harford Rifles, 1776.
    Paid subsistence for six weeks, two days, September 16, 1776.
    Signer, Association of Freemen, 1776, Bush River Upper.
    "Doratio Coop" signed Oath of Fidelity and Allegiance, 1778.
    "Horatio Coops" drafted in militia, 1781.
    Army Accounts No. 1, p.2; Intendants Orders No. 1, f.76.
    (E-123, F-400, I-320, E-132, A-32, B-30, J-247, N-16, HR-50,
     X-152)

COOP, JAMES.
    Private, Capt. Harris' Company.
    Paid subsistence for six weeks, two days, September 16, 1776.
    Signer, Association of Freemen, 1775/1776, Bush River Upper.
    (I-316, I-320, K-435)

COOP, RICHARD.
    Signer, Association of Freemen, 1775/1776, Bush River Upper.
    (I-317, I-320)

COOPER, CALVIN.
    Signer, Oath of Fidelity and Allegiance to Maryland, 1778.
    (A-32, B-29, J-246)

COOPER, HENRY.
    Signer, Association of Freemen, 1776, Spesutie Upper.
    Signer, Oath of Fidelity and Allegiance to Maryland, 1778.
    (A-32, B-28, I-319, J-245)

COOPER, JAMES.
    Private, Capt. Harris' Harford Rifles, 1776. (E-123)

COOPER, JOHN.
    Private, Capt. Taylor's Company No. 7, September 9, 1775.
    Rifleman, Battle of Fort Washington, November 16, 1776.
    Private, 4th Maryland Continental Line, 1776-1779.
    Signer, Association of Freemen, 1776, Bush River Lower.
    (E-113, E-129, E-136, F-301, I-320)

COOPER, WILLIAM.
    Private, Capt. John Love's Co. No. 10, September 14, 1775.
    Signer, Association of Freemen, 1775, Bush River Upper.
    Private, Capt. Bennett Bussey's Company, July 20, 1776.
    Rifleman, Battle of Fort Washington, November 16, 1776.
       (continued)

COOPER, WILLIAM (continued)
    Signer, Association of Freemen, 1776, Spesutie Upper Hundred.
    Private, 4th Maryland Continental Line, 1776-1779.
      Hospital, June-July, 1777.
    Signer, Oath of Fidelity and Allegiance to Maryland, 1778.
    (A-32, B-28, E-116, E-127, E-129, E-136, F-60, F-302, I-317, I-319, J-245, X-153)

COPELAND (CAPELAND), GEORGE.
    Private, Capt. Aquila Hall's Co. No. 4, September 9, 1775.
    Signer, Association of Freemen, 1776, Harford Lower Hundred.
    (E-109, I-324)

COPELAND, JOHN.
    Private, Capt. Josias Hall's Co. No. 1, September 12, 1775.
    Private, Capt. Francis Holland's Harford Rifles, 1776.
    (E-106, E-124)

CORBET (CORBIT), JAMES.
    Signer, Association of Freemen, 1776, Bush River Upper Hundred.
    Ensign, Capt. George Vaghan's Company, Deer Creek Battalion, April 9, 1778.
    (C-44, C-9, I-320)

CORBETT (CORBIT), JESSE.
    Signer, Association of Freemen, 1775/1776, Bush River Upper.
    Private, 4th Maryland Continental Line, 1776-1777, July.
    Rifleman, Battle of Fort Washington, November 16, 1776.
    "At Hospital" June-July, 1777.
    (E-129, E-136, F-302, I-317, I-320)

CORBETT (CORBET, CORBITT), JOHN.
    Private, Capt. Taylor's Company No. 7, September 9, 1775.
    Private, Capt. Baker's Company No. 15, January 27, 1776.
    Signer, Association of Freemen, 1776: one signer with this name in Eden Hundred, and one in Gunpowder Upper Hundred.
    Signer, Oath of Fidelity and Allegiance to Maryland, 1778.
    (E-120, E-113, A-32, B-23, J-241, I-324, I-326)

CORBETT (CORBITT), JOSEPH.
    Signer, Oath of Fidelity and Allegiance to Maryland, 1778.
    (A-32, B-30, J-247)

CORBETT (CORBIT), LEWIS.
    Private, Capt. Baker's Co. No. 15, January 27, 1776. (E-120)

CORBETT (CORBIT), SAMUEL.
    Signer, Association of Freemen, 1776, Bush River Upper. (I-320)

CORBETT (CORBET, CORBIT), WILLIAM.
    Signer, Association of Freemen, 1775/1776, Bush River Upper.
    Signer, Oath of Fidelity and Allegiance to Maryland, 1778.
    (A-32, B-28, I-317, I-320, J-245)

CORD, ABRAHAM.
    Signer, Oath of Fidelity and Allegiance to Maryland, 1778.
    (A-32, B-17, J-237)

CORD, ASHBERRY.
    Private, Capt. Dorsey's Company No. 8, October 31, 1775.
    Signer, Association of Freemen, 1775, Spesutie Lower.
    (E-114, I-317)

CORSBY (CORSLEY), RICHARD.
    Signer, Oath of Fidelity and Allegiance to Maryland, 1778.
    (A-32, B-26, J-243)

CORVIN, ALEXANDER.
    Colonel, 8th Battalion, April 9, 1778.   (C-46)

COSTLET, THOMAS.
    Signer, Association of Freemen, 1775, Gunpowder Neck. (I-327)

COTMAN (COLTMAN), JOHN.
    Private, 4th Maryland Continental Line, 1776-July, 1777.
    Rifleman, Battle of Fort Washington, November 16, 1776.
    (E-129, E-136, F-302)

COUPLAND, GEORGE.
    Signer, Oath of Fidelity and Allegiance to Maryland, 1778.
    (A032, B-21, J-239)

COUPLAND, JOHN.
    Signer, Oath of Fidelity and Allegiance to Maryland, 1778.
    (A-32, B-22, J-240)

COURTNEY, THOMAS.
    Signer, Association of Freemen, 1775/1776, Susquehanna.
    Signer, Oath of Fidelity and Allegiance to Maryland, 1778.
    (A-32, B-25, D-357, I-321, J-242)

COWEN (COWAN), ALEXANDER.
    Married: Elinora Boyce in 1771.
    Signer and solicitor, Association of Freemen, 1775/1776,
      Gunpowder Neck, Gunpowder Lower, Deer Creek Upper.
    War Committee, Correspondence, June 11, 1775.
    1st Lieutenant, Capt. Rumsey's Co. No. 6, Sept. 16, 1775.
    Captain, 8th Battalion, September 18, 1776.
    (D-358, D-359, E-96, E-112, E-263, E-267, I-315, I-323,
     I-327, K-281, M-41)

COWEN (COWAN), EDWARD.
    Signer, Oath of Fidelity and Allegiance to Maryland, 1778.
    (A-32, B-19, J-238)

COWEN (COWAN), JOHN.
    Private, Capt. Aquila Hall's Co. No. 4, September 9, 1775.
    Signer, Association of Freemen, 1775, Spesutie Lower.
    (E-109, I-317)

COWEN (COWAN), WILLIAM.
    Signer, Association of Freemen, 1776, Deer Creek Upper. (I-323)

COWLEY, MATHEW.
    Signer, Oath of Fidelity and Allegiance to Maryland, 1778.
    (A-32, B-23, J-241)

COWLEY, THOMAS.
    Private, Capt. Aquila Hall's Co. No. 4, Sept. 9, 1775. (E-109)

COX, JAMES.
    Private, Capt. Taylor's Company No. 7, September 9, 1775.
    Private, Capt. Bennett Bussey's Company, July 20, 1776.
    Signer, Association of Freemen, 1776, Gunpowder Upper.
    (E-113, E-127, F-60, I-326)

COYN (COYNE), DOMINICK.
    Private, Capt. Robert Harris' Company Payroll. (E-130, F-304)

COYNE, EDWARD.
    Signer, Association of Freemen, 1776, Gunpowder Upper. (I-326)

CRAIL, PHILIP.
    Private, Capt. Rigdon's Co., No. 12, December 2, 1775. (E-118)

CRAVEN, ANDREW.
    Private, Capt. Charles Baker's Co. No. 15, January 27, 1776.
    Private, Capt. Bennett Bussey's Company, July 25, 1776.
    Signer, Association of Freemen, 1776, Eden Hundred.
    Signer, Oath of Fidelity and Allegiance to Maryland, 1778.
    (A-32, B-24, E-120, E-128, F-60, I-324, J-242)

CRAWFORD, ALEXANDER.
    Private, Capt. William Bradford's Co. No. 13, Sept. 30, 1775.
    Signer, Association of Freemen, 1776, Harford Upper Hundred.
    Signer, Oath of Fidelity and Allegiance to Maryland, 1778.
    Secretary to County Lieutenant, Harford County, 1781.
    Sold 19 horses and 2 wagons to the State for military use.
    Army Accounts No. 1, p. 137. (HR-50)
    (A-32, B-21, E-119, E-131, F-399, F-400, F-401, I-325, J-239)

CRAWFORD, MORDECAI.
    Signer, Association of Freemen, 1776, Deer Creek Lower. (I-322)

CREETER, JOS.
    Signer, Association of Freemen, 1776, Bush River Upper. (I-320)

CREIGHTON, JAMES.
    Signer, Oath of Fidelity and Allegiance to Maryland, 1778.
    (A-32, B-30, J-247)

CRESWELL (CRISWELL), MATTHEW.
    Private, Capt. Baker's Company No. 15, January 27, 1776.
    Signer, Association of Freemen, 1776, Eden Hundred.
    Signer, Oath of Fidelity and Allegiance to Maryland, 1778.
    (A-32, B-23, E-120, I-324, J-241)

CRESWELL, MATHEW.
    Private, Capt. Robert Harris' Harford Rifles, 1776.
    Paid subsistence for four weeks, two days, October 5, 1776.
    Signer, Association of Freemen, 1776, Bush River Upper.
    Signer, Oath of Fidelity and Allegiance to Maryland, 1778.
    (A-32, B-23, E-123, I-320, J-241, K-435)

CRESWELL, ROBERT SR.
    Private, Capt. John Patrick's Company No. 17, April 1, 1776.
    Signer, Oath of Fidelity and Allegiance to Maryland, 1778.
    Grand Juror, Harford County, 1780.
    (A-32, B-25, E-76, E-122, J-242)

CRESWELL, ROBERT JR.
    Private, Capt. Patrick's Co. No. 17, April 1, 1776. (E-122)

CRETIN (CRATON, CREATON), JAMES.
    Private, Capt. John Love's Co. No. 10, September 14, 1775.
    Signer, Association of Freemen, 1776, Spesutie Upper.
    Signer, Oath of Fidelity and Allegiance to Maryland, 1778.
    Ensign, Deer Creek Battalion, County Militia, 1779.
    (A-32, B-28, C-43, E-116, I-318, J-245)

CRETIN (CRATON, CREATON), JOHN.
    Private, Capt. John Love's Co. No. 10, September 14, 1775.
    Signer, Association of Freemen, 1776, Spesutie Upper.
    Signer, Oath of Fidelity and Allegiance, February 7, 1778.
    (B-25, E-116, I-318, J-243)

CRETIN, JOHN JR.
    Signer, Association of Freemen, 1776, Spesutie Upper.
    Signer, Oath of Fidelity and Allegiance to Maryland, 1778.
    (A-32, B-26, I-319, J-243)

CRETIN, JOHN F.
    Signer, Oath of Fidelity and Allegiance, 1778. (A-32)

CRETIN, PATRICK.
    Private, Capt. John Archer's Co. No. 2, September 16, 1775.
    Signer, Oath of Fidelity and Allegiance to Maryland, 1778.
    "Patrick Creaton" was a Harford County Grand Juror, 1779.
    (A-32, B-25, E-107, E-75, J-242)

CRISWELL (CHRISWELL), ROBERT.
    Private, Capt. Archer's Company No. 2, September 16, 1775.
    Signer, Association of Freemen, 1776, Spesutie Upper.
    Signer, Oath of Fidelity and Allegiance to Maryland, 1778.
    (A-32, B-25, E-107, I-319, J-242)

CRISWELL, WILLIAM.
    Signer, Oath of Fidelity and Allegiance to Maryland, 1778.
    (A-32, B-26, J-243)

CROCKETT, GILBERT.
    Private, Capt. William Webb's Co. No. 16, October 14, 1775.
    Signer, Association of Freemen, 1776, Deer Creek Upper.
    Signer, Oath of Fidelity and Allegiance to Maryland, 1778.
    (A-32, B-14, E-121, I-323, J-235)

CROCKETT, JOHN.
    Private, 4th Maryland Continental Line, 1776-July, 1777.
    Rifleman, Battle of Fort Washington, November 16, 1776.
    (E-129, E-136, F-302)

CROCKETT, SAMUEL.
    Private, Capt. Webb's Company No. 16, October 14, 1775.
    Signer, Oath of Fidelity and Allegiance to Maryland, 1778.
    (A-32, B-14, E-121, J-235)

CROESEN (KROESEN), JOHN.
    Private, Capt. Archer's Company No. 2, September 16, 1775.
    Signer, Oath of Fidelity and Allegiance to Maryland, 1778.
    (E-108, A-34, B-25)

CROESEN (KROESEN), NICHOLAS.
    Signer, Oath of Fidelity and Allegiance to Maryland,
      February 21, 1778. (A-34, B-25, J-242)

CROESEN (KROESEN), RICHARD.
    Private, Capt. Archer's Company No. 2, September 16, 1775.
    Signer, Association of Freemen, 1776, Susquehanna Hundred.
    Signer, Oath of Fidelity and Allegiance to Maryland, 1778.
    "Richard Courson" was a Harford County Grand Juror, 1779.
    (A-34, B-25, E-75, E-107, I-321, J-242)

CROMWELL, JAMES.
    Militia Substitute, 1781 "to 10th Dec." (E-133, F-401)

CROMWELL, JOSEPH.
    Private, Capt. Rumsey's Company No. 6, September 16, 1775.
    Signer, Association of Freemen, 1775, Gunpowder Neck.
    (E-112, I-327)

CROMWELL, RICHARD.
    Captain, Gunpowder Upper Battalion, Oct. 31, 1780. (C-4)

CROOK, WILLIAM.
    Private, Capt. Harris' Company. Paid subsistence for four
      weeks, three days, October 4, 1776. (K-435)

CROOKE, THOMAS.
    Private, Capt. Webb's Co. No. 16, Oct. 14, 1775. (E-121)

CROOKER, JAMES.
    Signer, Oath of Fidelity and Allegiance to Maryland, 1778.
    (A-32, B-14, J-236)

CROOKS, HENRY.
　　Signer, Oath of Fidelity and Allegiance to Maryland, 1778.
　　(A-32, B-14, J-235)

CROOKS, ROBERT.
　　Signer, Oath of Fidelity and Allegiance to Maryland, 1778.
　　(A-32, B-14, J-236)

CROOKS, THOMAS.
　　Signer, Association of Freemen, 1776, Deer Creek Upper. (I-323)

CROOKS, WILLIAM.
　　Private, Capt. Robert Harris' Harford Rifles, 1776.
　　Signer, Association of Freemen, 1776, Deer Creek Upper.
　　(E-123, I-323)

CROOKS, WILLIAM JR.
　　Private, Capt. Webb's Company No. 16, October 14, 1775.
　　Signer, Association of Freemen, 1776, Deer Creek Upper.
　　(E-121, I-323)

CROP, JAMES.
　　Signer, Oath of Fidelity and Allegiance to Maryland, 1778.
　　(A-32, B-30, J-247)

CROSBY, RICHARD.
　　Continental Army, 1777-80 (Family Support Allowance). (F-661)
　　　　　　　　(Wife, Elizabeth, and 5 children, 1780)

CROSS, RICHARD.
　　Signer, Association of Freemen, 1776, Bush River Upper.
　　Signer, Oath of Fidelity and Allegiance to Maryland, 1778.
　　(A-32, B-29, I-320, J-246)

CROUCH, STEPHEN.
　　Private, Capt. Aquila Hall's Company No. 4, September 9, 1775.
　　Private, Capt. Paca's Company, August 5, 1776.
　　Signer, Association of Freemen, 1776, Harford Lower.
　　Signer, Oath of Fidelity and Allegiance to Maryland, 1778.
　　(A-32, B-22, E-110. E-127, F-59, I-324, J-240)

CUDDY, JAMES.
　　Born 1754. Died 1839. Married: Alcey Dunlap.
　　Was an Artificer in Md., S.C. and Penn.
　　Signer, Oath of Fidelity and Allegiance to Maryland, 1778.
　　(A-32, X-167)

CUDDY, JOHN.
　　Signer, Association of Freemen, 1776, Spesutie Upper Hundred.
　　Signer, Oath of Fidelity and Allegiance, February 26, 1778.
　　(B-26, I-319, J-243)

CULTRAUGH (CULOUGH, COLTHOUGH), WILLIAM.
　　Signer, Association of Freemen, 1775, Bush River Upper.
　　Signer, Oath of Fidelity and Allegiance to Maryland, 1778.
　　"William Colthough" was a Harford County Grand Juror, 1783.
　　(A-32, B-26, E-77, I-317, J-243)

CULVER, BENJAMIN.
Private, Capt. Anderson's Company No. 3, September 23, 1775.
Signer, Association of Freemen, 1776, Susquehanna Hundred.
Signer, Oath of Fidelity and Allegiance to Maryland, 1778.
Drafted, Militia, 1781; "discharged by Govt. and Council."
(A-32, B-26, E-109, E-133, F-401, I-321, J-243)

CULVER, ROBERT.
Private, Capt. Anderson's Company No. 3, September 23, 1775.
Signer, Association of Freemen, 1776, Susquehanna Hundred.
Signer, Oath of Fidelity and Allegiance to Maryland, 1778.
(A-32, B-26, E-108, I-321, J-243)

CUMMINS, JOB.
Signer, Association of Freemen, 1776, Susquehanna. (I-321)

CUMMINS, JOHN.
Private, Capt. Anderson's Company No. 3, September 23, 1775.
"John Cummings", born 1760, Private, Cont. Line Pensioner.
(E-108, N-17)

CUNNING, PHILLIP.
Signer, Oath of Fidelity and Allegiance to Maryland, 1778.
(A-32, B-27, J-244)

CUNNINGHAM, CLOTHWORTH or CLOTWORTHY.
Signer, Association of Freemen, 1775, Gunpowder Neck.
Signer, Oath of Fidelity and Allegiance to Maryland, 1778.
(A-32, B-17, I-327, J-237)

CUNNINGHAM, EDWARD.
Signer, Association of Freemen, 1775, Gunpowder Neck.
Signer, Oath of Fidelity and Allegiance to Maryland, 1778.
(A-32, B-14, I-327, J-235)

CUNNINGHAM, GEORGE.
Private, Capt. Bradford's Co. No. 13, September 30, 1775.
Signer, Association of Freemen, 1775, Gunpowder Neck.
Signer, Oath of Fidelity and Allegiance to Maryland, 1778.
(A-32, B-17, E-119, I-327, J-237)

CUNNINGHAM, JAMES.
Signer, Association of Freemen, 1776, Gunpowder Upper. (I-326)

CUNNINGHAM, JOHN.
Ensign, Deer Creek Battalion, Harford County Militia, 1778.
Signer, Oath of Fidelity and Allegiance to Maryland, 1778.
(A-32, B-26, C-44, J-243)

CUNNINGHAM, JONATHAN.
Private, Capt. Baker's Company No. 15, January 27, 1776.
Private, Capt. Bennett Bussey's Company, July 25, 1776.
Signer, Association of Freemen, 1776, Bush River Upper.
(E-120, E-128, F-60, I-320)

CUNNINGHAM, THOMAS.
    Private, Capt. Bradford's Company No. 13, September 30, 1775.
    Signer, Association of Freemen, 1775, Gunpowder Neck.
    Private, Capt. Baker's Company No. 15, January 27, 1776.
    Signer, Oath of Fidelity and Allegiance to Maryland, 1778.
    (A-32, B-10, E-119, E-120, I-327, J-234)

CUNNINGHAM, WILLIAM.
    Signer, Association of Freemen, 1775, Bush River Upper.
    Private, Capt. Bussey's Company, July 25, 1776.
    (E-128, F-60, I-316)

CURL, JOHN.
    Militia Substitute, 1781. (E-132, F-400)

CURRY, JAMES.
    Private, Capt. Jacob Bond's Co. No. 11, December 9, 1775.
    Signer, Association of Freemen, 1776, Harford Upper.
    Signer, Oath of Fidelity and Allegiance to Maryland, 1778.
    (A-32, B-23, E-117, I-325, J-241)

CURRY, JAMES.
    Private, Capt. Baker's Company No. 15, January 27, 1776.
    Signer, Oath of Fidelity and Allegiance to Maryland, 1778.
    (A-32, B-29, E-120, J-246)

CURRY, JOHN.
    Private, Capt. Archer's Company No. 2, September 16, 1775.
    Signer, Association of Freemen, 1776, Harford Upper.
    Signer, Oath of Fidelity and Allegiance to Maryland, 1778.
    (A-32, B-26, E-107, I-325, J-243)

CURRY (CUREY), JOS.
    Signer, Association of Freemen, 1776, Bush River Upper. (I-320)

CURTIS, FRANCIS.
    Attorney at Law of Harford County Court, 1774-1775. (E-63)

CUSICK (CUSSICK, CUSACK), CHRISTOPHER.
    Married: Mary Cave in 1790.
    Served in Maryland Line; widow applied for pension.
    Warrant No. 11090, 100 acres, applied October 6, 1794.
    No. 85204, $80, paid January 1, 1782.
    No. 93030, $80, paid to November 16, 1783, 4th Md. Rgt.
    (N-17, N-62, N-112, P-131)

CUTHBERT, WILLIAM.
    Private, Capt. Bond's Company No. 11, December 9, 1775.
    Private, Capt. Robert Harris' Harford Rifles, 1776.
    Paid subsistence for five weeks, five days, Sept. 26, 1776.
    Signer, Association of Freemen, 1776, Bush River Lower.
    (E-117, E-123, I-328, K-436)

DAILEY, WILLIAM.
    Signer, Association of Freemen, 1775, Gunpowder Neck.
    Signer, Oath of Fidelity and Allegiance to Maryland, 1778.
    (A-32, B-14, I-327, J-236)

DALE, JAMES.
    Signer, Association of Freemen, 1776, Bush River Lower. (I-328)

DALE, JOHN.
    Signer, Oath of Fidelity and Allegiance to Maryland, 1778.
    (A-32, B-23, J-241)

DALLAM, FRANCIS.
    Born 1755. Married: Martha S. Dallam.
    Signer, Association of Freemen, 1776, Harford Upper.
    Signer, Oath of Fidelity and Allegiance to Maryland, 1778.
    One source stated he was a Government Auditor. (X-173)
    (A-32, B-21, I-325, J-239)

DALLAM, JOHN.
    Private, Capt. Patrick's Company No. 17, April 1, 1776.
    Signer, Oath of Fidelity and Allegiance to Maryland, 1778.
    (A-32, B-22, E-122, J-240)

DALLAM, JOHN WINSTON.
    Signer and solicitor, Association of Freemen, 1775/1776, Deer Creek Lower Committee. (E-262, I-315, I-322)

DALLAM, JOSIAS WILLIAM.
    Born 1747. Died 1820. Married: (1) Sarah Smith (2) Henrietta Jones. Buried at Aberdeen Proving Grounds, Md.
    Signer, Oath of Fidelity and Allegiance to Maryland, 1778.
    (A-32, B-27, J-244, X-173)

DALLAM, RICHARD.
    Born c.1714. Died 1805, Abingdon, Md.
    Married: Francis Wallace and/or Francis Paca.
    Son of Richard Dallam II who died prior to the Revolution.
    Referred to as Richard Dallam Sr. in some sources, and as Richard Dallam III in others.
    Signer, Bush Declaration, March 22, 1775.
    War Committee, Harford County, June 11, 1775.
    Representative to Maryland Convention, June 26. 1775.
    Signer, Association of Freemen, 1776, Deer Creek Lower.
    Private, Capt. Patrick's Company No. 17, April 1, 1776.
    Private, Capt. Francis Holland's Harford Rifles, 1776.
    Signer, Oath of Fidelity and Allegiance to Maryland, 1778.
    Owned a factory that made muskets, boasting in July 16, 1776, "I have not the least doubt but my arms will please and be found as good as any made in Maryland."
    County Lieutenant, Harford County, August 4, 1780.
    Quartermaster and Deputy Paymaster General, 1781.
    (A-32, B-17, B-26, D-355, D-358, D-361, E-95, E-122, E-124, E-97, F-344, I-322, J-243, K-59, K-389, M-46, X-173, O-4, R)

DALLAM, WINSTON SMITH.
    Son of Richard and Frances Dallam. Married: Margaret Gover
      in 1772, daughter of Ephraim and Elizabeth Gover.
    Children: Winston, Frances, Elizabeth, Cassandra.
    Signer, Association of Freemen, 1776, Deer Creek Lower.
    1st Lieutenant, Capt. Patrick's Co. No. 17, April 1, 1776.
    1st Lieutenant, Deer Creek Battalion.
    Died 1778.
    (C-44, I-322, D-359, E-122, E-265, M-46, R)

DALY, JOHN.
    Signer, Association of Freemen, 1776, Bush River Upper. (I-328)

DARBY, DANIEL.
    Private, Capt. Bussey's Company, July 25, 1776.
    Recruit, New Regiment, August 3, 1780.
    (E-128, E-131, F-60, F-343)

DARBY, ROBERT.
    Signer, Association of Freemen, 1776, Deer Creek Lower. (I-322)

DARLEY, SAMUEL.
    Signer, Association of Freemen, 1775, Spesutie Lower. (I-317)

DARLEY, WILLIAM.
    Signer, Association of Freemen, 1775, Spesutie Lower. (I-317)

DARS, RICHARD TOOTILL.
    Signer, Oath of Fidelity and Allegiance to Maryland, 1778.
    (A-32, B-17, J-237)

DAUGHERTY. See Dougherty.

DAVIDSON, JOHN.
    Private, Capt. Archer's Company No. 2, September 16, 1775.
    Private, Capt. Robert Harris' Harford Rifles, 1776.
    Paid subsistence for two weeks, one day, October 15, 1776.
    Private, Maryland Line, pensioner.
    Signer, Oath of Fidelity and Allegiance to Maryland, 1778.
    Records indicate there were two signers with this name.
    (A-32, B-23, B-26, E-108, E-123, J-241, J-243, K-436, N-17)

DAVIS, DAVID.
    Signer, Oath of Fidelity and Allegiance to Maryland, 1778.
    (A-32, B-30, J-247)

DAVIS, JACOB.
    Private, Capt. Baker's Co. No. 15, January 27, 1776. (E-120)

DAVIS, JOHN.
    Private, Capt. Baker's Company No. 15, January 27, 1776.
    Signer, Association of Freemen, 1776, Bush River Upper.
    Signer, Oath of Fidelity and Allegiance to Maryland, 1778.
    (A-32, B-30, E-120, I-320, J-247)

DAVIS, JOHN REV.
    War Committee, Harford County, 1775.
    Signer, Association of Freemen, 1776, Bush River Upper.
    Signer, Oath of Fidelity and Allegiance to Maryland, 1778.
    (A-32, B-29, D-358, I-320, J-246)

DAVIS, THOMAS.
    Signer, Oath of Fidelity and Allegiance to Maryland, 1778.
    (A-32, B-30, J-247)

DAWES, ELIJAH.
    Born c.1750. Died c.1788. Married: Mary Morgan.
    Daughter: Martha.
    Private, Capt. Francis Holland's Harford Rifles, 1776.
    (E-124, G-262, X-181)

DAY, EDWARD SR.
    Private, Capt. Rumsey's Company No. 6, September 16, 1775.
    Signer, Association of Freemen, 1775, Gunpowder Neck.
    (E-112, I-327)

DAY, HENRY.
    Private, Capt. Baker's Co. No. 15, January 27, 1776. (E-120)

DAY, JOHN, OF Edward.
    Born 1754. Died 1794. Married: Mary Maxwell.
    War Committee, Harford County, 1775.
    Signer, Association of Freemen, 1775, Gunpowder Neck.
    Ensign, 8th Battalion, 1778. One source says Captain.
    Signer, Oath of Fidelity and Allegiance to Maryland, 1778.
    (A-32, B-14, C-47, D-358, I-327, J-235, X-182)

DAY, JOHN JR.
    Born 1755. Died 1791. Married: Mary Goldsmith Presbury.
    Signer and solicitor, Association of Freemen, 1775/1776,
      Gunpowder Lower Hundred.
    Private, Capt. Rumsey's Company No. 6, September 16, 1775.
      One source lists him as a Corporal.
    Signer, Oath of Fidelity and Allegiance to Maryland, 1778.
    (A-32, B-14, E-112, I-327, J-236, M-48, X-182)

DAY, NICHOLAS.
    Born c.1750. Died c.1815. Married: Grace Angelly (2nd wife).
    Private, Capt. Charles Baker's Co. No. 15, January 27, 1776.
    Signer, Association of Freemen, 1776, Eden Hundred.
    (E-120, I-324, X-182)

DAY, ROBERT.
    Signer, Oath of Fidelity and Allegiance to Maryland, 1778.
    (A-32, B-24, J-242, X-182)

DAY, SAMUEL.
    Signer, Association of Freemen, 1776, Eden Hundred.
    Signer, Oath of Fidelity and Allegiance to Maryland, 1778.
    Constable, Bush River Upper, during Revolutionary era.
    (A-32, B-24, E-64, I-324, J-242)

DEACON, FRANCIS.
    Signer, Association of Freemen, 1776, Harford Lower. (I-324)

DEAL, JAMES.
    Private, Capt. Bond's Co. No. 11, December 9, 1775. (E-117)

DEALE, JAMES.
    Private, Capt. Love's Co. No. 10, September 14, 1775. (E-116)

DEALY, JOHN.
    Signer, Oath of Fidelity and Allegiance to Maryland, 1778.
    (A-32, B-30, J-247)

* DEARMOTT (DERMOTT, DEARMON), JOHN.
    Signer, Association of Freemen, 1775, Bush River Upper, and
      Eden Hundred, 1776.
    Drafted, Militia, 1781; "Taken ill with the flux."
    (E-132, F-400, I-317, I-323)

DEARMOTT (DERMOTT, DEARMON), THOMAS.
    Signer, Association of Freemen, 1775, Bush River Upper, and
      Eden Hundred, 1776.
    Private, 4th Maryland Continental Line, 1776-July, 1777.
    Rifleman, Battle of Fort Washington, November 16, 1776.
    (E-129, E-136, F-302, I-317, I-320, I-323)

DEARMON, FRANCIS.
    Signer, Oath of Fidelity and Allegiance to Maryland, 1778.
    (A-32, B-17, J-237)

DEAVER (DEVER), AQUILA.
    Born 1756. Died c1830. Buried In Angel Hill Cemetery,
      Havre de Grace, Maryland.
    Private, Capt. Rigdon's Company No. 12, December 2, 1775.
    Carried General Lafayette ashore from the Susquehanna River
      in 1781.
    Signer, Association of Freemen, 1776, Deer Creek Upper.
    Pensioner. Land Warrant No. 11150, 100 acres, applied for
      August 7, 1794.
    Pay Certificate No. 84613, $43.30, paid to Nov. 16, 1783.
    Pay Certificate No. 89196, $80.00, 3rd Maryland Regiment.
    Pay Certificate No. 86661, $31.86, paid to Jan. 1, 1783.
    (D-363, E-118, E-141, E-142, N-18, N-62, P-140, P-144)

DEAVER, DANIEL.
    Private, Capt. Rodgers' Co. No. 5, Sept. 15, 1775. (E-111)

---

* This name could be "DeMoss" because that family lived in Harford County, namely John DeMoss, Sr. (1718-1806) and John DeMoss, Jr. (died 1820).

DEAVER, DAVID.
    Private, Capt. Rodgers' Company No. 5, September 14, 1775.
    Drafted, Militia, 1781; "Discharged, having wife & children."
    (E-110, E-132, F-400)

DEAVER, GEORGE.
    Signer, Association of Freemen, 1776, Harford Lower. (I-324)

DEAVER, HUGH.
    Private, Capt. Archer's Company No. 2, September 16, 1775.
    Private, Capt. Patrick's Company No. 17, April 1, 1776.
    Signer, Association of Freemen, 1776, Harford Upper.
    Signer, Oath of Fidelity and Allegiance to Maryland, 1778.
    (A-32, B-25, E-107, E-122, I-325, J-242)

DEAVER, JAMES.
    Private, Capt. Rigdon's Company No. 12, December 2, 1775.
    Signer, Association of Freemen, 1776, Deer Creek Upper.
    (E-118, I-322)

DEAVER, JAMES.
    Sergeant, Capt. Dorsey's Company No. 8, Oct. 31, 1775. (E-114)

DEAVER, JOHN.
    Private, Capt. Dorsey's Co. No. 8, Oct. 31, 1775. (E-115)

DEAVER (DEAVOUR), MICAJAH.
    Private, Capt. Dorsey's Co. No. 8, October 31, 1775.
    Signer, Association of Freemen, 1776, Spesutie Lower.
    (E-115, I-318)

DEAVER (DEVER), RICHARD.
    2nd Lieutenant, Capt. Rigdon's Co. No. 12, December 2, 1775.
    Signer, Association of Freemen, 1776, Deer Creek Upper.
    (D-359, E-118, I-322)

DEAVER, RICHARD JR.
    Married: Sarah Pritchard.
    Signer, Association of Freemen, 1776, Deer Creek Upper.
    (I-322, M-49)

DEAVER, THOMAS.
    Private, Capt. Dorsey's Co. No. 8, Oct. 31, 1775. (E-115)

DEBRULAR (DEBRULER), ANTHONY.
    Signer, Oath of Fidelity and Allegiance to Maryland, 1778.
    (A-32, B-22, J-240)

DEBRULER, JAMES.
    Signer, Oath of Fidelity and Allegiance to Maryland, 1778.
    (A-32, B-14, J-236)

DEBRULER, JOHN.
    Born 1751.
    Private, Maryland Line (pensioner).
      (continued)

DEBRULER, JOHN (continued)
    Private, 4th Maryland Line, 1776-1779.
    Hospital, June-July, 1777.
    Rifleman, Battle of Fort Washington, November 16, 1776.
    (E-129, F-301, E-136, N-18)

DEBRULER (DEBUELER), WILLIAM.
    Married: Sarah Watters in 1764.
    Signer, Association of Freemen, 1775, Gunpowder Neck.
    Signer, Oath of Fidelity and Allegiance to Maryland, 1778.
    (A-32, B-14, I-327, J-236, M-49)

DEINGAN, DANIEL.
    Signer, Oath of Fidelity and Allegiance to Maryland, 1778.
    (A-32, B-15, J-236)

DELANY, NICHOLAS.
    Private, Capt. Robert Harris' Company Payroll. (E-130, F-304)

DELANEY (DELENEY), JOHN.
    Born 1740. Private, Maryland Line.
    Signer, Association of Freemen, 1776, Deer Creek Upper.
    Land Warrant No. 1343, 100 acres, applied July 31, 1828.
    Pay Certificates: 82088, $43.30, 2nd Md. Regt. monthly pay;
      85314, $80.00, Md. Regt. paid to Jan. , 1782; 86667, $80,
      Md. Regt. paid to Jan. 1, 1783; 93081, $80, 4th Md. Regt.
      paid to Nov. 16, 1783.
    (I-323, N-18, N-62, P-141)

DELONG, JAMES.
    Private, Capt. Rigdon's Co. No. 12, Dec. 2, 1775. (E-118)

DENEY (DENNY), JAMES.
    Signer, Oath of Fidelity and Allegiance to Maryland, 1778.
    (A-22, B-30, J-247)

DENEY (DENNY), WALTER.
    Signer, Oath of Fidelity and Allegiance to Maryland, 1778.
    (A-32, B-30, J-247)

DENISON (DENNISON), JAMES.
    Private, Capt. Dorsey's Company No. 8, October 31, 1775.
    Signer, Association of Freemen, 1775, Spesutie Lower.
    Private, 4th Maryland Line, 1776-1779.
    Rifleman, Battle of Fort Washington, November 16, 1776.
    Hospital, September, 1777 - February, 1778.
    (E-115, E-129, E-136, F-301, I-317)

DENNIS, JOHN.
    Private, Capt. Bussey's Co., July 27, 1776. (E-128, F-60)

DENNY, JAMES.
    Signer, Association of Freemen, 1776, Deer Creek Upper. (I-322)

DENNY, MICHAEL.
    Signer, Oath of Fidelity and Allegiance to Maryland, 1778.
    (A-32, B-26, J-243)

DENNY, OLIVER.
    Militia Substitute, 1781, 3 years. (E-133, F-401)

DENNY, SIMON.
    Signer, Oath of Fidelity and Allegiance to Maryland, 1778.
    (A-32, B-13, J-235)

DENNY (DUNNY), SIMON, JR.
    Signer, Oath of Fidelity and Allegiance to Maryland, 1778.
    (A-33, B-17, J-237)

DENNY, WALTER.
    Private, Capt. Rigdon's Co. No. 12, December 2, 1775.
    Signer, Association of Freemen, 1775, Bush River Upper,
        and Deer Creek Upper, 1776.
    (E-118, I-316, I-322)

DENT, JOHN.
    Born 1760.
    Corporal, Maryland Line. Pensioner (maimed soldier), 1778.
    Widow applied for pension.
    Pay Certificates: 86335, $70.60, Md. Regt. paid to Jan. 1,
        1782; 87027, $80.00, Md. Regt. paid to Jan. 1, 1783.
    (F-661, N-18, P-143, X-188)

DEREALE, MICHAEL.
    Signer, Oath of Fidelity and Allegiance to Maryland, 1778.
    (A-32, B-29, J-246)

DERROW, JOHN.
    Signer, Oath of Fidelity and Allegiance to Maryland, 1778.
    (A-32, B-30, J-247)

DEIVER (DEVIER), HUGH.
    Born 1752. Died 1787. Married: Margaret Ann Smith.
    Private, Flying Camp. Lt. John Smith enlisted July 15, 1776
        at age 24; born in America. (6'$1\frac{1}{2}$" tall with black hair)
    Served in Col. Thomas Ewing's Battalion.
    (E-125, F-56, X-190)

DEVIN (DIVAN), JOHN.
    Private, Capt. Rumsey's Co. No. 6, September 16, 1775.
    Signer, Association of Freemen, 1775, Gunpowder Neck.
    (E-112, I-327)

DEVINE, BARNEY.
    Private, Capt. Bussey's Company, July 25, 1776. (E-128, F-60)

DEVINE, CHARLES.
    Signer, Association of Freemen, 1775, Gunpowder Neck. (I-327)

DEW, GEORGE.
  Grand Juror, Harford County, 1780. (E-76)

DICK, DAVID.
  Signer, Oath of Fidelity and Allegiance to Maryland, 1778.
  (A-32, B-30, J-247)

DICKSON, DAVID.
  Private, Capt. Archer's Co. No. 2, September 16, 1775.
  Signer, Association of Freemen, 1776, Spesutie Upper.
  Signer, Oath of Fidelity and Allegiance to Maryland, 1778.
  (A-32, B-25, E-108, I-319, J-242)

DICKSON, HENRY.
  Signer, Association of Freemen, 1776, Deer Creek Upper. (I-322)

DICKSON, JOHN.
  Records indicate there were two signers with this name:
  Signer, Association of Freemen, 1776, Bush River Upper.
  Signer, Association of Freemen, 1776, Eden Hundred.
  (I-320, I-323)

DIEMER (DEIMER), JOHN.
  Private, Capt. Josias Hall's Co. No. 1, September 12, 1775.
  Signer, Association of Freemen, 1776, Harford Lower.
  Signer, Oath of Fidelity and Allegiance to Maryland, 1778.
  (A-32, B-17, E-106, I-324, J-237)

DIGNAN, PATRICK.
  Signer, Association of Freemen, 1776, Gunpowder Upper. (I-326)

DILLION, GEORGE.
  Grand Jury Bailiff, Harford County, 1779. (E-75)

DINES (DINSE), FRANCIS.
  Hosted the War Committee elections for the Bush River Upper
    Hundred in 1775.
  Signer, Oath of Fidelity and Allegiance to Maryland, 1778.
  (A-32, B-29, D-358, J-246)

DINHAM, JOHN, of Jesse.
  Signer, Oath of Fidelity and Allegiance to Maryland, 1778.
  (A-32, B-15, J-236)

DIVERS, CHRISTOPHER.
  Signer, Association of Freemen, 1775, Gunpowder Neck. (I-327)

DIXON, MORRIS.
  Signer, Oath of Fidelity and Allegiance to Maryland, 1778.
  (A-32, B-21, J-239)

DIXON, PETER.
  Signer, Oath of Fidelity and Allegiance to Maryland, 1778.
  (A-32, B-17, J-237)

DOBBINS, JAMES.
    Private, Capt. Bradford's Co. No. 13, September 30, 1775.
    Signer, Association of Freemen, 1776, Harford Upper.
    Signer, Oath of Fidelity and Allegiance to Maryland, 1778.
    (A-32, B-10, E-119, I-325, J-233)

DOHERTY, SAMUEL.
    Private, Capt. Archer's Co. No. 2, September 16, 1775.
    Signer, Association of Freemen, 1776, Spesutie Upper.
    (E-108, I-319)

DOME, WILLIAM.
    Signer, Oath of Fidelity and Allegiance to Maryland, 1778.
    (A-32, B-19, J-238)

DONAHEY (DONAHAY, DONAHUY), JOHN.
    Signer, Bush Declaration, March 22, 1775.
    War Committee, 1775.
    Private, Capt. Rigdon's Co. No. 12, December 2, 1775.
    Signer, Association of Freemen, 1776, Deer Creek Upper.
    (D-355, D-359, E-118, I-322)

DONOVAN (DONAVIN), DANIEL.
    Signer, Association of Freemen, 1776, Susquehanna. (I-321)

DONOVAN (DONAVIN, DUNNAVIN), DANIEL SR.
    Signer, Association of Freemen, 1776, Susquehanna. (I-321)

DONOVAN, JOHN.
    Maryland Line, last date August, 1780. (F-414)

DONOVAN (DONNOVAN), PETER.
    Born 1748, Ireland.
    Private, Flying Camp, Lt. John Smith enlisted July 15, 1776
      in Col. Ewing's Battalion. (5'5" tall; thin visage)
    (E-126, F-56)

DONOVAN (DONAVIN), PHILIP.
    Private, Capt. Anderson's Co. No. 3, September 23, 1775.
    Signer, Association of Freemen, 1776, Susquehanna.
    (E-108, I-321)

DONOVAN (DONAVIN), THOMAS.
    Signer, Association of Freemen, 1776, Susquehanna. (I-321)

DONOVAN (DONAVIN), WILLIAM.
    Private, Capt. Anderson's Co. No. 3, September 23, 1775.
    Signer, Association of Freemen, 1776, Susquehanna.
    (E-108, I-321)

DONEL, MICHAEL.
    Private, Capt. Archer's Co. No. 2, Sept. 16, 1775. (E-107)

DONOHOE, DANIEL.
   Signer, Association of Freemen, 1776, Bush River Upper. (I-320)

DONOHOO, JOHN.
   Signer and solicitor, Association of Freemen, Deer Creek Upper
      Committee. (E-262)

DONOLEY (DONNELLY), JAMES.
   Private, Capt. Baker's Co. No. 15, January 27, 1776.
   Private, Capt. Robert Harris' Harford Rifles, 1776.
   Paid subsistence for four weeks, two days, Oct. 5, 1776.
      Name spelled "Jas. Donnaly."
   Signer, Oath of Fidelity and Allegiance to Maryland, 1778.
   (A-32, B-24, E-120, E-123, J-242, K-435)

DOOLEY, SAMUEL.
   Private, Capt. Aquila Hall's Co. No. 4, Sept. 9, 1775. (E-110)

DOOLY, EDWARD.
   Signer, Oath of Fidelity and Allegiance to Maryland, 1778.
   (A-32, B-17, J-237)

DORAN, HUGH.
   Signer, Oath of Fidelity and Allegiance to Maryland, 1778.
   (A-32, B-19, J-238)

DORAN, JOHN.
   Signer, Oath of Fidelity and Allegiance to Maryland, 1778.
   9A-32, B-19,J-238)

DORAN, PATRICK.
   Private, Capt. Bussey's Company, July 27, 1776.
   Signer, Oath of Fidelity and Allegiance to Maryland, 1778.
   (A-32, B-19, F-60, J-238)

DORNEY, JOHN.
   Signer, Association of Freemen, 1775, Gunpowder Neck. (I-327)

DORRAH, JOHN.
   Private, Capt. Aquila Hall's Co. No. 4, Sept. 9, 1775. (E-109)

DORSEY, FRISBY.
   Private, Capt. Dorsey's Co. No. 8, October 31, 1775.
   Signer, Association of Freemen, 1775, Spesutie Lower.
   Private, Capt. Francis Holland's Harford Rifles, 1776.
   Signer, Oath of Fidelity and Allegiance to Maryland, 1778.
   (A-32, B-22, E-114, E-124, I-317, J-240)

DORSEY, GREENBERRY.
   Born 1729. Died c.1798. Married: (1) Frances Henderson;
      (2) Sophia Clark; (3) Mary Hollis Copeland.
   Signer, Bush Declaration, March 22, 1775.
   War Committee, 1775.
      (continued)

DORSEY, GRENNBERRY (continued)
    Signer, Association of Freemen, 1775, Spesutie Lower Hundred.
    Captain, Company No. 8, Harford County Militia, Oct. 31, 1775.
    (D-355, D-358, D-359, E-114, I-317, Z-14)

DORSEY, JOHN HAMMOND.
    Born 1754. Died 1826. Married: Ann Maxwell in 1772.
    Signer, Association of Freemen, 1775, Gunpowder Neck.
    Private, Capt. Rumsey's Co. No. 6, September 16, 1775.
    One source lists him as "Jr.", and a Sergeant.
    Militia Substitute, 1781 "to 10th December."
    Signer, Oath of Fidelity and Allegiance to Maryland, 1778.
    (A-32, B-14, E-112, E-133, F-401, I-327, J-236, M-53, X-199)

DORSEY, LEVEN.
    Born 1735. Died 1781. Married: Elizabeth Keene Home.
    Private, Capt. Paca's Company, August 5, 1776.
    "Leaven Dorsey" listed as Private, Maryland Line.
    "Levin Dorsey" listed as Guard.
    (E-127, F-59, N-18, X-199)

DORSEY, STEPHEN.
    Born 1758. Died 1825. Married: Rachel Ewing.
    Cadet, Flying Camp, Capt. James Young enlisted July 7, 1776,
      under Col. Ewing's Battalion.
    Born in America. (In 1776: 5'9 3/4" tall; dark hair)
    (E-125, F-54, X-199)

DOUGHERTY (DAUGHERTY), BARNET
    Private, Capt. Patrick's Co. No. 17, April 1, 1776.
    Signer, Association of Freemen, 1776, Deer Creek Lower.
    (E-122, I-321)

DOUGHERTY, EDWARD.
    Private, Capt. Robert Harris' Harford Rifles, 1776.
    Paid subsistence for two weeks, four days, Oct. 16, 1776,
      listed as "Edwd. Daugharty."
    Signer, Association of Freemen, 1776, Spesutie Upper.
    (E-123, I-318, K-435)

DOUGHERTY, GEORGE.
    Private, Capt. Dorsey's Co. No. 8, October 31, 1775.
    Signer, Association of Freemen, 1776, Spesutie Lower.
    Signer, Association of Freemen, 1776, Deer Creek Upper.
    (E-114, I-318, I-323)

DOUGHERTY, HUGH.
    Signer, Association of Freemen, 1776, Harford Hundred. (I-325)

DOUGHERTY (DAUGHERTY), MICHAEL.
    Private, Capt. Webb's Company No. 16, October 14, 1775.
    Private, Capt. Robert Harris' Harford Rifles, 1776.
    Paid subsistence for four weeks, three days, Oct. 4, 1776.
    Signer, Association of Freemen, 1776, Deer Creek Upper.
      (continued)

DOUGHERTY, MICHAEL (continued)
    2nd Lieutenant, Capt. Harris' Company Payroll.
    Recruit, 8th Maryland Regiment, 1780.
    (E-121, E-123, E-130, E-131, I-323, F-304, F-343, K-435)

DOUGHERTY, SAMUEL.
    Signer, Oath of Fidelity and Allegiance to Maryland, 1778.
    (A-32, B-22, J-240)

DOUGHERTY (DAUGHERTY, DAUGHTY), WILLIAM.
    Private, Capt. Dorsey's Company No. 8, October 31, 1775.
    Signer, Association of Freemen, 1775, Spesutie Lower.
    (E-115, I-317)

DOWNEY, JOHN.
    Private, Capt. Bussey's Company, July 27, 1776. (E-128, F-60)

DOWNS, BARTHOLOMEW.
    Private. Capt. Bussey's Company, July 27, 1776. (E-128, F-60)

DOWNS, DENNIS.
    Recruit, New Regiment, July 17, 1780. (E-130, F-343)

DOWNS (DOWNES), WILLIAM.
    Signer, Association of Freemen, 1775/1776, Bush River Upper.
    2nd Lieutenant, Flying Camp. Capt. Robert Harris' Harford Rifles.
    "William Down" furnished two musquets to the county, June, 1776.
    2nd Lieutenant, 8th Battalion, 1776.
    1st Lieutenant, 8th Battalion, 1778.
    (C-47, D-359, E-123, E-267, I-317, I-320, E-328)

DOZENS (DUZENT, DUGAN), ISAAC.
    Private, Capt. Dorsey's Company No. 8, October 31, 1775.
    Private, Capt. Paca's Company, July 24, 1776.
    Signer, Association of Freemen, 1776, Spesutie Lower.
    (E-115, E-126, F-59, I-318)

DOZENS (DUZART, DAZAN), JACOB.
    Private, Capt. Dorsey's Company No. 8, October 31, 1775.
    Private, Capt. Paca's Company, July 24, 1776.
    Signer, Association of Freemen, 1776, Spesutie Lower.
    (E-115, E-126, F-59, I-318)

DOZENS (DUGAN), PETER.
    Signer, Association of Freemen, 1776, Spesutie Lower. (I-318)

DOZENS (DUZAN, DUGAN), WILLIAM GRAY.
    Private, Capt. Dorsey's Company No. 8, October 31, 1775.
    Private, Capt. Paca's Company, July 24, 1776.
    Signer, Association of Freemen, 1776, Spesutie Lower.
    (E-115, E-126, F-59, I-318)

DRENNEN, JOHN.
    Private, Capt. Bond's Co. No. 11, Dec. 9, 1775. (E-117)

DREW, ANTHONY.
    Signer, Association of Freemen, 1776, Harford Lower Hundred.
    Signer, Oath of Fidelity and Allegiance to Maryland, 1778.
    (A-32, B-22, I-324, J-240)

DREW, GEORGE.
    Private, Capt. Aquila Hall's Co. No.4, September 9, 1775.
    Signer, Oath of Fidelity and Allegiance to Maryland, 1778.
    (A-32, B-22, E-109, J-240)

DREW, HENRY.
    Signer, Oath of Fidelity and Allegiance to Maryland, 1778.
    (A-32, B-21, J-239)

DREW, JAMES.
    Private, Capt. Aquila Hall's Co. No. 4, September 9, 1775.
    Signer, Association of Freemen, 1776, Harford Lower Hundred.
    Signer, Oath of Fidelity and Allegiance to Maryland, 1778.
    (A-32, B-22, E-110, I-324, J-240)

DRIVER, WILLIAM.
    Signer, Association of Freemen, 1776, Bush River Lower. (I-319)

DRUMMOND, THOMAS.
    Signer, Oath of Fidelity and Allegiance to Maryland, 1778.
    (A-32, B-13, J-235)

DUBLIN, JOHN STEWART.
    Signer, Oath of Fidelity and Allegiance to Maryland, 1778.
    (A-32, B-23, J-241)

DUEBERRY, JOSEPH.
    Private, Capt. Robert Harris' Harford Rifles, 1776.
    Paid subsistence for three weeks, one day, October 9, 1776.
    (E-124, K-436)

DUFF, THOMAS.
    Private, Capt. Webb's Company No. 16, October 14, 1775.
    Signer, Association of Freemen, 1776, Deer Creek Upper.
    "Thomas Dufft" was Private in Capt. Paca's Co., July 24, 1776.
    Recruit, 8th Maryland Regiment, 1780.
    (E-121, E-126, E-131, F-59, F-343, I-323)

DUFFY, MICHAEL.
    Pensioner (maimed soldier), 1778.   (F-661)

DUKE, THOMAS.
    Private, Capt. Holland's Harford Rifles, 1776. (E-124)

DULANY, ISAAC.
    Private, Capt. Dorsey's Company No. 8, October 31, 1775.
    Signer, Association of Freemen, 1776, Spesutie Lower.
    (E-114, I-318)

DULEY, JAMES.
    Signer, Oath of Fidelity and Allegiance to Maryland, 1778.
    (A-32, B-10, J-233)

DULY, WILLIAM.
    Private, Capt. Paca's Company, July 24, 1776. (E-126, F-59)

DUNAHOO (DONAHO), DANIEL.
    Private, Capt. Anderson's Company No. 3, September 23, 1775.
    Signer, Association of Freemen, 1776, Susquehanna Hundred.
    (E-108, I-321)

DUNCAN, BENJAMIN.
    Signer, Oath of Fidelity and Allegiance to Md., 1778. (A-33)

DUNCAN, JAMES.
    Signer, Oath of Fidelity and Allegiance to Maryland, 1778.
    (A-33, B-23, J-241)

DUNGAN, BENJAMIN.
    Signer, Oath of Fidelity and Allegiance to Maryland, 1778.
    (B-20, J-239)

DUNGAN, DAVID.
    Signer, Association of Freemen, 1776, Bush River Lower. (I-319)

DUNHAM, AQUILA.
    Private, Capt. Robert Harris' Harford Rifles, 1776.
    Paid subsistence for five weeks, September 29, 1776.
    (E-123, K-436)

DUNHAM (DONHAM), DENNIS.
    Private, Capt. Anderson's Company No. 3, September 23, 1775.
    Signer, Association of Freemen, 1776, Susquehanna Hundred.
    (E-108, I-321)

DUNNAHOE, DENT.
    Signer, Oath of Fidelity and Allegiance to Maryland, 1778.
    (A-33, B-19, J-238)

DUNSHEATH, WILLIAM.
    Signer, Oath of Fidelity and Allegiance to Maryland, 1778.
    (A-33, B-30, J-247)

DURBIN, DANIEL.
    Born 1729. Died 1827, Harford County, Md.
    Married: Molly Johns in 1764, daughter of Richard and Anne
        Johns. Child: Nathaniel.
    Signer, Oath of Fidelity and Allegiance to Maryland, 1778.
    (A-33, B-26, G-286, J-243, M-55, X-208)

DURBIN, FRANCIS.
    Signer, Association of Freemen, 1776, Susquehanna. (I-321)

DURBIN, SAMUEL.
    Private, Capt. Rodgers' Co. No. 5, Sept. 15, 1775. (E-111)

DURBIN, THOMAS.
    Harford County Grand Juror, 1783. (E-77)

DURHAM, AQUILA.
    Private, Capt. Bond's Company No. 11, December 9, 1775.
    Signer, Association of Freemen, 1776, Gunpowder Neck.
    Signer, Oath of Fidelity and Allegiance to Maryland, 1778.
    (A-33, B-15, E-117, I-327, J-236)

DURHAM, DAVID.
    Born c.1744. Died 1815. Married: Sarah Smithson or Thompson.
    Signer, Association of Freemen, 1775, Bush River Upper.
    Signer, Oath of Fidelity and Allegiance to Maryland, 1778.
    (A-33, B-30, I-317, J-247, M-55, Y-63)

DURHAM, JAMES.
    Signer, Association of Freemen, 1776, Bush River Lower. (I-328)

DURHAM, JOHN.
    Born 1738. Died 1801. Married: Elizabeth Smithson.
    Signer, Bush Declaration, March 22, 1775.
    War Committee, 1775.
    Signer and solicitor, Association of Freemen, 1776, Gunpowder
      Lower Committee. Signer at Gunpowder Neck in 1775.
    Signer, Oath of Fidelity and Allegiance to Maryland, 1778.
    (D-355, D-358, E-263, I-327, A-33, B-10, X-208)

DURHAM, JOHN, of Joshua.
    Private, Capt. Bond's Company No. 11, December 9, 1775.
    Signer, Association of Freemen, 1776, Bush River Lower.
    (E-117, I-328)

DURHAM, JOSHUA.
    Born 1733. Died 1829. Married: Sarah Thompson in 1754.
    Signer, Association of Freemen, 1776, Bush River Lower.
    (I-328, M-55, Y-63)

DURHAM, MORDECAI.
    Private, Capt. Bond's Company No. 11, December 9, 1775.
    Signer, Association of Freemen, 1776, Bush River Lower.
    (E-117, I-328)

DURHAM, SAMUEL.
    Private, Capt. Bond's Company No. 11, December 9, 1775.
    Signer and solicitor, Association of Freemen, 1775, Bush
      River Lower, and signer again in 1776.
    Signer, Oath of Fidelity and Allegiance to Maryland, 1778.
    Petit Juror, Harford County, 1783.
    (A-33, B-15, E-117, I-315, I-328, E-77, J-236)

DURHAM, WILLIAM.
    Born 1760. Died 1818. Married: Ann Tolby.
    Private. Capt. Paca's Company, July 24, 1776.
    Private, Maryland Line. Widow pensioned.
    Maryland Line, last date, May 7, 1781.
    (E-126, F-414, F-59, N-19, X-208)

DURNER, THOMAS.
    Signer, Oath of Fidelity and Allegiance to Maryland, 1778.
    (A-33, B-29, J-246)

DUZAN, DUZART. See Dozens.

DYRE, JAMES.
    Pensioner (maimed soldier), 1778. (F-661)

E

EADIN, WILLIAM.
    Private, Capt. Bradford's Co. No. 13. Sept. 30, 1775. (E-119)

EAGLE, JAMES.
    Signer, Oath of Fidelity and Allegiance to Maryland, 1778.
    (A-33, B-22, J-240)

EAGON, PATRICK.
    Private, Capt. Harris' Company Payroll. (E-130, F-304)

EAGON, SAMSON.
    Born c.1745. Died c.1792. Married: Mary_____.
    Private, Capt. Baker's Company No. 15, January 27, 1776.
    Signer, Association of Freemen, 1776, Eden Hundred.
    Signer, Oath of Fidelity and Allegiance to Maryland, 1778.
    (A-33, B-24, E-120, I-324, J-242, Y-65)

EAGON (or EAGER), THOMAS.
    Signer, Association of Freemen, 1776, Gunpowder Upper. (I-326)

EAVS, NATH.
    Signer, Oath of Fidelity and Allegiance to Maryland, 1778.
    (A-33, B-29, J-246)

ECKSEN (ECKSON, ECKSTON), NICHOLAS.
    Private, Capt. Rumsey's Co. No. 6, September 16, 1775.
    Signer, Association of Freemen, 1775, Gunpowder Neck.
    2nd Lieutenant, 8th Battalion, 1778.
    Signer, Oath of Fidelity and Allegiance to Maryland, 1778.
    (A-33, B-17, C-47, E-112, I-327, J-237)

EDDY, JONATHAN.
>Private, Capt. Robert Harris' Harford Rifles, 1776.
>Paid subsistence for five weeks, one day, Sept. 28, 1776.
>(E-123, K-436)

EDMONSTON, ALEXANDER.
>Private, Capt. Paca's Company, August 5, 1776. (E-127, F-59)

EDWARDS, JAMES.
>Private, Capt. Rodgers' Co. No. 5, Sept. 15, 1775. (E-110)

EKEN, WILLIAM.
>Private, Capt. Rigdon's Company No. 12, December 2, 1775.
>Signer, Association of Freemen, 1776, Deer Creek Upper.
>(E-118, I-322)

ELDER, ROBERT.
>Signer, Association of Freemen, 1776, Gunpowder Upper.
>Signer, Oath of Fidelity and Allegiance to Maryland, 1778.
>(A-33, B-24, I-326, J-242)

ELLIOTT, JAMES.
>Signer, Association of Freemen, 1776, Gunpowder Upper. (I-326)

ELLIOTT, ROBERT.
>Private, Maryland Line; widow applied for pension.
>Born 1742. Married: Martha Creswell in 1787.
>Marriage proven through Maryland pension application.
>(N-113, N-20)

ELLIOTT (ELLETT), SAMUEL.
>Born 1757. Died 1841. Married: Keziah Webb.
>Private, Capt. William Webb's Co. No. 16, October 14, 1775.
>Signer, Association of Freemen, 1776, Deer Creek Upper.
>(E-121, I-323, X-218)

ELLIOTT, SAMUEL.
>Born 1748. Died 1795. Married: Mary Richardson.
>Private, Capt. Francis Holland's Harford Rifles, 1776.
>(E-124, X-218)

ELLIOTT (ELLETT), THOMAS.
>Private, Capt. Webb's Company No. 16, October 14, 1775.
>Signer, Oath of Fidelity and Allegiance to Maryland, 1778.
>(A-33, B-19, E-121)

ELLIS, ELLIS.
>Signer, Association of Freemen, 1776,Deer Creek Lower. (I-322)

ELLIS, JOHN.
>Private, Capt. Bradford's Company No. 13, September 30, 1775.
>Signer, Association of Freemen, 1776, Spesutie Upper and
> Harford Upper Hundred.
>Signer, Oath of Fidelity and Allegiance to Maryland, 1778.
>(A-33, B-17, E-119, I-319, I-325, J-237)

ELLIS, WILLIAM.
    Signer, Association of Freemen, 1776, Deer Creek Upper. (I-323)

ELLISON, RALPH.
    Private, Capt. Webb's Co. No. 16, October 14, 1775. (E-121)

ELY, THOMAS (QUAKER).
    Drafted, Militia, 1781; "Never taken up." (E-133, F-400)

ELY, WILLIAM.
    Pensioner (maimed soldier), 1778. (F-661)

ENLOWS, HENRY.
    Private, Capt. Baker's Co. No. 15, January 27, 1776. (E-120)

ENSOR, THOMAS.
    Married: Mary Talbott in 1770. Died c.1815.
    Signer, Oath of Fidelity and Allegiance to Maryland, 1778.
    (A-33, B-23, M-59, J-241, Z-15)

ERATT, WILLIAM.
    Signer, Oath of Fidelity and Allegiance to Maryland, 1778.
    (A-33, B-26, J-243)

ERWIN, JAMES.
    Signer, Association of Freemen, 1776, Spesutie Upper.
    Signer, Oath of Fidelity and Allegiance to Maryland, 1778.
    (A-33, B-28, I-319, J-245)

ESELDEIN, JOHN.
    Signer, Oath of Fidelity and Allegiance to Maryland, 1778.
    (A-33, B-17, J-237)

ESTHER, JAMES.
    Signer, Oath of Fidelity and Allegiance to Maryland, 1778.
    (A-33, B-26, J-243)

EVANS, BENJAMIN.
    Signer, Oath of Fidelity and Allegiance to Maryland, 1778.
    (A-33, B-21, J-239)

EVANS (EVINS), DAVID.
    Signer, Association of Freemen, 1776, Bush River Upper.
    Signer, Oath of Fidelity and Allegiance to Maryland, 1778.
    (A-33, B-30, I-320, J-247)

EVANS, EDWARD.
    Private, Capt. Dorsey's Company No. 8, October 31, 1775.
    Continental Army, 1777-1780 (Family Support Allowance).
    Land Warrant No. 11179, 100 acres, February 1, 1790.
    Land Warrant No. 11190, 100 acres, September 12, 1792.
    Seven Pay Certificates listed between 1780 and 1783.
    Records indicate there may have been others with this name
      who served in the 2nd and 4th Maryland Regiments.
    (E-114, F-661, N-64, Z-15) This Edward Evans served in the
      4th Maryland Regiment and had a wife, Sophia, and two children
      in Dec., 1778 (Minutes of the Harford County Court).

EVANS, ELIJAH.
    Born 1752. Died 1806. Married: Catherine Schaeffer.
    Lieutenant, 4th Maryland Line, 1776-October, 1777.
    Claimed Captaincy, April 10, 1778, in Maryland part of the
      Rifle Regiment. Supernumerary, January 1, 1781.
    Captain, Land Warrant No. 673, 300 acres (no date given).
    Pay Certificates for Officer's Pay in the Maryland Regiment:
      No. 89440, $58.70; No. 89441, $26.41; No. 89442, $1573.30.
    (E-129, F-301, F-365, N-64, X-224)

EVANS, EVAN.
    Private, Capt. Dorsey's Company No. 8, October 31, 1775.
    Signer, Association of Freemen, 1776, Spesutie Lower.
    Signer, Oath of Fidelity and Allegiance to Maryland, 1778.
    (A-33, B-23, E-115, I-318, J-241)

EVANS, GRIFFITH.
    Born 1760. Died 1818, Baltimore County. Married: Mary Burgess.
    Children: Sarah, Ann, George, Mary, Louisa, Margaret, Eli.
    Signer, Association of Freemen, 1775/1776, Bush River Upper.
    Private, Capt. Robert Harris' Harford Rifles, 1776.
    Paid subsistence for three weeks, three days, Oct. 7, 1776.
    Signer, Oath of Fidelity and Allegiance to Maryland, 1778.
      Records indicate there were two signers with this name.
    1st Lieutenant, Deer Creek Battalion, Commissioned 1779.
    Militia Substitute, 1781.
    (A-33, B-24, B-29, C-43, E-124, E-132, I-316, I-320, J-242,
    J-246, F-400, K-436, G-299, G-300, X-224)

EVANS, JOHN.
    Private, Capt. Baker's Company No. 15, January 27, 1776.
    Land Warrant No. 11194, 100 acres, February 1, 1790.
    (E-120, N-64)

EVANS, NATHAN.
    Signer, Association of Freemen, 1775, Bush River Upper. (I-316)

EVANS, WILLIAM.
    Private, Capt. Dorsey's Company No. 8, October 31, 1775.
    Signer, Association of Freemen, 1775, Spesutie Lower.
    Pensioner (maimed soldier), 1778.
    (E-115, I-317, F-661)

EVANS, WILLIAM JR.
    Private, Capt. Dorsey's Co. No. 8, October 31, 1775. (E-115)

EVERETT, JAMES.
    Private, Capt. Baker's Company No. 15, January 27, 1776.
    Signer, Association of Freemen, 1775, Bush River Upper.
    Signer, Oath of Fidelity and Allegiance to Maryland, 1778.
    (A-33, B-10, E-120, I-316, J-233)

EVERETT, JAMES, of Samuel.
    Private, Capt. Taylor's Co. No. 7, September 9, 1775. Signer,
    Association of Freemen, Gunpowder Upper Hundred, 1776. Signer,
    Oath of Allegiance to Maryland, 1778. (B-29, E-113, I-326, J-246)

EVERETT, RICHARD.
Private, Captain Baker's Company No. 15, January 27, 1776. (E-120)
Signer, Association of Freemen, Eden Hundred, 1776. (I-324)

EVERETT, SAMUEL.
Born April 5, 1763 in Harford County, MD. Served in Col. Alexander Cowan's Regiment in 1780, and in Capt. Jacob Norris' Company in 1781. Later in 1781 he joined the marines commanded by Capt. Jesse Bussey and went on board the "Jolly Tar" commanded by Capt. Belt. Was captured in a battle with British ship "Perseverance" at Hampton Roads, VA. Held prisoner in New York aboard British ship "Old Jersey" for one year and then parolled. Moved to North Carolina in 1786 and Tennessee in 1821. Living in Carroll Co., Tenn. when he applied for pension in Dec., 1832. (Zella Armstrong's Some Tennessee Heroes of the Revolution, 1933, page 67). This Samuel was too young to sign the Oath of Allegiance in 1778, so it must have been his father who did (A-33, B-10).

EVERIST, BENJAMIN.
Private, Capt. Dorsey's Company No. 8, October 31, 1775. (E-114)

EVERIST (EVEREST), JOHN.
Private, Capt. Dorsey's Company No. 8, October 31. 1775. (E-114)
Signer, Association of Freemen, Spesutie Lower Hundred, 1775. (I-317)

EVERIST (EVEREST), JOSEPH.
Private, Capt. Dorsey's Company No. 8, October 31, 1775. (E-114)
Signer, Association of Freemen, Spesutie Lower Hundred, 1775. (I-317)

EVERIST (EVEREST), THOMAS.
Signer, Association of Freemen, Spesutie Lower Hundred, 1775. (I-317)

EVITT, ANDREW.
Private, Capt. Rodgers' Company No. 5, September 15, 1775. (E-111)

EVITT, WILLIAM.
Private, Capt. Rodgers' Company No. 8, September 15, 1775. (E-110)

EWING (EWEN), ALEXANDER.
Signer, Association of Freemen, Bush River Lower Hundred, 1776. (A-33, B-10)
Signer, Oath of Allegiance to Maryland, 1778. (I-320, J-234)

EWING, JOSEPH.
Signer, Association of Freemen, Bush River Lower Hundred, 1776. (I-320)

EWING, THOMAS.
Captain in Gen. Smallwood's Maryland Regiment, January 14, 1776.
Colonel of 3rd Maryland Battalion of the Flying Camp, July to December, 1776. His battalion included soldiers from Baltimore and Harford Counties.
(L-220, E-125, F-54)

EWING, WILLIAM.
Private, Capt. Taylor's Company No. 7, September 9, 1775.
Signer, Association of Freemen, Gunpowder Upper Hundred, 1776.
Ensign, 8th Battalion, 1778. (C-46, E-113, I-326)

EYRE, JOHN.
Maryland Line, May, 1780, last date. (F-414)

F

FARISH (or TAVISH), GREGGS.
    Signer, Association of Freemen, Harford Hundred, 1776. (I-325)

FARMER, JOHN.
    1st Lieutenant, Deer Creek Battalion, 1778.
    Captain, Deer Creek Battalion, 1779.
    (C-44)

FAULKNER, ROBERT.
    Private, Capt. Aquila Hall's Co. No. 4, September 9, 1775.
    Signer, Association of Freemen, 1776, Harford Lower.
    (E-109, I-324)

FAUST, FRANCIS.
    Private, Capt. Rodgers' Co. No. 5, September 15, 1775, (E-110)

FAWCETT, JONATHAN.
    Signer, Association of Freemen, 1775, Spesutie Lower. (I-317)

FEAT, DAVID.
    Signer, Oath of Fidelity and Allegiance to Maryland, 1778.
    (A-33, B-30, J-247)

FEELY, WILLIAM.
    Signer, Association of Freemen, 1775/1776, Bush River Upper.
    Private, Capt. Robert Harris' Harford Rifles, 1776.
    Paid subsistence for six weeks, two days, September 16, 1776.
    (E-123, I-317, I-320, K-435)

FELL, STEPHEN.
    Private, Capt. Taylor's Com. No. 7, September 9, 1775.
    Signer, Association of Freemen, 1776, Gunpowder Upper.
    (E-113, I-326)

FELL, WILLIAM.
    Private, Capt. Francis Holland's Harford Rifles, 1776. (E-124)

FERGUSON, ANDREW.
    Signer, Association of Freemen, 1775/1776, Susquehanna.
    Private, Capt. Anderson's Co. No. 3, September 23, 1775.
    Signer, Oath of Fidelity and Allegiance to Maryland, 1778.
    (A-33, B-26, D-357, E-108, I-321, J-243)

FERGUSON, JAMES.
    Born 1752. Died c.1783. Married: Ruth Hallsall.
    Corporal, 4th Maryland Line, Capt. Thomas Bell's Co., 1777.
    (E-129, F-301, X-233)

FIE, BALTUS.
    Corporal, Capt. Dorsey's Company No. 8, October 31, 1775.
    Signer, Association of Freemen, 1776, Spesutie Lower.
    (E-114, I-318)

FIE, GODFREY.
    Private, Capt. Webb's Company No. 16, October 14, 1775.
    Signer, Oath of Fidelity and Allegiance to Maryland, 1778.
    (A-33, B-28, E-121, J-245)

FIELDS, JOSEPH.
    Corporal, Capt. Dorsey's Co. No. 8, October 31, 1775. (E-114)

FINCHAM, EDWARD.
    Militia Substitute, 1781. (E-132, F-400)

FING, JAMES.
    Signer, Association of Freemen, 1776, Bush River Upper. (I-328)

FINLEY, JAMES.
    Signer, Oath of Fidelity and Allegiance to Maryland, 1778.
    (A-33, B-29, J-246)

FINLEY, JAMES JR.
    Signer, Oath of Fidelity and Allegiance to Maryland, 1778.
    (A-33, B-29, J-246)

FINLEY, JOHN.
    Signer, Oath of Fidelity and Allegiance to Maryland, 1778.
    (A-33, B-29, J-246)

FINLEY, JOSEPH.
    Private, Capt. Josias Hall's Co. No. 1, September 12, 1775.
    Signer, Association of Freemen, 1776, Bush River Lower.
    Signer, Oath of Fidelity and Allegiance to Maryland, 1778.
    (A-33, B-15, J-236, E-106, I-319)

FINLEY, JOSEPH.
    Private, Capt. Rumsey's Co. No. 6, September 16, 1775.
    Signer, Association of Freemen, 1775, Gunpowder Neck.
    Signer, Oath of Fidelity and Allegiance to Maryland, 1778.
    (A-33, B-15, J-236, E-112, I-327)

FINLEYSON, GEORGE.
    Pensioner (maimed soldier), 1778.
    "George Finliston" received Pay Certificate No. 89463 for
      $8.00 as an Officer in the Maryland Regiment.
    (F-661, P-176)

FINN (or FIRM), BARTHO.
    Private, Capt. Bussey's Co., July 20, 1776. (E-127, F-60)

FINNAGON, PATRICK.
    Signer, Oath of Fidelity and Allegiance to Maryland, 1778.
    (A-33, B-10, J-233)

FINNCH, JOHN.
    Militia Substitute, 1781, 3 years. (E-133, F-401)

FINNEY, MANNASSAH.
    Signer, Association of Freemen, 1776,Deer Creek Upper. (I-323)

FISHER, WILLIAM.
    Signer, Association of Freemen, 1776, Deer Creek Lower.
    2nd Lieutenant, 8th Battalion, 1776.
    Captain, Deer Creek Battalion, 1778.
    Harford County Grand Juror, 1780.
    (C-43, E-267, I-321, E-76)

FISHER, WILLIAM JR.
    Signer, Bush Declaration, March 22, 1775.
    War Committee, 1775.
    2nd Lieutenant, Capt. Webb's Co. No. 16, October 14, 1775.
    Signer, Association of Freemen, 1776, and Solicitor for the
      Deer Creek Upper Hundred Committee.
    Constable, Deer Creek Upper, during the Revolutionary era.
    (D-355, D-359, E-121, E-262, E-265, E-64, I-323)

FITZGERALD (or FitzGerrald), JAMES.
    Private, Capt. Dorsey's Company No. 8, October 31, 1775.
    Signer, Association of Freemen, 1776, Spesutie Lower.
    Recruit, 8th Maryland Regiment, 1780.
    (E-114, E-131, F-343, I-318)

FLANIGAN, JOHN.
    Signer, Association of Freemen, 1776, Gunpowder Upper. (I-326)

FLANNAGAN, TORRANCE.
    Private, Capt. Taylor's Company No. 7, Sept. 9, 1775. (E-113)

FLATT (FLAT), JOHN.
    Private, Capt. Rigdon's Company No. 12, December 2, 1775.
    Signer, Association of Freemen, 1776, Deer Creek Upper.
    Signer, Oath of Fidelity and Allegiance to Maryland, 1778.
    (A-33, B-19, E-118, I-322, J-238)

FLYNN (FLENN), JOHN.
    Private, Capt. Patrick's Company No. 17, April 1, 1776.
    Signer, Association of Freemen, 1776, Deer Creek Lower.
    (E-122, I-321)

FORD, BENJAMIN.
    Born 1755. Died 1782/1783. Married: Mary Anderson.
    Private, Capt. Dorsey's Company No. 8, October 31, 1775.
    Wife applied for pension.
    Signer, Association of Freemen, 1775, Spesutie Lower.
    (E-115, I-317, N-22, X-244)

FORD, GEORGE.
    Signer, Association of Freemen, 1775, Spesutie Lower. (I-317)

FORD, JAMES.
    Signer, Association of Freemen, 1776, Susquehanna Hundred.
    1st Lieutenant, 23rd Battalion, 1778.
    (C-44, I-321)

FORD, JAMES.
    Private, Capt. Dorsey's Company No. 8, October 31, 1775.
    Signer, Association of Freemen, 1776, Spesutie Lower.
    (E-114, I-318)

FORD, JOHN.
    One source listed his name as "John Howard Ford."
    Born 1754. Died c.1810. Married: Esther Jessup.
    Corporal, 4th Maryland Line, 1777.
    "With Baggage at Chads Ford" June 6, 1778.
    "Sick at New Castle" June-July 24, 1778.
    Sergeant, Maryland Line.
    Signer, Association of Freemen, 1775, Gunpowder Neck.
    (E-129, F-301, I-327, N-22, Z-16)

FORD, THOMAS.
    Born 1744. Son of John Ford. Died c.1782.
    Married: Elizabeth Ford or Fortt in 1764.
    Private, Capt. Taylor's Company No. 7, September 9, 1775.
    Signer, Association of Freemen, 1776, Gunpowder Upper.
    (E-113, I-326, N-91, M-63, X-245)

FORRISDALE, STANFORD.
    One source listed his name as "Stafford Forestdale."
    Signer, Association of Freemen, 1776, Gunpowder Upper.
    Signer, Oath of Fidelity and Allegiance to Maryland, 1778.
    (A-33, B-24, I-326, J-242)

FORT, CHRISTOPHER.
    Private, Capt. Rigdon's Company No. 12, December 2, 1775.
    Private, Capt. Robert Harris' Harford Rifles, 1776.
    Paid subsistence for five weeks, September 28, 1776.
    Signer, Association of Freemen, 1776, Deer Creek Upper.
    (E-118, E-123, I-322, K-436)

FORT, PETER.
    Private, Capt. Rodgers' Co. No. 5, Sept. 15, 1775. (E-110)

FORWOOD, JACOB.
    2nd Lieutenant, Capt. Aquila Hall's Co. No. 4, Sept. 9, 1775.
    Signer and solicitor, Association of Freemen, 1776, Spesutie
    Lower Committee.
    Captain, 23rd Battalion, 1778.
    (C-45, D-359, E-109, E-262, E-324, N-91)

FORWOOD, JOSEPH.
    Signer, Association of Freemen, 1776, Harford Hundred.
    (I-325)

FOSTER, HENRY.
    Signer, Oath of Fidelity and Allegiance to Maryland, 1778.
    (A-33, B-19, J-238)

FOSTER, JAMES.
    Private, Capt. Rumsey's Co. No. 6, Sept. 16, 1775. (E-112)

FOSTER, SAMUEL.
    Private, Capt. Baker's Co. No. 15, January 27, 1776.
    Signer, Association of Freemen, 1776, Eden Hundred.
    Signer, Oath of Fidelity and Allegiance to Maryland, 1778.
    (A-33, B-19, E-120, I-324, J-238)

FOWLER, PATRICK.
    Born 1755, Ireland.
    Private, Capt. Anderson's Company No. 3, September 23, 1775.
    Private, Flying Camp, Lt. John Smith enlisted July 15, 1776,
      in Col. Thomas Ewing's Battalion. (5'4½" tall with sandy hair)
    (E-108, E-125, F-56)

FOWLER, PERRY.
    Signer, Association of Freemen, 1776, Spesutie Lower. (I-318)

FOWLER, SAMUEL.
    Private, Capt. Rodgers' Company No. 5, September 15, 1775.
    Signer, Association of Freemen, 1776, Spesutie Lower.
    (E-111, I-318)

FOWLER, WILLIAM PERRY.
    Private, Capt. Rodgers' Co. No. 5, Sept. 15, 1775. (E-111)

FOX, RICHARD.
    Signer, Oath of Fidelity and Allegiance to Maryland, 1778.
    (A-33, B-19, J-238)

FRALEY, DANIEL.
    Private, Capt. Taylor's Co. No. 7, Sept. 9, 1775. (E-114)

FRANCE, JOSHUA.
    Private, Capt. Rumsey's Co. No. 6, September 16, 1775.
    Signer, Association of Freemen, 1775, Gunpowder Neck.
    (E-112, I-327)

FRAULKNOR, ROBERT.
    Signer, Oath of Fidelity and Allegiance to Md., 1778. (A-33)

FRAZIER, SAMUEL.
    Married Penelope Johnson in 1792, Harford County, Md.
    Marriage proven through Maryland pension application.
    Private, Maryland Continental Line.
    (N-22, N-114)

FREEMAN, EDWARD.
    Private, Capt. Love's Company No. 10, September 14, 1775.
    Private, Capt. Bussey's Company, July 20, 1776.
    Recruit, New Regiment, July 16, 1780.
    (E-116, E-127, E-130, F-60, F-343)

FREEMAN, THOMAS.
    Private, Capt. Taylor's Company No. 7, September 9, 1775.
    Signer, Oath of Fidelity and Allegiance to Maryland, 1778.
    (A-33, B-10, E-113, J-234)

FREMBLE, ROBERT.
    Private, Capt. Bond's Co. No. 11, December 9, 1775. (E-117)

FRENCH, OTHO.
    Private, Capt. Rumsey's Company No. 6, September 16, 1775.
    Signer, Association of Freemen, 1775, Gunpowder Neck.
    (E-112, I-327)

FRENCH, PETER.
    Militia Substitute, 1781, 3 years. (E-133, F-401)

FREW, ALEXANDER.
    Signer, Association of Freemen, Bush River Lower, 1776. (I-328)

FREW, JAMES.
    Signer, Association of Freemen, Bush River Upper, 1776. (I-320)

FREW, JOHN.
    Records indicate there was more than one signer with this name.
    Signer, Association of Freemen, Bush River Upper, 1776.
    Signer, Association of Freemen, Eden Hundred, 1776.
    Signer, Association of Freemen, Gunpowder Upper, 1776.
    Signer, Oath of Fidelity and Allegiance to Maryland, 1778.
    (A-33, B-30, I-320, I-323, I-326, J-247)

FRIER (FRYER), ISAAC.
    Private, Capt. Bradford's Company no. 13, September 30, 1775.
    Signer, Association of Freemen, 1776, Harford Upper Hundred.
    Signer, Oath of Fidelity and Allegiance to Maryland, 1778.
    (A-33, B-10, E-119, I-325, J-233)

FRISBEY, THOMAS PEREGRINE.
    Son of Capt. Peregrine Frisbey and Mary Holland.
    Private, Capt. Josias Hall's Company No. 1, September 12, 1775.
    Signer, Association of Freemen, 1775, Spesutie Lower Hundred.
    Signer, Oath of Fidelity and Allegiance to Maryland, 1778.
    (A-33, B-22, E-105, I-317, J-240, M-65)

FROST, JAMES.
    Private, Capt. Rigdon's Co. No. 12, Dec. 2, 1775. (E-118)

FROST, JOHN.
    Private, Capt. Rigdon's Co. No. 12, Dec. 2, 1775. (E-118)

FULFET (FULFIT), JOHN.
    Signer, Oath of Fidelity and Allegiance to Maryland, 1778.
    Militia Substitute, 1781, 3 years.
    (A-33, B-30, E-133, F-401, J-247)

FULTON, JOHN.
Signer, Association of Freemen, 1776, Gunpowder Neck.
Signer, Oath of Fidelity and Allegiance to Maryland, 1778.
Harford County Grand Juror, 1783.
(A-33, B-20, E-77, I-328, J-239)

FULTON, WILLIAM.
Private, Capt. Love's Company No. 10, September 14, 1775.
Pensioner (maimed soldier), 1778.
Signer, Oath of Fidelity and Allegiance to Maryland, 1778.
(A-33, B-28, E-116, F-661, J-245)

FURREY, PATRICK.
Signer, Association of Freemen, 1776, Bush River Lower. (I-328)

GADDIS, WILLIAM.
Private, Capt. Bussey's Company, July 27, 1776.
Signer, Association of Freemen, 1775/1776, Bush River Upper.
(E-128, F-60, I-315, I-328)

GALE (GAIL, GAILE), WILLIAM.
Private, Capt. Bradford's Co. No. 13, September 30, 1775.
Signer, Association of Freemen, 1775, Gunpowder Neck.
Signer, Oath of Fidelity and Allegiance to Maryland, 1775.
(A-33, B-17, E-119, I-327, J-237)

GALLION, GREGORY.
Signer, Association of Freemen, 1776, Deer Creek Lower. (I-322)

GALLION, JAMES.
Signer, Association of Freemen, 1776, Susquehanna. (I-321)

GALLION, JOHN.
Private, Capt. Anderson's Co. No. 3, September 23, 1775.
Signer, Association of Freemen, 1776, Susquehanna.
(E-109, I-321)

GALLION, NATHAN.
Private, Capt. Aquila Hall's Co. No. 4, September 9, 1775.
Signer, Association of Freemen, 1776, Harford Lower.
Drafted, Militia, 1781; "infirm and sickly."
(E-110, E-132, F-400, I-324)

GALLION, SAMUEL.
Private, Capt. Dorsey's Co. No. 8, Oct. 31, 1775. (E-115)

GALLION, THOMAS.
 Private, Capt. Anderson's Company No. 3, September 23, 1775.
 Private, Capt. Webb's Company No. 16, October 14, 1775.
 Signer, Association of Freemen, 1776, Susquehanna Hundred.
 (E-108, E-121, I-321)

GALLOWAY, WILLIAM.
 Signer, Association of Freemen, 1775, Gunpowder Neck. (I-327)

GAMERY, GODFREY.
 Signer, Association of Freemen, 1775, Gunpowder Neck. (I-327)

GARDNER (GARDER), GEORGE.
 Private, Capt. Bussey's Co., July 25, 1776. (E-128, F-60)

GARDNERS, GEORGE.
 Militia Substitute, 1781, 3 years. (E-133, F-401)

GARLAND (GARLON), FRANCIS.
 Private, Capt. Aquila Hall's Co. No. 4, September 9, 1775.
 Signer, Association of Freemen, 1775, Spesutie Lower.
 Signer, Oath of Fidelity and Allegiance to Maryland, 1778.
 (A-33, B-21, E-110, I-317, J-239)

GARLAND, HENRY.
 Signer, Association of Freemen, 1775, Spesutie Lower. (I-317)

GARREGUIES (GARRIGUES), JOHN.
 8th Maryland Regiment, 1780. (E-131, F-343)

GARRETT, AMOS.
 Married Frances Drew in 1744.
 Harford County Court Justice, 1774.
 War Committee, Correspondence, June 11, 1775.
 Chairman, War Committee, 1776.
 Signer, Association of Freemen, 1776, Spesutie Lower.
 Army Ledger No. 4, f. 39, February 16, 1776.
 Agent's Ledger No. 1, f. 22, 1776-1777.
 "I am very unfit for the task entrusted to me being so deprived
 of my sight as to be unable to distinguish any writing or print
 but desirous to promote the service all in my power." Part of
 a letter written by Garrett to the Md. Council, Oct. 14, 1776.
 Signer, Oath of Fidelity and Allegiance to Maryland, 1778.
 (A-33, B-26, D-358, E-266, E-61, E-96, I-318, J-243, K-414,
 K-350, M-67, HR-50) Furnished a musquet, Sept., 1776. (E-335)

GARRETT, HENRY.
 Private, Capt. Rumsey's Co. No. 6, Sept. 16, 1775. (E-112)

GARRETT, JESSE.
 Signer, Oath of Fidelity and Allegiance to Maryland, 1778.
 (B-24, J-242)

GARRETT, JOHN.
    Private, Capt. Bussey's Co., July 25, 1776. (E-128, F-60)

GARRETT (GARROTT), WILLIAM.
    Signer, Oath of Fidelity and Allegiance to Maryland, 1778.
    (A-33, B-24, J-242)

* GARRETSON (GARRETTSON), CARNS. (CORNELIUS).
    2nd Lieutenant, 8th Battalion, 1778.
    Intendant's Orders No. 1, f.44, May 29, 1782.
    (C-46, HR-50)

GARRETTSON (GANETSON), FREEBORN.
    Private, Capt. Dorsey's Co. No. 8, October 31, 1775.
    Signer, Association of Freemen, 1775, Spesutie Lower.
    Signer, Association of Freemen, 1776, Harford Lower.
    Signer, Oath of Fidelity and Allegiance to Maryland, 1778.
    (A-33, B-17, E-115, I-317, I-324, J-237)

GARRETTSON (GARRITTSON), GARRETT.
    Married Susannah Robinson in 1760.
    Private, Capt. Josias Hall's Co. No. 1, September 12, 1775.
    Signer, Association of Freemen, 1775, Spesutie Lower.
    Signer, Oath of Fidelity and Allegiance to Maryland, 1778.
    (A-33, B-22, E-105, I-317, J-240)

GARRETTSON, GARRETT, of Edward.
    Private, Capt. Aquila Hall's Company No. 4, Sept. 9, 1775.
    Signer, Association of Freemen, 1776, Harford Lower.
    (E-110, I-324)

GARRETTSON, GEORGE.
    Married Martha Presbury in 1768.
    Private, Capt. Taylor's Company No. 7, September 9, 1775.
    Signer, Association of Freemen, 1776, Gunpowder Upper.
    (E-113, I-326, M-67)

GARRETTSON, JAMES.
    Private, Capt. Webb's Co. No. 16, October 14, 1775. (E-121)

GARRETTSON, JAMES.
    Private, Capt. Baker's Co. No. 15, January 27, 1776. (E-120)

GARRETTSON (GANETSON), RICHARD.
    Signer, Association of Freemen, 1775, Spesutie Lower.
    Signer, Oath of Fidelity and Allegiance to Maryland, 1778.
    (A-33, B-17, I-317, J-237)

* GARRISON, CORNELIUS.
    Signer, Association of Freemen, 1776, Gunpowder Upper.
    Signer, Oath of Fidelity and Allegiance to Maryland, 1778.
    (A-33, B-23, I-326, J-241)

* Data on Cornelius Garrison and Cornelius Garrettson applies only to Cornelius Garrison, son of John. There is no Cornelius in the family Garrettson in Harford County. Garrisons were from Bucks County, Pa.

GARRISON, JAMES.
　　Signer, Association of Freemen, 1776, Gunpowder Upper. (I-326)

GARRISON, JOHN.
　　Signer, Oath of Fidelity and Allegiance to Maryland, 1778.
　　(A-33, B-23, J-241)

GARRISON, PHILIP.
　　Signer, Association of Freemen, 1776, Gunpowder Upper. (I-326)

GARSON, JOHN SR.
　　Signer, Association of Freemen, 1776, Gunpowder Upper. (I-326)

GASH, THOMAS.
　　Sergeant, Capt. Rodgers' Co. No. 5, September 15, 1775.
　　Signer, Association of Freemen, 1776, Spesutie Lower.
　　(E-110, I-318)

GASH, WILLIAM.
　　Private, Capt. Bussey's Company, July 25, 1776.
　　Signer, Association of Freemen, 1776, Deer Creek Upper.
　　(E-128, F-60, I-322)

GATHERIDGE, EDWARD.
　　Private, Capt. Baker's Co. No. 15, January 27, 1776. (E-120)

GAVETT, JOHN.
　　Signer, Oath of Fidelity and Allegiance to Maryland, 1778.
　　(A-33, B-13, J-235)

GELLEY (HELLY), WILLIAM.
　　Signer, Association of Freemen, 1776, Harford Lower Hundred.
　　Signer, Oath of Fidelity and Allegiance to Maryland, 1778.
　　(A-33, B-22, I-324, J-240)

GIANT, ISAAC.
　　Private, Capt. Paca's Company, July 24, 1776. (E-126, F-59)

GIANT, JOHN.
　　Private, Capt. Dorsey's Co. No. 8, October 31, 1775. (E-115)

GIBB, JOHN.
　　Signer, Oath of Fidelity and Allegiance, 1778. (B-25, J-242)

GIBBONS (GIBBENS), JOSEPH.
　　Private, Capt. Rigdon's Co. No. 12, December 2, 1775.
　　1st Lieutenant, Deer Creek Battalion, November 17, 1779.
　　Signer, Association of Freemen, 1776, Deer Creek Upper.
　　　Records indicate there were two signers with this name.
　　(C-44, E-118, I-322)

GIBS, JOHN.
　　Signer, Oath of Fidelity and Allegiance to Maryland, 1778.
　　(A-33, B-30, J-247)

GIBSON, FRANCIS.
   Signer, Association of Freemen, 1775, Bush River Upper.
   Private, Capt. Robert Harris' Harford Rifles, 1776.
   Paid subsistence for two weeks, one day, October 15, 1776.
   Signer, Oath of Fidelity and Allegiance to Maryland, 1778.
   (A-33, B-19, E-123, I-316, J-238, K-436)

GIBSON, JOHN.
   Signer, Association of Freemen, 1775, Bush River Upper.
   Signer, Oath of Fidelity and Allegiance to Maryland, 1778.
   (A-33, B-19, I-316, J-238)

GIBSON, JOHN LEE.
   Signer, Oath of Fidelity and Allegiance to Maryland, 1778.
   Clerk for Harford County Court Justices, 1779.
   (A-33, B-21, E-75, J-239)

GIBSON, WILLIAM.
   Private, Capt. Rigdon's Co. No. 12, December 2, 1775.
   Signer, Association of Freemen, 1776, Deer Creek Upper.
   (E-118, I-322)

GIFFIN (GIFFEN), ROBERT.
   Signer, Association of Freemen, 1776, Deer Creek Upper.
   Signer, Oath of Fidelity and Allegiance to Maryland, 1778.
   (A-33, I-323)

GILBERT, AQUILLA.
   Son of Gervas Gilbert and Mary_____ (2nd wife).
   Born 1726/1727. Married: Elizabeth Butler in 1749.
   Private, Capt. Anderson's Co. No. 3, September 23, 1775.
   Signer, Association of Freemen, 1776, Susquehanna Hundred.
   Signer, Oath of Fidelity and Allegiance to Maryland, 1778.
   (A-33, B-26, E-108, I-321, J-243, M-68, U-12)

GILBERT, CHARLES, of Michael.
   Son of Michael Gilbert and Mary Taylor.
   Born 1723. Died 1796. Married: Mary_____.
   One source states he married Comfort Cole; died 1820.
   Daughter, Ann, married Amos Anderson.
   Signer, Oath of Fidelity and Allegiance to Maryland, 1778.
   (A-33, B-26, J-244, U-12, U-16, O-23)

GILBERT, CHARLES SR.
   Son of Gervais Gilbert and Mary_____.
   Born 1723/1724. Died 1798. Married: Elizabeth Hawkins,
      daughter of Robert Hawkins.
   Children: Michael, Mary, Martha, Elizabeth.
   War Committee, 1775.
   Signer, Association of Freemen, 1776, Susquehanna.
   Signer, Oath of Fidelity and Allegiance to Maryland, 1778.
   (A-33, B-26, D-358, I-321, J-244, M-68, U-12, U-16)

GILBERT, JAMES.
    Son of Micah Gilbert and Mary Gallion.
    Born 1755-1760. No further record.
    Signer, Association of Freemen, 1776, Susquehanna.
    (I-321, U-13)

GILBERT, JARVIS.
    Son of Michael Gilbert and Sarah Preston.
    Born 1731. Married: _____ Ricketts.
    Had a son Jarvis who died unmarried.
    Private, Capt. Francis Holland's Harford Rifles, 1776.
    Signer, Association of Freemen, 1776, Deer Creek Upper.
    (E-124, I-323, U-13)

GILBERT, JOHN.
    Son of Samuel Gilbert and Martha Webster.
    Born 1738 "John Webster Gilbert"
    Signer, Association of Freemen, 1776, Gunpowder Upper.
    (I-326, U-12)

GILBERT, JONAS.
    Private, Capt. Webb's Co. No. 16, October 14, 1775. (E-121)

GILBERT, MARTIN TAYLOR.
    Son of Michael Gilbert and Mary Taylor.
    Born 1739. Died 1797. Married Martha Gilbert in 1764.
    Children: Mary, Charles, Martin Taylor Jr., Wilson,
      Elizabeth, Sarah Ann, Martha, Julia.
    Signer, Oath of Fidelity and Allegiance to Maryland, 1778.
    Listed simply as "Taylor Gilbert."
    (A-33, B-25, J-243, M-68, U-15, U-16, O-23)

GILBERT, MICH. ("MICAH")
    Son of Michael Gilbert and Sarah Preston.
    Born 1734. Died 1827. Married Mary Gallion in 1757.
    Children: Aquilla, James, Sarah, Michael, Mary, Martha,
      William, Amos, Phoebe, Jacob, Naomi.
    Signer, Association of Freemen, 1776, Susquehanna Hundred.
    Signer, Oath of Fidelity and Allegiance to Maryland, 1778.
    (B-26, I-321, J-243, U-13, U-14)

GILBERT, MICHAEL.
    Son of Charles Gilbert and Elizabeth Hawkins.
    Born 1754. Died 1796. Married Elizabeth Presbury in 1782.
    Children: Charles, Elizabeth, William Presbury, Elizabeth,
      Clemency Hughes, William.
    Ensign, Capt. Anderson's Company No. 3, September 23, 1775.
    2nd Lieutenant, Capt. Paca's Company, August 5, 1776.
    Fought at Battle of White Plains, October 28, 1776.
    1st Lieutenant, 2nd Canadian Regt. (Hazen's), November 3, 1776.
    Captain, 2nd Canadian Regiment, April 1, 1777.
    Signer, Association of Freemen, 1776, Susquehanna Hundred.
      (continued)

GILBERT, MICHAEL (continued)
    Signer, Oath of Fidelity and Allegiance to Maryland, 1778.
    Ensign, 23rd Battalion, Harford County Militia, 1778.
    2nd Lieutenant, 23rd Battalion, 1779.
    Captain, County Militia; wife applied for pension.
    Resigned, April 20, 1781.
    Depreciation Pay No. 1, p. 25; No. 2, p. 37; No. 3, P. 139; August 14, 1782.
    Army Ledger No. 2, f. 84; No. 3, f.49; 1783 "Captain".
    Intendant's Ledger No. 15, p. 49; Intendant's Ledger A No. 9, ff. 46, 57; 1783 "Captain".
    Agent's Letter Book No. 1, p. 117; Intendant's Ledger A No. 10, ff. 64, 80; 1783-1785 "Captain".
    Harford County Grand Juror, 1783.
    (A-33, B-26, C-45, E-108, E-126, E-137, I-321, J-243, K-170, F-59, N-23, E-76, HR-50, G-330, H-85, L-247, N-114, X-267)

GILBERT, MICHAEL SR.
    Son of Gervais Gilbert and Margaret_____.
    Born 1707. Died 1784. Married: (1) Sarah Preston in 1728.
    Children: Martha, Jarvis, Micah. (2) Mary Taylor in 1738.
    Children: Martin Taylor, Parker, Michael, Charles, Elizabeth, Philip, Samuel, Mary.
    Signer and solicitor, Association of Freemen, 1775/1776, Harford Hundred, and Susquehanna Hundred.
    Signer, Oath of Fidelity and Allegiance to Maryland, 1778.
    One of the first Elders in Churchville Presbyterian Church.
    (A-33, B-25, D-357, I-315, I-321, I-325, J-243, M-68, U-14, U-15, Y-83) (O-23, O-25)

GILBERT, MICHAEL JR.
    Son of Michael Gilbert and Mary Taylor.
    Born 1741.
    Private, Capt. Josias Hall's Co. No. 1, September 12, 1775.
    Signer, Association of Freemen, 1776, Harford Hundred.
    (E-105, I-325, U-15, U-16)

GILBERT, PARKER.
    Son of Michael Gilbert and Mary Taylor.
    Born 1740. Died 1803/1808. Married: Elizabeth_____.
    Children: Sarah, Parker, Gidian, Abner, Michael, Priscilla.
    Private, Capt. Anderson's Co. No. 3, September 23, 1775.
    Signer, Oath of Fidelity and Allegiance to Maryland, 1778.
    (A-33, B-25, E-108, J-242, U-15, U-16, Y-83)

GILBERT, PHILIP.
    Son of Michael Taylor and Mary Taylor.
    Born c.1750. Married Sarah Ruff. Son, Shadrach.
    Signer, Oath of Fidelity and Allegiance to Maryland, 1778.
    (A-33, B-25, J-242, U-15, U-16)

GILBERT, TAYLOR. See "Martin Taylor Gilbert."

GILBERT, SAMUEL.
    Private, Capt. Anderson's Co. No. 3, September 23, 1775.
    Private, Capt. Francis Holland's Harford Rifles, 1776.
    Signer, Oath of Fidelity and Allegiance to Maryland, 1778.
    (A-33, B-25, E-108, E-124, J-242, U-15, U-16)

GILBERT, WILLIAM.
    Son of Samuel Gilbert and Martha Webster. Born 1743.
    Signer, Association of Freemen, 1776, Gunpowder Upper.
    (I-326, U-12)

GILCHRIST, ROBERT.
    Private, Capt. Webb's Co. No. 16, October 14, 1775. (E-121)

GILES, EDWARD.
    Son of Jacob Giles and Hannah Webster.
    Captain (later Major) and Aide-de-Camp to General Morgan
        during the Southern Campaign under General Nathaniel Greene.
    Signer, Oath of Fidelity and Allegiance to Maryland, 1778.
    Army Ledger No. 2, f. 82; Army Accounts No. 1, p. 46;
    Intendant's Orders No. 1, f. 10; Agent's Ledger No. 1,
        f. 27 (1780-1792, "Major Edward Giles").
    (A-33, B-21, J-239, HR-50, S-367)

GILES, JACOB.
    Married Hannah Webster in 1728.
    Children: Sarah, Jacob, James, Edward, Nathaniel.
    During the Revolution he became Assistant Quartermaster to
        Richard Dallam. This action and his reluctance to manumit
        slaves resulted in serious charges being brought against him
        by the Deer Creek Meeting, Society of Friends, in 1778, which
        stated: "Jacob Giles is charged with supplying the militia
        and troops with provisions and other war-like materials. It
        appears he has taken ye test (oath) prescribed by the present
        powers and other matters contrary to Quaker principles."
    Signer, Oath of Fidelity and Allegiance to Maryland, 1778.
    (A-33, B-16, J-237, S-367)

GILES, JACOB JR.
    War Committee, 1775.
    Signer, Oath of Fidelity and Allegiance to Maryland, 1778.
    (A-33, B-16, D-358, J-237, S-367)

GILES, JAMES.
    Son of Jacob Giles and Hannah Webster.
    2nd Lieutenant and Adjutant, Capt. Rodgers' Company No. 5,
        September 15, 1775.
    Signer, Association of Freemen, 1776, Harford Lower Hundred.
    Signer, Oath of Fidelity and Allegiance to Maryland, 1778.
    Harford County Court Justice, 1780.
    (A-33, B-23, D-359, E-110, E-76, I-324, J-241, S-367)

GILES, NATHANIEL.
    Son of Jacob Giles and Hannah Webster.
    Married Sarah Hammond in 1762.
    Committee of Correspondence, June 11, 1775.
    (E-95, M-69, S-367)

GILES, THOMAS.
    Private, Capt. Josias Hall's Co. No. 1, September 12, 1775.
    Private, Capt. Francis Holland's Harford Rifles, 1776.
    Signer, Association of Freemen, 1776, Spesutie Lower.
    Signer, Oath of Fidelity and Allegiance to Maryland, 1778.
    (A-33, B-17, E-106, E-124, I-318, J-237)

GILLASPEY, CHARLES.
    Private, Capt.Taylor's Co. No. 7, September 9, 1775.
    Signer, Association of Freemen, 1776, Gunpowder Upper.
    (E-113, I-326)

GILLASPEY (GILLESPEY), JOHN.
    Private, Capt. Taylor's Co. No. 7, September 9, 1775.
    Signer, Association of Freemen, 1776, Gunpowder Upper.
    (E-113, I-326)

GILLESPIE, GEORGE.
    Married Sarah Hall, Harford County, as proven through Maryland
      pension application; no details on service record. (N-114)

GILLIS, ROBERT.
    Born 1732. Died 1807. Married Elizabeth Sharp before 1766.
    Children: Thomas, John, James, William, Sarah, David, Elizabeth,
      Lavina, Hannah, Rebecca, William Robert.
    Came from Ireland in 1750 and settled in Harford County, Md.
    Served in Revolution as Private in Northumberland County, Pa.
      Militia.
    (G-332, X-269)

GILMORE, CHARLES.
    Signer, Oath of Fidelity and Allegiance to Maryland, 1778.
    (A-33, B-22, J-240)

GIVDON, RICHARD.
    Signer, Oath of Fidelity and Allegiance, 1778. (B-24, J-242)

GLADDEN, JACOB.
    Signer, Oath of Fidelity and Allegiance to Maryland, 1778.
    (A-33, B-30, J-247)

GLEEN, ROBERT.
    Signer, Oath of Fidelity and Allegiance to Maryland, 1778.
    (A-33, B-29, J-246)

GLENN (GLEN), ROBERT.
    Born 1722. Died 1799. Married Isabella Clendenin in 1755.
    Children: William.
    Captain, Harford County Militia Company, 1775-1776.
    Major, Deer Creek Battalion, 1778.

GLENN, ROBERT (continued)
    Signer, Association of Freemen, 1775, Bush River Upper.
    (C-43, I-316, G-335, X-271)

GLOURY (GLORY), WILLIAM.
    Recruit, 8th Maryland Regiment, 1780.
    Pay Certificates: No. 81353, $80, 2nd Md. Regt. pay;
    No. 82171, $43.30, 2nd Md. Regt. pay; No. 85483, $80,
    Md. Regt. paid to Jan. 1, 1782; No. 87122, $80, 2nd Md.
    Regt. paid to Nov. 16, 1783.
    (E-131, F-343, P-205)

GLYN, JOSEPH.
    Private, Capt. Paca's Co., July 24, 1776. (E-126, F-59)

GODDIN, AARON.
    Private, Capt. Bradford's Co. No. 13, September 30, 1775.
    Signer, Association of Freemen, 1776, Harford Upper.
    (E-119, I-325)

GODDIN, WILLIAM.
    Private, Capt. Bradford's Co. No. 13, September 30, 1775.
    Signer, Association of Freemen, 1776, Bush River Lower.
    (E-119, I-320)

GODFREY, THOMAS.
    Private, Capt. Bussey's Company, July 27, 1776. (E-128, F-60)

GODSGRACE, WILLIAM.
    1st Lieutenant, Capt. Rodgers Co. No. 5, September 15, 1775.
    From "A Walking Tour of Spesutie Cemetery": "Rebecca and
    William Godsgrace, died 1777/1778. These may be the oldest
    marked graves in the cemetery."
    (D-359, E-110)

GOFFEY, HENRY.
    Signer, Oath of Fidelity and Allegiance to Maryland, 1778.
    (A-33, B-14, J-235)

GOLDSMITH, VINCENT.
    Private, Capt. Love's Co. No. 10, September 14, 1775.
    Signer, Association of Freemen, 1776, Bush River Lower.
    Signer, Oath of Fidelity and Allegiance to Maryland, 1778.
    (A-33, B-28, E-116, I-319, J-245)

GOLDSMITH, WILLIAM COPELAND.
    Private, Capt. Rumsey's Co. No. 6, September 16, 1775.
    Signer, Association of Freemen, 1775, Gunpowder Neck.
    (E-116, I-327)

GOODWIN, WILLIAM.
    Signer, Oath of Fidelity and Allegiance to Maryland, 1778.
    (A-33, B-10, J-233)

GORDON, ALEXANDER.
    Private, Capt. Dorsey's Co. No. 8, October 31, 1775.
    Signer, Association of Freemen, 1775, Spesutie Lower.
    Signer, Oath of Fidelity and Allegiance to Maryland, 1778.
    (A-33, B-22, E-114, I-317, J-240)

GORDON, JAMES.
    Signer, Association of Freemen, 1775, Spesutie Lower. (I-317)

GORDON, JOHN.
    Private, Capt. Dorsey's Co. No. 8, October 31, 1775.
    Militia Substitute, 1781.
    (E-114, E-131, F-400)

GORDON, ROBERT.
    Signer, Association of Freemen, 1775, Bush River Upper.
    Signer, Association of Freemen, 1776, Deer Creek Upper.
    Private, Capt. Robert Harris' Harford Rifles, 1776.
    Paid Subsistence for six weeks, September 18, 1776.
    (e-123, I-316, I-323, I-328, K-435)

GORDON, WILLIAM.
    Private, Capt. Robert Harris' Harford Rifles, 1776.
    Signer, Oath of Fidelity and Allegiance to Maryland, 1778.
    (A-33, B-30, E-123, J-247)

GORMILLEY, OWEN.
    Signer, Oath of Fidelity and Allegiance to Maryland, 1778.
    (A-33, B-31, J-248)

GORRELL (GORREL), ABRAHAM.
    Signer, Association of Freemen, 1775, Susquehanna.
    Signer, Association of Freemen, 1776, Susquehanna.
    (D-357, I-321)

GORRELL, JOHN.
    Signer, Association of Freemen, 1775, Susquehanna.
    Signer, Association of Freemen, 1776, Susquehanna.
    (D-357, I-321)

GORRELL, THOMAS.
    Signer, Association of Freemen, 1775, Susquehanna.
    Signer, Association of Freemen, 1776, Susquehanna.
    Private, Capt. Anderson's Co. No. 3, September 23, 1775.
    (D-357, E-108, I-321)

GORRELL, WILLIAM.
    Signer, Association of Freemen, 1776, Susquehanna. (I-321)

GOTT, SAMUEL.
    Signer, Association of Freemen, 1775, Gunpowder Neck.
    (I-327)

GOUGH, HUGH M.
    Signer, Oath of Fidelity and Allegiance to Maryland, 1778.
    (A-33, B-14, J-236)

GOULDSMITH, THOMAS.
    Born 1758 in America.
    Cadet, Flying Camp. Lt. James Bond enlisted July 7, 1776,
      in Col. Thomas Ewing's Battalion.
    5'3" tall with short light hair.
    Signer, Association of Freemen, 1775, Gunpowder Neck.
    (E-125, F-54, I-327)

GOVER, GIDEON.
    Private, Capt. Patrick's Co. No. 17, April 1, 1776. (E-122)

GOVER, GITTINGS.
    Signer, Association of Freemen, 1776, Deer Creek Lower. (I-322)

GOVER, PHILIP.
    Private, Capt. Francis Holland's Harford Rifles, 1776.
    Signer, Oath of Fidelity and Allegiance to Maryland, 1778.
    (A-33, B-16, E-124, J-237)

GOVER, SAMUEL.
    Private, Capt. Josias Hall's Co. No. 1, September 12, 1775.
    Signer, Association of Freemen, 1776, Deer Creek Lower.
    (E-106, I-322)

GRACE, AARON.
    Born c.1734. Died c.1788. Married: Ann Boyer.
    Signer, Association of Freemen, 1776, Spesutie Lower.
    Signer, Oath of Fidelity and Allegiance to Maryland, 1778.
    Ensign, 23rd Battalion, 1778.
    Militia Draft, 1781; "discharged, being poor and having a
      wife and five children."
    Captain, Intendant's Day Book No. 2, p. 70. Oct. 21, 1785.
    (A-33, B-21, C-45, E-132, F-400, I-318, J-239, HR-50, X-278)

GRAFTON, DANIEL.
    Signer, Oath of Fidelity and Allegiance to Maryland, 1778.
    (A-33, B-28, J-245)

GRAFTON, SAMUEL.
    Signer, Association of Freemen, 1776, Bush River Upper.
    Signer, Oath of Fidelity and Allegiance to Maryland, 1778.
    (A-33, B-30, I-320, J-247)

GRAFTON, WILLIAM.
    Signer, Association of Freemen, 1776, Spesutie Upper.
    Signer, Oath of Fidelity and Allegiance to Maryland, 1778.
    Drafted, Militia, 1781; "discharged, a wife and children
      to support."
    (A-33, B-28, I-319, J-245, E-132, F-400)

GRANT, ALEXANDER.
Signer, Association of Freemen, 1776, Gunpowder Upper. (I-326)

GRANT, JONATHAN.
Private, Capt. Rodgers' Co. No. 5, Sept. 15, 1775. (E-110)

GRAY, JOHN.
Private, Capt. Rumsey's Co. No. 6, September 16, 1775.
Signer, Association of Freemen, 1775, Bush River Upper.
Signer, Association of Freemen, 1776, Gunpowder Neck.
(E-112, I-316, I-327, I-328)

GRAY, THOMAS.
Signer, Association of Freemen, 1776, Harford Hundred. (I-325)

GREEN, ABEL.
Married Lydia Palmer in 1770.
Private, Capt. Taylor's Co. No. 7, September 9, 1775.
Private, Capt. Robert Harris' Harford Rifles, 1776.
Paid subsistence for four weeks, six days, Sept. 27, 1776.
Signer, Association of Freemen, 1776, Gunpowder Upper.
(A-33, B-10, E-113, E-123, I-326, J-233, K-436, M-72)

GREEN, BENJAMIN.
Born 1730, Charles Co., Md. Died 1808, Harford Co., Md.
Married Elizabeth Thomas. Children: Teresa, Henrietta,
  Elanora, Leonard, Elizabeth, Benjamin, Clement, Sarah,
  Anastasia.
Signer, Association of Freemen, 1776, Spesutie Upper.
Signer, Oath of Fidelity and Allegiance to Maryland, 1778.
Enlisted in the Continental Army, September 11, 1778.
(A-33, B-28, G-343, I-319, J-245, X-282)

GREEN, BENNETT.
Private, Capt. Baker's Co. No. 15, January 27, 1776.
Signer, Association of Freemen, 1776, Bush River Upper.
(E-120, I-320)

GREEN, HENRY.
Private, Capt. Love's Co. No. 10, September 14, 1775.
Signer, Association of Freemen, 1776, Spesutie Upper.
Signer, Oath of Fidelity and Allegiance to Maryland, 1778.
(A-33, B-28, E-116, I-318, J-245, N-24)

GREEN, HENRY, of John.
Signer, Association of Freemen, 1776, Bush River Lower.
Signer, Oath of Fidelity and Allegiance to Maryland, 1778.
(A-33, B-28, I-328, J-245)

GREEN, JAMES.
Signer, Oath of Fidelity and Allegiance to Maryland, 1778.
(A-33, B-28, J-245)

GREEN, JOHN.
    Born 1726. Died 1787. Married Ann Hardesty in 1753.
    Children: Henry, Joshua, John Jr., Ann.
    Signer, Oath of Fidelity and Allegiance to Maryland, 1778.
    (A-33, B-28, G-344, J-245, M-72, X-283)

GREEN, LAWRENCE.
    Signer, Oath of Fidelity and Allegiance to Maryland, 1778.
    (A-33, B-28, J-245)

GREEN, LEONARD.
    Private, Capt. Love's Co. No. 10, September 14, 1775.
    Signer, Association of Freemen, 1776, Spesutie Upper.
    (E-116, I-318)

GREEN, LEONARD, of Benjamin.
    Private, Capt. Love's Co. No. 10, September 14, 1775.
    Signer, Association of Freemen, 1776, Spesutie Upper.
    (E-116, I-319)

GREEN, RICHARD B B
    Signer, Association of Freemen, 1775, Bush River Upper, (I-316)

GREENHILL (GREEN HILL), WILLIAM.
    Private, Capt. Bussey's Company, July 20, 1776. (E-127, F-60)

GREENLAND (GREEDLAND), RICHARD.
    Signer, Association of Freemen, 1776, Susquehanna Hundred.
    Drafted, Militia, 1781; "infirm and sickly."
    (E-132, F-400, I-321)

GREENLEE, SAMUEL.
    Signer, Association of Freemen, 1776, Bush River Lower. (I-319)

GREER, HENRY.
    Private, Capt. Bond's Co. No. 11, December 9, 1775. (E-117)

GREME, ANGUS.
    Born 1750, in France. Died 1800, Harford County, Md.
    Captain in the French Army under General Lafayette.
    He was so taken with the beauty of the countryside that he
    vowed to return to Harford County to live when the war
    was over. Lived in the Darlington area of northern
    Harford County. (Roadside marker on Route 136)

GRENE, PETER.
    Signer, Association of Freemen, 1775, Bush River Upper. (I-317)

GRIFFIN, ROBERT.
    Private, Capt. Webb's Co. No. 16, October 14, 1775.
    Signer, Oath of Fidelity and Allegiance to Maryland, 1778.
    (B-14, E-121, J-236)

GRIFFIN, SAMUEL.
    Signer, Association of Freemen, 1776, Gunpowder Upper. (I-326)

GRIFFITH, JOHN.
    Signer, Association of Freemen, 1775/1776, Susquehanna.
    (D-357, I-321)

GRIFFITH, SAMUEL.
    Born 1737. Died 1803.
    Married: (1) Frenettah Garrettson in 1764; (2) Mrs. Presbury.
    Children: George, Mary, John, Martha, Frances, Samuel Gouldsmith.
    Referred to in one source as "Samuel Griffith IV."
    Signer, Association of Freemen, 1775, Spesutie Lower Hundred.
    1st Lieutenant, Capt. Aquila Hall's Co. No. 4, Sept. 9, 1775.
    Signer, Association of Freemen, 1776, Harford Lower Hundred.
    Captain, Maryland Line, Flying Camp.
    Signer, Oath of Fidelity and Allegiance to Maryland, 1778.
    (A-33, B-21, D-359, E-109, I-317, I-324, J-239, G-349, M-74,
    N-24, X-287)

GRIFFITH, THOMAS.
    Signer, Oath of Fidelity and Allegiance to Maryland, 1778.
    (A-33, B-29, J-246)

GRIMES, WILLIAM.
    Private, Capt. Archer's Co. No. 2, September 16, 1775. (E-107)

GUFF, JAMES.
    Signer, Oath of Fidelity and Allegiance to Maryland, 1778.
    (A-33, B-30, J-247)

GUYTON, ISAAC.
    Private, Capt. Archer's Co. No. 2, September 16, 1775.
    Signer, Association of Freemen, 1776, Harford Upper.
    (E-108, I-325)

* GUYTON (GUYON), JOHN.
    Signer, Association of Freemen, 1776, Gunpowder Upper.
    Signer, Oath of Fidelity and Allegiance to Maryland, 1778.
    (A-33, B-23, I-326, J-241)

GUYTON, JOHN JR.
    Signer, Association of Freemen, 1775, Bush River Upper. (I-316)

GUYTON, JOSHUA.
    Married Hannah Whitaker in 1754.
    Signer, Association of Freemen, 1775/1776, Bush River Upper.
    (I-316, I-328, M-75)

GUYTON, UNDERWOOD.
    Married Priscilla Jackson in 1762.
    Private, Capt. Baker's Co. No. 15, January 27, 1776.
    (E-120, M-75)

* This is "John deGuyon" who was formerly from Bucks County, Pennsylvania.

H

HACKETT, RICHARD.
    Born 1748 in England.
    Private, Flying Camp, Capt. James Young enlisted July 7, 1776,
        in Col. Thomas Ewing's Battalion. (5'4" tall with black hair)
    Signer, Association of Freemen, 1775, Gunpowder Neck Hundred.
    Private, Capt. Rumsey's Company No. 6, September 16, 1775.
    (E-112, E-125, F-55, I-327)

HAGEN, HENRY.
    Signer, Association of Freemen, 1776, Spesutie Upper.
    Signer, Oath of Fidelity and Allegiance to Maryland, 1778.
    (A-33, B-25, I-319, J-242)

HAIG, JOHN.
    Private, Capt. Robert Harris' Harford Rifles, 1776.
    Paid subsistence for four weeks, October 4, 1776.
    (E-123, K-436)

HAILY, DANIEL.
    Signer, Association of Freemen, 1776, Deer Creek Upper. (I-323)

HAILY, JOHN.
    Signer, Association of Freemen, 1776, Deer Creek Upper.
    "John Haley" was a Private, Maryland Line (Invalid).
    (I-323, N-25, N-93)

HALFPENNY, PATRICK.
    Private, Capt. Webb's Company No. 16, October 14, 1775.
    Signer, Association of Freemen, 1776, Deer Creek Upper.
    (E-121, I-323)

HALL, AQUILA.
    Born 1727. Died 1779. Son of Aquila Hall.
    Married: Sophia White, daughter of Col. Thomas White, in 1750.
    Children: Thomas, Aquila, James White, William, Charlotte, Mary,
        John, Edward, Sophia, Martha, Elizabeth, Benedict.
    Signer, Bush Declaration, March 22, 1775.
    War Committee, Correspondence, June 11, 1775.
    Delegate to Maryland Assembly from Baltimore County, 1773.
    Attorney at Law of Harford County Court, 1774.
    Harford County Court Justice, 1774-1779.
    Raised one of the first companies of militia in 1775.
    Captain, Company No. 4, September 9, 1775.
    Member of Observation Committee, 1775.
    Colonel of two battalions of militia, 1776.
    1st Justice of Harford County Orphans Court, 1777.
    Signer, Oath of Fidelity and Allegiance to Maryland, 1778.
    Administered the oath ("Worshipfull Aquila Hall"), 1778.
    Gave money to be applied towards the saltpetre works to
        produce gunpowder, August 21, 1776.
    Gave two guns for use by the militia, August 24, 1776.
    (continued)

HALL, AQUILA (continued)
On October 13, 1776, he wrote that "agreable to the resolve of Convention of the 10th September last to select a company of volunteers out of the 23rd Battalion in Harford County, I now make a return of the officers names which are appointed to that company and I am of opinion a compleater company has not gone from Maryland, the officers are first, Francis Holland Captain, John Carlile first Lieutenant, William Young 2nd Lieut and Robert Morgan Ensign." (K-346)
Intendant's Ledger A No. 9, ff. 78, 80, 81.
Intendant's Letter Book No. 12, p. 228.
Intendant's Ledger A No. 10, ff. 69, 71, 76. (1784-1785)
Built the mansion called "Sophia's Dairy" in 1768, which still
 stands near the Riverside Development in Belcamp, Maryland.
Sons of the American Revolution Chapter named after him, 1920.
 Organized by Mayor James Harry Preston in Bel Air, Md. (O-7)
(A-33, B-21, D-355, D-358, D-359, E-109, E-95, E-75, E-61, M-76,
 G-356, K-229, K-230, K-346, J-239, J-240, E-63, L-267, K-294,
 HR-50; Roadside Marker of Bush Declaration, Rt. 7, Bush, Md.)

HALL, AQUILA JR.
Born 1750. Died 1815. Married Ann Tolley.
Signer, Bush Declaration, March 22, 1775.
War Committee, 1775.
Private, Capt. Josias Hall's Co. No. 1, September 12, 1775.
Signer, Association of Freemen, 1776, Harford Hundred.
Signer, Oath of Fidelity and Allegiance to Maryland, 1778.
(A-33, B-21, D-355, D-358, E-106, I-325, J-239, X-294)

HALL, BENEDICT EDWARD.
War Committee, Correspondence, June 11, 1775; August 24, 1776.
Representative to Maryland Convention, June 26, 1775.
Harford County Court Justice, 1774.
Private, Capt. Josias Hall's Co. No. 1, September 12, 1775.
Private, Capt. Francis Holland's Harford Rifles, 1776.
Signer, Oath of Fidelity and Allegiance to Maryland, 1778.
Agent's Ledger No. 1, f. 22, 1776-1777.
Agent's Account No. 1, p. 74, 1780-84.
(A-33, B-21, D-358, E-106, E-124, E-97, E-61, E-95, J-239,
 HR-50, K-230) Furnished a gun and bayonet, July, 1776. (E-331)

HALL, EDWARD.
Born 1748. Died 1787, Harford County, Md.
War Committee, 1775.
Signer and solicitor, Association of Freemen, 1775/1776,
 Spesutie Lower Hundred and Harford Lower Hundred.
Private, Capt. Josias Hall's Co. No. 1, September 12, 1775.
1st Lieutenant, Grayson's Additional Continental Regiment,
 February, 1777; Prisoner at Staten Island, August 22, 1777;
 Exchanged November 5, 1777 and did not return to his regiment.
Signer, Oath of Fidelity and Allegiance to Maryland, 1778.
Army Ledger No. 1, f. 12; No. 3, f. 55. Intendant's Ledger B,
 ff. 1, 34; Intendant's Day Book No. 1, p. 13; Depreciation Pay
 No. 1, p. 32; No. 2, p. 49; No. 3, p. 228; Agent's Letter Book
 No. 1, p. 101. (A-33, B-21, D-358, E-105, E-262, I-315, I-324,
 H-89, HR-50, J-239)

HALL, ISAAC.
Private, Capt. Rumsey's Co. No. 6, September 16, 1775.
Signer, Association of Freemen, 1775, Gunpowder Neck.
Signer, Oath of Fidelity and Allegiance to Maryland, 1778.
(A-33, B-14, E-112, I-327, J-236)

HALL, JAMES.
Born c.1750. Died 1822. Married Sarah Burk in 1772.
Private, Capt. Francis Holland's Harford Rifles, 1776.
(E-124, M-76, X-295)

HALL, JAMES WHITE.
Private, Capt. Josias Hall's Co. No. 1, September 12, 1775.
Captain, 23rd Battalion, 1778.
Signer, Oath of Fidelity and Allegiance to Maryland, 1778.
(A-33, B-21, C-44, E-106, J-239)

HALL, JOHN OF CRANBERRY.
Born 1718. Died 1779. Colonial Planter and Patriot.
Lived at Cranberry Hall and was very active in the affairs of
   St. George's Parish (Spesutie Church).
Son of Edward Hall and Avarilla Carvil.
Marriage to Sarah Hughes in 1741 not recognized by Church of
   England; one son by this marriage: John Hall Hughes.
Married second to Barthia Stansberry.
Signer, Association of Freemen, 1776, Harford Lower Hundred.
Signer, Oath of Fidelity and Allegiance to Maryland, 1778.
(A-33, B-21, I-324, J-239, V-37,38,96,98)

HALL, JOHN BEADLE.
Son of John Hall of Cranberry.
Married in 1777 to Sarah Hall, daughter of John Hall of Swan
   Town.
2nd Lieutenant, Capt. Josias Hall's Co. No. 1, Sept. 12, 1775.
1st Lieutenant, Capt. Paca's Company, August 5, 1776.
Signer, Association of Freemen, 1776, Harford Lower.
Presented a gun for use by the militia, August 21, 1776.
Fought in the Battle of White Plains, October 28, 1776.
Signer, Oath of Fidelity and Allegiance to Maryland, 1778.
Major, 23rd Battalion, April 9, 1778.
(A-33, B-21, C-44, D-359, E-105, E-126, E-137, C-21, I-324,
   F-59, H-90, J-239, K-170, K-230, K-229, L-268, M-77)

HALL, JOSIAS.
Private, Capt. Josias Carvil Hall's Co. No. 1, Sept. 12, 1775.
Signer, Association of Freemen, 1776, Harford Lower Hundred.
Signer, Oath of Fidelity and Allegiance to Maryland, 1778.
(A-33, B-21, E-106, I-324, J-239)

HALL, JOSIAS CARVIL (Doctor).
Born 1746, Baltimore County. Died 1814, Baltimore County.
Signer, Bush Declaration, March 22, 1775, Harford County.
Signer, Association of Freemen, 1775, Spesutie Lower.
   (continued)

HALL, JOSIAS CARVIL (continued)
    Captain, Company No. 1, Harford County Militia, 1775.
    War Committee, 1775.
    Colonel of two Harford County companies and seven Baltimore
    County companies. His Captains in Baltimore County were:
    James Disney, Zachariah Maccubbin, John Eager Howard,
    Daniel Dorsey, Edward Norwood, Thomas Hammond, Thomas Yates;
    in Harford County: Aquila Paca and Bennett Bussey.
    Colonel, 2nd Battalion, Flying Camp. July, 1776.
    Colonel, 4th Maryland Regiment, December 10, 1776.
    Fought in Battle of White Plains, October 28, 1776.
    Declared supernumerary, January 1, 1781.
    Pay Certificates: No. 91991, $293.00; No. 91992, $78.40;
      No. 91993, $4425.00; No. 93577, $81.15.
    Army Accounts No. 1, p. 50; Pay Account No. 1, p. 11;
      Intendant's Ledger No. 15, P. 41 (1777-1784).
    Army Ledger No. 2, f. 65; Army Ledger No. 3, f. 10;
      Intendant's Ledger A No. 9, ff. 31, 44, 66; No. 15, p. 10.
      (1779-1783).
    Depreciation Pay No. 1, p. 28; no. 2, p. 42; No. 3, p. 45.
      (July 28-30, 1781).
    Intendant's Ledger A No. 10, f. 9. (August 27, 1783).
    Intendant's Orders No. 2, f. 12. (November 10, 1785).
    Army Journal, No. 1, p. 79. (August 7, 1780).
    (D-355, D-358, D-359, E-105, E-137, I-317, K-170, K-171,
    H-90, L-268, P-223)
    Col. Hall was an Original Member of the Society of the
    Cincinnati of Maryland.

HALL, THOMAS.
    Ensign, Capt. Josias Hall's Co. No. 1, September 12, 1775.
    Private, Capt. Francis Holland's Harford Rifles, 1776.
    Signer, Association of Freemen, 1776, Harford Hundred.
    Signer, Oath of Fidelity and Allegiance to Maryland, 1778.
    (A-33, B-17, E-105, E-124, I-325, J-237)

HALL, WILLIAM.
    Private, Capt. Josias Hall's Co. No. 1, September 12, 1775.
    Private, Capt. Francis Holland's Harford Rifles, 1776.
    Paid subsistence for five weeks, September 21, 1776.
    Signer, Oath of Fidelity and Allegiance to Maryland, 1778.
    (A-33, B-21, E-106, E-123, J-239, K-435)

HALL, WILLIAM, of Aquila.
    Private, Capt. Josias Hall's Co. No. 1, September 12, 1775.
    Signer, Association of Freemen, 1775, Spesutie Lower.
    Private, Capt. Francis Holland's Harford Rifles, 1776.
    Signer, Oath of Fidelity and Allegiance to Maryland, 1778.
    (B-29, E-106, E-124, I-317, J-246)

HALL, WILLIAM JR.
    Signer, Oath of Fidelity and Allegiance to Maryland, 1778.
    (A-33, B-22, J-240)

HALL, WILLIAM SR.
    Private, Capt. Francis Holland's Harford Rifles, 1776.
    Signer, Oath of Fidelity and Allegiance to Maryland, 1778.
    (A-33, E-124)

HAMBLETON, EDWARD.
    Signer, Oath of Fidelity and Allegiance to Maryland, 1778.
    (A-33, B-15, J-236)

HAMILTON, EDWARD.
    Private, Capt. Bond's Co. No. 11, December 9, 1775.
    Signer, Association of Freemen, 1776, Bush River Lower.
    (E-117, I-328)

HAMLIN, PATRICK.
    Signer, Association of Freemen, 1776, Bush River Lower. (I-319)

HAMMOND, LARKIN.
    Private, Capt. Josias Hall's Co. No. 1, Sept. 12, 1775. (E-106)

HAMON, JOHN.
    Signer, Oath of Fidelity and Allegiance to Maryland, 1778.
    (A-33, B-17, J-237)

HAMPTON, DAVID.
    Signer, Association of Freemen, 1775/1776, Susquehanna Hundred.
    (D-357, I-321)

HANESEY, PATRICK.
    Signer, Oath of Fidelity and Allegiance to Maryland, 1778.
    (A-33, B-17, J-237)

HANEY, BARNEY.
    Private, Capt. Paca's Company, July 24, 1776. (E-126, F-59)

HANEY, PATRICK.
    Signer, Association of Freemen, 1776, Spesutie Upper. (I-319)

HANNA, ALEXANDER.
    Private, Capt. Anderson's Co. No. 3, September 23, 1775.
    Signer, Oath of Fidelity and Allegiance to Maryland, 1778.
    (A-33, B-26, E-108, J-243)

HANNA, CALEB.
    Signer, Oath of Fidelity and Allegiance to Maryland, 1778.
    (A-33, B-23, J-241)

HANNA, HUGH.
    Signer, Oath of Fidelity and Allegiance to Maryland, 1778.
    (A-33, B-23, J-241)

HANNA, JAMES.
    Born 1752. Died 1827. Married Hannah Bayless.
    Private, Capt. Anderson's Co. No. 3, September 23, 1775.
        (continued)

HANNA, JAMES (continued)
> Born in Ireland.
> Private, Flying Camp. Lt. John Smith enlisted July 15, 1776, in Col Ewing's Battalion. (5'8½" tall, thin visage)
> Signer, Association of Freemen, 1776, Susquehanna Hundred.
> Signer, Oath of Fidelity and Allegiance to Maryland, 1778.
> (A-33, B-15, E-108, E-126, F-56, I-321, X-301)

HANNA, JAMES.
> Private, Capt. Bond's Co. No. 11, December 9, 1775.
> Signer, Association of Freemen, 1776, Spesutie Upper.
> Signer, Oath of Fidelity and Allegiance to Maryland, 1778.
> Grand Juror, Harford County, 1783.
> (A-33, B-25, E-117, I-319, J-242, E-77)

HANNA, JOHN.
> Signer, Association of Freemen, 1776, Spesutie Upper.
> Signer, Oath of Fidelity and Allegiance to Maryland, 1778.
> (A-33, B-26, I-319, J-243, O-20, O-23, O-25)

HANNA (HANNAH), ROBERT.
> Born 1755. Died c.1833. Married Mary Thomas.
> Private, Capt. Robert Harris' Harford Rifles, 1776.
> Paid subsistence for six weeks, two days, September 16, 1776.
> Signer, Oath of Fidelity and Allegiance to Maryland, 1778.
> (A-33, B-29, E-123, J-246, K-435, X-301, O-22)

HANNAH, SAMUEL.
> Signer, Oath of Fidelity and Allegiance to Maryland, 1778.
> (A-33, B-30, J-247)

HANNAH, WILLIAM.
> Signer, Oath of Fidelity and Allegiance to Maryland, 1778.
> (A-33, B-28, J-245)

HANSON, BENJAMIN.
> Signer, Association of Freemen, 1776, Harford Lower. (I-324)

HANSON, EDWARD.
> Private, Capt.Bradford's Co. No. 13, September 30, 1775.
> Signer, Association of Freemen, 1776, Harford Hundred.
> Signer, Oath of Fidelity and Allegiance to Maryland, 1778.
> (A-33, B-10, E-119, I-325, J-234)

HANSON, HOLLIS.
> Private, Capt.Aquila Hall's Co. No. 4, September 9, 1775.
> Signer, Association of Freemen, 1776, Harford Lower.
> Signer, Oath of Fidelity and Allegiance to Maryland, 1778.
> (A-33, B-21, E-109, I-324, J-239)

HANSON, JACOB.
> Signer, Oath of Fidelity and Allegiance to Maryland, 1778.
> (A-33, B-26, J-243)

HANSON, JOHN.
    Private, Capt.Aquila Hall's Co. No. 4, September 9, 1775.
    Private, Capt. Francis Holland's Harford Rifles, 1776.
    Signer, Association of Freemen, 1776, Harford Lower.
    (E-110, E-124, I-324)

HANSON, JOHN JR.
    Signer, Association of Freemen, 1776, Harford Lower.
    Signer, Oath of Fidelity and Allegiance to Maryland, 1778.
    (A-33, B-21, I-324, J-239)

HANSON, SAMUEL.
    Private, Capt. Aquila Hall's Co. No. 4, September 9, 1775.
    Signer, Association of Freemen, 1776, Spesutie Lower.
    (E-109, I-318)

HANSON, THOMAS.
    Private, Capt. Aquila Hall's Co. No. 4, Sept. 9, 1775. (E-109)

HARDGROVE, WILLIAM.
    Signer, Association of Freemen, 1776, Susquehanna. (I-321)

HARGRASS, STEPHEN.
    Private, Capt. Rodgers' Co. No. 5, Sept. 15, 1775. (E-111)

HARMER, SAMUEL.
    Signer, Oath of Fidelity and Allegiance to Maryland, 1778.
    (A-33, B-30, J-247)

HARPAN, ANDREW.
    Signer, Oath of Fidelity and Allegiance to Maryland, 1778.
    (A-33, B-30, J-247)

HARPER, FRANCIS.
    Signer, Association of Freemen, 1776, Deer Creek Upper.(I-323)

HARPER, FRANCIS JR.
    Association of Freemen, Signer, 1776, Deer Creek Upper. (I-323)

HARPER, GEORGE.
    Signer, Oath of Fidelity and Allegiance to Maryland, 1778.
    (A-33, B-19, J-238)

HARPER, MOSES.
    Signer, Association of Freemen, 1776, Gunpowder Upper.
    Signer, Oath of Fidelity and Allegiance to Maryland, 1778.
    (A-33, B-23, I-326, J-241)

HARPER, SAMUEL.
    Signer, Association of Freemen, 1775, Bush River Upper.
    Signer, Oath of Fidelity and Allegiance to Maryland, 1778.
    (A-33, B-29, I-317, J-246)

HARRINGTON, THOMAS.
　　Signer, Oath of Fidelity and Allegiance to Md., 1778. (A-33)

HARRIOT (HERRIOTT), ANDREW.
　　Private, Capt. Archer's Co. No. 2, September 16, 1775.
　　Signer, Association of Freemen, 1776, Harford Upper.
　　(E-107, I-325)

HARRIS, DANIEL.
　　Signer, Association of Freemen, 1776, Deer Creek Lower.(I-322)

HARRIS, JAMES.
　　Signer, Bush Declaration, March 22, 1775.
　　War Committee, Harford County, 1775.
　　Private, Capt. Archer's Co. No. 2, September 16, 1775.
　　Private, Capt. Robert Harris' Harford Rifles, 1776.
　　Signer, Association of Freemen, 1776, Spesutie Lower.
　　　Records indicate there were two signers with this name.
　　Paid subsistence for five weeks, September 21, 1776.
　　Tested ("proved") gun barrels made by Richard Dallam's
　　　factory, 1776.
　　Signer, Oath of Fidelity and Allegiance to Maryland, 1778.
　　(A-33, B-28, D-355, D-358, E-108, E-123, I-318, I-319, J-245,
　　K-435, K-59)

HARRIS, JOSEPH.
　　Private, Capt. Anderson's Co. No. 3, September 23, 1775.
　　Signer, Association of Freemen, 1776, Deer Creek Upper.
　　(E-108, I-323)

HARRIS, JOSEPH ESQ.
　　Signer, Association of Freemen, 1776, Susquehanna. (I-321)

HARRIS, ROBERT.
　　Married Susannah Wheeler, daughter of Thomas Wheeler and
　　　Elizabeth Hillen (Ravin).
　　Signer and solicitor, Association of Freemen, 1775 and
　　　1776, Bush River Upper Hundred.
　　Granted warrant by Maryland Convention to raise a company,
　　　September 23, 1776.
　　Captain, Co. No. 1, Flying Camp, Harford Rifles, 1776.
　　Paid 429 lbs. for Bounty and one months's pay, Sept., 1776.
　　Part of letter to Maryland Convention from Hon. Benjamin
　　　Rumsey, September 18, 1776: "Today the field officers
　　　meet in order to decide who shall go (agreeable to the
　　　resolves of the Convention) and I believe the lott will
　　　fall on Captain Harris as he is a single man of spirit
　　　very desirous of going and the furthest from the water
　　　and internal enemies in case of an attack."
　　Captain, 8th Battalion, September 18, 1776.
　　Raised 76 men into Harford County Militia, 1776.
　　Captain, 2nd Battalion, September 23, 1776.
　　Captain, 6th Maryland Regiment, December 10, 1776.
　　Resigned, November 9, 1777.

　　　(continued)

HARRIS, ROBERT (continued)
    Pay Certificate No. 93614, $930.46.
    Army Accounts No. 1, p. 91; Intendant's Orders No. 2, f. 12;
    Intendant's Day Book No. 2, p. 81. (1777-1785)
    Signer, Oath of Fidelity and Allegiance to Maryland, 1778.
    (A-33, B-31, J-248, D-359, E-123, N-93, I-316, E-262, E-267,
        I-320, K-281, K-282, L-276, H-94, HR-50, P-232, K-293, R)

HARRIS, THOMAS.
    Private, 4th Maryland Line.
    Enlisted, August 21, 1777; Missing, September 11, 1777.
    (E-129, F-302)

HARRISON, HORATIO.
    Private, Capt. Dorsey's Co. No. 8, Oct. 31, 1775. (E-115)

HARRISON, JOHN ROBERT.
    Private, Capt. Rumsey's Co. No. 6, September 16, 1775.
    Signer, Association of Freemen, 1775, Gunpowder Neck.
    (E-112, I-327)

HARRISON, RICHARD.
    Private, Capt. Dorsey's Co. No. 8, Oct. 31, 1775. (E-114)

HARRISON, WILLIAM.
    Private, Capt. Archer's Co. No. 2, September 16, 1775.
    Signer, Association of Freemen, 1776, Spesutie Upper.
    (E-107, I-319)

HARROD, HENRY.
    Drafted, Militia, 1781; "Never taken up." (E-133, F-400)

HARROD, ROBERT.
    Signer, Association of Freemen, 1776, Bush River Upper. (I-320)

HARROD, THOMAS.
    Private, Capt. Paca's Co., August 5, 1776. (E-127, F-59)

HARROD, WILLIAM.
    Signer, Oath of Fidelity and Allegiance to Maryland, 1778.
    (A-34, B-23, J-241)

HARRY, DAVID.
    Private, Capt. Taylor's Co. No. 7, Sept. 9, 1775. (E-113)

HART (HEARTT), AUGUSTUS.
    Signer, Association of Freemen, 1776, Deer Creek Upper. (I-323)

HART, JOHN.
    Signer, Association of Freemen, 1776, Spesutie Upper.
    Signer, Oath of Fidelity and Allegiance to Maryland, 1778.
    (A-33, B-25, I-319, J-242)

HART, ROBERT.
    Private, Capt. Archer's Co. No. 2, September 16, 1775.
    Signer, Association of Freemen, 1776, Spesutie Upper.
    (E-107, I-319)

HART, WILLIAM.
    Private, Capt. Webb's Co. No. 16, October 14, 1775.
    Private, Capt. Paca's Company, August 5, 1776.
    Signer, Association of Freemen, 1776, Deer Creek Upper.
    (E-121, E-127, F-59, I-323)

HARTLEY (HARTHEY), JOSEPH.
    Signer, Association of Freemen, 1776, Gunpowder Upper.
    Signer, Oath of Fidelity and Allegiance to Maryland, 1778.
    Grand Juror, Harford County, 1779.
    (A-33, B-23, E-75, I-326, J-241)

HASLET, MOSES.
    Private, Capt. Rumsey's Co. No. 6, Sept. 16, 1775. (E-112)

HASLETT, MOSES (Doctor).
    War Committee, Harford County, 1775. (D-358)

HASSET (HASSETT), WILLIAM.
    Private, Capt. Archer's Co. No. 2, September 16, 1775.
    Private, Capt. Paca's Company, August 5, 1776.
    Signer, Oath of Fidelity and Allegiance to Maryland, 1778.
    (A-33, B-26, E-107, E-127, F-59, J-243)

HAWEY, WILLIAM.
    Signer, Oath of Fidelity and Allegiance to Maryland, 1778.
    (A-33, B-19, J-238)

HAWKINS, GREGORY.
    Private, Capt. Rigdon's Co. No. 12, December 2, 1775.
    Signer, Association of Freemen, 1776, Deer Creek Upper.
    (E-118, I-322)

HAWKINS, JEREMIAH.
    Private, Capt. Rigdon's Co. No. 12, December 2, 1775.
    Signer, Association of Freemen, 1776, Deer Creek Upper.
    (E-118, I-322)

HAWKINS, JOHN.
    War Committee, Harford County, 1775.
    Signer, Association of Freemen, 1776, Deer Creek Lower.
    (D-358, I-322)

HAWKINS, RICHARD.
    Born 1748. Died 1811, Harford County, Md.
    Married: (1) Elizabeth Cox, 1774; (2) Avarilla Durbin, 1777.
    Children: (1) Elizabeth; (2) Robert, Thomas, Cassandra, Lydia,
       Hosea, Richard, John, Nancy Ann, William. (G-376)
    Signer, Association of Freemen, 1776, Deer Creek Lower.(I-322)
    Served as Clerk, 5th Battalion, Washington Co., Pa. (X-314)

HAWKINS, ROBERT.
    Private, Capt. Rigdon's Co. No. 12, December 2, 1775.
    Signer, Association of Freemen, 1776, Deer Creek Upper.
    Signer, Oath of Fidelity and Allegiance to Maryland, 1778.
    (A-33, B-19, E-118, I-322, J-238)

HAWKINS, SAMUEL.
    Private, Capt. Patrick's Co. No. 17, April 1, 1776.
    Signer, Association of Freemen, 1776, Deer Creek Lower.
    (E-122, I-322)

HAWLEY, WILLIAM.
    Private, Capt. Harris' Company Payroll. (E-130, F-304)

HAWTHORN (HATHORN), JOHN.
    Private, Capt. Archer's Co. No. 2, September 16, 1775.
    Signer, Association of Freemen, 1776, Susquehanna.
    Signer, Oath of Fidelity and Allegiance to Maryland, 1778.
    (A-33, B-26, E-107, I-321, J-243)

HAYS, ARCHER.
    Private, Capt. Archer's Co. No. 2, September 16, 1775.
    Signer, Association of Freemen, 1776, Spesutie Upper.
    Signer, Oath of Fidelity and Allegiance to Maryland, 1778.
    (A-33, B-26, E-107, I-319, J-243)

HAYS, HENRY. (HENRY HAY)
    Private. Capt. Rumsey's Co. No. 6, September 16, 1775.
    Signer, Association of Freemen, 1775, Gunpowder Neck.
    (E-112, I-327)

HAYS, JOHN. (JOHN HAY)
    Signer, Association of Freemen, 1776, Spesutie Upper.
    Signer, Oath of Fidelity and Allegiance to Maryland, 1778.
    Harford County Grand Juror, 1780.
    (A-33, B-27, I-319, E-76)

HAYS, JOHN.
    Signer, Association of Freemen, 1776, Bush River Lower. (I-319)

HAYS, JOHN JR.
    Signer, Oath of Fidelity and Allegiance to Maryland, 1778.
    (A-33, B-21, J-239)

HAZEL, CALEB.
    "Lt. Caleb Hazle", Maryland Militia.
    Pensioner (maimed soldier), 1778.
    (F-661, N-26)

HEALY, JOHN.
    Signer, Association of Freemen, 1776, Deer Creek Upper. (I-323)

HEANY, PATRICK
    Private, Capt. Archer's Co. No. 2, September 16, 1775. (E-107)

HEAPS, ARCHIBALD.
    Born 1758. Died c.1841. Married Sarah Bay.
    Private,Maryland Militia. Pensioner in 1840.
    (E-262, N-26, X-318)

HEAPS, JOHN.
    Private, Maryland Militia. Born 1754.
    Pensioner in 1840. ("John Heap"). (E-262, N-26)

HEAPS, ROBERT.
    Signer, Association of Freemen, 1775/1776, Bush River Upper.
    (I-317, I-320)

HEARN, JAMES.
    Signer, Association of Freemen, 1776, Spesutie Lower. (I-318)

HEARN, JOHN.
    Signer, Association of Freemen, 1775, Gunpowder Neck, and
      1776, Harford Lower. (I-324, I-327)

HEATON, JOHN.
    Signer, Association of Freemen, 1776, Deer Creek Lower. (I-322)

HENDERSIDES, FRANCIS.
    Signer, Oath of Fidelity and Allegiance to Maryland, 1778.
    (A-33, B-29, J-246)

HENDERSIDES, WILLIAM.
    "William Henderside" married Mary Williams in 1771.
    "William Handersides" was Private, Capt. Taylor's Co. No. 7,
      September 9, 1775.
    "William Hendersides" was in Continental Army, 1777-1780
      (Family Support Allowance.
    (F-661, E-113, M-83)

HENDERSON, ANDREW.
    Signer, Association of Freemen, 1775/1776, Bush River Upper.
    Signer, Oath of Fidelity and Allegiance to Maryland, 1778.
    (A-33, B-29, I-316, I-328, J-246)

HENDERSON, FRANCIS.
    Signer, Association of Freemen, 1776, Bush River Upper. (I-328)

HENDERSON, PHILIP.
    Married Elizabeth Smith in 1768.
    Private, Capt. Josias Hall's Co. No. 1, September 12, 1775.
    Signer, Association of Freemen, 1776, Harford Hundred.
    Signer, Oath of Fidelity and Allegiance to Maryland, 1778.
    (A-33, B-21, E-106, I-325, J-239, M-84)

HENDERSON, THOMAS.
    Signer, Association of Freemen, 1775, Bush River Upper. (I-316)

HENION (HENLON), PATRICK.
    Signer, Oath of Fidelity and Allegiance to Maryland, 1778.
    (A-33, B-10, J-233)

HENLEY, PETER.
    Private, Capt. Love's Co. No. 10, Sept. 14, 1775. (E-116)

HENRY, BARNY.
    Signer, Association of Freemen, 1776, Susquehanna. (I-321)

HENRY, JAMES.
    Association of Freemen Committee, 1775. (D-357)

HENRY, MICHAEL.
    Signer, Oath of Fidelity and Allegiance to Maryland, 1778.
    (A-33, B-30, J-247)

HENRY, THOMAS.
    Signer, Association of Freemen, 1775, Bush River Upper. (I-317)

HERBERT, CHARLES.
    Private, Capt. Taylor's Co. No. 7, September 9, 1775.
    Signer, Association of Freemen, 1776, Gunpowder Upper.
    Signer, Oath of Fidelity and Allegiance to Maryland, 1778.
    (A-33, B-12, E-113, I-326, J-234)

HERBERT, RICHARD.
    Signer, Association of Freemen, 1776, Harford Hundred. (I-325)

HERD, FRANCIS ("A Servant")
    Fifer, Flying Camp, Lt. John Smith enlisted July 15, 1776,
        in Col. Ewing's Battalion.
    Born 1756 in America. (5'6" tall with short curled hair).
    (E-125, F-54)

HEWETT, JOSEPH.
    Private, Capt. Rumsey's Co. No. 6, September 16, 1775.
    Signer, Association of Freemen, 1775, Gunpowder Neck.
    Signer, Oath of Fidelity and Allegiance to Maryland, 1778.
    (A-33, B-20, E-112, I-327, J-239)

HEWS, JAMES.
    Private, Capt. Archer's Co. No. 2, Sept. 16, 1775. (E-108)

HICKS, ZEBEDEE.
    Signer, Association of Freemen, 1775/1776, Bush River Upper.
    Private, Capt. Robert Harris' Harford Rifles, 1776.
    Paid subsistence for six weeks, two days, Sept. 16, 1776.
    Signer, Oath of Fidelity and Allegiance to Maryland, 1778.
    (A-33, B-30, E-123, I-316, I-320, J-247, K-435)

HILL, HERMAN.
    Born 1758.
    Signer, Association of Freemen, 1776, Spesutie Lower.
        (continued)

HILL, HERMAN (Contined)
"Herman Hill" signed Association of Freemen, 1776, Susquehanna.
"Harmon Hill" was Private, Capt. Dorsey's Co. No. 8, 1775.
"Hermon Hill" was Private, Maryland Militia (pensioner).
(D-357, E-114, I-318, I-321, N-27)

HILL, JOHN.
Association of Freemen, 1775/1776, Signer, Susquehanna Hundred.
(D-357, I-321)

HILL, SAMUEL.
Private, Capt. Rigdon's Co. No. 12, December 2, 1775. (E-118)

HILL, STEPHEN.
3rd Sergeant, Capt. Love's Co. No. 10, September 14, 1775.
Signer, Association of Freemen, 1776, Spesutie Upper Hundred.
Signer, Oath of Fidelity and Allegiance to Maryland, 1778.
(A-33, B-13, E-115, E-77, I-318, J-235)

HILL, THOMAS.
Private, Capt. Love's Co. No. 10, September 14, 1775.
Signer, Association of Freemen, 1776, Spesutie Upper.
(E-116, I-319)

HILL, THOMAS.
Private, Capt. Archer's Co. No. 2, Sept. 16, 1775. (E-108)

HILL, THOMAS (SAILOR).
Signer, Oath of Fidelity and Allegiance to Maryland, 1778.
(A-33, B-14, J-235)

HILL, WILLIAM.
Private, Capt. Rodgers' Co. No. 5, Sept. 15, 1775. (E-110, N-94)

HILLIDAY, ROBERT.
Signer, Oath of Fidelity and Allegiance to Maryland, 1778.
(A-34, B-21, J-239)

HILTON, JOHN.
Private, Capt. Patrick's Co. No. 17, April 1, 1776. (E-122)

HINDS, LAURENCE (Hines, Lawrence).
Private, Capt. Bussey's Company, July 27, 1776.
Militia Substitute, 1781, 3 years.
(E-128, E-133, F-60, F-401)

HINKS, THOMAS.
Private, Capt. Bond's Co. No. 11, December 9, 1775.
Private, Capt. Bussey's Company, July 20, 1776.
Signer, Association of Freemen, 1776, Bush River Lower.
(E-117, E-127, I-319, F-60)

HIPKINS, CHARLES.
Private, Capt. Dorsey's Co. No. 8, Oct. 31, 1775. (E-115)

HITCHCOCK, ASAEL SR.
    Born 1719, Baltimore County. Died 1790, Harford County.
    Married Sarah Norris in 1741. Children: Josiah, John,
      Isaac, Nancy Ann, Mary, Asael Jr., William.
    Signer, Association of Freemen, 1776, Bush River Upper.
    Signer, Oath of Fidelity and Allegiance to Maryland, 1778.
    Harford County Grand Juror, 1779.
    (A-33, B-23, E-75, I-320, J-241, G-391, M-86, X-332)

HITCHCOCK, ASAEL JR.   Born 1750. Married Sarah Baker.
    2nd Lieutenant, Capt. Bussey's Company, July 24, 1776.
    Fought at Battle of White Plains, October 28, 1776.
    1st Lieutenant, 2nd Maryland Battalion, December, 1776.
    Signer, Association of Freemen, 1776, Bush River Upper
      Hundred and Eden Hundred.
    Signer, Oath of Fidelity and Allegiance to Maryland, 1778.
    (A-33, B-23, E-126, E-137, I-320, I-324, J-241, F-59, E-267,
      K-170, L-291)

HITCHCOCK, HENRY.
    Private, Capt. Baker's Co. No. 15, January 27, 1776.
    Signer, Association of Freemen, 1776, Eden Hundred.
    Signer, Oath of Fidelity and Allegiance to Maryland, 1778.
    (A-34, B-24, E-120, I-324, J-242)

HITCHCOCK, ISAAC.
    Signer, Association of Freemen, 1776, Deer Creek Upper. (I-322)

HITCHCOCK, JOHN.
    Signer, Oath of Fidelity and Allegiance to Maryland, 1778.
    (A-34, B-24, J-242)

HITCHCOCK, JOSEPH.
    Elected Ensign at Upper Cross Roads, Nov. 30, 1776. (K-496)

HITCHCOCK, JOSIAH.
    Married Susanna Garland in 1755.
    Signer, Association of Freemen, 1776, Bush River Upper and
      Eden Hundred. Records indicate two signers with this name.
    Signer, Oath of Fidelity and Allegiance to Maryland, 1778.
    (A-34, B-24, I-320, I-324, J-242, M-87)

HITCHCOCK, JOSIAH JR.
    Signer, Oath of Fidelity and Allegiance to Maryland, 1778.
    (A-34, B-23, J-241)

HITCHCOCK, JOSIAS.
    Private, Capt. Baker's Co. No. 15, January 27, 1776.
    2nd Lieutenant, 8th Battalion, 1778.
    (C-47, E-120)

HITCHCOCK, RANDEL.
    Signer, Association of Freemen, 1776, Eden Hundred. (I-324)

HITCHCOCK, WILLIAM.
    Married Cordelia Robison in 1769.
    Private, Capt. Baker's Co. No. 15, January 27, 1776.
    Signer, Association of Freemen, 1776, Eden Hundred.
    Signer, Oath of Fidelity and Allegiance to Maryland, 1778.
    (A-34, B-24, E-120, I-324, J-242, M-87)

HODGES, GYKES.
    Private, Capt. Robert Harris' Harford Rifles, 1776.
    Paid subsistence for four weeks, October 4, 1776.
    (E-123, K-436)

HODGSKINS (HODGKINS), SAMUEL.
    Born 1757.
    Private, Capt. Bussey's Company, July 25, 1776.
    Signer, Association of Freemen, 1776, Bush River Upper.
    Militia Substitute, 1781.
    Wife applied for pension.
    (E-128, E-132, I-320, F-60, F-400, N-27)

HOLLAND, FRANCIS (1745-1795).
    Son of Francis Holland and Cordelia Knight.
    Signer, Bush Declaration, March 22, 1775.
    War Committee, Harford County, 1775.
    Private, Capt. Josias Hall's Co. No. 1, September 12, 1775.
    Signer and solicitor, Association of Freemen, 1775, Spesutie Lower Committee.
    "Warrant granted to Francis Holland of Harford County to raise a Company of Militia agreeable to the Resolves of late Convention." September 23, 1776. (K-293)
    Paid 429 lbs. for Bounty and one month's pay, Sept. 23, 1776.
    Captain, Co. 2, Flying Camp, Harford Rifles, 1776.
    Colonel, 23rd Battalion, Harford County, April 9, 1778.
    Army Accounts No. 1, p. 67, October 6, 1787.
    (C-44, D-355, D-358, D-359, E-106, E-262, I-315, I-317, E-124, L-296, K-293, N-94, M-87, HR-50)

HOLLINGSWORTH, GEORGE.
    Married Hannah Nelson in 1737.
    Signer, Association of Freemen, 1776, Harford Lower.
    (I-324, M-88)

HOLLIS, AMOS.
    Married Martha Everett in 1761.
    Signer, Association of Freemen, 1776, Harford Lower.
    Private, Capt. Aquila Hall's Co. No. 4, September 9, 1778.
    Signer, Oath of Fidelity and Allegiance to Maryland, 1778.
    (A-34, B-21, E-110, I-324, J-239, M-88)

HOLLIS, CLARK.
    Signer, Association of Freemen, 1776, Harford Lower.
    (I-324)

HOLLIS, WILLIAM SR.
    Married Sarah Gallion in 1748.
    Signer, Association of Freemen, 1775, Harford Lower,
      and Solicitor, 1776.
    Signer, Oath of Fidelity and Allegiance to Maryland, 1778.
    (A-34, B-22, I-315, I-324, J-240, M-88)

HOLLIS, WILLIAM JR.
    Private, Capt. Josias Hall's Co. No. 1, September 12, 1775.
    Signer, Association of Freemen, 1776, Harford Lower.
    Signer, Oath of Fidelity and Allegiance to Maryland, 1778.
    (A-34, B-22, E-106, I-324, J-240)

HOLLOWAY, RICHARD.
    Private, Capt. Rumsey's Co. No. 6, September 16, 1775.
    Signer, Association of Freemen, 1775, Gunpowder Neck.
    (E-112, I-327)

HOLMES, JAMES.
    Hosted the War Committee elections for Bush River Upper
      Hundred in 1775.
    Private, Capt. Josias Hall's Co. No. 1, September 12, 1775.
    Signer, Association of Freemen, 1776, Bush River Lower.
    (A-34, B-25, D-358, E-106, I-320, J-242)

HONNOLL, WILLIAM.
    Signer, Oath of Fidelity and Allegiance to Maryland, 1778.
    (A-34, B-28, J-245)

HOOPER, ABRAHAM.
    Born 1756.
    Private, Capt. Harris' Company Payroll. (E-130, F-304)
    Private, Maryland Line. Wounded. Pensioner.
    (E-130, F-304, N-28)

HOPE, RICHARD.
    Signer, Association of Freemen, 1776, Bush River Upper.
    Signer, Oath of Fidelity and Allegiance to Maryland, 1778.
    (A-34, B-29, I-320, J-246)

HOPE, THOMAS.
    Born 1742. Died 1815, Harford County, Md.
    Married Hannah Nelson. Children: Ezra, William, Thomas Jr.,
      Hannah, Annie, Lovisee.
    War Committee, Harford County, 1775.
    Signer, Association of Freemen, 1775, and Solicitor, 1776,
      Bush River Upper Committee.
    Captain, Deer Creek Battalion, April 9, 1778.
    Signer, Oath of Fidelity and Allegiance to Maryland, 1778.
    (A-34, B-29, C-43, D-358, C-21, I-315, I-328, J-246, G-398,
      X-341)

HOPKINS, JOSEPH JR.
    Son of Joseph Hopkins and Ann Chew. Born 1728. Died 1795.
    Married Elizabeth Gover, daughter of Ephraim and Elizabeth
      Gover, in 1769. Son, Samuel, married Rachel Worthington.
    Signer, Association of Freemen, 1776, Deer Creek Lower.
    (I-322, M-90) Buried in Kicksite Quaker Cemetery, Darlington.

HOPKINS, RICHARD.
    Son of Gerrard Hopkins.
    Married Ann Snowden, daughter of Samuel Snowden, in 1774.
    Private, Capt. Robert Harris' Harford Rifles, 1776.
    Paid subsistence for five weeks, September 21, 1776.
    Private, Capt. Bussey's Company, July 25, 1776.
    (E-123, E-128, F-60, K-435, M-90)

HOPKINS, SAMUEL.
    Son of Philip and Elizabeth Hopkins.
    Married Mary Gover, daughter of Ephraim and Elizabeth Gover,
      in 1769.
    Private, Capt. Patrick's Co. No. 17, April 1, 1776.
    Signer, Association of Freemen, 1776, Deer Creek Lower.
    Signer, Oath of Fidelity and Allegiance to Maryland, 1778.
    (A-34, B-16, I-322, E-122, J-237, M-90)

HOPKINS, WILLIAM JR. (Quaker)
    Signer. Oath of Fidelity and Allegiance to Maryland, 1778.
    (A-34, B-28, J-245)

HORMOTT, ANDREW.
    Signer, Oath of Fidelity and Allegiance to Maryland, 1778.
    (A-34, B-25, J-242)

HORNER, HOLLIS.
    Harford County Grand Juror, 1783. (E-77)

HORNER, JAMES.
    War Committee, 1775.
    Signer and Solicitor, Association of Freemen, 1775/1776,
      Susquehanna Committee.
    Signer, Oath of Fidelity and Allegiance to Maryland, 1778.
    Third Sheriff of Harford County, 1780.
    (A-34, B-25, D-358, E-263, E-357, I-315, J-242)

HORNER, THOMAS.
    Signer, Association of Freemen, 1776, Harford Lower. (I-324)

HORNER, WILLIAM.
    Signer, Association of Freemen, 1776, Susquehanna. (I-321)

HORTON, WILLIAM.
    Signer, Association of Freemen, 1776, Susquehanna. (I-321)

HORNER, NATHAN.
    Furnished a gun to Harford County Committee, June, 1776. (E-330)

HOSHAL, JESSE.
    Born 1758. Died 1830. Married Mary Hurst in 1779.
    Marriage proven through Maryland pension application.
    Private, Continental Line, German Regiment.
    Widow applied for pension.
    (N-116, N-28, X-344)

HOSKINS, THOMAS.
    Signer, Association of Freemen, 1776, Bush River Upper.(I-320)

HOWARD, JOHN BEALE.   Son of John Howard and Elizabeth Gassaway.
    Born in 1735 in Md. Died in 1799, Harford County, Md.
    Married: Blanche Carvel Hall in 1765, daughter of Parker Hall.
    Children: Parker, Matthias, John Beale, Edward, Acquilla,
        Elizabeth.
    War Committee, Harford County, 1775.
    Signer, Association of Freemen, 1775, Gunpowder Neck.
    2nd Lieutenant, Capt. Rumsey's Co. No. 6, Sept. 16, 1775.
    1st Lieutenant, 8th Battalion, Harford County Militia, 1776.
    Delegate to Maryland Legislature, 1781.
    Harford County Court Justice, 1774.
    First Register of Wills of Harford County, 1774.   (O-3)
    (D-358, D-359, E-112, E-267, I-327, E-359, G-405, M-91, X-347)

HOWARD, JOHN.
    Pensioner (maimed soldier), 1778. (F-661, N-28)

HOWARD, LEMUEL.
    Married Martha Scott in 1760.
    Private, Capt. Love's Co. No. 10, September 14, 1775.
    Signer, Association of Freemen, 1776, Spesutie Upper.
    (E-116, I-318, M-91)

HOWARD, SAMUEL.
    Signer, Oath of Fidelity and Allegiance to Maryland, 1778.
    (A-34, B-10, J-234)

HOWARD, SIMON.
    Private, Capt. Bussey's Company, July 20, 1776. (E-127, F-60)

HOWARD, THOMAS GASSAWAY.   Son of John Howard & Elizabeth Gassaway.
    Born 1740. Died 1803. Married Frances Holland in 1765,
        daughter of Francis Holland.
    Private, Capt. Rumsey's Co. No. 6, September 16, 1775.
    Signer, Association of Freemen, 1775, Gunpowder Neck.
    (E-112, I-327, M-91, X-347)

HOWE, JOHN.
    Corporal, 1st Company of Maryland Riflemen under Col. Rawlings,
        4th Maryland Line, 1776-July, 1777.
    Fought at Battle of Fort Washington, November 16, 1776.
    (D-361, E-129, F-301, E-136)

HOWE, WILLIAM.
    Private, Capt. Bussey's Company, July 20, 1776. (E-127, F-60)

HOWELL, JOHN.
    Sergeant, Capt. Dorsey's Co. No. 8, October 31, 1775. (E-114)

HOWELL, SAMUEL.
    Corporal, Capt. Rodgers' Co. No. 5, September 15, 1775.
    Signer and Solicitor, Association of Freemen, 1775/1776,
      Susquehanna Committee.
    (E-110, E-263, I-315. I-321, N-28)

HOWLETT, ANDREW.
    War Committee, 1775.
    Signer, Oath of Fidelity and Allegiance to Maryland, 1778.
    (A-34, B-14, D-358, J-235)

HOWLETT, JAMES.
    Signer, Oath of Fidelity and Allegiance to Maryland, 1778.
    (A-34, B-14, J-235)

HUDSON, JOHN.
    Private, Capt. Rigdon's Co. No. 12, Dec. 2, 1775. (E-118)

HUDSON, THOMAS.
    Private, Capt. Rigdon's Co. No. 12, Dec. 2, 1775. (E-118,N-28)

HUFF, ABRAHAM.
    Signer, Association of Freemen, 1776, Harford Upper.
    Signer, Oath of Fidelity and Allegiance to Maryland, 1778.
    (A-34, B-25, I-325, J-242)

HUFF, JOHN.
    Signer, Oath of Fidelity and Allegaince to Maryland, 1778.
    (B-30, J-247)

HUGESTON, JOHN.
    Signer, Oath of Fidelity and Allegiance to Maryland, 1778.
    (A-34)

HUGG, JOHN.
    Signer, Oath of Fidelity and Allegiance to Md., 1778. (A-34)

HUGGINS, JAMES.
    Private, Capt. Taylor's Co. No. 7, September 9, 1775.
    Signer, Association of Freemen, 1776, Gunpowder Upper.
      Records indicate there were two signers with this name,
      one signed "Huggins" and one signed "Hugins".
    Signer, Oath of Fidelity and Allegiance to Maryland, 1778.
    (A-34, B-10, E-113, I-326, J-234)

HUGHES, AARON.
    Married Elizabeth Taylor in 1769.
    Signer, Association of Freemen, 1776, Bush River Upper.
    (I-328, M-92)

HUGHES, ABM.
    Signer, Association of Freemen, 1775, Bush River Upper.(I-316)

HUGHES, ANDREAS.
    Private, Capt. Taylor's Co. No. 7, Sept. 9, 1775. (E-114)

HUGHES, ANDREW.
    Signer, Association of Freemen, 1776, Gunpowder Upper. (I-326)

HUGHES, ARAM.
    Signer, Oath of Fidelity and Allegiance to Maryland, 1778.
    (A-34, B-19, J-238)

HUGHES, JOHN.
    Signer, Oath of Fidelity and Allegiance to Maryland, 1778.
    (A-34, B-14, J-236)

HUGHES, JOHN JR.
    Signer, Association of Freemen, 1775, Gunpowder Neck, and
      Susquehanna Hundred, 1776.
    (D-357, I-3321, I-327)

HUGHES, JOHN HALL.
    Born 1742. Died 1802, Harford County, Md.
    Married: Ann Everett in 1769. Children: Everett, John Hall Jr.,
      Scott, James, Martha, Sarah, Mitchell, Ann.
    Son of John Hall of Cranberry and Sarah Hughes.
    Private, Capt. Aquila Hall's Co. No. 4, September 9, 1775.
    1st Lieutenant, Capt. Samuel Griffith's Co., May 16, 1776.
    Signer, Association of Freemen, 1776, Harford Lower Hundred.
    Signer, Oath of Fidelity and Allegiance to Maryland, 1778.
    Harford County Grand Juror, 1779.
    (A-34, B-21, E-109, I-324, E-75, J-239, G-409, M-92, V-98,
      V-99, V-100, X-353)

HUGHES, NAASSON.
    Signer, Association of Freemen, 1775/1776, Bush River Upper.
    (I-316, I-320)

HUGHES, NATHAN.
    Signer, Association of Freemen, 1775/1776, Susquehanna Hundred.
    (D-357, I-321)

HUGHES, PATRICK.
    Private, Capt. Bond's Co. No. 11, December 9, 1775.
    Signer, Association of Freemen, 1776, Bush River Lower.
    (E-117, I-319)

HUGHES,ZENAS.
    Signer, Association of Freemen, 1775/1776, Bush River Upper.
    (I-317, I-320)

HUGHSTON, HUGH.
    Signer, Association of Freemen, 1776, Bush River Lower. (I-328)

HUGHSTON, JOHN.
  Married Hannah Waltham in 1771.
  Signer, Association of Freemen, 1775, Gunpowder Neck.
  Signer, Oath of Fidelity and Allegiance to Maryland, 1778.
  (B-14, I-327, J-236, M-93)

HUNT, HENRY.
  Signer, Association of Freemen, 1776, Bush River Upper. I-320)

HUNT, JAMES.
  Private, Capt. Baker's Co. No. 15, January 27, 1776. (E-120, N-29)

HUNT, ROBERT.
  Private, Capt. Rodgers' Co. No. 5, September 15, 1775.
  Signer, Oath of Fidelity and Allegiance to Maryland, 1778.
  (A-34, B-15, E-110, J-236)

HURLEY, JAMES.
  Fifer, Capt. Rodgers' Co. No. 5, September 15, 1775.
  Private, Capt. Paca's Company, August 5, 1776.
  (E-110, E-127, F-59)

HUSBAND, WILLIAM.
  Private, Capt. Patrick's Co. No. 17, April 1, 1776.
  Signer, Association of Freemen, 1776, Deer Creek Lower.
  (E-122, I-321)

HUSKINS, THOMAS.
  Signer, Association of Freemen, 1776, Eden Hundred.
    Record indicated two signers with this name.
  Signer, Oath of Fidelity and Allegiance to Maryland, 1778.
  (A-34, B-31, I-323, J-248)

HUSTON, ALEXANDER.
  Private, Capt. Love's Co. No. 10, September 14, 1775. (E-116)

HUSTON, HUGH.
  Private, Capt. Harris' Company, Harford Rifles, 1776.
  Paid subsistence for one week, four days, October 19, 1776.
  Signer, Oath of Fidelity and Allegiance to Maryland, 1778.
  (A-34, B-28, J-245, K-436)

HUSTON, JAMES.
  Signer, Oath of Fidelity and Allegiance to Maryland, 1778.
  (A-34, B-26, J-243)

HUSTON, JOHN.
  Private, Capt. Rumsey's Co. No. 6, September 16, 1775. (E-112)

HUTCHESON, JAMES.
  Private, Capt. Webb's Co. No. 16, October 14, 1775.
  Signer, Association of Freemen, 1776, Deer Creek Upper.
  (E-121, I-323)

HUTCHINS, HENRY.
Signer, Association of Freemen, 1775, Gunpowder Neck. (I-327)

HUTCHINS, JACOB.
Signer, Oath of Fidelity and Allegiance to Maryland, 1778.
(A-34, B-23, J-241)

HUTCHINS (HUTCHINGS), RICHARD.
Born 1741. Died 1826. Married: Zana Phyllis Standiford (or
Philliszanner Standeford) in 1767.
2nd Lieutenant, Capt. Baker's Co. No. 15, January 27, 1776.
Signer, Association of Freemen, 1776, Eden Hundred.
2nd Lieutenant, 8th Battalion, 1778.
Signer, Oath of Fidelity and Allegiance to Maryland, 1778.
(A-34, B-23, C-46, D-359, E-120, J-241, M-93, X-358)

HUTCHINS (HUTCHINGS), THOMAS.
2nd Lieutenant, Capt. Taylor's Co. No. 7, September 9, 1775.
1st Lieutenant, 8th Battalion, appointed in 1776.
Signer, Association of Freemen, 1776, Gunpowder Upper.
Signer, Oath of Fidelity and Allegiance to Maryland, 1778.
Captain, 8th Battalion, appointed 1778.
(A-34, B-12, C-46, D-359, E-113, E-266, I-326, J-234)

HUTCHINS (HUTCHINGS), THOMAS.
Private, Capt. Taylor's Co. No. 7, Sept. 9, 1775. (E-113)

HUTCHINS, WILLIAM.
Signer, Oath of Fidelity and Allegiance to Maryland, 1778.
(A-34, B-23, J-241)

HUTON, HUGH.
Signer, Association of Freemen, 1775, Bush River Upper. (I-316)

HUTSON, HUGH.
Private, Capt. Harris' Harford Rifles, 1776. (E-123)

HUTSON, JAMES.
Militia Substitute, 1781, 3 years. (E-133, F-401)

HUTSON, JOHN.
Militia Substitute, 1781, 3 years. (E-133, F-401)

HYNDS, LAWRENCE.
(See "Lawrence Hines")
Private, Capt. Bussey's Co., July 20, 1776. (E-127, F-60)

J

INGRAM, ARCHIBALD.
    Private, Capt. Webb's Co. No. 16, October 14, 1775.
    Private, Capt. Francis Holland's Harford Rifles, 1776.
    Signer, Association of Freemen, 1776, Deer Creek Upper.
    (E-121, E-124, I-323)

INGRAM, LEVIN.
    Married Hannah Legoe in 1761.
    Private, Capt. Rumsey's Co. No. 6, September 16, 1775.
    Signer, Association of Freemen, 1775, Gunpowder Neck.
    (E-112, I-327, M-94)

IRE, FREDERICK.
    Pensioner(maimed soldier), 1778. (F-661)

IRONS, JOHN.
    Private, 4th Maryland Line, 1776-1779.
    Rifleman, Battle of Fort Washington, November 16, 1776.
    Hospital, June-July, 1777.
    Pay Certificate No. 81454, Md. Regt., $80.00.
    Pay Certificate No. 82257, Md. Regt., $43.30.
    (E-129, E-136, F-302, P-268)

ISAACS, JAMES.
    Pensioner (maimed soldier), 1778. (F-661)
    Pay Certificate No. 86339, $76.40, Md. Regt. paid to Jan. 1,
       1782; No. 87033, $80.00, Md. Regt. paid to July 11, 1784;
       No. 87034, $30.00, Md. Regt. paid to July 11, 1784.
    (P-269, F-661)

ISLANDER, FRANCIS SR.
    Signer, Association of Freemen, 1775, Bush River Upper. (I-316)

J

JACKSON, JAMES.
    Private, Capt. Webb's Co. No. 16, October 14, 1775.
    Signer, Association of Freemen, 1776, Deer Creek Upper.
    Recruit, 8th Maryland Regiment, 1780.
    (E-122, E-131, F-343, I-323)

JACKSON, JOHN.
    Private, Capt. Webb's Co. No. 16, October 14, 1775.
    Signer, Association of Freemen, 1776, Deer Creek Upper.
    (E-121, I-323)

JACKSON, JOHN.
    Signer, Association of Freemen, 1776, Gunpowder Upper. (I-325)

JACKSON, THOMAS.
    Signer, Association of Freemen, 1776, Harford Lower. (I-324)

JACKSON, THOMSON.
    Signer, Oath of Fidelity and Allegiance to Maryland, 1778.
    (A-34, B-22, J-240)

JAMES, HENRY.
    Married: (1) Mary Henley, 1745; (2) Mary Smith, 1771.
    Signer, Oath of Fidelity and Allegiance to Maryland, 1778.
    (A-34, B-30, J-247, M-96)

JAMES, JOHN.
    Married Avarilla Standeford in 1761.
    Signer, Association of Freemen, 1776, Deer Creek Upper.
    (I-323, M-96)

JAMES, JOSHUA.
    Private, Capt. Robert Harris' Co., Harford Rifles, 1776.
    Paid subsistence for six weeks, two days, September 16, 1776.
    Signer, Association of Freemen, 1776, Bush River Upper.
    Signer, Oath of Fidelity and Allegiance to Maryland, 1778.
    (A-34, B-30, E-123, I-320, J-247, K-435)

JAMES, JOSHUA, of Joshua.
    Signer, Association of Freemen, 1775, Bush River Upper. (I-316)

JAMES, RICHARD.
    Private, Capt. Webb's Co. No. 16, October 14, 1775.
    Signer, Association of Freemen, 1776, Deer Creek Upper.
    (E-121, I-323)

JAMES, ROBERT.
    Married Sarah Jones in 1767.
    Private, Capt. Patrick's Co. No. 17, April 1, 1776.
    Signer, Association of Freemen, 1776, Deer Creek Lower.
    (E-122, I-321, M-96)

JAMES, SEDWICK (SEDGWICK).
    Private, Capt. Webb's Co. No. 16, October 14, 1775.
    Signer, Association of Freemen, 1776, Deer Creek Upper.
    Ensign, Deer Creek Battalion, Harford Militia, 1778.
    Signer, Oath of Fidelity and Allegiance to Maryland, 1778.
    (A-34, B-10, C-43, E-122, I-323, J-234)

JAMES, THOMAS.
    Private, Capt. Bussey's Company, July 25, 1776.
    Signer, Association of Freemen, 1775/1776, Bush River Upper.
      Another Thomas James signed in 1776 in Bush River Lower.
    Signer, Oath of Fidelity and Allegiance to Maryland, 1778.
    (A-34, B-30, E-128, F-60, I-317, I-319, I-320, J-247)

JAMES, THOMAS JR.
Private, Capt. Baker's Co. No. 15, January 27, 1776.
Signer, Association of Freemen, 1776, Bush River Upper.
Signer, Oath of Fidelity and allegiance to Maryland, 1778.
(A-34, B-30, E-120, I-320, J-247)

JAMES, WALTER.
Married Cordelia Legoe in 1762.
Private, Capt. Rumsey's Co. No. 6, September 16, 1775.
Signer, Association of Freemen, 1775, Gunpowder Neck.
Signer, Oath of Fidelity and Allegiance to Maryland, 1778.
(A-34, B-14, E-112, I-327, J-235, M-96)

JAMES, WILLIAM.
Signer, Association of Freemen, 1775, Bush River Upper, and Eden Hundred, 1776.
Signer, Oath of Fidelity and Allegiance to Maryland, 1778.
Records indicate there were two signers with this name.
2nd Lieutenant, Deer Creek Battalion, Militia, 1778.
(A-34, B-23, B-29, C-44, I-316, I-324, J-241, J-246)

JAMESON, ALEXANDER.
Signer, Oath of Fidelity and Allegiance to Maryland, 1778.
(A-34, B-25, J-242)

JAMISON, CLADIUS.
Private, Capt. Bussey's Co., July 25, 1776. (E-128, F-60)

JAMISON, JOHN (Farmer).
Private, Capt. Archer's Co. No. 2, September 16, 1775.
Signer, Oath of Fidelity and Allegiance to Maryland, 1778.
(A-34, B-26, E-107, J-243)

JAMISON, JOHN (Innkeeper).
Association of Freemen, Signer, 1775, Susquehanna, and 1776.
Private, Capt. Archer's Co. No. 2, September 16, 1775.
Signer, Oath of Fidelity and Allegiance to Maryland, 1778.
(A-34, B-25, D-357, E-107, I-321, J-242)

JARMAN, JOHN.
Signer, Association of Freemen, 1775, Gunpowder Neck. (I-327)

JARRETT, ABRAHAM.
Born 1735. Died 1776. Married: Martha Bussey.
Captain of Militia Company he organized in 1775.
Children: Jesse, Abraham, Bennett, Eli, Elishs, Eleanor, Mary.
(G-421, X-366)

JARRETT, ABRAHAM JR.
Signer, Association of Freemen, 1776, Gunpowder Upper. (I-326)

JARRETT, HENRY.
Signer, Association of Freemen, 1775, Gunpowder Neck.
Signer, Oath of Fidelity and Allegiance to Maryland, 1778.
(A-34, B-20, I-327, J-239)

JARRETT, JESSE.
  Born c.1758. Died 1839, Jarrettsville, Md.
  Married: (1) Alice Anna Bond; (2) Elizabeth Bosley, 1803.
  Children: (1) Asbury; (2) Abraham, Elizabeth, Martha, Luther, Ariel.
  Signer, Association of Freemen, 1776, Gunpowder Upper Hundred.
  Signer, Oath of Fidelity and Allegiance to Maryland, 1778.
  Ensign, 8th Battalion, commissioned April 4, 1778.
  (A-34, C-47, I-326, G-422, X-366)

JARVIS, JAMES.
  Private, Capt. Bond's Company No. 11, December 9, 1775.
  Signer, Association of Freemen, 1776, Bush River Lower.
  (E-117, I-319)

JARVIS (JARVES, JERVES), JOHN.
  Signer, Association of Freemen, 1776, Spesutie Upper.
  Signer, Oath of Fidelity and Allegiance to Maryland, 1778.
  Private, Maryland Line. Pay Certificate No. 81459, $80.00,
  2nd Md. Regt.; No. 82246, $43.30; No. 87091, $80, paid 1783.
  (A-34, B-10, I-319, J-234, N-29, P-272)

JARVIS, JOSHUA.
  Signer, Association of Freemen, 1776, Spesutie Upper. (I-319)

JARVIS, WILLIAM.
  Private, Capt. Anderson's Company No. 3, September 23, 1775.
  Signer, Association of Freemen, 1776, Susquehanna Hundred.
  (E-108, I-321, N-95)

JAY, DANIEL.
  Signer, Association of Freemen, 1776, Eden Hundred. (I-324)

JEFFERS, WILLIAM.
  Signer, Association of Freemen, 1775, Spesutie Lower. (I-317)

JEFFREY, ALEXANDER.
  Private, Capt. Archer's Company No. 2, September 16, 1775.
  Signer, Association of Freemen, 1776, Harford Upper Hundred.
  (E-107, I-325)

JEFFREY, HUGH.
  "Hugh Jefferys" was a Constable, Spesutia Upper, 1774.
  "Hugh Jeffrey" signed Association of Freemen, 1776, Harford Upper.
  Signer, Oath of Fidelity and Allegiance to Maryland, 1778.
  Grand Juror, Harford County, 1783.
  (A-34, B-26, E-77, E-64, I-325, J-243)

JEFFREY, ROBERT.
  Signer, Association of Freemen, 1776, Harford Upper Hundred.
  Signer, Oath of Fidelity and Allegiance to Maryland, 1778.
  Grand Juror, Harford County, 1779.
  (A-34, B-25, E-75, I-325, J-242)

JEFFREY, THOMAS.
  Signer, Association of Freemen, 1776, Harford Upper. (I-325)

JEFFRIES, THOMAS.
    Signer, Oath of Fidelity and Allegiance to Maryland, 1778.
    (A-34, B-28, J-245)

JENKINS, FRANCIS.
    Private, Capt. Webb's Company No. 16, October 14, 1775.
    Signer, Association of Freemen, 1776, Deer Creek Upper.
    (E-121, I-323)

JENKINS, SAMUEL.
    Constable, Deer Creek Lower, 1774.
    War Committee, 1775.
    Private, Capt. Dorsey's Co. No. 8, October 31, 1775.
    Signer, Association of Freemen, 1776, Deer Creek Upper.
    Signer, Oath of Fidelity and Allegiance to Maryland, 1778.
    (A-34, B-14, E-64, E-115, I-323, J-235, D-359)

JENKINS (JINKINS), SAMUEL.
    Signer, Association of Freemen, 1776, Spesutie Lower.
    Signer, Oath of Fidelity and Allegiance to Maryland, 1778.
    (A-34, B-14, I-318, J-235)

JENKINS, WILLIAM.
    Private, Capt. Taylor's Co. No. 7, September 9, 1775.(I-113)

JENKINS, WILLIAM.
    Private, Capt. Rigdon's Co. No. 12, December 2, 1775.(E-118)

JERVIS, JAMES.
    Signer, Oath of Fidelity and Allegiance to Maryland, 1778.
    (A-34, B-15, J-236)

JERVIS, JOHN.
    Signer, Oath of Fidelity and Allegiance to Maryland, 1778.
    (A-34, B-25, J-242)

JERVIS, JOSEPH.
    Private, Capt. Archer's Company No. 2, September 16, 1775.
    Signer, Oath of Fidelity and Allegiance to Maryland, 1778.
    (A-34, B-26, E-107, J-243)

JERVIS, WILLIAM.
    Signer, Association of Freemen, 1775/1776, Susquehanna.
    (D-357, I-321)

JEWETT, CHARLES.
    Signer, Oath of Fidelity and Allegiance to Maryland, 1778.
    (A-34, B-29, J-246)

JEWETT, ROBERT.
    Signer, Association of Freemen, 1776, Spesutie Upper and Deer
    Creek Upper. Records indicate two signers. (I-318, I-322)

JEWETT, THADDEUS.
    "Dr. Thaddeus Jewett" married Ann Webster in 1773.
    Signer, Association of Freemen, 1776, Spesutie Upper.
    Private, Capt. Josias Hall's Company No. 1, September 12, 1775.
    (E-106, I-319, S-369)

JIBB (JEBB, JYB), JOHN.
    Private, Capt. Archer's Co. No. 2, September 16, 1775.
    Signer, Association of Freemen, 1776, Spesutie Upper.
    Signer, Oath of Fidelity and Allegiance to Maryland, 1778.
    (A-34, E-107, I-319)

JIVDON, RICHARD.
    Signer, Oath of Fidelity and Allegiance to Md., 1778. (A-34)

JOHNSON, ARCHIBALD.
    Private, Capt. Aquila Hall's Co. No. 4, September 9, 1775.
    Signer, Association of Freemen, 1775, Spesutie Lower.
    Private, Maryland Line (Forage Master).
    Pay Certificate No. 85633, $120.00, Md. Regt. pd. to Jan., 1782;
        No. 87170, $80.00, Md. Regt., paid to July 11, 1784.
    (E-109, I-317, N-30, P-274)

JOHNSON, BARNET.
    Signer, Oath of Fidelity and Allegiance to Maryland, 1778.
    (A-34, B-28, J-245)

JOHNSON, BERNARD.
    Signer, Association of Freemen, 1776, Spesutie Upper Hundred.
    Private, Capt. Love's Company No. 10, September 14, 1775.
    (E-116, I-318)

JOHNSON, CHARLES.
    Born 1750. Died c.1821.
    Private, Capt. Rigdon's Co. No. 12, December 2, 1775.
    (E-118, X-370)

JOHNSON, EDWARD.
    Private, Capt. Bussey's Co., July 20, 1776.(E-127,F-60,N-30,N-95)

JOHNSON, GEORGE.
    Signer, Association of Freemen, 1776, Deer Creek Upper. (I-322)

JOHNSON, ISAAC.
    Private, Capt. Anderson's Company No. 3, September 23, 1775.
    Private, Capt. Paca's Company, July 24, 1776.
    Signer, Association of Freemen, 1776, Deer Creek Upper.
    Signer, Oath of Fidelity and Allegiance to Maryland, 1778.
    (A-34, B-14, E-108, I-323, E-126, F-59, J-235, N-95)

JOHNSON, JACOB.
    Private, Capt. Love's Company No. 10, September 14, 1775.
    Signer, Oath of Fidelity and Allegiance to Maryland, 1778.
    (A-34, B-28, E-116, J-245)

JOHNSON, JOHN.
Private, Capt. Aquila Hall's Co. No. 4, Sept. 9, 1775. (E-109)

JOHNSON, JOHN.
Private, Capt. Rigdon's Co. No. 12, Dec. 2, 1775. (E-118)

JOHNSON, JOSEPH.
Private, Capt. Aquila Hall's Co. No. 4, September 9, 1775.
Signer, Association of Freemen, 1775, Spesutie Lower, and Deer Creek Upper, 1776.
Drafted, Militia, 1781; "A wife and children to support."
Private, Maryland Line.
(E-109, E-132, F-400, I-317, I-323, N-30)

JOHNSON, MOSES.
Married Priscilla Standeford in 1757.
1st Lieutenant, Capt. Baker's Co. No. 15, January 27, 1776.
Company Election Judge ("Guge"), Upper Cross Roads, Nov.,1776.
Signer, Association of Freemen, 1776, Bush River Upper. Another Moses Johnson signed this declaration in Eden Hundred, 1776.
Signer, Oath of Fidelity and Allegiance to Maryland, 1778.
1st Lieutenant, 8th Battalion, Militia, 1778.
(A-34, B-24, C-46, D-359, E-119, J-242, K-496, M-98)

JOHNSON, ROBERT.
Private, Capt. Bond's Co. No. 11, December 9, 1775.
Signer, Oath of Fidelity and Allegiance to Maryland, 1778.
(A-34, B-28, E-117, J-245)

JOHNSON, THOMAS.
1st Lieutenant, Capt. Bond's Co. No. 11, December 9, 1775.
Signer, Bush Declaration, March 22, 1775.
War Committee, Harford County, 1775. Lord Justice, 1783.
Signer, Association of Freemen, 1776, Spesutie Upper.
Signer, Oath of Fidelity and Allegiance to Maryland, 1778.
Administered the oath ("Worshipfull Thomas Johnson").
(A-34, B-13, D-355, D-358, D-359, E-116, I-319, E-77)

JOHNSON, THOMAS.
Private, Capt. Rigdon's Co. No. 12, December 2, 1775.
Signer, Association of Freemen, 1776, Deer Creek Upper.
(E-118, I-322, N-30)

JOHNSON, THOMAS JR.
Born 1760. Private, Militia, Flying Camp.
Signer, Oath of Fidelity and Allegiance to Maryland, 1778.
(A-34, B-13, J-235, N-30)

JOHNSON, WILLIAM.
Private, Capt. Aquila Hall's Co. No. 4, September 9, 1775.
Signer, Association of Freemen, 1776, Spesutie Upper.
Signer, Oath of Fidelity and Allegiance to Maryland, 1778.
Letter to W. Johnson from Md. Council, October 10, 1776:
"Captain Holland and Capt. Harriss of Harford County have
(Continued)

JOHNSON, WILLIAM (continued)
    orders to apply to you to make up tents for their Companies which you will be paid for by us. You Will be pleased to take receipts therefor when you make a delivery thereof, and furnish this Board therewith." (K-331)
    (A-34, B-22, E-110, I-319, J-240)

JOHNSON, WILLIAM.
    Private, Capt. Bond's Co. No. 11, December 9, 1775.
    Signer, Oath of Fidelity and Allegiance to Maryland, 1778.
    (B-29, J-246, E-117)

JOHNSON, WILLIAM JR.
    Signer, Association of Freemen, 1776, Bush River Upper. (I-328)

JOHNSTON, CHARLES.
    Signer, Association of Freemen, 1776, Deer Creek Upper. (I-322)

JOHNSTON, GEORGE.
    Private, Capt. Rigdon's Co. No. 12, December 2, 1775. (I-118)

JOHNSTON, JOHN.
    Signer, Association of Freemen, 1776, Deer Creek Upper. (I-322)

JOHNSTON, THOMAS.
    Private, Capt. Love's Co. No. 10, September 14, 1775. (E-116)

JOLLY (JOLLEY), JOHN.
    Captain, Deer Creek Battalion, March 10, 1776-1778.
    Signer, Association of Freemen, 1776, Deer Creek Lower.
    (C-44, E-266, I-322)

JONES, AMOS.
    Born 1754. Died 1827, Married: Ann Lewin, 1783.
    Children: Hugh, Daniel, Phineas, Mary.
    Buried in small family plot near Rochelle Road, Fallston, Md.
    Private, Capt. Taylor's Co. No. 7, September 9, 1775.
    Signer, Association of Freemen, 1776, Gunpowder Upper.
    (E-114, I-326, G-429, X-373, O-25)

JONES, AQUILA LEE.
    Private, Capt. Paca's Company, July 24, 1776. (E-126,F-59,N-95)

JONES, AWBRAY.
    Signer, Oath of Fidelity and Allegiance. (A-34, B-17, J-237)

JONES, BENJAMIN.
    Signer, Association of Freemen, 1776, Deer Creek Upper. (I-323)

JONES, BENJAMIN JR.
    Private, Capt. Rigdon's Co. No. 12, December 2, 1775.(E-118,N-95)

JONES, GILBERT.
> Signer, Association of Freemen, 1776, Bush River Lower.
> Signer, Oath of Fidelity and Allegiance to Maryland, 1778.
> 1st Lieutenant, 8th Battalion, 1778.
> Harford County Grand Juror, 1780.
> (A-34, B-12, C-47, E-76, I-319, J-234)

JONES, ISAAC.
> Private, Capt. Rigdon's Co. No. 12, December 2, 1775.
> Signer, Association of Freemen, 1776, Deer Creek Upper.
> (E-118, I-322)

JONES, ISAAC, of William.
> Private, Capt. Rigdon's Co. No. 12, December 2, 1775. (E-118)

JONES, JACOB.
> Private, Capt. Rigdon's Co. No. 12, December 2, 1775.
> Signer, Association of Freemen, 1776, Deer Creek Upper.
> (E-118, I-322, N-95)

JONES, JOHN.
> Private, Capt. Aquila Hall's Co. No. 4, September 9, 1775.
> Private, Capt. Bradford's Co. No. 13, September 30, 1775.
>   Records indicate there were two men with this name.
> Signer, Association of Freemen, 1775, Gunpowder Neck.
> Signer, Oath of Fidelity and Allegiance to Maryland, 1778.
> (A-34, B-17, E-110, E-119, I-327, J-237, N-95)

JONES, JOSEPH.
> Private, Capt. Baker's Co. No. 15, January 27, 1776.
> Signer, Association of Freemen, 1776, Bush River Upper.
> Company Election Judge ("Guge") Upper Cross Roads, Nov., 1776.
> Signer, Oath of Fidelity and Allegiance to Maryland, 1778.
> (A-34, B-24, E-120, I-320, K-496, J-242)

JONES, REESE.
> Private, Captain Paca's Company, July 24, 1776.
> "Rees Jones" listed as Private, Pennsylvania (1749-1801).
> (E-126, F-59, X-375)

JONES, REUBEN.
> Private, Capt. Patrick's Co. No. 17, April 1, 1776.
> Signer, Association of Freemen, 1776, Deer Creek Lower.
> (E-122, I-322)

JONES, ROBERT.
> Militia Substitute, 1781 "to 10th December." (E-132, F-400)
> Drafted, Militia, 1781; "Never taken up." (E-133, F-401)

JONES, THOMAS.
> Private, Capt. Rigdon's Co. No. 12, December 2, 1775.
> Signer, Association of Freemen, Deer Creek Upper, 1776.
> (E-118, I-322)

JONES, THOMAS.
    Private, Capt. Webb's Co. No. 16, October 14, 1775.
    Signer, Association of Freemen, 1776, Harford Upper.
    (E-121, I-325)

JONES, WILLIAM.
    Private, Capt. Aquila Hall's Co. No. 4, September 9, 1775.
    Signer, Association of Freemen, 1776, Bush River Lower, and
        Signer and Solicitor, 1775.
    Signer, Oath of Fidelity and Allegiance to Maryland, 1778.
    (A-34, B-17, J-237, E-109, I-316, I-319)

JONES, WILLIAM.
    Ensign, Capt. Rigdons' Co. No. 12, December 2, 1775.
    Signer, Association of Freemen, 1776, Deer Creek Upper.
    Signer, Oath of Fidelity and Allegiance to Maryland, 1778.
    Ensign, Deer Creek Battalion, Militia, 1779.
    (A-34, B-21, J-239, C-44, E-118, I-322, N-30)

JONES, WILLIAM JR.
    Signer, Association of Freemen, 1776, Spesutie Upper. (I-319)

JORDON, HENRY.
    Signer, Association of Freemen, 1776, Gunpowder Upper. (I-326)

JORDON, JAMES.
    Recruit, New Regiment, July 29, 1780. (E-130, F-343)

JORDON, RICHARD.
    Private, Capt. Robert Harris' Harford Rifles, 1776. (E-123)
    "Richard Jourdan", Maryland Marine (N-95).
    Paid subsistence for six weeks, September 25, 1776. (K-436)

JORDON, SIMON.
    "Simon Jordin" was Private, Capt. Webb's Co. No. 16, Oct.14,1775.
    "Simon Jrudir" was Signer, Oath of Fidelity to Maryland, 1778.
    (E-121, B-14, J-235)

JORDON (JORDAN), WILLIAM.
    Private, Capt. Harris' Company, Harford Rifles, 1776.
    Paid subsistence for one week, four days, October 19, 1776.
    (K-436)

JOYCE (JOICE), ELIJAH, Carpenter.
    Private, Capt. Bond's Co. No. 11, December 9, 1775.
    Signer, Association of Freemen, 1776, Bush River Lower.
    Signer, Oath of Fidelity and Allegiance to Maryland, 1778.
    (A-34, B-15, E-117, I-319, J-236)

JUDD, DANIEL.
    Signer, Association of Freemen, 1775/1776, Susquehanna.
    (D-357, I-321)

JUDD, WILLIAM.
    Signer, Association of Freemen, 1776, Susquehanna. (I-321)

K

KAIGER, JAMES.
Ensign, 23rd Battalion, 1778. (C-45)

KEAN, JOHN.
Private, Capt. Bradford's Co. No. 13, September 30, 1775.
Signer, Association of Freemen, 1775, Bush River Upper.
(E-119, E-262, I-316)

KEAN, JOSEPH.
Signer, Oath of Fidelity and Allegiance to Maryland, 1778.
(A-34, B-29, J-246)

KEARNS, JAMES.
Private, Capt. Harris' Co. Payroll, 1776. (E-130, F-304)

KEARNS, JOHN.
Private, Capt. Rigdon's Co. No. 12, December 2, 1775. (E-118)

KEEPS, ROBERT.
Signer, Oath of Fidelity and Allegiance to Maryland, 1778.
(A-34, B-29, J-246)

KEER, JOHN.
Signer, Association of Freemen, 1775, Bush River Upper. (I-316)

KEITH, DANIEL.
Pensioner (maimed soldier), 1778. (F-661)

KELLEY, JOHN.
Signer, Oath of Fidelity and Allegiance to Maryland, 1778.
(A-34, B-29, J-246)

KELLY, ARTHUR.
Signer, Oath of Fidelity and Allegiance to Maryland, 1778.
(A-34, B-23, J-241)

KELLY, JAMES.
Records indicate there were several patriots with this name.
Private, Capt. Dorsey's Company No. 8, October 31, 1775.(E-114)
Private, Capt. Bond's Company No. 11, December 9, 1775. (E-117)
Private, Capt. Bradford's Co. No. 13, September 30, 1775(E-119)
Continental Army, 1777-1780, Family Support Allowance. (F-661)
"James Kelley" signed Association of Freemen, 1775, Spesutie Lower Hundred. (I-317)

KENLEY, SAMUEL.
2nd Lieutenant, Deer Creek Battalion, Militia, 1779. (C-44)

KENLY, RICHARD.
Baptized 1761. Died 1825. Married: Avis Ward. (X-382)
Draft, Militia, 1781; "Infirm and sickly." (E-132, F-400)

KENNARD (KINNARD), MICHAEL.
    Born 1744. Died 1810. Married: Johanna Drew.
    Private, Capt. Aquila Hall's Co. No. 4, September 9, 1775.
    Signer, Association of Freemen, 1776, Harford Lower.
    Signer, Oath of Fidelity and Allegiance to Maryland, 1778.
    (A-34, B-22, E-110, I-324, J-240, Y-120)

KENNEDY, JAMES.
    Signer, Association of Freemen, 1776, Harford Upper.
    Signer, Oath of Fidelity and Allegiance to Maryland, 1778.
    (A-34, B-25, I-325, J-242)

KENNEDY, JOHN.
    Private, Capt. Taylor's Co. No. 7, September 9, 1775. (E-114)
    Signer, Association of Freemen, 1776, Gunpowder Upper. (I-326)

KENNEDY, ROBERT.
    Private, Capt. Rigdon's Co. No. 12, December 2, 1775. (E-118)
    Signer, Association of Freemen, 1776, Deer Creek Upper. (I-322)

KENNEDY, THOMAS.
    Signer, Oath of Fidelity and ALlegiance to Maryland, 1778.
    (A-34, B-25, J-242)

KENT, CHRISTOPHER.
    Signer, Association of Freemen, 1776, Bush River Lower. (I-319)

KENT (KANT), JESSE.
    Private, Capt. Rigdon's Co. No. 12, December 2, 1775. (E-118)
    Signer, Association of Freemen, 1776, Deer Creek upper. (I-322)

KERNE, JOHN.
    Signer, Oath of Fidelity and Allegiance to Maryland, 1778.
    (A-34, B-29, J-246)

KERNS, JOSEPH.
    Private, Capt. Rigdon's Co. No. 12, December 2, 1775. (E-118)

KERR, JOHN.
    Signer, Association of Freemen, 1776, Bush River Upper. (I-328)

* KERR, NEVIN ("Norm Ker")
    Private, Capt. Archer's Co. No. 2, September 16, 1775. (E-108)
    Signer, Association of Freemen, 1776, Harford Upper. (I-325)

KEY, JOB.
    2nd Lieutenant, Capt. Love's Co. No. 10, September 14, 1775.
    Signer, Association of Freemen, 1776, Spesutie Upper.
    Signer, Oath of Fidelity and Allegiance to Maryland, 1778.
    (A-34, B-28, D-359, E-115, I-318, J-245)

* Nevin Kerr also furnished a musquet with bayonet and steel rammer
    to the Harford County Committee in 1776. (E-335)

KEYS, JAMES.
    "James Key": Born 1740. Died 1817. Married: Judith Keith.
    "James Keys": Militia Substitute, 1781. (E-132, F-400, X-384)

KIDD, JAMES.
    Signer, Oath of Fidelity and Allegiance to Maryland, 1778.
    (A-34, B-31, J-248)

KIDD, JOHN.
    Signer, Oath of Fidelity and Allegiance to Maryland, 1778.
    (A-34, B-30, J-247, Y-121)

KIDD, WILLIAM.
    Signer, Association of Freemen, 1776, Bush River Upper. (I-320)

KIMBLE, GILES.
    Private, Capt. Dorsey's Co. No. 8, October 31, 1775. (E-115)
    Signer, Association of Freemen, 1776, Spesutie Lower.(I-318)

KIMBLE (KEMBOL), JAMES.
    Born c.1740. Died c.1778. Signer, Oath of Fidelity and
    Allegiance to Maryland, 1778. (A-34, B-10, X-386)
    Private, Capt. Dorsey's Co. No. 8, October 31, 1775. (E-115)
    Signer, Association of Freemen, 1776, Spesutie Lower. (I-318)

KIMBLE, JAMES, JR.
    Private, Capt. Aquila Hall's Co. No. 4, September 9, 1775.
    Signer, Association of Freemen, 1776, Spesutie Lower.
    Signer, Oath of Fidelity and Allegiance to Maryland, 1778.
    (A-34, B-21, E-109, I-318, J-239)

KIMBLE (KEMBLE), JOHN.
    Private, Capt. Dorsey's Co. No. 8, October 31, 1775. (E-114)
    Signer, Association of Freemen, 1776, Spesutie Lower.(I-318)

KIMBLE (KEMBLE), JONES.
    Signer, Association of Freemen, 1776, Spesutie Lower. (I-318)

KIMBLE (KIMBAL), JOSIAS.
    Private, Capt. Dorsey's Co. No. 8, October 31, 1775. (E-114)
    Private, 4th Maryland Line, 1776-1779. (E-129, F-302)
    Rifleman, Battle of Fort Washington, November 16, 1776.
    Black River Hospital, June-July, 1777; Hospital, Dec., 1778;
    Died January 1, 1779.   (E-136, F-302)

KIMBLE (KEMBLE), ROLAND.
    Private, Capt. Dorsey's Co. No. 8, October 31, 1775. (E-115)
    Signer, Association of Freemen, 1776, Spesutie Lower.(I-318)

KIMBLE, SAMUEL.
    Signer, Association of Freemen, 1776, Spesutie Lower.
    Signer, Oath of Fidelity and Allegiance to Maryland, 1778.
    (A-34, B-22, I-318, J-240)

KIMBLE, STEPHEN.
    Born 1738. Died 1782. Married: Mrs. Margaret Barkey Daugherty.
    Private, Capt. Dorsey's Company No. 8, October 31, 1775.
    Signer, Association of Freemen, 1776, Spesutie Lower Hundred.
    (E-114, I-318, X-387)

KING, FRANCIS.
    Private, Capt. Webb's Co. No. 16, October 14, 1775. (E-121)

KING, JAMES.
    Private, Capt. Webb's Co. No. 16, October 14, 1775. (E-121)

KING, WILLIAM.
    Born 1745 in America. Private, Flying Camp. Lt. John Smith
        enlisted July 15, 1776, in Col. Ewing's Battalion (5'8" tall
        with sandy complexion). (E-126, F-56)
    Private, Capt. Webb's Co. No. 16, October 14, 1775. (E-121)
    Private, Capt. Bond's Co. No. 11, December 9, 1775. (E-117)
    Signer, Association of Freemen, 1776, Bush River Lower. (I-319)

KINNEER, JOSEPH.
    Signer, Association of Freemen, 1775/1776, Bush River Upper.
    (I-316, I-328)

KIRK, JOHN.
    Private, Capt. Dorsey's Co. No. 8, October 31, 1775. (E-115)
    Private, Militia; born 1754; prisoner; pensioner. (N-32)

KIRKPATRICK, HUGH.
    2nd Lieutenant, Capt. Bradford's Co. No. 13, September 30, 1775.
    Signer, Association of Freemen, 1776, Harford Upper Hundred.
    Signer, Oath of Fidelity and Allegiance to Maryland, 1778.
    2nd Lieutenant, 23rd Battalion, 1778.
    (A-34, B-25, C-45, D-359, E-119, C-23, I-325, J-242)

KIRKPATRICK, WILLIAM.
    Private, Capt. Harris' Harford Rifles, 1776. (E-123)
    Paid subsistence for four weeks, one day, Oct. 3, 1776. (K-436)

KIRKWOOD, ROBERT.
    Signer, Association of Freemen, 1776, Bush River Upper. (I-328)
    Signer, Oath of Fidelity and Allegiance, 1778. (A-34, B-29, J-246)

KIRKWOOD, WILLIAM.
    Signer, Association of Freemen, 1776, Bush River Upper. (I-328)

KITELY, JOHN.
    Private, Capt. Bradford's Co. No. 13, September 30, 1775. (E-119)

KITELY, JOHN THOMAS.
    Signer, Association of Freemen, 1775, Gunpowder Neck. (I-327)

KNIGHT, DAVID.
>Private, 4th Maryland Line, enlisted August 28, 1777;
Hospital, Sept.-Oct.,1777; With Baggage, Chad's Ford,
June 6, 1778. (E-129, F-320)

KNIGHT, JONATHAN.
>Private, Capt. Rodgers' Co. No. 5, September 15, 1775. (E-111)

KNIGHT, MICHAEL.
>Private, Capt. Patrick's Co. No. 17, April 1, 1776. (E-122)

KNIGHT, THOMAS.
>Private, Capt. Rodgers' Co. No. 5, September 15, 1775. (E-111)
Private, Capt. Bond's Co. No. 11, December 9, 1775. (E-117)
Signer, Association of Freemen, 1776, Bush River Lower. (I-328)
Signer, Oath of Fidelity and Allegiance to Maryland, 1778.
(A-34, B-15, J-236)

KNIGHT, WILLIAM.
>Born c.1721. Died c.1789. Married: (1) Sarah_____; (2) Sarah
Cox in 1752. Signer, Oath of Fidelity and Allegiance to Maryland
1778. (B-23, J-241, M-104, X-393)

KNOTT, WILLIAM.
>Signer, Association of Freemen, 1776, Deer Creek Lower. (I-322)

KNOWLMAN, ANTHONY.
>Signer, Association of Freemen, 1775, Gunpowder Neck. (I-327)

KROESEN. See Croesen.

KYLE, WILLIAM.
>Signer, Oath of Fidelity and Allegiance to Maryland, 1778.
(A-34, B-13, J-235)

L

LACY, THOMAS.
>Private, Capt. Bussey's Co., 1776. (E-127, F-60)
Signer, Association of Freemen, 1776, Eden. (I-323)

LANCASTER, THOMAS.
>Born 1758. Died c.1806. Married: Charity Posey. (Y-126)
Private, Capt. Dorsey's Co. No. 8, October 31, 1775. (E-114)
Signer, Association of Freemen, 1776, Spesutie Lower. (I-318)

LANDON, ROBERT B.
>Harford County Grand Juror, 1783. (E-77)

LANE, MORRIS.
    Private, Capt. Baker's Co. No. 15, January 27, 1776. (E-120)

LANGHIN, PETER.
    Signer, Oath of Allegiance to Md., 1778. (A-34, B-25, J-242)

LARRAMORE, JOHN.
    Private, Capt. Taylor's Co. No. 7, September 9, 1775. (E-113)

LARY, LAWRENCE.
    Signer, Association of Freemen, 1775, Spesutie Lower. (I-317)

LATTIMORE (LATIMORE, LATTIMONE), JOHN.
    "John Lattamore" married Ann Wright in 1766. (M-107)
    Signer, Association of Freemen, 1775, Bush River Upper, and 1776, Eden Hundred. (I-317, I-320, I-323)
    Signer, Oath of Allegiance to Md., 1778. (A-34, B-15, J-236)
    Private, Capt. Harris' Harford Rifles, 1776. (E-123)
    Paid subsistence fro 5 weeks, September 29, 1776. (K-436)

LATTIMORE (LATOMORE, LETTEMORE), WILLIAM.
    Signer, Association of Freemen, 1775, Bush River Upper. (I-316)
    Private, Capt. Robert Harris' Harford Rifles, 1776. (E-123)
    Paid subsistence for 2 weeks, 1 day, October 15, 1776. (K-436)

LAUGHLIN, PETER.
    Signer, Association of Freemen, 1776, Susquehanna Hundred. (I-321)
    Private, Capt. Archer's Company No. 2, September 16, 1775. (E-107)

LAVERTY, JACKSON.
    Private, Capt. Rodgers' Company No. 5, September 15, 1775. (E-110)

LAWRENCE, JOHN.
    Born 1743. Died 1782. Married: Martha West. (X-404)
    Signer, Association of Freemen, 1775/1776, Susquehanna.(D-357, I-321)

LEAKIN, JAMES.
    Private, Capt. Rigdon's Company No. 12, December 2, 1775. (E-118)
    Signer, Association of Freemen, 1776, Deer Creek Upper. (I-322)
    Signer, Oath of Allegiance to Md., 1778. (A-34, B-19, J-238)

LEAQUER, AQUILA.
    Signer, Association of Freemen, 1776, Spesutie Lower. (I-318)

LEE, DAVID.
    Quaker from Bucks Co., Pa. Built Jerusalem Mills in 1772. (D-170)
    A roadside historic marker states "a gun manufactury back of the mill furnished guns for the Revolution in 1776."
    Source D-172 states that David Lee actually made wooden stocks for guns in a two-story building behind the mill.

LEE, JAMES, of Samuel.
    Private, Capt. Archer's Company No. 2, September 16, 1775. (E-107)
    Ensign, 23rd Battalion, Harford Militia, 1778. (C-46)

LEE, JOHN.
    Private, Capt. Dorsey's Co. No. 8, October 31, 1775.
    Signer, Association of Freemen, 1776, Spesutie Lower.
    Signer, Oath of Fidelity and Allegiance to Maryland, 1778.
    (A-34, B-30, E-115, I-318, J-247, N-33, N-117)

LEE, JOSIAH.
    Signer, Association of Freemen, 1776, Deer Creek Upper. (I-323)

LEE, PARKER.
    Private, Capt. Josias Hall's Co. No. 1, September 12, 1775.
    "Parker Hall Lee" (1759-1829) married Elizabeth Dallam, and
      this source (X-408) indicates he was a Lieutenant. (E-106)

LEE, SAMUEL.
    Signer, Association of Freemen, 1776, Spesutie Upper. (I-319)

LEECANS, BENJAMIN.
    Signer, Association of Freemen, 1776, Gunpowder Upper. (I-326)

LEGOE, BENEDICT.
    Married Sally Hick in 1770. Signer, Oath of Fidelity and
    Allegiance to Maryland, 1778. (A-34, B-21, J-239, M-109)
    "Benedict Legs" signed Association of Freemen, 1775,
    Gunpowder Neck. (I-327)

LEMMON, ROBERT. (Doctor)
    Signer, Bush Declaration, March 22, 1775.
    Harford County War Committee, 1775. (D-355, D-358)

LENAGIN, JAMES.
    Private, Capt. Aquila Hall's Co. No. 4, Sept. 9, 1775. (E-110)
    Signer, Association of Freemen, 1776, Harford Lower. (I-324)
    Signer, Oath of Fidelity and Allegiance to Md., 1778. (A-34)

LEONARD, EDWARD.
    Signer, Oath of Fidelity and Allegiance to Maryland, 1778.
    (A-34, B-19, J-238)

LERTER, NORRIS.
    Signer, Oath of Fidelity and Allegiance to Maryland, 1778.
    (A-34, B-17, J-237)

LESTER, WILLIAM.
    Signer, Association of Freemen, 1776, Harford Upper. (I-325)

LEVISTON, JOHN.
    Private, 4th Maryland Line, 1776-1779. Rifleman, Battle of
      Fort Washington, November 16, 1776. (E-129, E-136, F-302)

LEWES, JESSEE.
    Signer, Oath of Fidelity and Allegiance to Maryland, 1778.
    (A-34, B-10, J-234)

LEWIN, JOHN.
    Recruit, New Regiment, July 31, 1780. Pay Certificate No.
    81518, $80, 2nd Md. Regt.; No. 82289, $43.30, 2nd Md. Regt.;
    85740, $80, Md. Regt. paid to Jan.1,1782. (F-343, P-308)

LEWIS, CLEMENT.
    Private, Capt. Rumsey's Co. No. 6, September 16, 1775.
    Signer, Oath of Fidelity and Allegiance to Maryland, 1778.
    (A-34, B-21, E-112, J-239)

LEWIS, JAMES.
    Born 1751. Died 1811. Married: Polly_____. (X-413)
    Private, Capt. Webb's Co. No. 16, Oct. 14, 1775. (E-121)
    Signer, Association of Freemen, 1776, Deer Creek Upper. (I-323)

LEWIS, JOHN.
    Private, Capt. Bond's Co. No. 11, Dec. 9, 1775. (E-117)
    Signer, Association of Freemen, 1776, Bush River Lower.(I-319)
    Recruit, New Regiment, July 25, 1780. (E-130)

LEWIS, JONATHAN W.
    Private, Capt. Rumsey's Co. No. 6, Sept. 16, 1775. (E-112)

LEWIS, JOSEPH.
    Born 1753. Died 1791. Married: Elizabeth Duncan. (X-413)
    2nd Lieutenant, 8th Battalion, 1776. (E-266)
    Signer, Association of Freemen, 1776, Gunpowder Upper. (I-326)
    Harford County Grand Juror, 1783. (E-77)

LEWIS, THOMAS.
    Born 1742. Died c.1814. Married: Mary Ellis.
    Signer, Oath of Fidelity and Allegiance to Maryland, 1778.
    (A-34, B-30, J-247, X-414)

LEWIS, WALTER.
    Private, Capt. Rigdon's Co. No. 12, Dec. 2, 1775. (E-118)
    Signer, Association of Freemen, 1776, Deer Creek Upper.(I-322)

LIANG, JOHN.
    Signer, Association of Freemen, 1776, Bush River Lower. (I-320)

LIGON, JONATHAN.
    Signer, Association of Freemen, 1776, Eden Hundred. (I-324)

LILLY, WILLIAM.
    Signer, Association of Freemen, 1776, Deer Creek Lower. (I-322)

LINAM, JAMES.
    Private, Capt. Webb's Co. No. 16, October 14, 1775. (E-121)

LINDSAY (LINDSEY), ANDREW.
    Private, Capt. Webb's Co. No. 16, October 14, 1775. (E-121)
    Signer, Association of Freemen, 1776, Deer Creek Upper.(I-323)

LINDSAY (LINSEY), DANIEL.
    Private, Capt. Webb's Co. No. 16, October 14, 1775. (E-121)
    Signer, Association of Freemen, 1776, Deer Creek Upper.(I-323)

LINTON, ISAIAH.
    Ensign, Capt. Rumsey's Co. No. 6, September 16, 1775. (E-112)
    Signer, Association of Freemen, 1775, Gunpowder Neck. (I-327)

LITTLE, GEORGE.
    Private, Capt. Aquila Hall's Co. No. 4, Sept. 9, 1775. (E-109)
    Signer, Association of Freemen, 1776, Harford Lower. (I-324)
    Signer, Oath of Fidelity and Allegiance to Maryland, 1778.
    (A-34, B-21, J-239)

LITTLE, JACOB.
    Signer, Association of Freemen, 1776, Spesutie Upper. (I-319)

LITTON, JOHN.
    Harford County War Committee, 1775. (D-358)

LITTON, SAMUEL.
    Harford County Grand Juror, 1783. (E-77)

LIVELY, THOMAS.
    Fifer, 1st Company of Maryland Riflemen under Col. Rawlings.(D-361)

LOCKART (LOCKHEARD), SAMUEL.
    Signer, Association of Freemen, 1776, Deer Creek Upper. (I-323)
    Signer, Oath of Fidelity and Allegiance to Maryland, 1778.
    (A-34, B-14, J-236)

LOGAN, JESSE (or Jessy).
    Private, Capt. Robert Harris' Co., Harford Rifles, 1776. (E-123)
    Paid subsistence for three weeks, three days, Oct. 7, 1776.(K-436)

LOGAN, WILLIAM.
    Private, Capt. Paca's Company, August 5, 1776. (E-127, F-59)
    Signer, Association of Freemen, 1776, Bush River Upper. (I-320)

LOGUE (LOGNE), WILLIAM SR.
    Signer, Oath of Fidelity and Allegiance to Maryland, 1778.
    One source (N-118) states he married Martha Vogan in 1794 in
    Harford County. The same source (N-33) states he was born
    in 1760 and was a Private, Sea Service, and his wife applied
    for a pension. (A-34, B-26, J-243, N-71)

LONEY, AMOS.
    Signer, Oath of Fidelity and Allegiance to Maryland, 1778.
    (A-34, B-26, J-243)

LONEY, JOHN.
    Private, Capt. Paca's Company, July 24, 1776. (E-126, F-59)

LONEY, MOSES (MOSEY).
    Private, Capt. Dorsey's Co. No. 8, October 31, 1775. (E-114)
    Signer, Association of Freemen, 1776, Spesutie Lower.(I-318)

LONEY, THOMAS.
    Signer, Association of Freemen, 1776, Susquehanna. (I-321)

LONEY, WILLIAM.
    Private, Capt. Josias Hall's Co. No. 1, September 12, 1775.
    Private, Capt. Francis Holland's Company, Harford Rifles, 1776.
    Signer, Association of Freemen, 1776, Spesutie Lower Hundred.
    Signer, Oath of Fidelity and Allegiance to Maryland, 1778.
    (A-34, B-22, E-106, E-124, I-318, J-240)

LONG, DANIEL.
    Signer, Oath of Fidelity and Allegiance to Maryland, 1778.
    (A-34, B-19, J-238)

LONG, HENRY.
    Pensioner in 1840, Harford County. (E-262)

LONG, JOHN.
    Crier of Harford County, 1774.
    Signer, Association of Freemen, 1775/1776. Bush River Upper.
    Private, Capt. Bussey's Company, July 25, 1776.
    Signer, Oath of Fidelity and Allegiance to Maryland, 1778.
    Widow applied for pension, July 17, 1797, Warrant No.11445.
    (A-34, B-29, E-128, E-62, F-60, I-317,320, J-246, N-34,71)

LONG, JOHN JR.
    Married Anne Scott in 1779, Harford County.
    Signer, Association of Freemen, 1776, Bush River Upper.
    Signer, Oath of Fidelity and Allegiance to Maryland, 1778.
    1st Lieutenant, Deer Creek Battalion, 1778. According to Capt.
    Vanhorne, Long was offered a 1st Lieutenant's rank on April 9,
    1778, but "refused by said Long, April 14, 1778, being much
    disabled by an accident happening while in service of the
    Flying Camp is therefore under the necessity refusing this
    commission." (C-24,43, A-34, B-30, I-320, N-118, J-247)

LONG, PETER.
    Signer, Oath of Fidelity and Allegiance to Maryland, 1778.
    (A-34, B-19, J-238)

LORAN, JOHN.
    Signer, Association of Freemen, 1775, Bush River Upper. (I-316)

LORDEN (LORDON), MICHAEL.
    Private, Capt. Love's Co. No. 10, September 14, 1775. (E-116)
    Signer, Association of Freemen, 1776, Spesutie Upper. (I-318)

LOTT, NATHAN.
    Signer, Association of Freemen, 1776, Bush River Upper. (I-320)

LOVATT, JOHN.
    Private, Capt. Dorsey's Co. No. 8, October 31, 1775. (E-115)

LOVE, JAMES.
    Private, Capt. Patrick's Co. No. 17, April 1, 1776. (E-122)

LOVE, JOHN.
    War Committee, Correspondence, June 11, 1775.
    Capt., Company No. 10, Harford Militia, September 14, 1775.
    Signer, Association of Freemen, 1775, and Solicitor, 1776,
        Spesutie Upper Hundred.
    Lieutenant, 23rd Battalion, January 3, 1776, under Colonel
        Aquila Hall.
    Signer, Oath of Fidelity and Allegiance to Maryland, 1778.
    Administered the oath ("Worshipfull John Love"), 1778.
    Harford County Court Justice, March 23, 1779/1780.
    Pay Certificate No. 81519, $80, 2nd Md. Regt. pay; No.82287,
        $43.30, 2nd Md. Regt. pay; No.84746, $43.30, Md. Regt. paid to
        November 16, 1783; No.85725, $80, Md. Regt. paid to January 1,
        1783; No.93141, Md. Regt. paid to January 1, 1780.
    Pay Account No. 1, pp. 80, 114; Army Account No. 2, f. 54,
        (1780-1784); Depreciation Pay No. 1, f. 38; No. 2, f. 62;
        No. 3, f. 115, (1782). Listed as "Lt." in Intendant's Ledger
        A No. 10, f. 6, on June 19, 1783; Listed as "Colonel" in
        Intendant's Day Book No. 1, p. 53, on December 21, 1786.
    (A-34, B-28, D-358, D-359, E-115, I-315, I-318, C-23, E-75,
        E-76, E-95, J-245, P-316, HR-50)

LOVELL, JOHN.
    Private, Capt. Rodgers' Co. No. 5, September 15, 1775. (E-110)

LOVELL (LOVEL), PETER.
    Private, Capt. Aquila Hall's Co. No. 4, Sept. 9, 1775. (E-110)
    Signer, Association of Freemen, 1776, Spesutie Lower. (I-318)

LOVELY, THOMAS.
    Fifer, 4th Maryland Line, 1777; promoted to Fife Major,
        February 10, 1778; reduced to Fifer, July 1, 1778.
    In Battle of Fort Washington, November 16, 1776.
    (E-129, E-136, F-301)

LOVETT, JOHN.
    Signer, Association of Freemen, 1776, Spesutie Lower, (I-318)

LOW, EDWARD.
    Private, Capt. Paca's Company, August 5, 1776. (E-127, F-59)

LOW, LEVI.
    Private, Capt. Webb's Company No. 16, October 14, 1775.(E-121)
    Private, Capt. Robert Harris' Co., Harford Rifles,1776.(E-123)
    Paid subsistence for six weeks, two days, Sept.16,1776.(K-435)
    Signer, Association of Freemen, 1776, Deer Creek Upper.(I-323)

LOWERY, JOHN.
    Born 1735. Died 1790. Married Hannah Phinney. (X-427)
    Pensioner (maimed soldier), 1778. (F-661)

LOWRY, WILLIAM.
    Recruit, 8th Maryland Regiment, 1780. (E-131, F-343)

LOYD, THOMAS.
    Signer, Oath of Fidelity and Allegiance to Maryland, 1778.
    Married: Anna Chew Ward. (A-34, B-30, J-247, X-420)

LUCAS, JOHN.
    Maryland Line, last date August, 1780. (F-414)

LURK, JAMES.
    Signer, Oath of Fidelity and Allegiance to Maryland, 1778.
    (A-34, B-30, J-247)

LUSHODY, FRANCIS.
    Signer, Oath of Fidelity and Allegiance to Maryland, 1778.
    (A-34, B-21, J-239)

LYNCH, ABRAHAM.
    Signer, Association of Freemen, 1776, Harford Upper. (I-325)

LYNCH, ANTHONY.
    Signer, Association of Freemen, 1776, Harford Upper. (I-325)

LYNCH, DANIEL.
    Private, Capt. Bradford Co. No. 13, Sept. 30, 1775. (E-119)

LYNCH, JOHN.
    Signer, Association of Freemen, 1776, Harford Upper. (I-325)

LYNCH, MATTHIAS.
    Signer, Association of Freemen, 1776, Bush River Lower.(I-319)

LYON, JOHN.
    Private, Capt. Bussey's Company, July 25, 1776. (E-128, F-60)
    Signer, Oath of Fidelity and Allegiance, 1778. (A-34, B-19)

LYON, JONATHAN.
    Signer, Oath of Allegiance to Md., 1778. (A-34, B-23, J-241)

LYTLE, GEORGE.
    Ensign, 23rd Battalion, Harford Militia, 1778. (C-45)

LYTLE, JAMES.
    Signer, Bush Declaration, March 22, 1775. (D-355)
    War Committee, Harford County, 1775. (D-358)
    Signer/solicitor, Association of Freemen, 1775, Eden. (I-315)
    Signer, Association of Freemen, 1776, Bush River Upper.(I-316)

LYTLE, THOMAS.
    Signer, Association of Freemen, 1775, Bush River Upper. (I-316)

LYTLE, WILLIAM.
    Private, Capt. Webb's Company No. 16, October 14, 1775. (E-121)
    Continental Army, 1777-1780 (Family Support Allowance). (F-661)
    Recruit, New Regiment, July 28, 1780. (E-130, F-343)

Mc

McADOW (McADOO), ANDREW.
    Private, Maryland Militia. Born 1761. Pensioner in 1840.
    Name spelled "Andrew McAdon" in one source. (N-34, E-262)

McADOW (McADOO), JOHN.
    Sergeant, Maryland Line. Born 1745. Pensioner. (N-34)
    Signer, Association of Freemen, 1776, Harford Upper. (I-325)
    Harford County Grand Juror, 1780. (E-76)

McARTY, DANIEL.
    Signer, Association of Freemen, 1775, Spesutie Lower. (I-317)

McAWAY, HENRY.
    Maryland Line, last date July 1780. (F-414)

McBRIDE, JOHN.
    Private, Capt. Aquila Hall's Co. No. 4, September 9, 1775.
    Signer, Association of Freemen, 1776, Harford Hundred.
    Drummer, 4th Maryland, 1777, under Capt. Richard Davis.
    Signer, Oath of Fidelity and Allegiance to Maryland, 1778.
    (A-34, B-25, E-110, E-129, F-301, I-325, J-242)

McCALL, JOHN.
    Signer, Association of Freemen, 1776, Deer Creek Upper, (I-323)
    Militia Substitute, 1781, three years. (E-133, F-401)

McCANDLEY, WILLIAM.
    Harford County Grand Juror, 1779. (E-75)

McCANN, ARTHUR (Weaver).
    Private, Capt. Josias Hall's Co. No. 1, September 12, 1775.
    Signer, Association of Freemen, 1776, Deer Creek Lower.
    Signer, Oath of Fidelity and Allegiance to Maryland, 1778.
    (A-34, b-26, E-106, I-322, J-243)

McCANN, ARTHUR (Miller).
    Signer, Oath of Fidelity and Allegiance to Maryland, 1778.
    (A-34, B-26, J-243)

McCANN, JOHN.
Private, Capt. Archer's Co. No. 2, September 16, 1775. (E-107)
Signer, Association of Freemen, 1776, Spesutie Upper. (I-319)
Private, Land Warrant No. 11522, applied Dec.18,1794. (N-71)
"John McChan" was Private and Pensioner, Md. Line. (N-35)
Pay Certificates: No. 93149, $80, 4th Md. Line, paid to
Nov. 16, 1783; No. 82365, $43.30, 2nd Md. Regt.; No. 85793,
$80, Md. Regt. paid to Jan. 1, 1782; No. 86815, $80, Md. Regt.
paid to Jan. 1, 1783. (P-322)

McCANN, MICHAEL.
Private, Capt. Harris' Company Payroll, 1776. (E-130, F-304)
Private, Maryland Line, born 1728; pensioner. (N-35)
Private, Land Warrant No.11482, applied Feb.1,1790. (N-71)
Pay Certificates: No. 81572, $80, 2nd Md. Regt.; No. 82324,
$43.30, 2nd Md. Regt.; No. 85810, $80, Md. Regt. paid to
Jan. 1, 1782; No. 87315, $80, 2nd Md. Regt. paid to Nov.,1783.
(P-322)

McCANN, PATRICK.
Born 1760. Died 1853. Married: Hannah Johnson. (X-448)
Private, 4th Maryland; Rifleman, Battle of Fort Washington,
    November 16, 1776. (E-136)

McCANNY, GEORGE.
Signer, Association of Freemen, 1775, Bush River Upper. (I-317)

McCARTY, JAMES.
Private, Capt. Aquila Hall's Company No. 4, September 9, 1775.
Signer, Association of Freemen, 1776, Harford Upper Hundred.
Continental Army, 1777-1780 (Family Support Allowance).
Signer, Oath of Fidelity and Allegiance to Maryland, 1778.
(A-34, B-22, E-109, F-661, I-325, J-240)

McCASKEY, JOSEPH.
Signer, Association of Freemen, 1776, Bush River Upper. (I-320)

McCLAIN, JOHN.
Private, Capt. Rigdon's Co. No. 12, December 2, 1775. (E-118)
Militia Substitute, 1781, 3 years. (E-133, F-401)

McCLAIN, PATRICK.
Private, Capt. Dorsey's Co. No. 8, October 31, 1775. (E-114)

McCLANE, FRANCIS.
Recruit, 8th Maryland Regiment, 1780. (E-131, F-343)

McCLELLAN, JOHN.
Signer, Association of Freemen, 1776, Susquehanna. (I-321)

McCLELLAN (McCLELAN), NATHAN.
Signer, Association of Freemen,1776, Gunpowder Upper. (I-326)
Signer, Oath of Allegiance to Md., 1778. (A-34, B-24, J-242)

McCLELLAND, CARY.
A pensioned soldier from Harford County, Maryland who settled
in Greene County, Pennsylvania after the war.

McCLINTOCK, MATHEW.
    Private, Capt. Archer's Company No. 2, September 16, 1775.
    Signer, Association of Freemen, 1776, Spesutie Upper.
    Signer, Oath of Fidelity and Allegiance to Maryland, 1778.
    1st Lieutenant, 23rd Battalion, Harford Militia, 1778.
    (A-34, B-25, C-45, E-108, I-319, J-242)

McCLINTOCK, MATHEW JR.
    Signer, Association of Freemen, 1776, Spesutie Upper. (I-319)
    Signer, Oath of Allegiance to Md., 1778. (A-34, B-25, J-242)

McCLOSKEY, JAMES.
    Signer, Oath of Allegiance to Md., 1778. (A-34, B-29, J-246)

McCLOSKEY, JOSEPH.
    Signer, Oath of Allegiance to Md., 1778, (A-34, B-29, J-246)

McCLUNG (McCLONG), ADAM.
    Born 1740. Died 1780. Married: Letitia Richardson in 1764.
    Signer, Oath of Fidelity and Allegiance to Maryland, 1778.
    (A-34, B-30, J-247, M-113, Y-141)

McCLUNG (McCLMONG), PATRICK.
    Signer, Association of Freemen, 1776, Deer Creek Lower. (I-322)

McCLURE, JAMES.
    Signer, Oath of Allegiance to Md., 1778. (A-34, B-26, J-243)

McCLURE, JOHN.
    Signer, Oath of Allegiance to Md., 1778. (A-34, B-29, J-246)

McCLURE, ROBERT.
    Signer, Association of Freemen, 1776, Spesutie Upper. (I-319)
    Signer, Oath of Allegiance to Md., 1778. (A-34, B-25, J-242)

McCLURE, WILLIAM.
    Private,Capt. Archer's Co. No. 2, September 16, 1775. (E-108)
    Signer, Association of Freemen, 1776, Spesutie Upper. (I-319)
    Signer, Oath of Allegiance, 1778. (A-34, B-25, J-242) (N-97)

McCLUSE (McCLURE), LUKE.
    Signer, Association of Freemen, 1775, Bush River Upper. (I-316)

McCOLOUGH, ALEXANDER.
    Signer, Oath of Allegiance to Md., 1778. (A-34, B-29, J-246)

McCOLOUGH, JAMES.
    Signer, Oath of Allegiance to Md., 1778. (A-34, B-29, J-246)

McCOLOUGH, JAMES JR.
    Signer, Oath of Allegiance to Md., 1778. (A-34, B-29, J-246)

McCOLOUGH, JAMES SR.
    Signer, Oath of Allegiance to Maryland, 1778. (A-34)

McCOLOUGH, DAVID.
    Signer, Oath of Allegiance to Md., 1778. (A-34, B-31, J-248)

McCOMAS, AARON, son of Solomon.
    Private, Capt. Bradford's Co. No. 13, Sept. 30, 1775. (E-119)
    Signer, Association of Freemen, 1775, Gunpowder Neck, and,
      1776, Bush River Lower. (I-320, I-327)

McCOMAS, ALEXANDER.
    Private, Capt. Bradford's Co. No. 13, Sept. 30, 1775. (E-119)
    Signer, Oath of Allegiance to Md., 1778. (A-34, B-17, J-237)

McCOMAS, ALEXANDER JR.
    Private, Capt. Bradford's Co. No. 13, Sept. 30, 1775. (E-119)

McCOMAS, BENJAMIN.
    Private, Capt. Bradford's Co. No. 13, Sept. 30, 1775. (E-119)

McCOMAS, DANIEL. (Doctor)
    Signer, Association of Freemen, 1776, Bush River Lower, (I-320)

McCOMAS, DANIEL, of John.
    Signer, Association of Freemen, 1776, Bush River Upper. (I-320)
    Signer, Oath of Allegiance to Md., 1778. (A-34, B-19, J-238)

McCOMAS, EDWARD DAY.
    Ensign, Capt. Bradford's Co. No. 13, Sept. 30, 1775. (E-119)
    Signer, Association of Freemen, 1776, Bush River Lower. (I-320)
    Ensign, 23rd Battalion, 1778; Captain, 1779. (C-45)
    Signer, Oath of Allegiance to Md., 1778. (A-34, B-17, J-237)
    Intendant's Day Book No. 2, p. 70, October 31, 1785. (HR-50)

McCOMAS, GEORGE.
    Signer, Association of Freemen, 1776, Bush River Upper. (I-320)

McCOMAS, JAMES.
    Signer, Bush Declaration, March 22, 1775. (D-355)
    War Committee, Harford County, 1775. (D-358)
    Signer, Association of Freemen, 1775/1776, and Solicitor
      for Bush River Lower. (I-315, I-319)   (D-359)
    2nd Lieutenant, Capt. Bond's Co. No. 11, Dec. 9, 1775. (E-116)
    Captain, 8th Battalion, Militia, appointed Sept. 18, 1776.
      (E-266, K-281) Records indicate another James McComas was
      2nd Lt., Deer Creek Battalion, in 1779. (C-43)
    Lt. Col., 8th Battalion, appointed April 9, 1778; resigned
      October 30, 1778. (C-46, C-25)
    Signer, Oath of Allegiance to Md., 1778. (A-34, B-9, J-233)
    Administered the oath ("Worshipfull James McComas").(B-10,J-234)

McCOMAS, JOHN, of Daniel.
    Private, Capt. Dorsey's Co. No. 8, October 31, 1775. (E-115)
    Signer, Association of Freemen, 1776, Bush River Lower.(I-319)
    Signer, Oath of Allegiance to Md., 1778. (A-34, B-10, J-233)
    Harford County Grand Juror, 1779. (E-75)

McCOMAS, JOHN, of William.
  Private, Capt. Bradford's Co. No. 13, Sept. 30, 1775. (E-119)
  Signer, Oath of Allegiance to Md., 1778. (A-35, B-10, J-234)
  Harford County Grand Juror, 1780. (E-76)

McCOMAS, JOHN JR.
  Signer, Association of Freemen, 1776, Bush River Lower. (I-320)
  Harford County Petit Juror, 1783. (E-77)

McCOMAS, MOSES.
  Private, Capt. Taylor's Co. No. 7, Sept. 9, 1775. (E-113)
  Signer, Association of Freemen, 1776, Gunpowder Upper. (I-326)

McCOMAS, SOLOMON.
  Private, Capt. Bradford's Co. No. 13, Sept. 30, 1775. (E-119)
  Signer, Association of Freemen, 1776, Bush River Lower. (I-320)
  Signer, Oath of Allegiance to Md., 1778. (A-35, B-10, J-234)

McCOMAS, WILLIAM.
  War Committee, Harford County, 1775. (D-358)
  Private, Capt. Bradford's Co. No. 13, Sept. 30, 1775. (E-119)
  Signer, Association of Freemen, 1776, Bush River Upper. (I-320)
  Captain, 8th Battalion, Militia, 1776. (E-267)   (I-328)
  Signer, Oath of Allegiance to Md., 1778. (A-35, B-30, J-247)
  Harford County Petit Juror, 1783. (E-77)

McCOMAS, WILLIAM, of Solomon.
  Signer, Association of Freemen, 1776, Bush River Lower. (I-320)
  Signer, Oath of Allegiance to Md., 1778. (A-35, B-10, J-233)

McCOMAS, WILLIAM JR.
  Signer/Solicitor, Association of Freemen, 1776, Bush Upper.(E-262)

McCONAL, WILLIAM.
  Signer, Association of Freemen, 1776, Deer Creek Upper. (I-322)

McCONNER, DANIEL.
  Signer, Oath of Allegiance to Md., 1778. (A-35, B-29, J-246)

McCORD, ARTHUR.
  Signer, Association of Freemen, 1775/1776, Bush River Upper.
  Signer, Oath of Fidelity and Allegiance to Maryland, 1778.
  (A-35, B-29, I-316, I-328, J-246)

McCORD, JAMES.
  Signer, Oath of Allegiance to Md., 1778. (A-35, B-12, J-235)

McCORMICK, JOHN.
  Signer, Association of Freemen, 1775, Gunpowder Neck. (I-327)

McCOURTIE, JAMES.
  Signer, Oath of Fidelity and Allegiance to Maryland, 1778. (A-35)

McCRACKEN, JAMES.
    Private, Capt. Dorsey's Co. No. 8, October 31, 1775. (E-114)
    Signer, Association of Freemen, 1775, Spesutie Lower. (I-317)

McCRACKEN, JOSEPH.
    Born 1748. Married: Mary Smith in 1789. Marriage proven through Maryland pension application. (N-118)
    Private, Maryland Line; widow applied for pension. (N-35)

McCRADEY (McCROADY), ROBERT.
    Private, Capt. Webb's Co. No. 16, October 14, 1775. (E-121)
    Signer, Association of Freemen, 1776, Deer Creek Upper. (I-323)

McCREARY, ANGUIS.
    Militia Substitute, 1781. (E-132, F-400)

McCREARY (McCRERY), BENJAMIN.
    Private, Capt. Rigdon's Co. No. 12, December 2, 1775. (E-118)
    Signer, Association of Freemen, 1776, Deer Creek Upper. (I-322)

McCREARY (McCRERY), ROBERT.
    Signer, Association of Freemen, 1776, Deer Creek Upper. (I-322)

McCULLOCH, DAVID.
    Signer, Association of Freemen, 1776, Bush River Upper. (I-328)

McCULLOCH (McCULLOCK), THOMAS.
    Signer, Association of Freemen, 1776, Deer Creek Lower. (I-322)

McCULLOCH (McCULLOCK), WILLIAM.
    Signer, Association of Freemen, 1776, Gunpowder Upper. (I-326)

McCULLOGH (McCULLOCH), DAVID.
    Private, Capt. Robert Harris' Harford Rifles, 1776. (E-123)
    Paid subsistence for two weeks, one day, Oct. 20, 1776. (K-436)

McCULLOUGH (McCULAH), James.
    Signer, Association of Freemen, 1775/1776, Bush River Upper. (I-317, I-320)

McCULLOUGH, WILLIAM.
    Born 1753, Private, Maryland Line; pensioner. (N-35)
    Private, 4th Maryland, 1776–July, 1777; Waggoner. (F-302)
    Signer, Association of Freemen, 1776, Bush River Upper. (I-320)

McCUNE, ANDREW.
    Married Sarah Gist in 1772. (M-114)
    Recruit, New Regiment, July 31, 1780. (E-130, F-343)

McCUNE (McCURE), JOHN.
    Signer, Association of Freemen, 1776, Bush River Upper. (I-321)

McCURDY, ARCHIBALD.
    Private, Capt. Rodgers' Co. No. 5, Sept. 15, 1775. (E-110)

McCURTY, JAMES.
   Private, Capt. Taylor's Co. No. 7, September 9, 1775. (E-113)

McDANIEL, JAMES.
   Private, Capt. Webb's Co. No. 16, October 14, 1775. (E-121)

McDANIEL, JOHN.
   1st Lieutenant, Deer Creek Battalion,"regular service",1778. (C-43)

McDANIEL, JOSEPH.
   Signer, Oath of Allegiance to Md., 1778. (A-35, B-29, J-246)

McDANIEL, THOMAS.
   Private, Capt. Paca's Company, July 24, 1776. (E-126, F-59)

McDONAL, JAMES.
   Recruit, New Regiment, July 25, 1780. (E-130, F-343)

McDONAL, JOHN.
   Recruit, 1st Maryland Regiment, 1780. (E-130, F-343)

McDONALD, CORNELIUS.
   Signer, Oath of Allegiance to Md., 1778. (A-35,B-23, J-241)

McDONALD, HUGH.
   Signer, Oath of Allegiance to Md., 1778. (A-35, B-23, J-241)

McDONALD, JAMES.
   Maryland Line, last date July 7, 1781. (F-414)

McDONALD, JOHN.
   Signer, Oath of Allegiance to Md., 1778. (A-35, B-23, J-241)

McDONALD, JOSEPH.
   Maryland Line, last date August, 1780. (F-414)

McDONALD, PATRICK.
   Private, Capt. Rodgers' Co. No. 5, September 15, 1775. (E-110)
   Signer, Oath of Allegiance to Maryland, 1778. (A-35)

McDONALD, PHILIP.
   Private, Capt. Rodgers' Co. No. 5, September 15, 1775. (E-110)
   Militia Substitute, 1781, thre years. (E-133, F-401)

McDONNELL, PATRICK.
   Signer, Association of Freemen, 1776, Bush River Lower. (I-319)
   Signer, Oath of Allegiance to Maryland, 1778. (B-25, J-242)

McDOWNS, JOHN.
   Signer, Association of Freemen, 1776, Bush River Upper. (I-320)

McEHNEN, JOHN.
   Signer, Association of Freemen, 1776, Deer Creek Lower. (I-322)

McELHANEY (McILHINNY, MacKALHENY), MATHEW.
    Private, Capt. Robert Harris' Harford Rifles, 1776. (E-123)
    Paid subsistence for six weeks, two days, Sept.16,1776.(K-435)
    Signer, Association of Freemen, 1775/1776, Bush River Upper.
    Signer, Oath of Fidelity and Allegiance to Maryland, 1778.
    (A-34, B-30, I-316, I-320, J-247)

McELMAREY, PATRICK.
    Signer, Oath of Allegiance to Md., 1778. (A-35, B-14, J-236)

McFADDEN, JOSEPH.
    Private, Capt. Anderson's Co. No. 3, Sept. 23, 1775. (E-108)

McFADDIN, DANIEL.
    Signer, Oath of Allegiance to Md., 1778. (A-35, B-27, J-244)

McFADDIN (McFADEN), JOHN.
    Private, Capt. Webb's Co. No. 16, October 14, 1775. (E-121)
    Signer, Association of Freemen, 1776, Deer Creek Upper. (I-323)

McGAW, JAMES.
    Signer, Oath of Allegiance to Md., 1778. (A-35, B-10, J-234)
    Drafted, Militia, 1781; "Never taken up." (E-133, F-400)

McGAW, JOHN.
    Private, Capt. Rigdon's Co. No. 12, December 2, 1775. (E-118)
    Drafted, Militia, 1781; "Never taken up." (E-132, F-400)

McGAW, ROBERT.
    Private, Capt. Aquila Hall's Co. No. 4, Sept. 9, 1775. (E-110)
    Signer, Association of Freemen, 1776, Harford Lower. (I-324)
    Signer, Oath of Allegiance to Md., 1778. (A-35, B-22, J-240)

McGAY, ROBERT.
    Signer, Oath of Allegiance to Md., 1778. (A-35, B-22, J-240)

McGEAUGH, JOHN.
    Signer, Association of Freemen, 1776, Deer Creek Upper. (I-322)

McGEAUGH, MILES.
    Signer, Association of Freemen, 1776,Deer Creek Upper. (I-322)

McGEE (MAGEE), THOMAS.
    Signer, Association of Freemen, 1776, Harford Lower. (I-324)
    Pensioner (maimed soldier), 1778. (F-661)

McGETTEGAN, THOMAS.
    Signer, Association of Freemen, 1776, Gunpowder Upper. (I-326)

McGILL, WILLIAM.
    Signer, Association of Freemen, 1776, Susquehanna. (I-321)

McGOUGH, HUGH.
    Private,Capt. Webb's Co. No. 16, October 14, 1775. (E-121)
    Signer, Association of Freemen, 1776, Deer Creek Upper. (I-323)

McGRILL, PATRICK.
    Signer, Association of Freemen, 1776, Gunpowder Upper. (I-326)

McGRUIGEN, _____.
    Signer, Oath of Allegiance to Md., 1778. (B-30, J-247)

McGUIRE, PHILLIP.
    Private, Capt. Love's Co. No. 10, September 14, 1775. (E-116)
    Signer, Association of Freemen, 1776, Spesutie Upper. (I-319)
    Signer, Oath of Allegiance to Md., 1778. (A-35, B-28, J-245)

McINTIRE, JAMES.
    Signer, Association of Freemen, 1776, Harford Hundred. (I-325)

McINTOSH, HUGH.
    Private, Capt. Francis Holland's Harford Rifles, 1776. (E-124)

McKELL (McKILL), JAMES.
    Signer, Association of Freemen, 1776, Eden Hundred. (I-323)
    Signer, Oath of Allegiance to Md., 1778. (A-35, B-30, J-247)

McKENZIE (McKINZIE), RODERICK.
    Private, Capt. Bond's Co. No. 11, December 9, 1775. (E-117)
    Signer, Association of Freemen, 1776, Bush River Lower. (I-328)

McKINLEY, RICHARD.
    Private, Capt. Taylor's Co. No. 7, September 9, 1775. (E-114)
    Signer, Association of Freemen, 1776, Gunpowder Upper. (I-326)

McKINLEY, ROGER.
    Signer, Oath of Allegiance to Md., 1778. (A-35, B-31, J-248)

McKINNEY (McKENNEY), JOSEPH.
    Private, Capt. Patrick's Co. No. 17, April 1, 1776. (E-122)
    Signer, Association of Freemen, 1776, Deer Creek Lower. (I-322)

McKINSEY, EDWARD.
    Private, Capt. Bradford's Co. No. 13, September 30, 1775. (E-119)

McKNIGHT, JAMES.
    Private, Capt. Rodgers' Co. No. 5, September 15, 1775. (E-111)
    Private, Capt. Paca's Company, August 5, 1776. (E-127, F-59, O-14)

McLANEY, WILLIAM.
    Private, Capt. Patrick's Co. No. 17, April 1, 1776. (E-122)
    Signer, Association of Freemen, 1776, Deer Creek Lower. (I-322)

McLAUGHLIN (McGLAUGHLAN), GEORGE.
    Private, Capt. Archer's Co. No. 2, September 16, 1775. (E-107)
    Signer, Association of Freemen, 1776, Spesutie Upper. (I-319)
    Signer, Oath of Allegiance to Md., 1778. (A-35, B-25, J-242)

McLAUGHLIN, JOHN.
    Signer, Oath of Allegiance to Md., 1778. (A-35, B-26, J-243)

McLAUGHLIN (McGLAUGHLIN), PATRICK.
Signer, Association of Freemen, 1776, Harford Lower. (I-324)

McLAUGHLIN (McGLOUGHLAN), ROBERT.
Private, Capt. Archer's Co. No. 2, September 16, 1775. (E-107)
Signer, Association of Freemen, 1776, Spesutie Upper. (I-319)
Signer, Oath of Allegiance, Feb. 21, 1778. (A-35, B-25, J-242)

McLAUGHLIN, WILLIAM.
Signer, Association of Freemen, 1776, Deer Creek Lower. (I-322)

McLEES, JAMES.
Signer, Association of Freemen, 1775. Bush River Upper. (I-316)

McMATH, SAMUEL.
Private, Capt. Bond's Co. No. 11, December 9, 1775. (E-117)

McMATH, WILLIAM.
Private, Capt. Bond's Co. No. 11, December 9, 1775. (E-116)
Signer, Association of Freemen, 1776, Bush River Lower. (I-328)

McMILLAN, SAMUEL.
Born 1750. Died 1832. Married: Isabella Long. (X-458)
Private, Capt. Bond's Co. No. 11, December 9, 1775. (E-117)

McMILLAN, WILLIAM.
Private, Capt. Bond's Co. No. 11, December 9, 1775. (E-117)

McMILLEN, HUGH.
Born 1750. Died 1791. Married: Anne Boone. (X-458)
Private and Sergeant, Capt. Bussey's Co., 1776. (E-128, F-60)

McMULLIN, WILLIAM.
Private, Capt. Love's Co. No. 10, September 14, 1775. (E-116)

McMURPHY, ARCHIBALD.
Signer, Association of Freemen, 1776, Spesutie Lower. (I-318)

McMURRAY, PATRICK.
Private, Capt. Patrick's Co. No. 17, April 1, 1776. (E-122)

McNABB, JAMES.
Drafted, Militia, 1781 "to Dec. 10th." (E-133, F-401)

McNAMARA, _____.
Pensioner (maimed soldier), 1778. (F-661)

McNAMARA, JOSEPH.
Recruit, New Regiment, July 25, 1780. (E-130, F-343)

McNEAR (McNAIR), ARCH.
Private, Capt. Bussey's Co., July 20, 1776. (E-127, F-60)
Signer, Association of Freemen, 1776, Deer Creek Upper. (I-322)

McNEAR (McNEARE), ROBERT.
    Private, Capt. Webb's Co. No. 16, October 14, 1775. (E-121)
    Signer, Association of Freemen, 1776, Deer Creek Upper. (I-323)

McNEILE, MICHAEL.
    Private, Capt. Bussey's Company, July 27, 1776. (E-128, F-60)

McNELY, GEORGE.
    Signer, Association of Freemen, 1776, Gunpowder Upper. (I-326)

McNUTT, GEORGE.
    Signer, Association of Freemen, 1775/1776, Bush River Upper. (I-316, I-328)

McOWEN, NEAL.
    Militia Substitute, 1781, three years. (E-133, F-401)

McPHAIL, DANIEL.
    Sergeant and Company Clerk, Capt. Rodgers' Co. No. 5, September 15, 1775. (E-110, E-111)

McQUELAND, EVER.
    Signer, Association of Freemen, 1775, Gunpowder Neck. (I-327)

McSWAIN, DAVID.
    2nd Lieutenant, Deer Creek Battalion, 1778. (C-44)

M

MACKEN, ARTHUR.
    Private, Capt. Patrick's Co. No. 17, April 1, 1776, (E-122)

MACKEY, GEORGE.
    Signer, Association of Freemen, 1776, Harford Lower. (I-324)

MADDIN, PHILIP.
    Signer, Association of Freemen, 1776, Bush River Upper. (I-320)

MADDON, JAMES.
    Signer, Association of Freemen, 1776, Bush River Upper. (I-328)

MADFORD, WILLIAM.
    Signer, Oath of Allegiance to Md., 1778. (A-34, B-17, J-237)

MAHAN, JNO.
    Signer, Association of Freemen, 1776, Susquehanna. (I-321)

MAHAN, WILLIAM W.
    Signer, Association of Freemen, 1776, Susquehanna. (I-321)

MAJOR (MAJORS), JOHN.
    "John Majors" born 1759; died c.1820. Married: Rachel Baxter.
    Private, Maryland Line; pensioner. (N-36, X-434)
    "John Majers" pay certificate no. 85764, $10.00, Maryland
        Regiment paid to January 1, 1782. (P-339)
    "John Major" signed Association of Freemen, 1775, Spesutie
        Lower, and Deer Creek Upper, 1776. (I-317, I-322)
    Private, Capt. Aquila Hall's Co. No. 4, Sept. 9, 1775. (E-109)

MAJOR, THOMAS.
    Married Jemima Fuller in 1761. (M-116)
    Signer, Association of Freemen, 1776, Bush River Lower. (I-328)

MAJOR, WILLIAM.
    Drafted, Militia, 1781; "Never taken up." (E-132, F-400)

MAKEMSON (MAKIMSON, MEKEMSON), ANDREW.
    Signer, Association of Freemen, 1775/1776, Bush River Upper.
    Signer, Oath of Fidelity and Allegiance to Maryland, 1778.
    (A-34, B-29, I-316, I-328, J-245)

MAKEMSON (MACAMSON), ROBERT.
    2nd Lieutenant, Deer Creek Battalion, Militia, 1778. (C-43)

MAKEMSON (MEKEMSON), THOMAS.
    Signer, Oath of Allegiance to Md., 1778. (A-35, B-23, J-241)

MEKEMSON (MAKEMSON, MACAMSON), JOHN.
    Born c.1750. Died 1814. Married: Elizabeth Brown. (X-434)
    "John Macamson" was 1st Lieutenant, Deer Creek Battalion, 1779.
    "John Mekemson" was 1st Lieutenant under Capt. Vanhorn in Deer
        Creek Battalion in 1778; from Pennsylvania. (C-39, C-43)
    Signer, Association of Freemen, 1775/1776, Bush River Upper.
    Signer, Oath of Fidelity and Allegiance to Maryland, 1778.
    (A-35, B-23, I-316, I-328, J-241)

MEKEMSON (MAKEMSON, MACAMSON), JOSEPH.
    Ensign, Deer Creek Battalion under Capt. Hope, 1778. (C-43, C-28)
    Signer, Association of Freemen, 1776, Bush River Upper. (I-328)

MEKEMSON (MAKEMSON, MACAMSON), WILLIAM.
    Ensign, Deer Creek Battalion, 1779. (C-43)
    Signer, Oath of Allegiance, 1778. (A-35, B-23, J-241)

MAKSON, ANDREW.
    Signer, Association of Freemen, 1775, Bush River Upper. (I-316)

MANLY, JESSE.
    Born 1752. Private, Maryland Militia; pensioner. (N-36)
    Private, Capt. Aquila Hall's Co. No. 4, Sept. 9, 1775. (E-109)

MANLY, JOHN.
"John Manly" was Private, Capt. Aquila Hall's Company No. 4, September 9, 1775. (E-110)
"John Manley" was Private, Continental Line; pensioner; land warrant 13525, 100 acres, applied Dec. 21, 1799. (N-36, N-72)

MARFORD (MORFORD), STEPHEN.
Private, Capt. Webb's Co. No. 16, October 14, 1775. (E-121)
Signer, Association of Freemen, 1776, Deer Creek Upper Hundred.
Record indicates there were two signers with this name.(I-323)

MARKHAM, WILLIAM.
Signer, Oath of Allegiance to Md., 1778. (A-34, B-23, J-241)

MARMOLD, JAMES.
Signer, Oath of Allegiance to Md., 1778. (A-34, B-14, J-235)

MARRET, WILLIAM.
Private, Capt.Taylor's Co. No. 7, September 9, 1775. (E-113)

MARSH, JOHN.
Signer, Oath of Allegiance to Md., 1778. (A-34, B-24, J-242)

MARSHALL, JOHN.
Private, Capt. Rodgers' Co. No. 5, September 15, 1775. (E-110)

MARTIN (MARTIAN), ABEL.
Signer, Association of Freemen, 1776, Deer Creek Upper. (I-323)

MARTIN, ALEXANDER.
Signer, Association of Freemen, 1775/1776, Susquhanna.(D-357,I-321)

MARTIN, EDWARD.
Signer, Association of Freemen, 1776, Susquehanna. (I-321)

MARTIN, HOWARD.
Signer, Association of Freemen, 1775, Susquehanna. (D-357)

MARTIN, JAMES.
Signer, Association of Freemen, 1776, Susquehanna. (I-321)
Record indicates there were two signers with this name.

MARTIN, ROBERT.
Signer, Association of Freemen, 1776, Gunpowder Upper. (I-326)
Signer, Oath of Allegiance to Md., 1778. (A-34, B-12, J-234)

MARTIN, WALTER.
Private, Capt. Taylor's Co. No. 7, September 9, 1775. (E-114)
Signer, Association of Freemen, 1776, Gunpowder Upper.(I-326)

MARTIN, WILLIAM.
Private, Capt. Archer's Co. No. 2, September 16, 1775. (E-107)

MASH (MARSH), LLOYD (LOYD).
    "Loyd Mash" was Private, Capt. Dorsey's Co. No. 8, 1775.(E-114)
    Signer, Oath of Allegiance to Md., 1778. (A-34, B-22, J-240)
    "Lloyd Marsh" signed Association of Freemen, 1775, Spesutie
       Lower Hundred. (I-317)

MASON, THOMAS.
    Private, Capt. Bradford's Co. No. 13, September 30, 1775. (E-119)

MATHER, JAMES.
    Signer, Association of Freemen, 1776, Bush River Lower. (I-320)
    Signer, Oath of Allegiance to Md., 1778. (A-34, B-21, J-239)

MATHER, MICHAEL.
    Private, Capt. Bradford's Co. No. 13, September 30, 1775. (E-119)
    Signer, Association of Freemen, 1776, Bush River Lower. (I-320)
    Signer, Oath of Allegiance to Md., 1778. (A-34, B-10, J-233)
    Harford County Grand Juror, 1783. (E-77)

MATHER, THOMAS.
    Private, Capt. Bradford's Co. No. 13, September 30, 1775. (E-119)
    Signer, Association of Freemen, 1776, Bush River Lower. (I-320)
    Signer, Oath of Allegiance to Md., 1778. (A-34, B-10, J-233)

MATHEWS, BENNETT.
    War Committee, Harford County, 1775. (D-358)
    Signer, Association of Freemen, 1775, Spesutie Upper Committee,
       and signer/solicitor, 1776, Spesutie Upper. (I-318,319, E-262)
    Private, Capt. Josias Hall's Co. No. 1, September 12, 1775. (E-106)
    Signer, Oath of Allegiance to Maryland, 1778. (A-34, B-26, J-243)
    Letter, dated November 16, 1776, from John Archer to the Council:
       "As I understand some of the Gondolas are nearly ready for
       which your Honourable Board has the appointment of officers.
       Capt. Bennett Mathews is well acquainted with the Sea and is
       a Gentleman of Integrity and attachment to the American cause,
       he applies for a Captain's commission." (K-481)

MATHEWS, IGNATIUS.
    Signer, Oath of Allegiance to Maryland, 1778. (A-34, B-31, J-248)

MATHEWS (MATTHEWS), JAMES.
    Married: Sophia Hall in 1771. (M-119)
    Private, Capt. Josias Hall's Co. No. 1, September 12, 1775. (E-106)
    Private, Capt. Francis Holland's Harford Rifles, 1776. (E-124)
    Private, Capt. Bussey's Company, July 20, 1776. (E-127, F-60)
    Indications are there were two men with this name.
    Signer, Association of Freemen, 1776, Harford Lower. (I-324)
    Signer, Oath of Allegiance to Maryland, 1778. (A-34, B-21, J-239)

MATHEWS (MATTHEWS), JOHN.
    Signer, Association of Freemen, 1775, Spesutie Lower. (I-317)
    Private, Capt. Josias Hall's Co. No. 1, Sept. 12, 1775. (E-106)
    Corporal, Maryland Line; invalid; maimed soldier; pensioner,
       1778. (F-661, N-37)

MATHEWS, JOHN SR.
    Signer, Association of Freemen, 1775, Spesutie Lower. (I-317)
    Captain, War Committee, Correspondence, June 11, 1775. (D-358,E-96)
    Signer, Oath of Allegiance to Maryland, 1778. (A-34, B-22, J-240)

MATHEWS, JOHN JR.
    Private, Capt. Aquila Hall's Co. No. 4, September 9, 1775. (E-109)
    Signer, Oath of Allegiance to Maryland, 1778. (A-34, B-22, J-240)

MATHEWS, JOHN.
    1780-1784: Pay Account No. 1, pp. 25, 85, 80, 88; Army Account No.2, f.57; Intendant's Orders No. 1, f. 22.
    1781, May 24: Depreciation Pay No. 1, p. 46; No. 2, p. 69; No. 3, p.28. (HR-50)

MATHEWS, LEVIN.
    "Leven Matthews" married Mary Day, daughter of John and Philizanna Day, in 1764. (M-119)
    "Levin Mathews" was Private, Capt. Aquila Hall's Company No. 4, September 9, 1775. (E-109)
    Signer, Association of Freemen, 1775, Spesutie Lower. (I-317)

MATHEWS (MATTHEWS), ROGER.
    Private, Capt. Josias Hall's Co. No. 1, September 12, 1775. (E-106)
    Signer, Association of Freemen, 1775, Spesutie Lower. (I-317)
    Private, Capt. Francis Holland's Harford Rifles, 1776. (E-124)
    Signer, Oath of Allegiance to Maryland, 1778. (A-34, B-22,J-240)

MATTOCKS (MATTOX), JOHN.
    Signer, Association of Freemen, 1776, Bush River Lower. (I-320)
    Signer, Oath of Allegiance to Maryland, 1778. (A-34, B-10, J-234)

MAXWELL, JAMES.
    Signer, Oath of Allegiance to Maryland, 1778. (A-34, B-14, J-235)

MAXWELL, JAMES JR.
    Private, Capt. Rumsey's Co. No. 6, September 16, 1775. (E-112)
    Signer, Association of Freemen, 1775, Gunpowder Neck. (I-327)

MAY, JAMES.
    Private, Capt. Archer's Co. No. 2, September 16, 1775. (E-108)
    Signer, Association of Freemen, 1776, Harford Upper. (I-325)

MAY, WILLIAM.
    Private, Capt. Bradford's Co. No. 13, September 30, 1775. (E-119)
    Signer, Association of Freemen, 1776, Harford Hundred. (I-325)

MAYS, JAMES.
    Private, Capt. Bussey's Co., July 27, 1776. (E-128, F-60)

MEAD (MEADS), JAMES.
    Signer, Association of Freemen, 1776, Bush River Upper. (I-328)
    Signer, Oath of Allegiance to Maryland, 1778. (A-35, B-29, J-246)

MEADS, BENJAMIN.
    Furnished a gun to the Harford County Committee, 1776. (E-330)

MEAD (MEADS), JAMES JR.
    Signer, Oath of Allegiance to Maryland, 1778. (A-35, B-19, J-238)

MEEGAA, JAMES.
    Signer, Oath of Allegiance to Maryland, 1778. (A-35, B-23, J-241)

MEEK, ANDREW.
    Signer, Association of Freemen, 1776, Susquehanna. (I-321)

MEEKMOOR (MEKMOOR), ROBERT.
    Signer, Oath of Allegiance to Maryland, 1778. (A-35, B-29, J-246)

MEKEEM (McKEEM), JOSEPH.
    Signer, Oath of Allegiance to Maryland, 1778. (A-35, B-29, J-246)

MELANHY, MICHAEL.
    Private, Capt. Dorsey's Co. No. 8, October 31, 1775. (E-115)

MELOY, MICHAEL.
    Born 1750, in Ireland. Private, Flying Camp, Lt. John Smith, enlisted July 15, 1776, in Col. Ewing's Battalion. At time of enlistment he was 5'5" tall with straight hair. (E-125, F-56)

MERRARTER, MATHEW.
    Signer, Association of Freemen, 1776, Spesutie Upper. (I-319)

MICHAEL, BALSHER.
    Born c.1728, in Germany. Died 1795, in Harford County, Maryland. Married twice; second wife was Ann Osborn in 1766. Children: (1) John, James; (2) Bennett, Jacob, Susannah, Daniel, William, Josias, George, Martha, Aquilla, Elizabeth, Henry. (G-514, X-466)
    Private, Capt. Rodgers' Co. No. 5, September 15, 1775. (E-110)
    Signer "Belser Mical", Association of Freemen, 1776, Susquehanna.
    Signer, Oath of Allegiance to Md., 1778. (B-22, I-321, J-240)
    Buried in Grove Presbyterian Church Cemetery, Aberdeen, Maryland.
        (SAR Magazine, Winter, 1984, Vol. LXXVIII, No. 3, page 30)
                                                      (O-15, O-18, O-25)

MIDDLETON, JOSEPH.
    Signer, Association of Freemen, 1775, Gunpowder Neck. (I-327)

MIDDLETON, THOMAS.
    Signer, Association of Freemen, 1776, Spesutie Lower. (I-318)

MILES, AQUILA. Son of Thomas Miles, Jr. & Margaret Burk Taylor.
    Private, Capt. Baker's Co. No. 15, January 27, 1776. (E-120)
    Signer, Association of Freemen, 1776, Eden Hundred. (I-324)
    Signer, Oath of Allegiance to Maryland, 1778. (A-35, B-23, J-241)

MILES, HENRY.
    Signer, Association of Freemen, 1776, Eden Hundred.(I-324,O-22,O-23)

MILES, JOHN.
    Private, Capt. Bussey's Company, July 25, 1776. (E-128, F-60)
    Signer, Association of Freemen, 1776, Deer Creek Upper. (I-322)
    Militia Substitute, 1781. (E-132, F-400)

MILES, JOSHUA.
 Signer, Association of Freemen, 1776, Bush River Upper. (I-320)
 1st Lieutenant, 2nd Battalion, Capt. Bussey's Company, July 26,
    1776; Battle of White Plains, October 28, 1776; 1st Lieutenant,
    8th Battalion, 1776; 1st Lieutenant, 6th Regiment, December 10,
    1776. (E-126, F-59, E-137, K-170, E-267, H-112, L-391)
 Captain, 6th Regiment, October 12, 1777; Resigned May 18, 1779.
 Depreciation Pay No. 2, p. 67; No. 3, p. 193; Army Accounts No. 1,
    p. 31; Army Ledger No. 2, ff. 55, 59; 1779-1787 (HR-50)
 Army Accounts No. 1, p. 11, February 3, 1780.
 Captain, Maryland Line; widow applied for pension. (N-38)
 Married: Jane Glenn in 1785, Harford County. (N-119)

MILES, THOMAS.
 Private, Capt. Rigdon's Co. No. 12, December 2, 1775. (E-118)
 Warrant No. 14119, 100 acres, applied May 1, 1795. (N-73)

MILES, WILLIAM.
 Born 1757. Private, Maryland Line. (N-38)
 Private, Capt. Love's Co. No. 10, September 14, 1775. (E-116)
 Private, Capt. Bussey's Company, July 20, 1776. (E-127, F-60)
 Signer, Association of Freemen, 1776, Spesutie Upper. (I-318)

MILLER, JAMES.
 Private, Capt. Robert Harris' Co., Harford Rifles, 1776. (E-124)
 Paid subsistence for three weeks, three days, Oct.7,1776.(K-436)

MILLER, PETER.
 Private, Capt. Baker's Co. No. 15, January 27, 1776. (E-120)

MILLER, SAMUEL.
 Signer, Association of Freemen, 1776, Susquehanna. (I-321)

MILLER, THOMAS.
 Signer, Association of Freemen, 1776, Harford Hundred. (I-325)
 First Sheriff of Harford County, 1774, Bush, Maryland. (E-357)

MILLIEN, PATRICK.
 Signer, Oath of Allegiance to Maryland, 1778. (A-35, B-25, J-242)

MILLS, JOHN.
 Private, Capt. Archer's Co. No. 2, September 16, 1775. (E-107)

MILLS, RICHARD.
 Signer, Association of Freemen, 1775, Gunpowder Neck. (I-327)

MIRES, JOHN.
 Signer, Association of Freemen, 1776, Harford Lower. (I-324)

MITCHELL, JAMES.
 Born 1753, son of Richard Mitchell and Elizabeth Williams.
 Married: Martha _____. Children: Martha and Kent. (R)
 Private, Capt. Rodgers' Co. No. 5, Sept. 15, 1775. (E-110)
 Signer, Association of Freemen, 1776, Susquehanna. (I-321)

MITCHELL, JOHN.
    Born 1745, son of Richard Mitchell and Elizabeth Williams. (R)
    Private, Capt. Rodgers' Co. No. 5, September 15, 1775. (E-111)
    Married:Mary_____. Children: Elizabeth, Rachael, Frederick.

MITCHELL, JOHN.
    Born 1739, son of William and Elizabeth Mitchell. (R)
    Private, Capt. Rumsey's Co. No. 6, Sept. 16, 1775. (E-112)
    Signer, Association of Freemen, 1775, Gunpowder Neck. (I-327)

MITCHELL, JOHN.
    Private, Capt.Francis Holland's Harford Rifles, 1776. (E-124)

MITCHELL, KENT JR.
    Born 1743. Married: Hannah_____. Children: Shadrick,
    Elizabeth, Mary, Thomas, Sarah, Asel. (R)
    Signer, Association of Freemen, 1776, Susquehanna. (I-321)

MITCHELL, MICAJA.
    Born 1752. Married: Averilla_____. Daughter, Martha. (R)
    Private, Capt. Anderson's Co. No. 3, September 23, 1775. (E-108)

MITCHELL, ROBERT.
    Born 1736. Married: Elizabeth_____. Children: Sarah, John
    and William. (R)
    Militia Substitute, 1781. (E-132, F-400)
    Signer, Association of Freemen, 1776, Bush River Lower. (I-320)

MITCHELL, THOMAS.
    Born 1743, Baltimore County. Died 1830, Harford County. Son of
    Richard Mitchell and Elizabeth Williams. Married: Anne Preston
    in 1767. Children: Elizabeth, Sarah, Richard, Barnet, Aberilla,
    John V., Thomas, Mary. (G-522, X-473, R)
    Signer, Oath of Fidelity and Allegiance, 1778, Baltimore County,
    before the Worshipfull James Calhoun. (J-189, O-7, O-11, O-14)

MITCHELL, WILLIAM.
    Born 1730. Died 1782, Cecil Co., Md. Married: Sarah Osborne in
    1751. Children: Richard, Thomas, William, Martha, Mary, Sarah,
    Clemmency, Edward, Elizabeth, Ann. Son of Thomas and Ann
    Mitchell. (M-124, R, Will of William Mitchell, Jan., 1782)
    Signer, Association of Freemen, 1776, Susquehanna. (I-321)

MITCHELL, WILLIAM.
    Born 1748. Married: Clemmency_____. Children: Barker,
    Charlotte, Elizabeth. (R)
    Signer, Association of Freemen, 1775. (D-357)

MITCHELL, WILLIAM JR.
    Born c.1755-1760. Died prior to 1822, Harford County, Maryland.
    Married: Sarah Mitchell in 1796. Children: Clemency, Elizabeth,
    Martha, Thomas Harley, Richard, Anne, Sarah Ann. (R)
    Private, Capt. Rodgers' Co. No. 5, September 15, 1775. (E-110)

MOBSLER, JAMES.
    Signer, Oath of Allegiance to Maryland, 1778. (A-35, B-22, J-240)

MODIN, PATRICK.
    Signer, Oath of Allegiance to Maryland, 1778. (A-35, B-14, J-235)

MOFFET, ANDREW.
    Signer, Association of Freemen, 1775, Gunpowder Neck. (I-327)

MOGAN, JAMES.
    Signer, Oath of Allegiance to Maryland, 1778. (A-35, B-19, J-238)

MOLAND, RICHARD.
    Corporal, Capt. Harris' Company Payroll, 1776. (E-130, F-304)

MONK, RICHARD.
    Born 1735. Died 1805. Married: (1) Agness Taylor; (2) Jane_____.
    Signer, Association of Freemen, 1775, Gunpowder Neck Hundred.
    Signer, Oath of Fidelity and Allegiance to Maryland, 1778.
    (A-35, B-14, J-236, I-327, M-124, X-474) Furnished a gun in 1776.
    (E-330)

MONOHAN (MORNEHORN), ARTHUR.
    Private, Capt. Archer's Co. No. 2, September 16, 1775. (E-107)
    Signer, Association of Freemen, 1776, Harford Upper Hundred. (I-325)
    Signer, Oath of Allegiance to Maryland, 1778. (A-35, B-25, J-242)

MONOHAN, ARTHUR.
    Signer, Oath of Allegiance to Maryland, 1778. (B-26, J-243)

MONOHAN, JOHN.
    Private, Capt. Archer's Co. No. 2, September 16, 1775. (E-107)
    Signer, Association of Freemen, Harford Upper, 1776. (I-325)
    Signer, Oath of Allegiance to Maryland, 1778. (A-35, B-25, J-242)

MONOHAN (MONAHON), ROLAND.
    Signer, Association of Freemen, 1776, Harford Upper. (I-325)

MONOHAN (MONAHON), THOMAS.
    Militia Substitute, 1781. (E-132, F-400)

MONROE, WILLIAM.
    Signer, Association of Freemen, 1776, Harford Lower. (I-324)
    Signer, Oath of Allegiance to Maryland, 1778. (A-35, B-13, J-235)

MONTGOMERY, JOHN.
    1st Lieutenant, Deer Creek Battalion, 1776-1778. (C-44, E-266)
    Harford County Petit Juror, 1783. (E-77)

MONTGOMERY, JOSEPH.
    Private, Capt. Rodgers' Co. No. 5, September 15, 1775. (E-110)

MONTGOMERY, THOMAS.
    Signer, Association of Freemen, 1776, Deer Creek Upper. (I-322)
    Signer, Oath of Allegiance to Maryland, 1778. (A-35, B-19, J-238)

MONTGOMERY, MICHAEL.
    Married Nancy Evans. Resident of Harford County, Maryland at the
    time of the Revolution, but enlisted in Chester County, Pa.

MOOBERRY (MOOBRY, MUBERY), WILLIAM.
    Private, Capt. Aquila Hall's Co. No. 4, Sept. 9, 1775. (E-109)
    Signer, Association of Freemen, 1775, Spesutie Lower. (I-317)
    Signer, Oath of Allegiance to Maryland, 1778. (A-35, B-17, J-237)
    Also listed as a Patriot from Pennsylvania; born 1752; died 1829;
      married Elizabeth Ramsey. (X-476)

MOORE, CHARLES.
    Private, Capt. Archer's Co. No. 2, September 16, 1775. (E-107)

MOORE, HUGH.
    Signer, Association of Freemen, 1776, Gunpowder Upper. (I-326)

MOORE, JAMES.
    Born 1742. Died 1798. Married: Mary Rider. (X-477)
    Private, Capt. Archer's Co. No. 2, Sept. 16, 1775. (E-108)
    Private, Capt. Bussey's Company, July 20, 1776. (E-127, F-60)
    Signer, Association of Freemen, 1776, Spesutie Upper. (I-319)
    Harford County Grand Juror, 1780. (E-76) Signer, Oath of
                  Allegiance to Md., 1778. (A-35, B-13, J-235)

MOORE, JAMES.
    Born c.1748. Died c.1794. Married: Ann Kirby. (X-477)
    Private, Capt. Taylor's Co. No. 7, September 9, 1775. (E-113)
    Private, Capt. Bussey's Company, July 27, 1776. (E-128, F-60)
    Signer, Association of Freemen, 1776, Gunpowder Upper. (I-326)
    Harford County Grand Juror, 1783. (E-77)
    Signer, Oath of Allegiance to Maryland, 1778. (A-35, B-25, J-242)

MOORE, JAMES, of John.
    Signer, Oath of Allegiance to Maryland, 1778. (A-35, B-28, J-245)

MOORE (MOOR), JOHN.
    Signer, Association of Freemen, 1776, Deer Creek Upper. (I-323)

MOORE (MOOR), WILLIAM.
    Private, Capt. Webb's Co. No. 16, October 14, 1775. (E-121, N-73)
    Signer, Association of Freemen, 1776,Deer Creek Upper. (I-323)
    Record indicates there were two signers with this name.

MOORES, JAMES, of John.
    Private, Capt. Bond's Co. No. 11, December 9, 1775. (E-117)
    Signer, Association of Freemen, 1776, Spesutie Upper. (I-319)

MOORES, JAMES. (Tanner)
    Private, Capt. Bond's Co. No. 11, December 9, 1775. (E-117)
    Signer/Solicitor, Association of Freemen, 1776, Spesutie
      Upper Committee. (E-262, I-319)

MOORES, JOHN.
    Signer, Association of Freemen, 1776, Spesutie Upper. (I-319)
    Signer, Oath of Allegiance to Maryland, 1778. (A-35, B-15, J-236)

MOORN, JOHN.
    Signer, Association of Freemen, 1776, Harford Upper. (i-325)
    Signer, Oath of Allegiance to Maryland, 1778. (A-35, B-25, J-242)

MORE (MOOR), DANIEL.
    Married: Mary_____. Died 1792. (X-476)
    Private, Capt. Webb's Co. No. 16, October 14, 1775. (E-121)
    Signer, Association of Freemen, 1776, Deer Creek Upper. (I-323)

MORGAN, EDWARD.
    Private, Capt. Robert Harris' Harford Rifles, 1776. (E-123)
    Paid subsistence for 4 weeks, 4 days, October 1, 1776. (K-436)
    Signer, Association of Freemen, 1776, Spesutie Upper. (I-319)
    Signer, Oath of Allegiance to Maryland, 1778. (A-35, B-25, J-242)

MORGAN, GEORGE.
    Signer, Oath of Allegiance to Maryland, 1778. (A-35, B-19, J-238)

MORGAN, ROBERT.
    Signer, Bush Declaration, March 22, 1775. (D-355)
    War Committee, Harford County, 1775. (D-358)
    Private, Capt. Hall's Company No. 1, September 12, 1775. (E-106)
    Signer and Solicitor, Association of Freemen, 1775 and 1776,
        Deer Creek Upper Hundred. (I-315, I-323)
    Ensign, Capt. Holland's Harford Rifles, 1776. (E-124, K-350)
    1st Lieutenant, 23rd Battalion, 1778; pensioner. (C-46, N-39)

MORGAN, ROBERT JR.
    Private, Capt. Patrick's Company No. 17, April 1, 1776. (E-122)

MORGAN, SAMUEL.
    Private, Capt. Rigdon's Co. No. 12, December 2, 1775. (E-118)
    Signer, Association of Freemen, 1776, Deer Creek Upper. (I-322)

MORGAN, WILLIAM.
    Son of Edward Morgan. Born 1744, Trappe, Harford (then Baltimore)
        County, Md. Died 1795, Harford County, Md. (X-480, E-223)
    Married Cassandra Lee, a Quakeress, in 1760; daughter of James Lee.
        Children: Elizabeth Morgan married Thomas S. Chew; Sarah Morgan
        married Joseph Hopkins; Cassandra Morgan married Zaccheus O. Bond;
        Edward Morgan; Elliner Morgan married John Hopkins; James Morgan;
        Mary Morgan married Ephraim Hopkins; Martha Morgan; and, Margaret
        Morgan. (G-532, E-224)
    Signer, Bush Declaration, March 22, 1775. (D-355)
    War Committee, Harford County, 1775. (D-359)
    Signer and Solicitor, Association of Freemen, 1775 and 1776,
        Deer Creek Lower Hundred. (I-315, I-322)
    Captain, Deer Creek Battalion, April 9, 1778. (C-44, C-28)
    Depreciation Pay No. 1, p. 44; No. 2, p. 74; No. 3, p. 9;
        Intendants Ledger A No. 10, ff. 88, 102 (1781-1782). (HR-50)

MORIARITY (MARIERTY), DANIEL.
    Signer, Association of Freemen, 1776, Spesutie Upper. (I-319)

MORIARITY, JAMES.
    Private, Capt. Bond's Co. No. 11, December 9, 1775. (E-117)
    Signer, Association of Freemen, 1776, Harford Upper. (I-325)

MORRIS, EDWARD.
    Private, Capt. Aquila Hall's Co. No. 4, Sept. 9, 1775. (E-109)
    Signer, Association of Freemen, 1775, Spesutie Lower. (I-317)
    Private, Capt. Paca's Company, July 24, 1776. (E-126, F-59)

MORRIS, JAMES.
    Private, Capt. Patrick's Co. No. 17, April 1, 1776. (E-122,N-39)

MORRIS, JOHN.
    Private, Capt. Dorsey's Co. No. 8, October 31, 1775. (E-115)
    Signer, Association of Freemen, 1776, Spesutie Lower.(I-318)
    Signer, Oath of Allegiance to Maryland, 1778. (A-35, B-24, J-242)

MORRIS, JOHN.
    Private, Capt. Bradford's Co. No. 13, Sept. 30, 1775. (E-119)
    Signer, Association of Freemen, 1776, Harford Upper. (I-325)

MORRIS, JOHN.
    Private, Capt. Paca's Company, July 24, 1776. (E-126, F-59)
    Militia Substitute, 1781. (E-131, F-400, N-39)

MORRIS, JOSEPH, son of Ed.
    Constable, Bush River Lower, 1774. (E-64)
    Signer, Association of Freemen, 1776, Gunpowder Upper. (I-326)

MORRIS, MICHAEL.
    Private, Capt. Paca's Company, July 24, 1776. (E-126, F-59)
    Signer, Association of Freemen, 1776, Deer Creek Lower. (I-321)

MORRIS, RICHARD.
    Signer, Association of Freemen, 1775, Spesutie Lower. (I-317)

MORRIS, THOMAS.
    Signer, Association of Freemen, 1776, Deer Creek Lower. (I-321)

MORRISON, JAMES.
    Signer, Associations of Freemen, 1776, Gunpowder Upper. (I-326)

MORRISON, JOSEPH.
    Signer, Association of Freemen, 1776, Bush River Lower. (I-319)
    Signer, Oath of Allegiance to Maryland, 1778. (A-35, B-15, J-236)

MORROW, BENJAMIN.
    Signer, Association of Freemen, 1776, Gunpowder Upper. (I-326)
    Signer, Oath of Allegiance to Maryland, 1778. (A-35, B-12, J-234)

MORROW, JOHN.
    Private, Capt. Webb's Co. No. 16, October 14, 1775. (E-121)

MORSELL, KIDD.
    Signer, Oath of Allegiance to Maryland, 1778. (A-35, B-20, J-239)

MULLEN, MICHAEL.
    Private, Capt. Paca's Company, August 5, 1776. (E-127, F-59)

MULLEN, PATRICK.
    Militia Substitute, 1782, 3 years. (E-133, F-401)

MULTON, PATRICK.
    Signer, Oath of Allegiance to Maryland, 1778. (A-35, B-10, J-233)

MUNDAY (MUNDEY), JAMES.
    2nd Sergeant, Capt. Love's Co. No. 10, Sept. 14, 1775. (E-115)
    Private, Capt. Robert Harris' Harford Rifles, 1776. (E-123)
    Paid subsistence for five weeks, five days, Sept.26,1776.(K-436)
    Signer, Association of Freemen, 1776, Bush River Lower. (I-328)

MUNROE, HUGH.
    Private, Capt. Rodgers' Co. No. 5, September 15, 1775. (E-111)

MURDOCK (MURDOUGH), WILLIAM.
    Private, Capt. Webb's Co. No. 16, October 14, 1775. (E-121)
    Signer, Association of Freemen, 1776, Deer Creek Upper. (I-323)

MURFEY, JAMES.
    Private, Capt. Patrick's Co. No. 17, April 1, 1776. (E-122)

MURPHY, ARCHIBALD M.
    Signer, Oath of Allegiance to Maryland, 1778. (A-35, B-10, J-233)

MURPHY, EDWARD.
    Born 1751, in Ireland. Private, Flying Camp, Capt. James Young enlisted July 7, 1776, in Col. Ewing's Battalion. At time of enlistment he was 5'8" tall with short black hair and had a stoppage in his speech. (E-125, F-55)
    Signer, Oath of Allegiance to Maryland, 1778. (A-35, B-27, J-244)

MURPHY, JOAB.
    Private, Capt. Paca's Company, August 5, 1776. (E-127, F-59)

MURPHY (MORFEY), PATRICK.
    Signer, Association of Freemen, 1776, Spesutie Upper. (I-319)
    Signer, Oath of Allegiance to Maryland, 1778. (A-35, B-28, J-245)

MURPHY, THOMAS.
    Signer, Oath of Allegiance to Maryland, 1778. (B-30, J-247)

MURPHY, WILLIAM.
    Private, Capt. Aquila Hall's Co. No. 4, Sept.9, 1775. (E-109)
    Signer, Association of Freemen, 1775, Spesutie Lower. (I-317)

MURPHY, WILLIAM.
    Private, Capt. Rogers' Co. No. 5, Sept. 15, 1775. (E-111)
    Signer, Oath of Allegiance to Maryland, 1778. (A-35, B-20, J-247)

MURPHY, WILLIAM.
    Continental Army, 1777-80 (Family Support Allowance), (F-661)

MURRAY, ALEXANDER.
    Signer, Association of Freemen, 1776, Deer Creek Lower. (I-322)

N

NEAL, FRANCIS (Doctor).
   Signer, Association of Freemen,1776, Deer Creek Upper. (I-323)

NEAL, JOHN (of Charles County).
   Took Oath of Allegiance in Harford County, 1778. (B-28, J-245)

NEAL, WILLIAM FRANCIS (of Charles County).
   Took Oath of Allegiance in Harford County, 1778. (B-28, J-245)
   Also signed Association of Freemen, 1776, Deer Creek. (I-323)

NEGRO NORA.
   Captain's servant. Capt. Holland's Harford Rifles, 1776. (E-124)

NEGROE TOWER.
   Drafted, Militia, 1781; "discharged, having wife and children."
   (E-132, F-400)

NEILL, HENRY.
   Private, Capt. Josias Hall's Co. No. 1, Sept. 12, 1775. (E-106)

NELSON, HUGH.
   Signer, Oath of Allegiance to Maryland, 1778. (A-35, B-23, J-241)

NELSON, JAMES.
   Private, Capt. Bussey's Company, July 27, 1776. (E-128, F-60)

NELSON, JOHN.
   Signer, Association of Freemen, 1776, Harford Lower. (I-324)
   Signer, Oath of Allegiance to Maryland, 1778. (A-35, B-17, J-237)

NELSON, ROBERT.
   Signer, Oath of Allegiance to Maryland, 1778. (A-35, B-30, J-247)

NEWBERRY, WILLIAM.
   Militia Substitute, 1781, 3 years. (E-133, F-401)

NIGHT, WILLIAM.
   Private, Capt. Bussey's Company, July 25, 1776. (E-128, F-60)

NIXON (NINON), HUGH.
   Signer, Association of Freemen, 1776, Bush River Upper. (I-320)

NIXON, ROBERT.
   Private, Capt. Anderson's Co. No. 3, September 23, 1775. (E-109)

NOLAND, RICHARD.
   Private, Capt. Taylor's Co. No. 7, September 9, 1775. (E-114)

NOLSTONE, ALEXANDER.
   Private, Capt. Paca's Company, July 24, 1776. (E-126, F-59)

NORRINTON (NOVINTON), JOHN.
    "John Norrington" married Mary Hays in 1737. (M-131)
    "John Norrinton" signed Association of Freemen, 1776, Bush
    River Upper. (I-320)
    "John Novinton" signed Oath of Allegiance to Maryland, 1778.
    (A-35, B-30, J-247)

NORRIS, ABRAHAM.
    Married Rebecca Kitely in 1762. (M-131)
    Signed, Oath of Allegiance to Maryland, 1778. (A-35, B-10, J-233)

NORRIS, AQUILA, of Thomas.
    Son of Thomas Norris and Elizabeth McComas. (Q-74)
    Private, Capt.Taylor's Co. No. 7, Sept. 9, 1775. (E-112)

NORRIS, AQUILA, of Edward.
    Son of Edward Norris and Hannah Scott. Born 1754. Died 1825.
    Married: (1) Sarah Norris; (2) Mary Waltham Dutton. Children:
    Floyd, Rhesa, Cardiff, Silas, Mary, Susan, Silas, Gabriel.
    (Q-25, Q-26, G-546, X-498)
    Signer, Association of Freemen, 1776, Gunpowder Upper. (I-326)
    Signer, Oath of Allegiance to Maryland, 1778. (A-35, B-20, J-239)
    Captain, 8th Battalion, Milltia, April 9, 1778. (C-46, Q-26)

NORRIS, AQUILA.
    Born c.1750. Died 1812. Married: Priscilla Temperance Norris.
    Signer, Association of Freemen, Gunpowder Upper Hundred, 1776.
    Signer, Oath of Allegiance to Maryland, 1778.
    (A-35, B-10, I-326, J-234, X-498)

NORRIS, ALEXANDER.
    Son of John Norris and Susannah Bradford.
    Born 1759. Married Rebecca Moore. (Q-17)
    Signer, Oath of Allegiance, 1778. (B-12, J-234)

NORRIS, ALEXANDER.
    Born 1744. Died 1810/1820. Married Sarah Norrington. (X-498)
    Signer, Association of Freemen, 1776, Bush River Upper. (I-328)

NORRIS, BENJAMIN.
    Son of Joseph and Mary Norris. Born 1749. (Q-13)
    Signer, Association of Freemen, 1776, Bush River Lower. (I-319)

NORRIS, BENJAMIN.
    Signer, Association of Freemen, 1776, Gunpowder Upper. (I-326)

NORRIS, BENJAMIN BRADFORD.
    Son of John Norris and Susannah Bradford. Born 1745. Died 1790.
    Married Elizabeth Richardson in 1768. Children: Martha, Sarah,
    William Lee, Amelia, Susan, Harriett, Provey, Benj. Bradford.
    Signer, Bush Declaration, March 22, 1775; War Committee, 1775.
    Signer, Association of Freemen, 1776, Bush River Lower Hundred.
    Captain and Major, Maryland Militia, 1776-1778. Served under his
    brother Jacob in the 6th Md. Regt. and was with Washington in
    the New Jersey campaign. Also, member of Harford Safety Comm.
    (D-355, D-358, I-319, L-415, Q-27, G-546, M-131, X-499)

NORRIS, DANIEL.
    Born 1728. Died 1804. Married: (1) Sarah Beaver; (2) Catherine.
    Son of Edward Norris and Hannah Scott. Daniel had no children.
    Private, Capt. Taylor's Co. No. 7, September 9, 1775.
    Signer, Association of Freemen, 1776, Bush River Lower.
    Signer, Oath of Allegiance to Maryland, 1778.
    Harford County Grand Juror, 1780.
    (A-35, B-10, E-113, I-319, J-233, E-76, Q-21, M-131)

NORRIS, DAVID.
    Signer, Association of Freemen, 1776, Gunpowder Upper. (I-326)

NORRIS, EDWARD, of Edward.
    Son of Edward Norris and Hannah Scott. Born 1741. Died 1793.
    Married Elizabeth Amos in 1771. Children: Hannah, John, William,
        Susannah, Oliver, Mary, Ann. (M-131, Q-23, Q-24)
    Signer, Association of Freemen, 1776, Gunpowder Upper. (I-326)
    Signer, Oath of Allegiance to Maryland, 1778. (A-35, B-12, J-234)

NORRIS, EDWARD.
    Signer, Oath of Allegiance to Maryland, 1778. (A-35, B-29, J-246)

NORRIS, EDWARD, of James.
    Signer, Association of Freemen, 1776, Gunpowder Upper. (I-326)

NORRIS, EDWARD, of Joshua.
    Private, Capt. Taylor's Co. No. 7, September 9, 1775. (E-113)

NORRIS, JACOB.
    Son of John Norris and Susannah Bradford. Born 1753. Died 1807.
    Married Asarilla Gallion in 1785. Children: Sophia, Clarissa,
        George, Luther, John, Amanda, Catherine, Otho. (Q-29, Q-30)
    Signer, Association of Freemen, 1776, Bush River Lower. (I-319)
    2nd Lieutenant, 6th Maryland, October 10, 1777.
    1st Lieutenant, 6th Maryland, November 26, 1778.
    Served with Washington in the New Jersey campaign, was wounded
        and taken prisoner at Camden, August 16, 1780; transferred
        to 5th Maryland, January 1, 1781; prisoner to close of war
        on parole, invalided home. (Q-29, Q-30)
    Land Warrant No. 1236, 200 acres, applied by widow, 1827. (N-74)
    Captain, 1780: Army Journal No. 1, p.24; Pay Account No.1, p.12;
    Intendant;s Day Book No. 2, p. 97; Army Accounts No. 1, p. 11,
    1779; Army Ledger No. 1, f.81; No. 2, f.111; No. 3, f.6 (Lieut.);
    Army Journal No. 1, pp. 3, 28, 35, 43, 80; 1781: Depreciation
    Pay No. 1, p. 46; No. 2. p. 79; No. 3, p. 45. (HR-50)

NORRIS, JACOB.
    Signer, Association of Freemen, 1776, Gunpowder Upper. (I-326)

NORRIS, JAMES.
    Son of Thomas Norris and Elizabeth McComas. (Q-74)
    Signer, Association of Freemen, 1775, Gunpowder Neck. (I-327)
    Signer, Oath of Allegiance to Maryland, 1778. (B-24, J-242)

NORRIS, JAMES.
    Son of Joseph and Mary Norris. Born 1756. (Q-13)
    Signer, Association of Freemen, 1776, Eden. (I-324)

NORRIS, JAMES.
    Son of Edward Norris and Hannah Scott. Born 1742/1743.
    Married Mary Norris in 1765. Children: Daniel, Charlotte.
    Signer, Association of Freemen, 1775/1776, Bush River Upper.
    (I-317, I-320, Q-13, M-131)

NORRIS, JAMES SR.
    Born 1715. Died 1798. Married Elizabeth Davis in 1744.
    Children: William, James, Henry, Sarah. (M-131)
    Son of John and Ann Norris. (Q-75)
    Signer, Association of Freemen, 1776, Gunpowder Upper. (I-326)
    Signer, Oath of Allegiance to Maryland, 1778. (A-35, B-10, J-233)

NORRIS, JAMES JR.
    Son of James Norris and Elizabeth Davis. (Q-75)
    Signer, Association of Freemen, 1776, Gunpowder Upper. (I-326)
    Signer, Oath of Allegiance to Maryland, 1778. (B-12, J-234)

NORRIS, JOHN.
    Son of Edward Norris and Hannah Scott. Born 1747. (Q-12)
    Married Martha Long in 1772. (M-131)
    Signer, Association of Freemen, 1776, Bush River Lower. (I-319)
    Signer, Oath of Allegiance to Maryland, 1778. (A-35, B-19, J-238)
    8th Battalion, 1st Lieutenant, 1778. (C-46)

NORRIS, JOHN, of Benjamin.
    Son of Benjamin Norris and Mary Duvall. (Q-20)
    Private, Capt. Bond's Co. No. 11, Dec. 9, 1775. (E-117)

NORRIS, JOHN, of James.
    Private, Capt. Taylor's Co. No. 7, September 9, 1775. (E-113)

NORRIS, JOHN, of John.
    Son of John Norris and Susannah Bradford. Born 1747. Died 1835.
    Married Sarah Richardson in 1785. Children: Susan, Alexander,
      Sarah, Elizabeth. (Q-28)
    Signer, Association of Freemen, 1776, Gunpowder Upper. (I-326)
    Signer, Oath of Allegiance to Maryland, 1778. (B-12, J-235)
    Militia Substitute, 1781. (E-132, F-400)

NORRIS, JOSEPH.
    Born 1705. Died 1784. Married_____1734. Children:
    Elizabeth, John, Rachel, Susannah, May, Hannah, Joseph, Willimen,
    Benjamin, Edward, Temperance, James.
    Son of John Norris and Elizabeth Parsons. (Q-13)
    Signer, Oath of Allegiance to Maryland, 1778. (A-35, B-10, J-234)

NORRIS, JOSEPH, of Edward.
    Son of Edward Norris and Hannah Scott. Born 1725. Died 1780. (Q-20)
    Married Philiszana Barton in 1750. Children: William, Joseph. (X-499)
    Signer, Oath of Allegiance to Maryland, 1778. (A-35, B-28, J-245)

NORRIS, MICHAEL.
  Private, Capt. Patrick's Co. No. 17, April 1, 1776.(E-122)

NORRIS, RICHARD.
  Signer, Oath of Allegiance to Maryland, 1778. (A-35, B-10, J-234)

NORRIS, THOMAS.
  Born 1716. Son of John Norris and Mary Newman. Married, 1738,
    to Averilla Scott. Children: William, Nathaniel, Mary, John.
  Signer, Association of Freemen, 1776, Gunpowder Upper Hundred.
  (I-326, M-131, Q-14)

NORRIS, THOMAS.
  Son of Edward Norris and Hannah Scott. (Q-12)
  Might have married Hannah Norrington in 1762. (X-499)
  Signer, Association of Freemen, 1776, Bush River Lower. (I-328)

NORRIS, THOMAS, of John.
  Son of John Norris and Susannah Bradford. Born 1756. Died 1818.
  Married Sarah Ann Billingsley. Children: Benjamin, William, Otho,
    Luther, Mary, Ann, John. (Q-31, X-499)
  Signer, Association of Freemen, 1776, Bush River Lower. (I-319)
  Signer, Oath of Allegiance to Maryland, 1778. (A-35, B-10, J-233)
  Private, Maryland Militia. (X-499)

NORRIS, WILLIAM, of John.
  Son of John Norris and Susannah Bradford. Born 1749. Died 1837.
  Married Martha Amos in 1780. Children: Thomas, William, Jr.,
    Elizabeth, Susan, Martha, Jacob, Mary, Ellen, John.
  Signer, Association of Freemen, 1776, Gunpowder Upper Hundred.
  Private, Capt. Bradford's Co. No. 13, September 30, 1775.
  Signer, Oath of Fidelity and Allegiance to Maryland, 1778.
  (A-35, B-23, E-119, G-546, I-326, J-241, Q-17, Q-28, X-499)

NORRIS, WILLIAM, of Joshua.
  Private, Capt. Taylor's Co. No. 7, September 9, 1775. (E-113)
  Born 1760. Died 1853. Married Nancy Cornelius. (X-499)

NORRIS, WILLIAM.
  Born 1758. Died 1838/1839. Married Sarah Rigdon. (X-499)
  Signer, Association of Freemen, 1776, Gunpowder Upper. (I-326)

NORTON, PATRICK.
  Private, Capt. Bussey's Co., July 25, 1776. (E-128, F-60)

NOWER, JAMES.
  Private, Capt. Bradford's Co. No. 13, September 30, 1775. (E-119)

NOWLAN, PATRICK.
  Private, Capt. Robert Harris' Harford Rifles, 1776. (E-123)
  Paid subsistence for five weeks, September 21, 1776. (K-435)

NUTTERWELL, DANIEL.
  Signer, Association of Freemen, 1775, Gunpowder Neck. (I-327)
  Private, Capt. Francis Holland's Harford Rifles, 1776.(E-124)
  Signer, Oath of Allegiance to Maryland, 1778. (A-35, B-22, J-240)

O'BED, JOHN.
　　Signer, Association of Freemen, 1776, Harford Upper. (I-325)

O'BRIAN, JAMES.
　　Recruit, 8th Maryland Regiment, 1780. (E-131, F-343)

O'BRIAN, WILLIAM.
　　Signer, Association of Freemen, 1776, Gunpowder Upper. (I-326)

O'CLOSE, CHARLES.
　　Private, Capt. Taylor's Co. No. 7, September 9, 1775. (E-113)
　　"Charles Close" born 1756; died 1838; married (1) Sarah_____;
　　(2) Hannah Whitney.　(E-113, X-139)

O'DILLEN, LAWRENCE.
　　Signer, Oath of Allegiance to Maryland, 1778. (A-35, B-26, J-243)

ODLE, TALBOT.
　　Private, Capt. Archer's Co. No. 2, September 16, 1775. (E-108)

O'DONALD, SAMUEL.
　　Signer, Oath of Allegiance to Maryland, 1778. (A-35, B-30, J-247)

O'DONEL, JOHN.
　　Private, Capt. Bussey's Company, July 25, 1776. (E-128, F-60)

O'DONNELL (O'DANNEL), MICHAEL.
　　Signer, Association of Freemen, 1776, Harford Upper. (I-325)
　　Signer, Oath of Allegiance to Maryland, 1778. (A-35, B-26, J-243)

OFFIELD, JOHN.
　　Drafted, Militia, 1781. (E-132, F-400)

OGLE, ROBERT.
　　Signer, Association of Freemen, 1776, Gunpowder Upper. (I-326)
　　Private, Capt. Bussey's Company, July 20, 1776. (E-127, F-60)

O'HARA, JAMES.
　　Pensioner (maimed soldier), 1778. (F-661)

O'KEIL, GEORGE.
　　Drafted, Militia, 1781. (E-132, F-400)

OLDHAM, HENRY.
　　Signer, Association of Freemen, 1776, Gunpowder Upper. (I-325)
　　Signer, Oath of Allegiance to Maryland, 1778. (A-35, B-23, J-241)

OLIVER, JAMES.
　　Private, Capt. Aquila Hall's Co. No. 4, September 9, 1775. (E-109)
　　Signer, Association of Freemen, 1776, Harford Lower. (I-324)

OLIVER, JAMES SR.
    Signer, Association of Freemen, 1776, Harford Lower. (I-324)

O'MULLAN, PATRICK.
    Private, Capt. Harris' Company Payroll, 1776. (E-130, F-304)

O'NEAL, JOHN.
    Born 1745. Died c.1815. Married Mary Smith in 1777 in
      Montgomery Co., Md. Children: Daniel, Mary Anne, James,
      John, Jane, Charles. (G-550, M-132, X-505)
    Private, Capt. Paca's Co., Harford County, 1776. (E-126, F-59)
    Militia Substitute, 1781, 3 years. (E-133, F-401)

O'NEALE, CHARLES.
    Born 1736, in Ireland. Private, Flying Camp, Lt. John Smith
      enlisted July 15, 1776, in Col. Ewing's Battalion. At time of
      enlistment he was 5'5" tall with short black hair.(E-126,F-56)

O'QUEEN, JAMES.
    Signer, Association of Freemen, 1776, Deer Creek Upper. (I-322)

O'REILLY, LUKE.
    Signer, Association of Freemen, 1775, Bush River Upper. (I-316)

ORR, CHARLES.
    Signer, Association of Freemen, 1775, Bush River Upper. (I-317)

ORR, HUGH.
    Private, Capt. Dorsey's Co. No. 8, October 31, 1775. (E-115)

ORR, JAMES.
    Signer, Association of Freemen, 1776, Bush River Upper. (I-320)
    Signer, Oath of Allegiance to Maryland, 1778. (A-35,B-29,J-246)
    Record indicates there were two signers with this name.

ORR, JOHN.
    Born 1762. Died 1840. Married Elizabeth Johns in 1792 in
      Fayette County, Pennsylvania. (N-120, X-506)
    Drummer, Capt. Rodgers' Co. No. 5, Harford Co., Maryland,
      September 15, 1775. (E-110)

ORR, JOHN.
    Private, Capt. Robert Harris' Co., Harford Rifles, 1776. (E-124)
    Paid subsistence for 3 weeks, 5 days, October 6, 1776. (K-436)
    Signer, Oath of Allegiance to Maryland, 1778. (A-35, B-29, J-246)

ORR (ORE), JOSEPH.
    Signer, Association of Freemen, 1775, Bush River Upper. (I-317)

ORR, THOMAS.
    Private, Capt. Josias Hall's Co. No. 1, September 12, 1775. (E-106)

OSBORN (OSBORNE), BENJAMIN.
    Private, Capt. Aquila Hall's Co. No. 4, Sept. 9, 1775. (E-110)
    Private, Capt. Francis Holland's Harford Rifles, 1776. (E-124)
    (continued)

OSBORN, BENJAMIN (continued)
    Signer, Association of Freemen, 1776, Harford Lower. (I-324)
    Signer, Oath of Allegiance to Maryland, 1778.(A-35, B-14, J-235)

OSBORN, CYRUS.
    Signer, Association of Freemen, 1775, Spesutie Lower. (I-317)
    Ensign, Capt. Dorsey's Co. No. 8, October 31, 1775. (E-114)
    1st Lieutenant, 8th Battalion, 1778. (C-45)
    Signer, Oath of Allegiance to Maryland, 1778. (A-35, B-17, J-237)

OSBORN (OSBORNE), JAMES.
    Harford County Grand Juror, 1779. (E-75)

OSBORN (OSBOURN), JAMES JR.
    Private, Capt. Josias Hall's Co. No. 4, September 12, 1775. (E-106)
    Signer, Association of Freemen, 1776, Harford Lower. (I-324)
    Signer, Oath of Allegiance to Maryland, 1778. (A-35, B-21, J-239)

OSBORN, JOHN.
    Private, Capt. Rodgers' Co. No. 5, September 15, 1775. (E-111)
    Land Warrant 11784, 100 acres, applied June 11, 1795. (N-74)

OSBORN (OSBORNE), SAMUEL GROOME.
    Born 1752. Died c.1794. Married: Mary_____. (X-507)
    Signer, Association of Freemen, 1775, Gunpowder Neck. (I-327)
    Private, Capt. Rumsey's Co. No. 6, September 16, 1775. (E-112)
    2nd Lieutenant, 8th Battalion, 1776. (E-267)
    Ensign, 8th Battalion, 1778. (C-46)
    Signer, Oath of Allegiance to Md., 1778. (A-35, B-18, J-237)
    Administered the Oath, 1778 ("Worshipfull Samuel G. Osborne").
    Harford County Court Justice, March 23, 1779 and 1780.(E-75,76)
    Intendant's Ledger Book 11, pp. 314, 353; Book 12, pp. 19, 35,
       94 (1782-1783). Intendant's Ledger A No. 9, ff. 22, 26, 27, 42;
       No. 10, ff. 4, 44 (1783-1784). Agent's Ledger 1, f.106. (HR-50)

OSBORN, WILLIAM, of Benjamin.
    Private, Capt. Rumsey's Co. No. 6, September 16, 1775. (E-122)
    Signer, Association of Freemen, 1775, Gunpowder Neck. (I-327)
    Signer, Oath of Allegiance to Md., 1778. (A-35, B-14, J-235)

OSBORN (OSBORNE, OSBOURN), WILLIAM.
    Private, Capt. Aquila Hall's Co. No. 4, Sept. 9, 1775. (E-110)
    Signer, Association of Freemen, 1776, Harford Lower. (I-324)
    Signer, Oath of Allegiance to Md., 1778. (A-35, B-21, J-239)

OSBORN (OSBOURN), WILLIAM JR.
    Signer, Association of Freemen, 1776, Harford Lower. (I-324)
    Signer, Oath of Allegiance to Md., 1778. (A-35, B-21, J-239)

OSBOURN, WILLIAM.
    Born 1755, in America. Cadet, Flying Camp, Lt. James Bond
    enlisted July 7, 1776, in Col Ewing's Battalion. At time of
    enlistment he was $5'2\frac{1}{2}"$ tall with short black hair.(E-125,F-54)

OVERMAN, JOHN.
    Militia Substitute, 1781, 3 years. (E-133, F-401)

OVERSTOCK (ACOISTOCK), PETER.
    Born 1696. Residing in Robert Mitchell's residence on Bush
    River in 1776.
    Signer, Oath of Allegiance, 1778. (A-31, B-10, J-233, R)

OWENS, EDWARD.
    Signer, Oath of Allegiance to Maryland, 1778. (A-35,B-20,J-239)

OWENS, JAMES.
    Born 1721. Died c.1786. Married: (1) Eliza_____; (2) Ann
        Pritchard. (X-509)
    Signer, Oath of Allegiance to Md., 1778. (A-35, B-20, J-239)

PACA, AQUILA.
    Born 1738. Died 1788. Married: Ellen Tootle. (X-510)
    Harford County Court Justice, 1774, and 1779. (E-75, E-61)
    Signer, Bush Declaration, March 22, 1775. (D-358)
    Signer, Association of Freemen, 1775, Gunpowder Neck. (I-327)
    Captain, 2nd Battalion, Flying Camp. July, 1776-December,1776;
    Battle of White Plains, October 28, 1776. (E-126, E-137, F-59,
    War Committee, 1775. (D-358)   L-422, K-170)
    Signer, Oath of Allegiance to Maryland, 1778.(A-35,B-17, J-237)
    Administered the Oath, 1778 ("Worshipfull Aquila Paca").
    Lt. Colonel, 23rd Battalion, 1778. (C-44)
    Army Accounts No. 1, p. 49, August 27, 1776. (HR-50)

PACA. AQUILA JR.
    Private, Capt. Josias Hall's Co. No. 1, Sept. 12, 1775. (E-106)
    Signer, Association of Freemen, 1776, Spesutie Lower. (I-318)
    Private, Capt. Francis Holland's Harford Rifles, 1776. (E-124)
    Signer, Oath of Allegiance to Md., 1778. (A-35, B-22, J-240)
    Captain, 23rd Battalion, 1778. "Capt. Paca has a substitute
        and will not serve." (C-31, C-46)

PACA, JAMES.
    Born 1754, Baltimore County, Md. Died 1828, Harford County, Md.
    Married: Ann Reiley; daughter, Elizabeth. (G-556, X-510)
    Private, Capt. Josias Hall's Co. No. 1, Sept. 12, 1775. (E-106)
    Private, Capt. Francis Holland's Harford Rifles, 1776. (E-124)
    Signer, Association of Freemen, 1776, Spesutie Upper. (I-319)

PACA, JOHN. (Captain)
　Born 1712, Died 1785. War Committee, June 11, 1775. (E-95)
　Signer, Oath of Allegiance to Maryland, 1778. (A-35, B-21, J-239)

PACA, WILLIAM.
　Son of Captain John Paca and Elizabeth Smith. (S-368, D-412)
　Born 1740, near Abingdon, Harford County, Md. Died 1799 in Talbot
　County, Md. Married: (1) Mary Chew in 1763, daughter of Samuel
　Chew of Annapolis; died 1774; (2) Ann Harrison of Philadelphia in
　1777 (one source gives Anna Harrison White as his second wife).
　Son, John Philemon Paca. (G-556, X-510, L-422, D-412, S-368)
　Member of Provincial Legislature, 1768; First Continental Congress,
　1774; Second Continental Congress, 1775-1779; Signer of Declaration
　of Independence, 1776; Chief Judge of Superior Court of Maryland,
　1778-1780; Governor of Maryland, 1782-1785; appointed by President
　George Washington as Federal District Judge, 1789-1799. (D-412)
　Harford County Chapter, D.A.R., named in his honor, Bel Air, MD.

PAIN, BARNIT.
　Private, Capt. Love's Co. No. 10, September 14, 1775. (E-116)
　Signer, Oath of Allegiance to Md., 1778. (A-35, B-30, J-247)

PAIN, JOHN.
　Private, Capt. Bond's Co. No. 11, December 9, 1775. (E-117)

PAINE, JOHN.
　Private, Capt. Love's Co. No. 10, September 10, 1775. (E-116)
　Private, Capt. Robert Harris' Harford Rifles, 1776. (E-124)
　Paid subsistence for 3 weeks, 5 days, October 6, 1776. (K-436)
　Signer, Association of Freemen, 1776, Spesutie Upper. (I-318)

PANT (PLANT), STEPHEN.
　Signer, Association of Freemen, 1775 and 1776, Bush River Upper.
　(I-317, I-320)

PARIS (PARRIS), WILLIAM.
　Signer, Association of Freemen, 1776, Bush River Lower. (I-320)
　Signer, Oath of Allegiance to Md., 1778. (A-35, B-10, J-233)

PARK, JOHN.
　Recruit, New Regiment, August 28, 1780.
　"Broke gaol and made his escape." (E-131, F-343)

PARKE, MARTIN.
　Signer, Association of Freemen, 1776, Bush River Upper. (I-320)

PARKER, AQUILA.
　Signer, Association of Freemen, 1776, Eden Hundred. (I-324)
　Signer, Oath of Allegiance to Md., 1778. (A-35, B-23, J-241)

PARKER, JOHN.
　Signer, Association of Freemen, 1776, Bush River Upper. (I-320)
　Signer, Oath of Allegiance to Md., 1778. (A-35, B-23, J-241)

PARKER, JOHN.
　Signer, Association of Freemen, 1776, Eden Hundred. (I-324)

PARKER, MARTIN.
    Sergeant, Capt. Baker's Company No. 15, January 27, 1776,
    Jarrettsville Militia. (E-120)
    Signer, Oath of Allegiance to Md., 1778. (A-35, B-23, J-241)

PARKER, WILLIAM.
    Private, Capt. Baker's Co. No. 15, January 27, 1776. (E-120)
    Signer, Association of Freemen, 1776, Eden Hundred. (I-324)
    Record indicates there were two signers with this name.
    Signer, Oath of Allegiance to Md., 1778. (A-35, B-24, J-242)

PARSONS, ISAAC.
    Signer, Oath of Allegiance to Md., 1778. (A-35, B-19, J-238)

PARSONS, JOHN.
    Born c.1735. Died 1806/7. Married: Rebecca _____.
    Children: Mary, John, Rebecca, Ruth, Ann, Abner, Abraham,
    Amoss, Tace. (G-560, X-518)
    Signer, Oath of Allegiance, 1778. (A-35, B-19, J-238)

PARSONS, JOHN.
    Signer, Oath of Allegiance, 1778. (A-35, B-30, J-247)

PATRICK, GEORGE.
    Private, Capt. Webb's Co. No. 16, October 14, 1775. (E-122)
    Signer, Association of Freemen, 1776, Deer Creek Upper. (I-323)

PATRICK, JOHN.
    Born 1735. Died 1805. Married Elizabeth Cummings in 1765.
    Children: Mary, Elizabeth, Martha, Samuel. (G-562, X-519)
    Signer, Bush Declaration, March 22, 1775. (D-355)
    War Committee, Harford County, 1775. (D-358)
    Signer, Association of Freemen, Deer Creek Lower,
    and Solicitor, 1775/1776. (I-315, I-321)
    Captain of Company No. 17, April 1, 1776. (D-359, E-122, E-266)
    Captain in Deer Creek Battalion, Militia, 1778. (C-44)
    Agents Ledger No. 1, f.106, Captain, Oct. 16, 1781. (HR-50)

PATRICK, JOHN.
    Private, Capt. Robert Harris' Harford Rifles, 1776. (E-124)
    Paid subsistence for 3 weeks, 5 days, Oct. 6, 1776. (K-436)

PATTERSON, GEORGE.
    Signer, Bush Declaration, March 22, 1775. (D-355)
    War Committee, Harford County, 1775. (D-358)
    Signer, Association of Freemen, 1776, Susquehanna. (D-357,E-321)
    1st Lieutenant, Capt. Anderson's Co. No. 3, 1775. (D-359, E-108)
    Captain, 23rd Battalion, Militia, April 9, 1778. (C-32, C-45)
    Signer, Oath of Allegiance to Md., 1778. (A-35, B-22, J-240)
    Intendant's Orders No. 2, f.10, Captain, Oct. 28, 1785. (HR-50)

PATTERSON, JAMES.
    Signer, Association of Freemen, 1776, Bush River Upper. (I-328)
    Signer, Oath of Allegiance to Md., 1778. (A-35, B-29, J-246)

PATTERSON, JOHN.
    Private, Capt. Josias Hall's Co. No. 1, Sept. 12, 1775. (E-105)
    Ensign, 2nd Battalion, Flying Camp, Captain Paca's Company,
        August 5, 1776. (E-126, F-59, L-429, K-170)
    Battle of White Plains, October 28, 1776. (E-137)
    Signer, Oath of Allegiance to Md., 1778. (A-35, B-21, J-239)
    Intendant's Ledger B, ff.99, 144, April, 1785. (HR-50)

PATTERSON, SAMUEL.
    Signer, Association of Freemen, 1776, Bush River Upper. (I-328)
    Signer, Oath of Allegiance, 1778. (A-35, B-29, J-246).
    Record indicates there were two signers with this name.

PATTERSON, WILLIAM.
    Signer, Association of Freemen, 1776, Bush River Upper. (I-328)
    Signer, Oath of Allegiance to Md., 1778. (A-35, B-23, J-241)

PAUL, JAMES.
    Signer, Oath of Allegiance to Md., 1778. (A-35, B-18, J-237)

PAUL, JOHN.
    Signer, Oath of Allegiance to Md., 1778. (A-35, B-18, J-237)

PAYNE, WILLIAM.
    Militia Substitute, 1781. (E-132, F-400)

PEACH, WILLIAM.
    Signer, Association of Freemen, 1776, Harford Lower. (I-324)

PEACOCK, LUKE.
    Married Constant Sicklemore in 1753. (M-136)
    Corporal, Capt. Rigdon's Co. No. 12, December 2, 1775. (E-118)
    Signer, Association of Freemen, 1776, Deer Creek Upper. (I-322)

PEACOCK, SAMUEL.
    Corporal, Capt. Rigdon's Co. No. 12, December 2, 1775, (E-118)
    Private, Capt. Bussey's Company, July 25, 1776. (E-126, F-60)
    Signer, Association of Freemen, 1776, Deer Creek Upper. (I-322)

PEARCE, RICHARD.
    Private, Capt. Dorsey's Co. No. 8, October 31, 1775. (E-115)
    Signer, Association of Freemen, 1776, Spesutie Lower. (I-318)

PEARIS, JOHN.
    Signer, Oath of Allegiance to Md., 1778. (A-35, B-23, J-241)

PEARSON, ABEL.
    Signer, Association of Freemen, 1775/6, Susquehanna. (D-357, I-321)

PEARSON, JOSEPH.
    Private, Capt. Taylor's Co. No. 7, September 9, 1775. (E-114)

PEDEN, JAMES.
    Landowner, in northern Harford County, Md., 1777. (Land Records
    Liber JLG, No. A, folio 85). Patriot from York County, Pa., and
    related to Capt. Hugh Peden of Lancaster (Pa. Archives, 5th Series).

PEIKEN (PICTURN), PHILLIP.
    Private, Capt. Paca's Co., August 5, 1776. (E-127, F-59)

PENCHIEFF, PAUL.
    Signer, Association of Freemen, 1776, Deer Creek Upper. (I-323)

PENCHIEFF, STOPHEL.
    Private,Capt. Webb's Co. No. 16, October 14, 1775. (E-121)
    Signer, Association of Freemen, 1776, Deer Creek Upper. (I-323)

PENDALL, JOHN.
    Militia Substitute, 1781, 3 years. (E-133, F-401)

PENDEGAST (PENDERGRASS), THOMAS.
    Private, Capt. Bond's Co. No. 11, December 9, 1775. (E-117)
    Signer, Association of Freemen, 1776, Bush River Lower. (I-328)

PENNICK, THOMAS.
    Married Ann Almon in 1769. (M-137)
    Private, Capt. Bond's Co. No. 11, September 14, 1775. (E-116)

PENNITH, THOMAS.
    Signer, Oath of Allegiance to Md., 1778. (A-35, B-28, J-245)

PENTENNEY, JOSEPH.
    Signer, Oath of Allegiance to Md., 1778. (A-35, B-21, J-239)

PERKINS, JAMES.
    Private, Capt. Josias Hall's Co. No. 1, Sept. 12, 1775. (E-106)

PERKINS, JOHN.
    Private, Capt. Archer's Co. No. 2, September 16, 1775. (E-107)

PERKINS, RICHARD.
    Private, Capt. Baker's Co. No. 15, January 27, 1776. (E-120)

PERKINS, WILLIAM.
    Signer, Association of Freemen, 1775/6,Susquehanna.(D-357,I-321)
    Ensign, 23rd Battalion under Capt. Hall, Apr.9,1778.(C-45,C-31)

PERRY, JOHN.
    Signer, Association of Freemen, 1776, Harford Lower. (I-324)

PERRY, THOMAS.
    Signer, Oath of Allegiance to Md., 1778. (A-35, B-25, J-242)

PETEEL, THOMAS.
    Signer, Oath of Allegiance to Md., 1778. (A-35, B-19, J-238)

PHILLIPS, JAMES.
    Private, Capt. Aquila Hall's Co. No. 4, Sept. 9, 1775. (E-110)
    Signer, Oath of Allegiance to Md., 1778. (A-35, B-17, J-237)

PHILLIPS, JAMES.
    Private, Capt. Webb's Co. No. 16, October 14, 1775. (E-121)

PHILLIPS, JAMES.
    Recruit, New Regiment, August 1, 1780. (E-131, F-343)

PHIPS, JOHN.
    Private, Capt. Rumsey's Co. No. 6, September 16, 1775. (E-112)

PHIPS (PHIPPS), JOSEPH.
    Signer, Association of Freemen, 1775, Gunpowder Neck. (I-327)
    Signer, Oath of Allegiance to Md., 1778. (A-35, B-20, J-239)

PIKE, HUTCHINS.
    Signer, Association of Freemen, 1776, Harford Hundred. (I-325)
    Signer, Oath of Allegiance to Md., 1778. (A-35, B-22, J-240)

PILLET, THOMAS.
    Signer, Oath of Allegiance to Md., 1778. (A-35, B-30, J-247)

PINNICK, ISAAC.
    Private, Capt. Love's Co. No. 11, September 14, 1775. (E-116)

PINNICK, THOMAS.
    Signer, Association of Freemen, 1776, Spesutie Upper. (I-318)

PITT, FRANCIS LOVEL.
    Private, Capt. Aquila Hall's Co. No. 4, Sept. 9, 1775. (E-109)
    Private, Capt. Francis Holland's Harford Rifles, 1776. (E-124)
    Signer, Association of Freemen, 1776, Harford Lower. (I-324)

PLATT, RALPH.
    Private, Capt. Rodgers' Co. No. 5, September 15, 1775. (E-111)

POAK, SAMUEL.
    Signer, Association of Freemen, 1776, Deer Creek Upper. (I-323)

POCEER, SANIEL.
    Signer, Oath of Allegiance to Md., 1778. (A-35, B-19, J-238)

POCOCK, DANIEL.
    Married Sarah Jones in 1751. (M-141)
    Private, Capt. Baker's Co. No. 15, January 27, 1776. (E-120)
    Signer, Association of Freemen, 1776, Eden Hundred. (I-324)

POCOCK, JAMES.
    Married Jemima Barton in 1756. (M-141)
    Signer, Association of Freemen, 1776, Eden. (I-324)

POLSON (POULSON), JOHN.
    Married Elizabeth Stewart in 1751. (M-142)
    Signer, Oath of Allegiance, 1778. (A-35, B-24, J-242)

POLSON, JOSEPH.
    Married Frances Allen in 1739. (M-142)
    Signer, Oath of Allegiance, 1778. (A-35, B-14, J-236)

POOL, JOHN.
    Private, Capt. Bradford's Co. No. 13, Sept. 30, 1775. (E-119)

POPE, JAMES.
    Pensioner (maimed soldier), 1778. (F-661)

PORTER, CHARLES.
    Private, Capt.Bussey's Company, July 25, 1776. (E-128, F-60)
    Signer, Oath of Allegiance to Md., 1778. (A-35, B-10, J-233)

PORTER, JOHN.
    Private, Capt. Rodgers' Co. No. 5, September 15, 1775. (E-110)

POTEE, PETER.
    Private, Capt. Bond's Co. No. 11, December 9, 1775. (E-117)
    Signer, Association of Freemen, 1776, Bush River Lower. (I-319)

POTEET, JAMES.
    Married Elizabeth Crabtree in 1748. (M-142)
    Signer, Oath of Allegiance, 1778. (A-35, B-30, J-247)

POTEET, THOMAS JR.
    Married Ann McComas in 1762. (M-142)
    Signer, Oath of Allegiance, 1778. (A-35, B-30, J-247)

POTTER, THOMAS, of John.
    Signer, Association of Freemen, 1776, Bush River Upper. (I-320)

POTTS, RICHARD.
    Signer, Association of Freemen, 1776, Susquehanna. (I-321)

POUND, JOHN.
    Maryland Line, last date August 18, 1780. (F-414)

POWER, JOHN.
    Private, Capt. Bradford's Co. No. 13, Sept. 30, 1775. (E-119)

POWER (POWAR), NICHOLAS.
    Signer, Oath of Allegiance to Md., 1778. (A-35, B-25, J-242)

POWER, SAMUEL.
    Private, Capt. Bradford's Co. No. 13, September 30, 1775. (E-119)
    Private, 4th Maryland Regiment, 1776-1779; on furlough March of
    1778; at hospital in Peeks Kill, July-August, 1778.(E-129,F-301)
    Rifleman, Battle of Fort Washington, November 16, 1776. (E-136)
    Signer, Association of Freemen, 1776, Susquehanna. (I-321)

PRALL, EDWARD.
    Signer, Bush Declaration, March 22, 1775. (D-355)
    War Committee, Harford County, 1775. (D-358)
    1st Lieutenant, Capt. Archer's Co. No. 2, 1774-1775.(D-359,E-107)

PREBLE (PRIBLE), JOHN.
    Signer, Association of Freemen, 1776, Deer Creek Lower. (I-322)

PRESBURY, GEORGE JR.
  Signer, Association of Freemen, 1775, Gunpowder Neck. (I-327)

PRESBURY, GEORGE B.
  Private, Capt. Josias Hall's Co. No. 1, Sept. 12, 1775. (E-106)
  Signer, Association of Freemen, 1775, Gunpowder Neck. (I-327)
  Signer, Oath of Allegiance to Md., 1778. (A-35, B-20, J-239)

PRESBURY, GEORGE GOULDSMITH.
  "Goldsmith Presbury" married Elizabeth Tolley in 1756. (M-143)
  Private, Capt. Rumsey's Co. No. 6, September 16, 1775. (E-112)

PRESTON, BARNET.
  Son of Daniel Preston and Ann Grafton. Born 1753. (R)
  Private, Capt. Love's Co. No. 10, September 14, 1775. (E-116)

PRESTON, BERNARD, of Daniel.
  Married Sarah Ruff in 1749. Children: Sarah, Bernard, Mary, Anna.
  Signer, Association of Freemen, 1775, Spesutie Upper, and 1776,
    Bush River Lower. Oath of Allegiance to Maryland, 1778.
  (A-35, B-28, J-245, I-319, I-327, E-77, M-143, R)

PRESTON, BENJAMIN.
  Private, Capt. Bond's Co. No. 11, December 9, 1775. (E-117)

PRESTON, DANIEL.
  Married Ann Grafton in 1737. Children: Margaret, Daniel, Sarah,
    Grafton, Daniel, James, Barnett, Sarah, William, Corbin.
  Signer, Association of Freemen, 1776, Spesutie Upper.
  Signer, Oath of Allegiance to Maryland, 1778.
  (A-35, B-28, I-319, J-245. M-143, R)

PRESTON, GRAFTON.
  Son of Daniel Preston and Ann Grafton. Born 1746. (R)
  1st Lieutenant, Capt. Love's Co. No. 10, Sept. 14, 1775.
  Private, Capt. Bussey's Company, July 20, 1776.
  Signer, Association of Freemen, 1776, Spesutie Upper.
  1st Lieutenant, Deer Creek Battalion, Militia, 1778.
  Signer, Oath of Allegiance to Maryland, 1778.
  (A-35, B-29, C-43, D-359, E-115, I-318, J-246, R)

PRESTON, JAMES.
  Son of Daniel Preston and Ann Grafton. Born 1751. (R)
  Corporal, Capt. Love's Co. No. 10, Sept. 14, 1775. (E-115)
  Lieutenant, Deer Creek Battalion, Militia, 1779. (C-43)

PRESTON, JAMES.
  Married Clemency Bond in 1749. Children: Martin, Mary, Bernard.
  Signer, Association of Freemen, 1776, Spesutie Upper. (I-318, R)

PRESTON, JAMES.
  Born 1713. Married Sarah Putteets/Pottet, 1733. Child: Ann.
  Signer, Oath of Allegiance, 1778. (A-35, B-28, J0245, R)

PRESTON, MARTIN.
    Ensign, Capt. Bond's Co. No. 11, December 9, 1775. (E-116)
    2nd Lieutenant, 8th Battalion, Militia, 1776. (E-266)
    Signer, Association of Freemen, 1776, Bush River Lower. (I-328)
    Signer, Oath of Allegiance to Maryland, 1778. (A-35, B-28, J-245)
    1st Lieutenant, 8th Battalion, Militia, 1778. (C-46)

PRESTON, MARTIN.
    Private, Capt. Love's Co. No. 10, September 9, 1775. (E-116)

PRESTON, WILLIAM.
    Born 1758. Son of Daniel Preston and Ann Grafton. (R)
    Private, Capt. Bussey's Company, July 20, 1776. (E-127, F-60)
    Signer, Oath of Allegiance to Maryland, 1778. (A-35, B-28, J-245)

PRICE, BENJAMIN.
    Signer, Oath of Allegiance to Maryland, 1778. (A-35)

PRICE, DANIEL.
    Private, Capt. Archer's Co. No. 2, September 16, 1775. (E-108)
    Signer, Association of Freemen, 1776, Harford Upper. (I-325)
    Signer, Oath of Allegiance to Maryland, 1778. Record indicates
       two signers with this name. (A-35, B-19, B-25, J-238, J-242)

PRICE, JAMES.
    Private, Capt. Rumsey's Co. No. 6, September 16, 1775. (E-112)
    Signer, Association of Freemen, 1775, Gunpowder Neck. (I-327)

PRICE, JOHN.
    Private, Capt. Bond's Co. No. 11, December 9, 1775. (E-117)

PRICE, NATHAN.
    Drafted, Militia, 1781. (E-132, F-400)

PRICE, ROBERT.
    Signer, Association of Freemen, 1776, Bush River Lower. (I-320)

PRICE, STEPHEN.
    Corporal, Capt. Robert Harris' Company Payroll, 1776. (E-130, F-304)
    Sergeant, Maryland Line (pensioner). (N-43, X-548)
    "Stephen Rickards Price" married Jane Parks. Born 1757. Died 1832.
       Record also indicates he was a Sergeant from Maryland. (X-548)

PRICE, WALTER.
    Signer, Association of Freemen, 1776, Bush River Upper. (I-320)

PRICE, WILLIAM.
    Private, Capt. Rumsey's Co. No. 6, September 16, 1775. (E-112)
    Signer, Association of Freemen, 1775, Gunpowder Neck. (I-327)
    Born 1750, in England. Private, Flying Camp, Capt. James Young
    enlisted in Col. Ewing's Battalion, July 7, 1776. At time of
    enlistment he was 5'3" tall and fullfaced. (E-125, F-55)

PRIGG, EDWARD.
    Signer and solicitor, Association of Freemen, 1775 and 1776,
        Spesutie Upper Hundred. (I-315, I-318, I-319)
    1st Lieutenant, 23rd Battalion, Militia, 1778. (C-46)
    Drafted, Militia, 1781; "Infirm and sickly." (E-132, F-400)
                          Furnished a gun to county, 1776.(E-336)

PRIGG, WILLIAM.
    Married Susan Wells in 1776 in Lancaster County, Pa. Marriage
        proven through Maryland pension application. (N-121)
    Signer, Association of Freemen, 1776, Spesutie Upper. (I-319)
    Ensign, Deer Creek Battalion, under Capt. William Morgan,
        April 9, 1778. Widow applied for pension. (N-43, C-44, C-31)

PRIGG, WILLIAM JR.
    Signer, Association of Freemen, 1776, Deer Creek Upper. (I-323)

PRIM, WILLIAM.
    Signer, Association of Freemen, 1776, Eden Hundred. (I-323)

PRITCHARD, CHARLES.
    Private, Capt. Dorsey's Co. No. 8, October 31, 1775. (E-114)

PRITCHARD, HARMON.
    Signer, Association of Freemen, 1775/1776, Susquehanna. Name
        spelled "Harmon" (D-357) and "Hermon" (I-321) on the lists.
    Private, Capt. Anderson's Co. No. 3, Sept. 23, 1775. (E-108)

PRITCHARD, ELEAZER.
    Private, Capt. Anderson's Co. No. 3, Sept. 23, 1775. (E-108)
    Signer, Association of Freemen, 1776, Susquehanna. (I-321)

PRITCHARD, JAMES.
    Private, Capt. Anderson's Co. No. 3, Sept. 23, 1775. (E-108)
    Signer, Oath of Allegiance, Feb. 26, 1778. (A-35, B-26, J-243)

PRITCHARD, JAMES (Tanner).
    Signer, Association of Freemen, 1776, Susquehanna. (I-321)

PRITCHARD, JAMES JR.
    Signer, Oath of Allegiance to Md., 1778. (A-35, B-25, J-242)

PRITCHARD, JESSE.
    Ensign, Capt. Stewart's Co. No. 9, 1775. (E-115)
    Signer, Association of Freemen, 1776, Bush River Upper. (I-320)
    Ensign, Col. Benjamin Rumsey's Battalion, January 3, 1776,
        upon the resignation of Mathew Talbot. (C-30)

PRITCHARD, OBADIAH (OBEDIAH).
    Signer, Association of Freemen, 1775/1776, Susquehanna Hundred.
    Private, Capt. Anderson's Co. No. 3, September 23, 1775.
    Signer, Oath of Fidelity and Allegiance to Maryland, 1778.
    2nd Lieutenant, 23rd Battalion, Militia, 1778.
    1st Lieutenant, 23rd Battalion, Militia, 1779.
    (A-35, B-25, J-242, C-45, D-357, E-321, E-108, I-321)

PRITCHARD, OBEDIAH.
    Private, Capt. Dorsey's Co. No. 8, October 31, 1775. (E-114)
    Signer, Association of Freemen, 1776, Susquehanna. (I-321)
    Private, Capt. Francis Holland's Harford Rifles, 1776. (E-124)

PRITCHARD, SAMUEL.
    Private, Capt. Dorsey's Co. No. 8, October 31, 1775. (E-114)
    Signer, Association of Freemen, 1776, Spesutie Lower. (I-318)

PRITCHARD, SAMUEL.
    Private, Capt. Rodgers' Co. No. 5, September 15, 1775. (E-111)

PRITCHARD, THOMAS.
    Private, Capt. Dorsey's Co. No. 8, October 31, 1775. (E-114)
    Signer, Oath of Allegiance to Md., 1778. (A-35, B-25, J-242)

PRITCHARD, WILLIAM.
    Private, Capt. Dorsey's Co. No. 8, October 31, 1775. (E-114)
    Private, 4th Maryland Regiment, 1776-1777. (E-129)
    Rifleman, Battle of Fort Washington, November 16, 1776. (E-136)
    Died June 18, 1777. (F-302)

PRITCHETT, JOHN.
    Signer, Association of Freemen, 1776, Bush River Upper. (I-328)

PRYNE, JAMES.
    Signer, Oath of Allegiance to Md., 1778. (A-35, B-19, J-238)

PRYNE, JOHN.
    Signer, Oath of Allegiance to Md., 1778. (A-35, B-19, J-238)

PUGH, HUGH.
    Private, Capt. Love's Co. No. 10, September 14, 1775. (E-116)

PUNTENY (PUNTENEY), JOSEPH.
    Born 1728. Died c.1780. Married: Sarah_____. (X-551)
    Signer, Association of Freemen, 1776, Harford Lower, (I-324)

PYLE, RALPH.
    Private, Capt. Love's Co. No. 10, September 14, 1775. (E-116)
    Signer, Association of Freemen, 1776, Spesutie Upper. (I-319)

PYLE, RALPH JR.
    Signer, Association of Freemen, 1776, Spesutie Upper. (I-319)

QUEEN, JAMES.
    Private, Capt. Rigdon's Company No. 12, December 2, 1775.
    (E-118).

QUINN, JOHN.
    Private, Capt. Taylor's Company No. 7, September 9, 1775.
    (E-113).

QUINN, JOSEPH.
    Pensioner (maimed soldier), 1778. (F-661)
    Pay Certificate No. 81690, $80.00, 2nd Maryland Regiment pay.
    Pay Certificate No. 84855, $43.30, Maryland Regiment paid to
      November 16, 1783.
    Pay Certificate No. 85986, $10.56, Maryland Regiment paid to
      January 1, 1782.
    (P-416)

QUINN, PATRICK.
    Private, 4th Maryland Regiment, 1776-1779.
    Rifleman, Battle of Fort Washington, November 16, 1776.
    Sick and present, July, 1778.
    Pay Certificate No. 85988, $80.00, Maryland Regiment paid to
      January 1, 1782.
    Pay Certificate No. 86881, $67.50, Maryland Regiment paid to
      January 1, 1783.
    (E-129, F-302, E-136, P-416)

QUINNLIN (QUINDIN), JAMES.
    Signer, Association of Freemen, 1776, Spesutie Upper Hundred.
    (I-319)

QUINNLIN (QUINDIN, QUINLAN), PHILLIP.
    Signer, Association of Freemen, 1776, Spesutie Upper Hundred.
    Signer, Oath of Allegiance to Maryland, 1778.
    (A-35, B-10, J-234, I-319)

R

RAIN, BARNET.
    Private, Capt. Robert Harris' Company, 1776. (E-123)
    Paid subsistence for 2 weeks, Oct. 16, 1776. (K-436)

RAMPLY, JAMES.
    Signer, Association of Freemen, 1776, Deer Creek Upper. (I-322)
    Born in England. Married Sarah Gibson, 1771. Died 1817, Harford Co.

RAMSAY, ANDREW.
    Private, Capt. Anderson's Co. No. 3, Sept. 23, 1775. (E-109)

RAMSAY, ANDREW.
    Private, Capt. Patrick's Co. No. 17, April 1, 1776. (E-122)

RAMSAY, WILLIAM.
    Signer, Oath of Allegiance to Md., 1778. (A-35, B-25, J-242)

RAMSEY, ANDREW.
    Private, Capt. Francis Holland's Harford Rifles, 1776. (E-124)
    Ensign, Deer Creek Battalion, Militia, 1779. (C-44)

RANSHER, JAS.
    Ensign, Deer Creek Battalion, Militia, 1779. (C-44)

RANSON, JOHN.
    Militia Substitute, 1781, 3 years. (E-133, F-401)

RATAGAN, PETER.
    Militia Substitute, 1781. (E-132, F-400)

RATTICAN, JAMES.
    Private, Capt. Harris' Company Payroll, 1776. (E-130, F-304)

READING (REDDING), WILLIAM.
    Private, Capt. Aquila Hall's Co. No. 4, Sept. 9, 1775. (E-110)
    Signer, Oath of Allegiance to Md., 1778. (A-35, B-21, J-239)

REARDON, JAMES.
    Signer, Oath of Allegiance to Md., 1778. (A-35, B-17, J-237)

REARDON, JOHN.
    Private, Capt. Harris' Company Payroll, 1776. (E-130, F-304)

REASIN (REASON), JAMES.
    Born 1758, Baltimore County. Died after 1791, Kent Co., Md.
    Married:_____Dulin. Children: William Dulin. (G-601, X-559)
    Signer, Oath of Allegiance, Harford County, 1778.
    Private, Kent County Militia. (A-35, B-22, J-240, X-559)

REAVES (REEVES), NOAH.
    Private, Capt. Bussey's Company, July 25, 1776. (E-128, F-60)
    Signer, Association of Freemen, 1776, Gunpowder Upper. (I-326)

REDDING, WILLIAM.
    Signer, Association of Freemen, 1776, Harford Lower. (I-324)

REDMAN, JAMES.
    Private, Capt. Aquila Hall's Co. No. 4, Sept. 9, 1775. (E-109)
    Signer, Association of Freemen, 1776, Harford Lower. (I-324)

REE, GEORGE.
    Signer, Association of Freemen, 1776, Susquehanna. (I-321)

REED, JOHN SR.
    Signer, Association of Freemen, 1775, Gunpowder Neck. (I-327)

REED, WILLIAM.
    Private, Capt. Rumsey's Co. No. 6, Sept. 16, 1775. (E-112)
    Signer, Association of Freemen, 1775, Gunpowder Neck. (I-327)
    Signer, Association of Freemen, 1776, Harford Upper. (I-325)
    Private, Maryland Line (pensioner). (N-43)

REESE, JOHN.
    Private, Capt. Patrick's Co. No. 17, April 1, 1776. (E-122)

REEVES, JOSIAS.
    Married Letitia Reaven in 1756. (M-148)
    Signer, Oath of Allegiance, 1778. (A-35, B-14, J-236)

REID, PATRICK.
    Private, Capt. Bond's Co. No. 11, December 9, 1775. (E-117)

REILLY, JOHN.
    Signer, Association of Freemen, 1776, Spesutie Upper. (I-319)

RENSHAW, JAS.
    Ensign, Capt. Robert Harris' Harford Rifles, 1776. (E-123)
    2nd Lieutenant, 8th Battalion, Militia, 1778. (C-47)

RENSHAW, JOHN.
    Married Mary Bishop in 1762. (M-148)
    Signer, Association of Freemen, 1776, Eden. (I-323)
    Signer, Oath of Allegiance, 1778. (A-35, B-30, J-247)

RENSHAW, JOSEPH.
    Married Elizabeth Wells in 1742. (M-148)
    Signer, Association of Freemen, 1776, Bush River Lower. (I-328)
    Signer, Oath of Allegiance to Md., 1778. (A-35, B-29, J-246)

RENSHAW, JOSEPH JR.
    Signer, Association of Freemen, 1775, Bush River Upper,
        and Eden Hundred, 1776. (I-316, I-323)
    Signer, Oath of Allegiance, 1778. (A-35, B-29, J-246)

RENSHAW, JOSHUA JR.
    Ensign, 8th Battalion, Militia, 1776. (E-267)

RENSHAW, PHILIP.
    Signer, Association of Freemen, 1775, Bush River Upper. (I-317)
    Signer, Oath of Allegiance to Md., 1778. (A-35, B-30, J-247)

RENSHAW, ROBERT.
    Private, Capt. Francis Holland's Company, 1776. (E-124)
    Signer, Association of Freemen, 1776, Deer Creek Upper. (I-323)

RENSHAW, SAMUEL.
    Signer, Oath of Allegiance to Md., 1778. (A-35, B-30, J-247)

RENSHAW, THOMAS.
    Married Frances Clark in 1739. (M-148)
    Signer, Association of Freemen, 1775, Bush River Upper. (I-317)
    Signer, Oath of Allegiance to Md., 1778. (A-35, B-29, J-246)

REVES, NOAH.
    Signer, Oath of Allegiance to Md., 1778. (A-35, B-24, J-242)

REYNOL, CHRISTOPHER.
    Pensioner (maimed soldier), 1778. (F-661)

RHOADS, GEORGE LERTON.
    Signer, Association of Freemen, 1776, Harford Lower. (I-324)
    Signer, Oath of Allegiance to Md., 1778. (A-35, B-17, J-237)

RHOADES (RHOADS), THOMAS.
    Private, Capt. Love's Co. No. 10, September 14, 1775. (E-116)
    Drafted. Militia, 1781; "a wife and children to support."
      (E-132, F-400)

RHODES (RHOADS), BENJAMIN.
    Private, Capt. Love's Co. No. 10, September 14, 1775. (E-116)
    Private, Capt. Bussey's Company, July 20, 1776. (E-127, F-60)
    Signer, Oath of Allegiance to Md., 1778. (A-35, B-28, J-245)

RICE, JOHN.
    Signer, Association of Freemen, 1776, Bush River Lower. (I-328)

RICE, ROBERT.
    Signer, Association of Freemen, 1776, Bush River Upper. (I-320)

RICE, WALTER.
    Private, Capt. Baker's Co. No. 15, January 27, 1776. (E-120)
    Signer, Oath of Allegiance to Md., 1778. (A-35, B-24, J-242)

RICE, WILLIAM.
    Private, Flying Camp, Lt. John Smith enlisted July 15, 1776,
      in Col. Ewing's Battalion. Born 1738 in England. At time
      of enlistment he was 5' 9 3/4" tall with sandy hair. (E-125, F-56)
    Private, Capt. Aquila Hall's Co. No. 4, Sept. 9, 1775. (E-110)
    Signer, Association of Freemen, 1776, Bush River Upper. (I-320)

RICHARDS, BENJAMIN.
Signer, Association of Freemen, 1776, Deer Creek Upper.(I-322)

RICHARDSON, BENJAMIN.
Married Jemima Standiford in 1753. (M-150)
Signer, Oath of Allegiance, 1778. (A-35, B-19, J-238)

RICHARDSON, DANIEL.
Private, Capt. Josias Hall's Co. No. 1, Sept. 12, 1775. (E-106)
Private, Capt. Francis Holland's Harford Rifles, 1776. (E-124)
Signer, Association of Freemen, 1776, Harford Hundred. (I-325)

RICHARDSON, HENRY.
Signer, Association of Freemen, 1776, Gunpowder Upper. (I-326)
Signer, Oath of Allegiance to Md., 1778. (A-35, B-12, J-234)

RICHARDSON, JAMES.
Private, Capt. Baker's Co. No. 15, January 27, 1776. (E-120)

RICHARDSON, SAMUEL.
Private, Capt. Rodgers' Co. No. 5, September 15, 1775. (E-111)
Born 1753. Private, Maryland Line; pensioner. (N-44, N-76)
Signer, Association of Freemen, 1776, Deer Creek Upper. (I-322)
Signer, Oath of Allegiance to Md., 1778. (A-35, B-19, J-238)
Pay Certificates No. 81696, $80, 2nd Md. Regt.; No. 82422, $43.30,
2nd Md. Regt.; No. 86038, $80, Md. Regt. to January 1, 1782; No.
89271, $80, 3rd Md. Regt. (P-427)

RICHARDSON, THOMAS.
Signer, Association of Freemen, 1776, Gunpowder Upper. (I-326)
Signer, Oath of Allegiance to Md., 1778. (A-35, B-12, J-235)

RICHARDSON, THOMAS JR.
Private, Capt. Taylor's Co. No. 7, September 9, 1775. (E-113,N-76)
Signer, Association of Freemen, 1776, Gunpowder Upper.(I-326)

RICHARDSON, VINCENT.
Born in Maryland. Died c.1776. Married Martha Norris in 1771.
Children: Benjamin, Harriet, Arnold, Cynthia. (G-608, M-150)
Ensign, Capt. Taylor's Co. No. 7, September 9, 1775. (E-113)
Signer, Association of Freemen, 1776, Gunpowder Upper. (I-326)
Killed in an early battle, 1776. (G-608)

RICHARDSON, VINCENT.
Private, Capt.Taylor's Co. No. 7, September 9, 1775. (E-113)
Signer, Oath of Allegiance to Md., 1778. (A-35, B-12, J-234)

RICHARDSON, WILLIAM.
Private,Capt. Taylor's Co. No. 7, September 9, 1775. (E-113)
Signer, Association of Freemen, 1776, Gunpowder Upper. (I-326)
Signer, Oath of Allegiance to Md., 1778. (A-35, B-12, J-235)

RICHARDSON, WILLIAM.
Signer, Oath of Allegiance to Md., 1778. (A-35, B-30, J-247)

RICHMAN, SAMUEL.
    Private, Capt. Taylor's Co. No. 7, September 9, 1775. (E-113)

RICKETS, BENJAMIN.
    Born 1724. Died 1788. Married: (1) Eleanor Maxwell in 1746;
    (2) Mary Cutchin in 1759. (X-570, M-151)
    Private, Capt. Bradford's Co. No. 13, Sept. 30, 1775. (E-119)

RICKETTS, SAMUEL.
    Born 1731. Died 1799. Married Hannah Mead in 1753. (X-570)
    Children: Ann, Edward, Catherine, Samuel Jr. (G-509, M-151)
    Furnished musquets to the Harford County Committee of Safety.

RIDDLE, JOHN.
    Signer, Oath of Allegiance to Md., 1778. (A-35, B-30, J-247)

RIELY, BARNARD.
    Private, Capt. Taylor's Co. No. 7, September 9, 1775. (E-113)
    Signer, Association of Freemen, 1776, Gunpowder Upper. (I-326)

RIELY, NARMT (N. RIELY)
    Signer, Oath of Allegiance to Md., 1778. (A-36, B-17, J-237)

RIGBIE (RIGBY), JAMES, COLONEL.
    Hosted General Lafayette and his troops at his home in Harford
    County, on their march to Yorktown on April 13, 1781. (D-363,E-140)

RIGDON, ALEXANDER.
    Born 1742. Died 1820. Married Ann Johnson in 1781. Daughter Ann
    married James G. Amoss; daughter Elizabeth married Abraham Amoss.
    Signer, Bush Declaration, March 22, 1775. War Committee, 1775.
    Captain of Company No. 12, Militia, December 2, 1775.
    Signer and solicitor, Association of Freemen, 1776, Deer Creek.
    Lt.Colonel, Deer Creek Battalion, Militia, Harford County, 1778.
    Harford County Petit Juror, 1783.
    (C-43, D-355, D-359, E-118, E-77, E-262, I-315, I-322. R)

RIGDON, BAKER.
    Private, Capt. Webb's Co. No. 16, October 14, 1775. (E-121)
    Signer, Association of Freemen, 1776, Deer Creek Upper. (I-323)

RIGDON, BENJAMIN.
    Signer, Association of Freemen, 1776, Deer Creek Upper. (I-322)
    Ensign, Deer Creek Battalion, Militia, 1778. (C-44)

RIGDON, CHARLES.
    Signer, Oath of Allegiance to Md., 1778. (A-36, B-17, J-237)

RIGDON, JAMES.
    Born 1762. Private, Militia; widow filed for pension. (N-44)
    Private, Capt. Love's Co. No. 10, September 14, 1775. (E-116)
    Private, Capt. Robert Harris' Harford Rifles, 1776. (E-123)
    Paid subsistence for 2 weeks, 6 days, Oct. 16, 1776. (K-436)
    Land Warrant No. 26913, 215 acres. (N-76)
    Signer, Association of Freemen, 1776, Spesutie Upper. (I-318)
    Signer, Oath of Allegiance to Md., 1778. (A-36, B-13, J-235)

RIGDON, STEPHEN.
    Private, Capt. Rigdon's Co. No. 12, December 2, 1775. (E-118)
    Signer, Association of Freemen, 1776, Deer Creek Upper. (I-322)

RIGDON, THOMAS BAKER SR.
    Signer, Association of Freemen, 1776, Deer Creek Upper. (I-322)

RIGDON, WILLIAM.
    Private, Capt. Rigdon's Co. No. 12, December 2, 1775. (E-118)
    Signer, Association of Freemen, 1776, Deer Creek Upper. (I-322)
    Captain, Deer Creek Battalion, Militia, 1778. (C-44)

RIGGS, JOHN.
    Signer, Association of Freemen, 1776, Harford Lower. (I-324)

RILEY, CHARLES.
    Private, Capt. Taylor's Co. No. 7, September 9, 1775. (E-113)

ROADS, BENJAMIN.
    Signer, Association of Freemen, 1776, Spesutie Upper. (I-318)

ROADS, THOMAS.
    Private, Capt. Robert Harris' Co., Harford Rifles, 1776. (E-123)
    Paid subsistence for 2 weeks, October 16, 1776. (K-436)
    Signer, Association of Freemen, 1776, Spesutie Upper. (I-319)
    Signer, Oath of Allegiance to Md., 1778. (A-36, B-30, J-247)

ROBBARDS, WILLIAM.
    Signer, Association of Freemen, 1776, Deer Creek Upper. (I-322)

ROBERTS, BILLINGSLEY.
    Married Betty Manen in 1758. (M-152)
    Constable, Gunpowder Lower. 1774. (E-64)
    Signer, Association of Freemen, 1775, Gunpowder Neck. (I-327)
    Signer, Oath of Allegiance to Md., 1778. (A-36, B-20, J-239)

ROBERTS, JOHN.
    Private, Capt. Rigdon's Co. No. 12, December 2, 1775. (E-118)
    Signer, Association of Freemen, 1775, Gunpowder Neck, and
      Deer Creek Upper, 1776. (I-322, I-327)
    Private, Capt. Bussey's Company, July 25, 1776. (E-128, F-60)
    Signer, Oath of Allegiance to Md., 1778. (A-36, B-19, J-238)

ROBERTS, STEPHEN.
    Signer, Association of Freemen, 1775, Gunpowder Neck. (I-327)

ROBERTS, WILLIAM.
    Born 1751. Private, Maryland Line; pensioner. (N-44)
    Land Warrant No. 11628, 100 acres, February 1, 1790. (N-77)
    Private, Capt. Rigdon's Co. No. 12, December 2, 1775. (E-118)
    Signer, Oath of Allegiance to Md., 1778. (A-36, B-23, J-241)

ROBERTSON, DANIEL.
    Married Elizabeth Webster in 1768. (S-369)
    Signer, Association of Freemen, 1776, Harford Upper. (I-325)

ROBINS, JOB.
    Signer, Association of Freemen, 1776, Gunpowder Upper. (I-325)
    Signer, Oath of Allegiance to Md., 1778. (A-36, B-24, J-242)

ROBINSON, ABRAHAM.
    Married Sarah Simpson in 1744. (M-153)
    Private, Capt. Anderson's Co. No. 3, Sept. 23, 1775. (E-108)
    Signer, Association of Freemen, 1775/6, Susquehanna. (D-357,I-321)

ROBINSON, ARCHIBALD.
    Signer, Association of Freemen, 1776, Bush River Upper. (I-320)
    Signer, Oath of Allegiance to Md., 1778. (A-36, B-29, J-246)

ROBINSON, CHARLES.
    Signer, Oath of Allegiance to Md., 1778. (A-36, B-23, J-241)

ROBINSON, EDWARD.
    Private, Capt. Baker's Co. No. 15, January 27, 1776. (E-120)
    Signer, Association of Freemen, 1776, Gunpowder Upper. (I-325)
    Signer, Oath of Allegiance to Md., 1778. (A-36, B-23, J-241)

ROBINSON, JAMES.
    Signer, Association of Freemen, 1775/1776, Bush River Upper.
    (I-317, I-320)

ROBINSON, JOHN.
    Signer, Association of Freemen, 1776, Spesutie Upper. (I-318)
    Signer, Oath of Allegiance to Md., 1778. (A-36, B-30, J-247)

ROBINSON, JOSEPH (Quaker).
    Signer, Association of Freemen, 1776, Spesutie Upper. (I-319)
    Signer, Oath of Allegiance to Md., 1778. (A-36, B-28, J-245)

ROBINSON, RICHARD, of Edward.
    Private, Capt. Baker's Co. No. 15, January 27, 1776. (E-120)
    Signer, Association of Freemen, 1776, Gunpowder Upper. (I-325)
    Signer, Oath of Allegiance to Md., 1778. (A-36, B-23, J-241)
    Harford County Grand Juror in 1779 and 1783. (E-75, E-77)

ROBINSON, THOMAS.
    Private, Capt. Taylor's Co. No. 7, September 9, 1775. (E-114)

ROBINSON, WILLIAM.
    Private, Capt. Taylor's Co. No. 7, September 9, 1775. (E-113)
    Signer, Association of Freemen, 1776, Bush River Upper. (I-320)
    Signer, Oath of Allegiance to Md.,1778. (A-36, B-23, J-239)

ROBINSON, WILLIAM.
    Private, Capt. Paca's Company, July 24, 1776. (E-126, F-59)
    Signer, Association of Freemen, 1776, Harford Lower. (I-324)

ROBINSON, WILLIAM SR.
    Signer, Association of Freemen, 1776, Gunpowder Upper. (I-326)
    Signer, Oath of Allegiance to Md., 1778. (A-36, B-24, J-242)
    Harford County Petit Juror, 1783. (E-77)

ROBINSON, WILLIAM JR.
    Signer, Association of Freemen, 1776, Gunpowder Upper. (I-325)
    Signer, Oath of Allegiance to Md., 1778. (A-36, B-23, J-241)

ROBSON, RICHARD.
    Signer, Oath of Allegiance to Md., 1778. (A-36, B-29, J-246)

ROCKHOLD, ASAEL.
    Married Anne Rowe (Roe) in 1749. (M-154)
    Signer, Oath of Allegiance, 1778. (A-36, B-24, J-242)

ROCKHOLD, CHARLES.
    Private, Capt. Baker's Co. No. 15, January 27, 1776. (E-120)

ROCKHOLD, JOHN.
    Private, Capt. Baker's Co. No. 15, January 27, 1776. (E-120)
    Signer, Association of Freemen, 1776, Eden Hundred. (I-324)

ROCKHOLD, JOHN JR.
    Signer, Oath of Allegiance to Md., 1778. (A-36, B-24, J-242)

ROCKHOLD, NAT.
    Signer, Association of Freemen, 1776, Bush River Upper. (I-320)

ROCKHOLD, THOMAS.
    Signer, Association of Freemen, 1776, Gunpowder Upper. (I-326)

ROCKWELL, ASELL.
    Private, Capt. Bussey's Company, July 25, 1776. (E-128, F-60)

RODGERS, ALEXANDER.
    Signer, Association of Freemen, 1775, Bush River Upper. (I-316)

RODGERS, JOHN. (Emigrated from Scotland in 1755. D-417)
    Born c.1726. Died 1791. Married c.1760 to Elizabeth Reynolds.
    Children: Alexander, John, Thomas Reynolds, George Washington,
    Maria Ann, Mary, Rebecca. (G-619, X-578)   Colonel. (D-417)
    Signer and solicitor, Association of Freemen, 1775, Susquehanna,
      and 1776, Gunpowder Upper ("John Rodges"). (I-326,I-315,E-263)
    Captain of Company No. 5, Militia, September 15, 1775. (D-359,
      (E-110) under Col. Francis Holland and Major John B. Hall.
    Captain, 23rd Battalion, Militia, 1776-1778. (C-44, K-413)
    Captain, Army Accounts No. 1, p. 52, June 17, 1778. (HR-50)

ROE, WILLIAM.
    Signer, Association of Freemen, 1776, Gunpowder Upper. (I-326)

ROGERS, GEORGE.
    Private, Capt. Webb's Co. No. 16, October 14, 1775. (E-121)
    Signer, Association of Freemen, 1776, Deer Creek Upper. (I-323)

ROGERS, JOHN.
    Private, Capt. Bussey's Company, July 27, 1776. (E-128, F-60)
    Signer, Association of Freemen, 1775/1776, Bush River Upper.
    (I-316, I-328)

ROGERS, MICHAEL.
    Maryland Line, last date June, 1780. (F-414)

ROGERS, OWEN.
    Signer, Association of Freemen, 1776, Bush River Upper. (I-328)
    Signer, Oath of Allegiance to Md., 1778. (A-36, B-29, J-246)

ROGERS, ROBERT.
    Signer, Association of Freemen, 1776, Bush River Lower. (I-319)
    Signer, Oath of Allegiance to Md., 1778. (A-36, B-12, J-234)

ROGERS, THOMAS.
    Signer, Oath of Allegiance to Md., 1778. (A-36, B-10, J-234)

ROLSTON, ALEXANDER.
    Signer, Association of Freemen, 1776, Deer Creek Lower. (I-322)

RONEY, JOHN.
    Signer, Oath of Allegiance to Md., 1778. (A-36, B-26, J-243)

ROOT, DANIEL.
    2nd Lieutenant, Deer Creek Battalion, Militia, April 9, 1778.
        "Left State."   (C-34, C-44)

ROSE, ISAAC.
    Born c.1748. Died 1822. Married: Margaret Leyde. (X-581)
    Corporal, 1st Company of Maryland Riflemen under Colonel
        Moses Rawlings, 1776. (D-361)
    Signer, Association of Freemen, 1776, Bush River Lower. (I-328)
    Private, Capt. Bond's Co. No. 11, December 9, 1775. (E-117)
    Sergeant, 4th Maryland Regiment, appointed June 1, 1777; sick
        at New Hackensack, October, 1778. (E-129, F-301)
    Fought at Battle of Fort Washington, November 16, 1776. (E-136)

ROSE, JOHN.
    1st Lieutenant, Capt. Bradford's Co. No. 13, 1776. (D-359)

ROSE, JOSEPH.
    1st Lieutenant, Capt. Bradford's Co. No. 13, Sept. 30, 1775. (E-119)
    1st Lieutenant, 23rd Battalion, April 9, 1778, Militia. (C-34, C-45)
    Signer, Oath of Allegiance to Maryland, 1778. (A-36, B-10, J-233)

ROSE, REUBEN.
    Signer, Association of Freemen, 1776, Harford Hundred. (I-325)

ROSE, WILLIAM.
    Corporal, Capt. Rigdon's Co. No. 12, December 2, 1775. (E-118)

ROSS, REUBEN.
    Born 1760. Died c.1832. Married: Henrietta Biven. (X-582)
    Another source states he was born 1758; pensioner. (N-45)
    Private, Capt. Bradford's Co. No. 13, Sept. 30, 1775. (E-119)
    Private, 4th Maryland Regiment, 1776-1777; Hospital, September,
        1777-October, 1777. (E-129, F-301)
    Rifleman, Battle of Fort Washington, November 16, 1776. (E-136)

ROSS, WILLIAM.
    Private, Capt. Bradford's Co. No. 13, Sept. 30, 1775. (E-119)
    Private, Capt. Francis Holland's Harford Rifles, 1776. (E-124)
    Signer, Association of Freemen, 1776, Bush River Lower. (I-320)

ROWLAND (ROWLIN), HENRY.
    Private, 4th Maryland Regiment, 1776-1779. (E-129, F-302)
    Rifleman, Battle of Fort Washington, November 16, 1776. (E-136)
    Furlough, March, 1778; Waiter, September, 1778; Furlough,
      November 15, 1778-February, 1779. (E-302)

ROWNTREE, THOMAS.
    Private, Capt. Archer's Co. No. 2, September 16, 1775. (E-108)
    Signer, Oath of Allegiance to Md., 1778. (A-36, B-25, J-242)

RUCKMAN, JOHN.
    Private, Capt. Love's Co. No. 10, September 14, 1775. (E-116)
    Signer, Association of Freemen, 1776, Spesutie Upper. (I-319)

RUCKMAN, JOHN.
    Private, Capt. Bond's Co. No. 11, December 9, 1775. (E-117)

RUFF, HENRY.
    Born 1729. Died 1815. Married Hannah Preston in 1757. (R)
    Signer, Association of Freemen, 1776, Spesutie Upper. (I-319)
    Son of Richard Ruff and Sarah Peverlye. Buried at Watters
      Memorial Church near Thomas Run Road, Harford County. (R)

RUFF, HENRY JR.
    Private, Capt. Bond's Co. No. 11, December 9, 1775. (E-117)
    Son of Henry Ruff and Hannah Preston. Buried with father. (R)
    Born 1760. Died 1845. Married Anna Preston in 1788.
    Children: James, Sarah Watters, Elizabeth Bull, Hannah Whitaker.
      (Data from his will, and records in Maryland Historical Soc.)
    Signer, Oath of Allegiance to Maryland, 1778. (A-36, B-10, J-233)

RUFF, JOHN.
    Private, Capt. Aquila Hall's Co. No. 4, Sept. 9, 1775. (E-109)
    Signer, Association of Freemen, 1776, Harford Lower. (I-324)
    Signer, Oath of Allegiance to Md., 1778. (A-36, B-22, J-240)
    1st Lieutenant, 23rd Battalion, 1778; Captain, 1779. (C-45)

RUFF, RICHARD.
    Private, Capt. Josias Hall's Co. No. 1, Sept. 12, 1775. (E-105)
    Signer, Association of Freemen, 1775/1776, Harford Upper. Oath
      of Allegiance to Md., 1778. (A-36, B-21, J-239, D-357, I-325)

RUMAGE, GEORGE.
    Married Mary Noble in 1754. (M-157)
    Signer, Oath of Allegiance to Md., 1778. (A-36, B-10, J-233)

RUMSEY, BENJAMIN.
Attorney-at-Law, Harford County, beginning in 1774, and later a
distinguished Judge. (E-63 and Historic Marker in Joppatowne)
War Committee, Correspondence, June 11, 1775. (D-358, E-95)
Signer, and solicitor, Association of Freemen, 1775, Gunpowder
Neck, and 1776, Gunpowder Lower. (E-263, I-327)
Captain of Company No. 6, Militia, September 16, 1775. (D-359,E-112)
Harford County Council of Safety, July 6, 1776. (K-1)
Letter, dated September 18, 1776, from Rumsey to the Md. Council:
"I sett from our place of meeting to attend six companies
tomorrow at Deer Creek....and to endeavour to inspire as
many as I can with a love of their country and desire to
serve her..." (K-282)
Colonel. (K-294) Member of Continental Congress, 1776-1778.
1782-1784: Intendant's Ledger A No. 10, f. 24; Intendant's Orders
No. 1, f. 35, 6a; Intendant's Orders No. 2, f.8; Intendant's Letter
Book 10, p. 60; Book 11, p. 353. (HR-50)

RUMSEY, JOHN.
War Committee, Correspondence, June 11, 1775. (D-358, E-96)
Private, Capt. Josias Hall's Co. No. 1, Sept. 12, 1775. (E-106)
Signer, Association of Freemen, 1776, Susquehanna. (E-263)

RUSS, HENRY.
Drafted, Militia, 1781; "Never taken up." (E-132, F-400)

RUSSELL, JAMES.
Signer, Association of Freemen, 1776, Bush River Upper. (I-328)

RUSSELL (RUSSEL), THOMAS.
Signer, Association of Freemen, 1776, Bush River Upper. (I-328)
Signer, Oath of Allegiance to Md.,1778. (A-36, B-29, J-246)

RUTH, JOSEPH.
Signer, Association of Freemen, 1776, Harford Upper. (I-325)
signer, Oath of Allegiance to Md., 1778. (A-36, B-10, J-233)

RUTH, MOSES SR.
Signer, Association of Freemen, 1776, Harford Upper. (I-325)
Signer, Oath of Allegiance to Md., 1778. (A-35, B-17, J-237)

RUTH, MOSES JR.
Private, Capt. Bond's Co. No. 11, December 9, 1775. (E-117)
Signer, Association of Freemen, 1776, Bush River Lower. (I-328)
Signer, Oath of Allegiance to Md., 1778. (A-36, B-12, J-234)

RUTLEDGE, ABRAM (ABRAHAM).
Private, Capt. Baker's Co. No. 15, January 27, 1776. (E-120)
Signer, Association of Freemen, 1776, Eden Hundred. (I-324)

RUTLEDGE, JOHN.
Signer, Association of Freemen, 1776, Eden Hundred. (I-324)
Signer, Oath of Allegiance to Md., 1778. (A-36, B-24, J-242)
Harford County Grand Juror, 1779. (E-75)

RUTLEDGE, JOSHUA.
    Born 1759. Died 1825. Married Augusta Biddle in 1789.
    Children: Elizabeth, Edward, Abraham, John Biddle, Joshua Jr.,
      Nancy, Mary (or May), Jacob, Ruth, James, Thomas. (G-624)
    Entered Army at age 19. 2nd Lieutenant, 4th Maryland Regiment,
      May 1, 1780. Captured in one of the campaigns in Camden, SC,
      and was imprisoned in the British Hulks in Charleston Harbor,
      August 16, 1780; exchanged in December, 1780. (H-126, R)
    Records in the Maryland Historical Society indicate that "he told
      Otho Scott, a prominent Bel Air lawyer, that the most delicious
      morsel he had ever eaten in his life was a biscuit on which some
      lard was spread in place of butter, given him by a woman in
      Charleston after he left the British ship."
    Later granted by the State certain tracts of wild land west of
      Fort Cumberland in Allegheny (now Garrett) County, Maryland,
      for his Revolutionary War services. He moved to Washington
      County but returned to Harford County. (R)
    Retained in Gunby's Battalion, April 12, 1783. (H-126)
    Lieutenant, Maryland Line; widow applied for pension. (N-45)
    Pay Certificates for Md. Officers: 82946, $10.20; 82947, $187.66;
      82948, $173.30; 82949, $500.00; 82950, $500.00; 82951, $500.00;
      92952, $73.30. (P-442)
    1780-1784: Army Ledger No. 1, f.72; No. 2, f.124,136; No. 3, f.14;
      Pay Account No. 1, p. 13; Depreciation Pay No. 1, p.51; No. 2,
      p.91; No. 3, p.129; Intendant's Ledger A No.10; f.63. (HR-50)
    Original Member of the Society of the Cincinnati of Maryland, and,
      in later life, referred to as Colonel Rutledge. (H-126, R)

RUTLEDGE, MICHAEL.
    Married Elinor Deason in 1765. (M-157)
    Private, Capt. Baker's Co. No. 15, January 17, 1776. (E-120)

RUTLEDGE, THOMAS.
    Private, Capt. Baker's Co. No. 15, January 27, 1776. (E-120)

RUTLEDGE, WILLIAM.
    Private, Capt. Bussey's Company, July 25, 1776. (E-128, F-60)
    Signer, Association of Freemen, 1776, Bush River Upper. (I-320)

RUTTER, RICHARD.
    Private, Capt. Anderson's Co. No. 3, Sept. 23, 1775. (E-108)

RYAN (RYON), JOHN.
    Private, Capt. Paca's Company, August 5, 1776. (E-127, F-59)
    Signer, Association of Freemen, 1776, Harford Lower. (I-324)

RYDON, GEORGE.
    Private, Capt. Love's Co. No. 10, September 14, 1775. (E-116)

RYLIE (REILLY), NICHOLAS.
    Born 1749, in Ireland. Private, Flying Camp, Capt. Jas. Young
    enlisted, July 7, 1776, in Col. Ewing's Battalion. At time of
    enlistment he was 5' $3\frac{1}{2}$" tall, with a sandy complexion.
    (E-125, F-55)

SADLER, JAMES NORRIS.
    Signer, Oath of Allegiance to Md., 1778. (A-36, B-29, J-246)

SAIN,_____.
    Signer, Oath of Allegiance to Md., 1778. (B-30, J-247)

ST. CLAIR, JAMES.
    2nd Lieutenant, 8th Battalion, Militia, 1776. (E-267)

ST. CLAIR, WILLIAM.
    Signer, Oath of Allegiance to Md., 1778. (A-36, B-10, J-234)

ST. GOODMAN, CHARLES.
    Signer, Association of Freemen, 1776, Bush River Lower. (I-319)

SANDERS, JAMES.
    Signer, Association of Freemen, 1776, Bush River Lower. (I-320)

SANDERS, JOSEPH.
    Capt. Harris' Company, Harford Rifles. Paid subsistence for
    5 weeks, 5 days, September 26, 1776. (K-436)

SAPPINGTON, RICHARD, M.D.
    Born 1749/1755, Anne Arundel Co., Md. Died 1828, Harford Co., Md.
    Married: (1) Margaret Hamilton; (2) Cassandra Frances Durbin, in
    1784. Children: John, William, Gerrard, Robert, Mary, John K.,
    Edward, Thomas, Frederick. (G-628, X-592, N-122)
    Surgeon Assistant (Mate), 3rd Maryland Regiment, Feb. 20, 1777.
    Resigned January 11, 1779. Appointed by Council to full
    surgeoncy, August, 1780. Served in Army until 1782.
    Surgeon, 3rd Regiment; wounded in war. (G-628, H-127, N-45)
    Pay Certificate No. 93642, $56.23, paid up to July 1, 1784.(P-445)

SARGENT, WILLIAM JR.
    Private, Capt. Taylor's Co. No. 7, September 9, 1775. (E-113)

SARGENT, WILLIAM SR.
    Private, Capt. Taylor's Co. No. 7, September 9, 1775. (E-113)

SAUNDERS, JOHN.
    Private, Capt. Taylor's Co. No. 7, September 9, 1775. (E-113)

SAUNDERS, JOSEPH.
    Private, Capt. Bond's Co. No. 11, December 9, 1775. (E-117)
    Private, Capt. Robert Harris' Harford Rifles, 1776. (E-123)
    Signer, Association of Freemen, 1776, Bush River Lower. (I-320)

SAUNDERS, JOSHUA.
    Sergeant, 1st Company of Maryland Riflemen under Colonel Moses
    Rawlings. (D-361)
        (continued)

SAUNDERS, JOSHUA (continued)
    Sergeant, 4th Maryland Regiment, 1776-October, 1777.(E-129,F-301)
    In hospital, October, 1777-no further record. (F-301)
    Fought at Battle of Fort Washington, November 16, 1776. (E-136)
    Signer, Association of Freemen, 1776, Bush River Lower. (I-319)

SAUNDERS, ROBERT.
    Signer, Oath of Allegiance to Md., 1778. (A-36, B-14, J-236)

SAUNDERS, THOMAS. (Farmer)
    Signer, Association of Freemen, 1776, Bush River Lower. (I-320)
    Signer, Oath of Allegiance to Md., 1778. (A-36, B-10, J-233)

SAUNDERS, THOMAS.
    Signer, Association of Freemen, 1776, Gunpowder Upper. (I-326)

SAUNDERS, WILLIAM.
    Born 1751. Private, Maryland Line; wounded; pensioner. (N-46)
    Private, Capt. Bradford's Co. No. 13, Sept. 30, 1775. (E-119)
    Private, Capt. Paca's Company, July 24, 1776. (E-126, F-59)
    Signer, Association of Freemen, 1776, Bush River Lower. (I-320)
    Signer, Oath of Allegiance to Md., 1778. (A-36, B-10, J-233)

SAVAGE, BARTHOLOMEW.
    Private, Capt. Love's Co. No. 10, September 14, 1775. (E-116)
    Signer, Association of Freemen, 1776, Spesutie Upper. (I-319)

SCANTLIN, JOHN.
    Private, Capt. Patrick's Co. No. 17, April 1, 1776. (E-122)

SCARBOROUGH, EUCLIDUS SR.
    Born 1714, Bucks County, Pa. Died 1808, Harford County, Md.
    Married Mary Dean, in 1744. Children: Isaac, John, Euclidus,
        William, Joseph, Thomas, Mary, Sarah, Hannah, Samuel, James.
    Private, Capt. Patrick's Co. No. 17, April 1, 1776.
    Signer, Association of Freemen, 1776,Deer Creek Upper.
    (E-122, I-323, G-621, X-596, O-16)

SCARBOROUGH, EUCLIDUS JR.
    Private, Capt. Wm.Webb's Co. No. 16, October 14, 1775. (E-121)

SCARBOROUGH, JOHN.
    Private, Capt. Webb's Company No. 16, October 14, 1775. (E-121)
    Signer, Association of Freemen, 1776, Deer Creek Upper. (I-323)
                                                              (O-25)
SCARBOROUGH, JOSEPH.
    Signer, Association of Freemen, 1776, Deer Creek Upper. (I-323)

SCARBOROUGH, SAMUEL.
    Militia Substitute, 1781 (deserted). (E-132, F-400)

SCARBOROUGH, THOMAS.
    Private, Capt. Patrick's Co. No. 17, April 1, 1776. (E-122)

SCARBOROUGH, WILLIAM.
    Private, Capt. Patrick's Co. No. 17, April 1, 1776. (E-122)

SCARFF, BENJAMIN.
    Married Ann Bayley in 1763. (M-159)
    Private, Capt. Rumsey's Co. No. 6, Sept. 16, 1775. (E-112)
    Signer, Association of Freemen, 1775, Gunpowder Neck. (I-327)
    Signer, Oath of Allegiance to Md., 1778. (A-36, B-14, J-235)

SCARFF, HENRY.
    Private, Capt. Baker's Co. No. 15, January 27, 1776. (E-120)
    Signer, Association of Freemen, 1776, Eden Hundred. (I-324)

SCARFF (SCARF), JOHN.
    Signer, Association of Freemen, 1776, Gunpowder Upper. (I-325)
    Signer, Oath of Allegiance to Md., 1778. (A-36, B-24, J-242)
    Ensign, 8th Battalion, Militia, 1778. (C-46)

SCARFF, JOHN, son of John.
    Signer, Association of Freemen, 1776, Gunpowder Upper. (I-326)

SCARY, MARTIN.
    Private, Capt. Bussey's Company, July 25, 1776. (E-128, F-60)

SCHARFF, HENRY.
    Private, Capt. Baker's Co. No. 15, January 27, 1776. (E-120)

SCHIVINGTON, THOMAS.
    Pensioner in 1840, Harford County. (E-262)

SCHRIFE, MICHAEL.
    Private, Capt. Francis Holland's Harford Rifles, 1776. (E-124)

SCOFIELD, WILLIAM.
    Signer, Oath of Allegiance to Md., 1778. (A-36, B-24, J-242)

SCOTT, ALEXANDER.
    Signer, Association of Freemen, 1776, Spesutie Upper. (I-319)
    Signer, Oath of Allegiance to Md., 1778. (A-36, B-30, J-244)

SCOTT, ANDREW ("Andrew Scoat").
    Private, Capt. Patrick's Co. No. 17, April 1, 1776. (E-122)
    Signer, Association of Freemen, 1776,Deer Creek Lower. (I-321)

SCOTT, AQUILA, of Aquila.
    Private, Capt. Bond's Co. No. 11, December 9, 1775. (E-117)
    Ensign, 8th Battalion, Militia, 1778. (C-46)
    Signer, Oath of Allegiance, 1778. (A-36, B-28, J-245)
    Harford County Grand Juror, 1779. (E-75)

SCOTT, AQUILA, of James.
    Private, Capt. Bond's Co. No. 11, December 9, 1775. (E-116)
    Signer, Association of Freemen, 1776, Bush River Lower. (I-319)
    Signer, Oath of Allegiance to Md., 1778. (A-36, B-15, J-236)
    Harford County Petit Juror, 1783. (E-77)

SCOTT, BENJAMIN.
Private, Capt. Bond's Co. No. 11, December 9, 1775. (E-117)
Signer, Association of Freemen, 1776, Bush River Lower. (I-319)

SCOTT, BENJAMIN.
Signer, Association of Freemen, 1776, Gunpowder Upper. (I-325)
2nd Lieutenant, Flying Camp. October 19, 1776. (H-127)
1st Lieutenant, Capt. Harris' Company Payroll. (E-130, F-304)
1st Lieutenant, 6th Maryland Regiment, December 10, 1776. (L-485)
1st Lieutenant, 8th Battalion, Militia, 1776. (E-266)
Resigned, September 21, 1778. (H-127)
Army Accounts No. 1, p. 44, March 12, 1779. (HR-50)

SCOTT, DANIEL, son of Aquila. (Died 1828; only child, Otho Scott, Esq.)
Signer, Bush Declaration, March 22, 1775. (D-355)   (E-225)
War Committee, Harford County, 1775. (D-358)
Signer, Association of Freemen, 1775, Bush River Upper, and
Solicitor, 1775, Bush River Lower. (I-315, I-317, I-328)
Private, Capt. Bond's Co. No. 11, December 9, 1775. (E-117)
Captain, 8th Battalion, Militia, 1778. (C-46)
Intendant's Letter Book No. 12, p. 291, Nov. 15, 1785. (HR-50)

SCOTT, JAMES.
Signer and solicitor, Association of Freemen, 1775 and 1776,
Bush River Upper. (I-315, I-320)
1st Sergeant, Capt. Love's Co. No. 10, Sept. 14, 1775. (E-115)
Signer, Oath of Allegiance to Md., 1778. (B-30, J-247)

SCOTT, JAMES, son of James.
Private, Capt. Baker's Co. No. 15, January 27, 1776. (E-120)
Signer, Association of Freemen, 1776, Bush River Upper. (I-320)
Signer, Oath of Allegiance to Md., 1778. (B-21, J-239)
Pensioner (maimed soldier), 1778. (F-661)
Private, Land Warrant No. 11742, 100 acres, 1797. (N-77)

SCOTT. JAMES, of Aquila.
Signer, Association of Freemen, 1776, Bush River Lower. (I-328)
Signer, Oath of Allegiance to Md., 1778. (B-15, J-236)
Recruit, New Regiment, July 13, 1780. (E-130, F-343)

SCOTT, NATHAN.
Signer, Oath of Allegiance to Md., 1778. (A-36, B-28, J-243)

SCOTT, PETER.
Recruit, 8th Maryland Regiment, 1780. (E-131, F-343)

SCOTT, WILLIAM.
Signer, Association of Freemen, 1775, Gunpowder Neck. (I-327)

SEALE, JAMES JR.
Private, Capt. Rodgers' Co. No. 5, September 15, 1775. (E-111)

SEARS, JOHN.
    Born 1752. Died 1802. Married: (1) Teresa Cilison; (2) Mary
      Dutton. (X-601)
    Sergeant, 2nd Maryland Regiment, January 10, 1777.
    Ensign, 2nd Maryland Regiment, January 2, 1780.
    Transferred to 5th Maryland Regiment, January 1, 1781.
    2nd Lieutenant, 5th Maryland Regiment, January 1, 1781.
    Transferred to 1st Maryland Regiment, January 1, 1783.
    Retained in Gunby's Battalion, April 12, 1783. Served to
      November 15, 1783. (H-127)
    Pay Certificates No. 82884, $21.30; No. 82885, $23.88; No. 82886,
      $357.00; No. 82887, $198.00; No. 82888, $500.00; No. 82889,
      $500.00; No. 82890, $300.00; No. 82891, $273.30. (P-450)
    Original Member of the Society of the Cincinnati of Maryland.

SEDGWICK, JAMES.
    Harford County Petit Juror, 1783. (E-77)

SEEMER, CHRISTOPHER.
    "Christopher Seemer" was a Recruit, New Regiment, July 17, 1780.
    "Christopher Seemore" was in the 2nd Maryland Regiment and
      received Pay Certificates No. 81748, $80, and 82468, $43.30.
    (E-130, F-343, P-450)

SELBY, JOHN.
    Signer, Association of Freemen, 1775, Gunpowder Neck. (I-327)

SENEY, PATRICK.
    Signer, Oath of Allegiance to Md., 1778. (A-36, B-13, J-235)

SEWELL, JOHN.
    Private, Capt. Rumsey's Co. No. 6, September 16, 1775. (E-112)
    Signer, Association of Freemen, 1775, Gunpowder Neck. (I-327)
    Signer, Oath of Allegiance to Md., 1778. (A-36, B-20, J-239)
    Captain, 8th Battalion, Militia, 1778. (C-47)

SHAGNASSEY, JOSEPH.
    Private, Capt. Archer's Co. No. 2, September 16, 1775. (E-107)

SHANE (SHEAN), HENRY.
    Signer, Association of Freemen, 1775, Bush River Upper. (I-316)
    Private, Capt. Bussey's Company, July 27, 1776. (E-128, F-60)

SHARSWOOD, WILLIAM.
    Signer, Oath of Allegiance to Md., 1778. (A-36, B-26, J-243)

SHAW, JOHN.
    Sergeant; Pensioner (maimed soldier), 1778. (F-661)

SHEANES, HENRY.
    Signer, Oath of Allegiance to Md., 1778. (A-36, B-29, J-246)

SHEARER, THOMAS.
    Private, Capt. Anderson's Co. No. 3, September 23, 1775. (E-108)

SHEEDY, ROGER.
    Private, Capt. Dorsey's Co. No. 8, October 31, 1775. (E-114)

SHEELS, JOHN.
    Signer, Association of Freemen, 1776, Bush River Upper. (I-328)

SHELL, JOHN.
    Signer, Oath of Allegiance to Md., 1778. (A-36, B-29, J-246)

SHEPHERD, WILLIAM.
    Signer, Oath of Allegiance to Md., 1778. (A-36, B-28, J-245)

SHEREDINE, JAMES.
    Private, Capt. Archer's Co. No. 2, September 16, 1775. (E-107)
    Signer, Association of Freemen, 1776, Harford Upper. (I-325)
    Signer, Oath of Allegiance to Md., 1778. (A-36, B-26, J-243)

SHEREDINE, JEREMIAH.
    Harford County Court Justice during Revolutionary era. (E-61)
    War Committeeman, Correspondence, June 11, 1775. (D-358, E-95)

SHEREDINE (SHEREDIN), THOMAS.
    4th Sergeant, Capt. Love's Co. No. 10, Sept. 14, 1775. (E-115)
    Militia Substitute, 1781, 3 years. (E-133, F-401)

SHERWOOD, WILLIAM.
    Signer, Association of Freemen, 1776, Spesutie Upper. (I-319)

SHIELDS, JOHN.
    Militia Substitute, 1781. (E-132, F-400)

SHIELDS, PAUL.
    Signer, Association of Freemen, 1776, Harford Upper. (I-325)

SHINTON, JOHN.
    Signer, Association of Freemen, 1776, Bush River Lower.(I-319)
    Signer, Oath of Allegiance to Md., 1778. (A-36, B-22, J-240)

SHIPLEY, ELIJAH.
    Signer, Oath of Allegiance to Md., 1778. (A-36, B-15, J-236)

SHIPLEY, JOHN.
    Signer, Association of Freemen, 1776, Eden Hundred.(I-324)

SHIPLEY, RICHARD.
    Private, Capt. Baker's Co. No. 15, January 27, 1776. (E-120)
    Signer, Association of Freemen, 1776, Eden Hundred. (I-324)
    Signer, Oath of Allegiance to Md., 1778. (A-36, B-24, J-242)

SHORT, EDWARD.
    Private, Capt. Archer's Co. No. 2, September 16, 1775. (E-108)
    Signer, Association of Freemen, 1776, Harford Upper. (I-325)

SHY, WILLIAM.
    Private, Capt. Rodgers' Co. No. 5, September 15, 1775. (E-111)

SILAS, JOHN.
    Signer, Association of Freemen, 1776, Gunpowder Upper. (I-326)

SILK, JAMES.
    Militia Substitute, 1781. (E-132, F-400)

SILVER (SILVERS), BENJAMIN.
    Born 1753. Died 1818. Married: Euphemia Smith. (X-617)
    Signer, Association of Freemen, 1775/6, Susquehanna. (D-357, I-321)
    Private, Capt. Anderson's Co. No. 3, September 23, 1775. (E-109)
    Signer, Oath of Allegiance to Maryland, 1778. (A-36, B-26, J-243)
    Harford County Grand Juror, 1783. (E-77)

SILVER, WILLIAM.
    (1) Private, Capt. Anderson's Co. No. 3, Sept. 23, 1775. (E-109)
    (2) Private, Capt. Patrick's Co. No. 17, April 1, 1776. (E-122)
    (3) Private, Capt. Francis Holland's Harford Rifles, 1776. (E-124)

SIMPERS, THOMAS.
    Private, Capt. Dorsey's Co. No. 8, October 31, 1775. (E-114)

SIMPSON, WILLIAM.
    Signer, Oath of Allegiance to Maryland, 1778. (A-36, B-23, J-241)

SIMS, GEORGE.
    Signer, Oath of Allegiance to Maryland, 1778. (A-36, B-25, J-242)

SINCLAR (SINCKLER, SINKLER, SINKCLEARE), JAMES.
    Signer, Association of Freemen, 1776, Bush River Upper. (I-320)
    2nd Lieutenant, Capt. McComas' Company, 1776. (E-268)
    Signer, Oath of Allegiance to Md., 1778. (A-36, B-30, J-247)

SINCLAR (SINKLER), WILLIAM SR.
    Signer, Association of Freemen, 1776, Spesutie Upper. (I-319)
    Born c.1705. Died 1795. Married: Mary Hines, 1730. (X-619, M-164)

SINCLAR (SINKLER), WILLIAM.
    Married Mary Norris in 1769. (M-164)
    Signer, Association of Freemen, 1776, Bush River Lower. (I-320)

SINGLETON, JOHN.
    Private, Capt. Rodgers' Co. No. 5, September 15, 1775. (E-110)

SIVERS (SIVEST), MICHAEL.
    Private, Capt. Webb's Co. No. 16, October 14, 1775. (E-121)
    Signer, Association of Freemen, 1776, Deer Creek Upper. (I-323)

SIVKINS, JOHN.
    Signer, Association of Freemen, 1776, Susquehanna. (I-321)

SKELL (SKEL), MATTHEW.
    Private, Capt. Robert Harris' Harford Rifles, 1776. (E-123)
    Paid subsistence for 4 weeks, 3 days, Oct. 1, 1776. (K-436)

SKENMETT, THOMAS.
    Signer, Association of Freemen, 1776, Bush River Lower. (I-319)

SKWINGTON (SKIVINGTON), JAMES.
    Signer, Oath of Allegiance to Md., 1778. (A-36, B-29, J-246)

SLACK, JACOB.
    Private, Capt. Archer's Co. No. 2, September 16, 1775. (E-107)
    Signer, Association of Freemen, 1776, Harford Upper. (I-325)

SLACK, JOHN.
    Signer, Association of Freemen, 1776, Spesutie Upper. (I-319)
    Signer, Oath of Allegiance to Md., 1778. (A-36, B-25, J-242)

SLADE, EZEKIEL.
    Married Ann Whitaker in 1754. (M-165)
    Signer, Association of Freemen, 1776, Eden Hundred. (I-324)
    Signer, Oath of Allegiance to Md., 1778. (A-36, B-19, J-238)

SLADE, EZEKIEL JR.
    Signer, Oath of Allegiance to Md., 1778. (B-19, J-238)

SLADE, THOMAS.
    Married Hannah Miles in 1748. (M-165)
    Private, Capt. Baker's Co. No. 15, January 27, 1776. (E-120)
    Signer, Association of Freemen, 1776, Eden Hundred. (I-324)
    Signer, Oath of Allegiance to Md., 1778. (A-36, B-19, J-238)

SLADE (SLAID), WILLIAM.
    Born 1746. Died 1795. Married Elizabeth Stansbury, 1770. (M-165)
    Signer, Association of Freemen, 1775 and 1776. Bush River Upper.
    Signer, Oath of Allegiance and Fidelity to Maryland, 1778.
    (A-36, B-19, I-317, I-320, J-238)

SLATOR, THOMAS.
    Signer, Oath of Allegiance to Md., 1778. (A-36, B-15, J-236)

SLATRY, THOMAS.
    Private, Capt. Bussey's Company, July 27, 1776. (E-128, F-60)

SLOAN, WILLIAM.
    Harford County Pensioner in 1840. (E-262)

SMALL, JOHN.
    Signer, Oath of Allegiance to Md., 1778. (A-36, B-26, J-243)

SMALL, ROBERT.
    Private, Capt. Anderson's Co. No. 3, September 23, 1775. (E-108)
    Signer, Association of Freemen, 1776, Susquehanna. (I-321)
    Signer, Oath of Allegiance to Md., 1778. (A-36, B-10, J-234)

SMITH, ALEXANDER LAWSON.
    Born 1753. Died 1801. Married: Martha Griffith in 1792, a
      daughter of Samuel Griffith and Frenetta Garretson. (N-123)
    Clerk and Keeper of the Records of Harford County, 1774. (E-61)
    Private, Capt. Josias Hall's Co. No. 1, Sept. 12, 1775. (E-106)
    Signer, Association of Freemen, 1776, Harford Hundred. (I-325)
    Captain, 1st Company of Maryland Riflemen under Colonel Moses
      Rawlings, 1776. (D-361)
    Captain, 4th Maryland Regiment, commissioned July 13, 1776.
      (E-129, F-301)
    Captain, 1779: Army Ledger No. 2, f. 131; Army Journal No. 1,
      p. 51. (HR-50)
    Major, 1781-2: Intendant's Ledger A No. 10, f.63, 10; A No. 15,
      p. 45; A No. 9, f.45, 55. (HR-50)
    Lieutenant Colonel, Maryland. (X-623)
    Colonel, 1782-4: Depreciation Pay No. 1, p. 54; No. 2, p. 98;
      No. 3, p. 128; Army Accounts No. 1, p. 46, 64. *HR-50)
    Saw service at Battles of Princeton and Trenton, and Battle of
      Fort Washington, November 16, 1776. (E-136)
    On furlough, June and July, 1777; February, 1778; November 15,
      1778; December, 1778; January, 1779. (F-301)
    Pay Certificates No. 93677, $74.68, and No. 93678, $50.00;
      Maryland Officers Pay. (P-464)
    Captain, Harford County Militia; wife applied for pension. (N-47)
    Buried in Spesutia Cemetery (St. George's Parish).

SMITH, AMOS.
    Signer, Association of Freemen, 1775, Gunpowder Neck. (I-327)

SMITH, BAZIE (BASIL).
    Signer, Association of Freemen, 1775, Gunpowder Neck. (I-327)
    Private, Capt. Bradford's Co. No. 13, Sept. 30, 1775. (E-119)
    Signer, Oath of Allegiance to Md., 1778. (A-36, B-15, J-236)

SMITH, BENJAMIN.
    Signer, Association of Freemen, 1775 and 1776, Susquehanna.
      (D-357, I-321) Furnished a gun to committee, 1776. (E-336)
    Private, Capt. Anderson's Co. No. 3, Sept. 23, 1775. (E-108)
    Signer, Oath of Allegiance to Md., 1778. (A-36, B-26, J-243)
    Private, Maryland Line; pensioner. (N-47)

SMITH, DAVID.
    Born 1756, in America. (E-125, F-54)
    Private, Capt. Anderson's Co. No. 3, September 23, 1775. (E-109)
    4th Sergeant, Flying Camp, Lt. John Smith enlisted July 15, 1776
      in Col. Ewing's Battalion. At time of enlistment he was 5'8"
      and had light colored hair. (E-125, F-54)
    Signer, Association of Freemen, 1776, Harford Upper. (I-325)
    Signer, Oath of Allegiance to Md., 1778. (A-36, B-25, J-242)

SMITH, DAVIS.
    Private, Capt. Francis Holland's Harford Rifles, 1776. (E-124)

SMITH, HUGH.
Signer and solicitor, Association of Freemen, 1775 and 1776, Susquehanna Hundred. (D-357, I-315, I-321)
Signer, Oath of Alegiance to Md., 1778. (A-36, B-25, J-242)
1st Lieutenant, 23rd Battalion, 1778; Captain, 1779. (C-45)

SMITH, ICHABOD.
Private, Capt. Anderson's Co. No. 3, September 23, 1775. (E-108)

SMITH, JAMES.
Signer, Association of Freemen, 1775, Bush River Upper. (I-317)
Signer, Association of Freemen, 1776, Gunpowder Upper. (I-326)
(1) Private, Flying Camp. Lt. John Smith enlisted July 15, 1776 in Col. Ewing's Battalion. (E-126, F-56)
(2) Private, Capt. Bussey's Co., July 20, 1776. (E-127, F-60)
(3) Pensioner (maimed soldier), 1778. (F-661, N-48)
Signer, Oath of Allegiance and Fidelity to Maryland, 1778.
Records indicate there were three signers with this name.
(A-36, B-12, B-24, B-25, J-234, J-242)
Twenty-four Pay Certificates are listed in the name of James Smith in Maryland. (P-467)

SMITH, JOHN.
(1) Private, Capt. Archer's Co. No. 2, Sept. 16, 1775. (E-107, N-102)
(2) Private, Capt. Webb's Co. No. 16, Oct. 14, 1775. (E-121, N-102)
(3) 2nd Lieutenant, Deer Creek Battalion, Militia, 1778. (C-43)
(4) Signer, Association of Freemen, 1776. Record indicates there were two signers with this name in Deer Creek Upper (I-323) and one in Spesutie Lower (I-318).
(5) Signer, Oath of Allegiance and Fidelity to Maryland, 1778. Record indicates there were three signers with this name from Harford County. (A-36, B-19, B-23, B-24, J-238, J-241, J-242)
(6) Thirty-six Pay Certificates are listed in the name of John Smith in Maryland. (P-468, P-469)

SMITH, JOHN, of "The Old 3rd."
Born 1747. Died 1832. Married: Martha Van Cleve. (X-626)
2nd Lieutenant, 2nd Battalion, Flying Camp, Baltimore County, July 15, 1776. 1st Lieutenant, 3rd Regiment, December 10, 1776. Captain, 3rd Regiment, January 1, 1777. Wounded at Savannah, October 8, 1779. Wounded and prisoner at Camden, August 16, 1780. Transferred to 5th Regiment, January 1, 1781. Brevet Major, September 30, 1783. Prisoner on parole to the close of the war. Resident of Harford County, Return of 1791, Cincinnati records. Original Member of the Society of the Cincinnati of Maryland. Land Warrant No. 2045, 300 acres, applied for January 26, 1792.
(N-78, H-132, L-504)

SMITH, JOHN JR.
Private, Capt. Webb's Co. No. 16, October 14, 1775. (E-121, N-78)

SMITH, JONATHAN.
Private, Capt. Robert Harris' Harford Rifles, 1776. (E-123)
Paid subsistence for 2 weeks, 1 day, October 19, 1776. (K-435)

SMITH, JOSEPH.
    Private, Capt. Aquila Hall's Co. No. 4, Sept. 9, 1775. (E-109)
    Signer, Association of Freemen, 1776, Harford Lower. (I-324)
    Signer, Oath of Allegiance to Md., 1778. (A-36, B-17, J-237)

SMITH, JOSEPH.
    Private, Capt. Rigdon's Co. No. 12, December 2, 1775. (E-118)

SMITH, JOSEPH JR.
    Signer, Association of Freemen, 1776, Gunpowder Upper. (I-326)

SMITH, JOSIAS.
    Private, Capt. Rumsey's Co. No. 6, September 16, 1775. (E-112)
    Signer, Association of Freemen, 1775, Gunpowder Neck. (I-327)
    Signer, Oath of Allegiance to Md., 1778. (A-36, B-14, J-236)

SMITH, NATHAN.
    Married Blanch Dooley in 1757. (M-167)
    Private, Capt. Bussey's Company, July 25, 1776. (E-128, F-60)
    Signer, Association of Freemen, 1776, Bush River Upper. (I-328)
    Signer, Oath of Allegiance to Md., 1778. (A-36, B-19, J-238)

SMITH, NATHANIAL.
    Married Elizabeth Webster in 1752. (M-167)
    Private, Capt. Webb's Co. No. 16, October 14, 1775. (E-121)
    Signer, Association of Freemen, 1776, Deer Creek Upper. (I-323)
    Signer, Association of Freemen, 1776, Harford Upper. (I-325)
    Signer, Oath of Allegiance to Md., 1778. (A-36, B-26, J-243)

SMITH, PATRICK.
    Signer, Oath of Allegiance to Md., 1778. (A-36, B-26, J-243)

SMITH, PETER.
    Signer, Association of Freemen, 1776, Bush River Lower. (I-328)
    Signer, Oath of Allegiance to Md., 1778. (A-36, B-29, J-246)

SMITH, RALPH.
    Private, Capt. Archer's Co. No. 2, September 16, 1775. (E-107)
        Record indicates two Ralph Smith's in this Company. (E-108)
    Private, Capt. Francis Holland's Harford Rifles, 1776. (E-124)
    Signer, Association of Freemen, 1776, Deer Creek Lower.(I-322)
    Signer, Oath of Allegiance to Md., 1778. (A-36, B-25, J-242)
    1st Lieutenant, Deer Creek Battalion, Militia, 1779. (C-44)

SMITH, ROBERT.
    Private, Capt. Archer's Co. No. 2, September 16, 1775. (E-107)
    Signer, Association of Freemen, 1776, Harford Upper. (I-325)
    Signer, Oath of Allegiance to Md., 1778. (A-36, B-25, J-242)
    Record indicates two Robert Smith's were signers. (B-29, J-246)

SMITH, SAMUEL.
    Ensign, Capt. Hall's Co. No. 1, 1774-1775. (E-107)
    Signer, Association of Freemen, 1776, Harford Upper. (I-325)
    Captain, 23rd Battalion, Militia. (C-45)
    Signer, Oath of Allegiance to Md., 1778. (A-36, B-25, J-242)

SMITH, THOMAS.
    Signer, Association of Freemen, 1775, Gunpowder Neck. (I-327)
    Private, Capt. Bond's Co. No. 11, December 9, 1775. (E-117)
    Signer, Association of Freemen, 1776, Susquehanna. (I-321)
    Private, 4th Maryland Regiment, 1776-1779. (E-129, F-301)
    Rifleman, Battle of Fort Washington, Nov. 16, 1776. (E-136)
    Signer, Oath of Allegiance to Md., 1778. (A-36, B-25, J-242)
    Recruit, 8th Maryland Regiment, 1780. (E-131, F-343)
    Pensioner. (N-78)
    Seventeen Pay Certificates listed under this name. (P-472)

SMITH, VALENTINE.
    Pensioner (maimed soldier), 1778. (F-661)

SMITH, VINCENT.
    Signer, Oath of Allegiance to Md., 1778. (A-36, B-19, J-238)

SMITH, WILLIAM.
    (1) Private, Capt. Aquila Hall's Co. No. 4, Sept. 9, 1775. (E-109)
    (2) Private, Capt. Bond's Co. No. 11, December 9, 1775. (E-117)
    (3) Private, Capt. Rigdon's Co. No. 12, December 2, 1775. (E-118)
    (4) Private, Capt. Webb's Co. No. 16, October 14, 1775. (E-121)
    (5) Militia Substitute, 1781. (E-132, F-400)
    Source N-48 lists 4 William Smith pensioners:
    (1) Born 1751, Private, Militia.
    (2) Born 1752, Private, Maryland Line.
    (3) Born 1744, Private, Maryland Line.
    (4) Born 1755, Sergeant, Maryland Line.
    Source N-103 lists 4 William Smith non-pensioners:
    (1) Private, Flying Camp.
    (2) Sea Service.
    (3) Maryland Service.
    (4) Mate, Sea Service.
    Three William Smiths signed the Oath of Allegiance and Fidelity to Maryland, 1778. (A-36, B-17, B-21, B-29, J-237, 239, 246)
    One was a 2nd Lieutenant in the Militia, 1778. (C-43)
        Deer Creek Battalion.
    Another, or possibly the same one, was Captain and Esquire, on the War Committee of Harford County, June 11, 1775. (D-358, E-96)
    Several signed the Association of Freemen declaration:
    (1) Bush River Upper, 1775. (I-316)
    (2) Bush River Upper, 1776. (I-319)
    (3) Bush River Upper, 1776. (I-320)
    (4) Deer Creek Upper, 1776. (I-323)
    (5) Harford Lower, 1776. (I-324)
    Fifteen Pay Certificates listed under this name. (P-472)

SMITH, WILLIAM, of William.
    Private, Capt. Josias Hall's Co. No. 1, Sept. 12, 1775. (E-106)
    Signer, Association of Freemen, 1776 Bush River Upper. (I-320)
        William Smith, Jr. also listed in Spesutie Lower (I-318).
    Signer, Oath of Allegiance to Md., 1778. (A-36, B-25, J-242)
    It is possible that additional information on this William Smith might be found in the other William Smiths listed above.

SMITH, WINSTON.
    Signer, Association of Freemen, 1776, Bush River Upper. (I-328)
    "Winston Smith" married Priscilla Paca in 1740. (M-167)
    "Winstone Smith" married Susanna Stokes in 1743. (M-167)
    Private, Capt. Bussey's Company, July 25, 1776. (E-128, F-60)
    Non-pensioner, Flying Camp. (N-103)

SMITH, ZACHARIAH.
    Private, Capt. Bradford's Co. No. 13, Sept. 30, 1775. (E-119)
    Signer, Association of Freemen, 1775, Gunpowder Neck. (I-327)
    Signer, Oath of Allegiance to Md., 1778. (A-36, B-14, J-235)

SMITHE, W.
    Signer, Bush Declaration, March 22, 1775. (D-355)

SMITHSON, DANIEL.
    Born 1723, Baltimore County. Died 1798, Harford County.
    Married Susannah Taylor in 1785. Children: John Taylor, Thomas,
        Amelia, Gabriel, Martin, Luther, Edward, Daniel. (G-662, X-630)
    Signer, Association of Freemen, 1776, Gunpowder Upper. (I-326)
    Signer, Oath of Allegiance to Md., 1778. (A-36, B-28, J-245)
    Civil Service; Harford County Petit Juror, 1783. (E-77, X-630)

SMITHSON, DAVID.
    Signer, Association of Freemen, 1776, Eden Hundred. (I-323)
    Signer, Oath of Allegiance to Md., 1778. (A-36, B-23, J-241)

SMITHSON, NATHANIEL.
    Private, Capt. Bond's Co. No. 11, December 9, 1775. (E-117)
    Signer, Association of Freemen, 1776, Bush River Lower. (I-328)
    Signer, Oath of Allegiance to Md., 1778. (A-36, B-10, J-233)
    Ensign, 8th Battalion, 1778. (C-47)

SMITHSON, THOMAS.
    Married Sarah Bond in 1767. (M-167)
    Signer, Association of Freemen, 1776, Bush River Lower.(I-328)
    Signer, Oath of Allegiance to Md., 1778. (A-36, B-15, J-236)

SMITHSON, WILLIAM.
    Married Elizabeth Scott in 1766. (M-167) Born 1745. Died 1809.
    Signer, Bush Declaration, March 22, 1775. (D-355)   (E-220)
    War Committee, Correspondence, June 11, 1775. (D-358, E-96)
    Private, Capt. Bond's Co. No. 11, December 9, 1775. (E-117)
    Signer, Association of Freemen, 1776, Spesutie Upper. (I-319)
    Signer, Oath of Allegiance to Md., 1778. (A-36, J-234)
    Administered the Oath ("Worshipfull William Smithson").(B-12)
    Harford County Court Justice, 1780/1783. (E-76, E-77)

SMYTH, JOHN.
    Signer, Association of Freemen, 1775/6, Bush River Upper. (I-316, I-328)

SNODEY (SNODDY), MATTHEW.
    Private, Capt. Paca's Company, July 24, 1776. (E-126, F-59)
    Signer, Association of Freemen, 1776, Harford Lower. (I-324)

SNODGRASS, WILLIAM.
Private, Capt. Patrick's Co. No. 17, April 1, 1776. (E-122)

SOWARD, RICHARD.
Signer, Association of Freemen, 1776, Susquehanna. (I-321)

SPARKS (SPARK), WILLIAM.
Private, Capt. Webb's Co. No. 16, October 14, 1775. (E-121)
Signer, Association of Freemen, 1776, Deer Creek Upper. (I-323)

SPEAR, JAMES.
Signer, Association of Freemen, 1776, Deer Creek Upper. (I-322)

SPEAR (SPEIR), ROBERT.
Signer, Association of Freemen, 1776, Deer Creek Upper. (I-322)

SPENCE, HENRY.
Signer, Association of Freemen, 1775 and 1776, Susquehanna.
(D-357, I-321)

SPENCE, JAMES.
Signer, Association of Freemen, 1775 and 1776, Susquehanna.
(D-357, I-321)

SPENCE, JOHN.
Signer, Association of Freemen, 1775 and 1776, Susquehanna.
(D-357, I-321)

SPENCER, JAMES.
Signer, Association of Freemen, 1775, Gunpowder Neck.(I-327)

SPENCER, JOHN.
Private, Capt. Bussey's Co., July 27, 1776. (E-128, F-60)

SPENCER, ROBERT.
Private, Capt. Robert Harris' Harford Rifles, 1776. (E-124)
Paid subsistence for 3 weeks, 3 days, Oct. 7, 1776. (K-436)

SPENCER, ROWLAND.
Signer, Oath of Allegiance to Md., 1778. (A-36, B-10, J-234)

SPENCER, ZACHARIAH ("ZACARY SPENSER").
Signer, Association of Freemen, 1776, Deer Creek Upper. (I-322)
Signer, Oath of Allegiance to Md., 1778. (A-36, B-19, J-238)
Source M-169 lists one married to Christian Coob in 1728, and
Ann Pogue in 1755.

STACK, JACOB.
Signer, Oath of Allegiance to Md., 1778. (A-36, B-25, J-242)

STAFFORD, JOHN.
Corporal, 4th Maryland, appointed June 1, 1777. (E-129)
Sergeant, 4th Maryland, appointed January, 1778. (F-301)

STALLINGS (STALLINS), SAMUEL.
    Private, Capt. Bradford's Co. No. 13, Sept. 30, 1775. (E-119)
    Signer, Association of Freemen, 1776, Harford Upper. (I-325)

STANDIFORD, JAMES.
    Signer, Oath of Allegiance to Md., 1778. (A-36, B-24, J-242)

STANDIFORD (STANDERFORD), SAMUEL.
    Signer, Oath of Allegiance to Md., 1778. (A-36, B-12, J-234)

STANDIFORD, SAMUEL JR.
    Private, Capt. Taylor's Co. No. 7, September 9, 1775. (E-113)
    Signer, Association of Freemen, 1776, Gunpowder Upper. (I-326)

STANDLEY, JOHN.
    Signer, Association of Freemen, 1776, Harford Hundred. (I-325)
    Signer, Oath of Allegiance to Md., 1778. (A-36, B-22, J-240)

STANLEY, WILLIAM.
    Signer, Oath of Allegiance to Md., 1778. (A-36, B-15, J-236)

STAPLETON, EDWARD.
    Born c.1715. Died c.1780. Married: Rachel_____. (X-642)
    Signer, Oath of Allegiance to Md., 1778. (A-36, B-13, J-235)

STAPLETON, JOSIAH.
    Private, Capt. Patrick's Co. No. 17, April 1, 1776. (E-122)

STAPLETON (STIPLETON), THOMAS.
    Married Sarah Crook in 1756. (M-170)
    Private, Capt. Patrick's Co. No. 17, April 1, 1776. (E-122)
    Signer, Association of Freemen, 1776, Deer Creek Lower. (I-321)

STARR, WILLIAM.
    Signer, Association of Freemen, 1776, Spesutie Upper. (I-319)

STEEL (STEELE), JAMES.
    Private, Capt. Bond's Co. No. 11, December 9, 1775. (E-117)
    Ensign, 8th Battalion, October 19, 1776. (E-266, H-135)
    Signer, Association of Freemen, 1776, Bush River Lower. (I-319)
    Ensign, Deer Creek Battalion, under Capt. Vanhorn, 1778. (C-43)
    Signer, Oath of Allegiance to Md., 1778. (A-36, B-14, J-233)

STEEL, JOHN.
    Private, Capt. Bussey's Co., July 20, 1776. (E-127, F-60)
    Signer, Association of Freemen, 1776, Eden Hundred. (I-323)
    Signer, Oath of Allegiance to Md., 1778. (A-36, B-30, J-247)

STEEL, JOSEPH.
    Private, Capt. Rodgers' Co. No. 5, September 15, 1775. (E-111)
    Private, Capt. Robert Harris' Harford Rifles, 1776. (E-124)
    Paid subsistence for 3 weeks, 3 days, October 6, 1776. (K-436)

STEET, JOHN.
    Signer, Association of Freemen, 1776, Susquehanna. (I-321)

STENSON, JOHN.
    Harford County Grand Juror, 1780. (E-76)

STEPHENS, WILLIAM.
    Private, Capt. Bond's Co. No. 11, December 9, 1775. (E-117)

STEPHENSON, THOMAS.
    Born 1754. Died 1829. Married: Sarah Evens. (X-648)
    Private, Capt. Patrick's Co. No. 17, April 1, 1776. (E-122)

STERRETT, JONATHAN.
    Signer, Association of Freemen, 1776, Deer Creek Lower. (I-322)
    Private, Capt. Patrick's Co. No. 17, April 1, 1776. (E-122)

STEUART, JAMES.
    Signer, Oath of Allegiance to Md., 1778. (A-36, B-22, J-240)

STEUART (STEWART), THOMAS.
    Private, Capt. Robert Harris' Harford Rifles, 1776. (E-123)
    Paid subsistence for 4 weeks, 1 day, Oct. 3, 1776. (K-436)

STEUART, WILLIAM.
    Signer, Oath of Allegiance to Md., 1778. (A-36, B-10, J-234)

STEVENSON (STEPHENSON), ALEXANDER.
    Private, Capt. Robert Harris' Harford Rifles, 1776. (E-123)
    Fifer, Capt. Harris' Company Payroll, 1776. (E-130, F-304)
    Paid subsistence for 6 weeks, 2 days, Sept. 16, 1776. (K-435)

STEVENSON, JOHN.
    Private, Capt. Archer's Co. No. 2, September 16, 1775. (E-107)
    Signer, Association of Freemen, 1776, Susquehanna. (I-321)
    Signer, Oath of Allegiance to Md., 1778. (A-36, B-17, J-237)
    Letter, dated November 26, 1776, from John Archer to the Md. Council, in part: "As I understand some of the Gondolas are nearly ready for which your Honourable Board has the appointment of officers, I would therefore beg leave to remind you ....John Stevenson is a worthy deserving young man as well acquainted with Military Discipline as most young men in our country. He applies for a First Lieutenancy and should your Honors think proper to appoint him he would be desirous of serving under Captain Mathews." (K-481)

STEVENSON, JONAS.
    Born 1751. Died 1801. Married: (1) Rebecca_____; (2) Rachel Hughes. (X-647)
    Private, Capt. Aquila Hall's Co. No. 4, September 9, 1775. (E-109)
    Signer, Association of Freemen, 1776, Harford Lower. (I-324)
    Signer, Oath of Allegiance to Md., 1778. (A-36, B-10, J-234)

STEVENSON, ROBERT.
    Born in America. Private, Flying Camp, Lt. John Smith enlisted July 15, 1776, in Col. Ewing's Battalion. At time of enlistment he was 5'7 3/4" tall with a sandy complexion. (E-125, F-56)
    Signer, Association of Freemen, 1776, Deer Creek Upper. (I-323)

STEVENSON, THOMAS.
    Private, Capt. Paca's Company, July 24, 1776. (E-126, F-59)
    Signer, Association of Freemen, 1776, Deer Creek Lower. (I-322)

STEWARD, JAMES.
    Private, Capt. Aquila Hall's Co. No. 4, September 9, 1775. (E-109)

STEWART, GEORGE.
    Private, Capt. Paca's Company, August 5, 1776. (E-127, F-59)

STEWART, HUGH.
    Private, Capt. Rumsey's Co. No. 6, September 16, 1775. (E-112)
    Signer, Association of Freemen, 1775, Gunpowder Neck. (I-327)

STEWART, JAMES.
    Born 1746/1747. Died 1781. Married: Elizabeth _____. (X-648)
    Captain of Company No. 9, Harford Militia, 1775. (D-359, E-115)
    Signer, Association of Freemen, 1776, Spesutie Lower. (I-318)

STEWART, JAMES.
    Signer, Association of Freemen, 1776, Gunpowder Upper. (I-325)

STEWART, JOHN.
    Private, Capt. Rumsey's Co. No. 6, September 16, 1775. (E-112)
    Signer, Association of Freemen, 1775, Gunpowder Neck. (I-327)
    Signer, Oath of Allegiance to Md., 1778. (A-36, B-23, J-241)

STEWART, ROBERT.
    Born 1747. Private, Maryland Line; pensioner. (N-50)
    Private, Capt. Rumsey's Co. No. 6, September 16, 1775. (E-112)
    Signer, Association of Freemen, 1775, Gunpowder Neck. (I-327)

* STILES, JOSEPH.
    Private, Capt. Bradford's Co. No. 13, September 30, 1775. (E-119)
    Signer, Association of Freemen, 1776, Harford Hundred. (I-325)
    Signer, Oath of Allegiance to Md., 1778. (A-36, B-21, J-239)
    Harford County Grand Juror, 1780. (E-76)

STOCKSDALE, THOMAS.
    Private, Capt. Rumsey's Co. No. 6, September 16, 1775. (E-112)

STOKES, ROBERT.
    Private, Capt. Josias Hall's Co. No. 1, Sept. 12, 1775. (E-106)
    Private, Capt. Francis Holland's Harford Rifles, 1776. (E-124)
    1st Lieutenant, 23rd Battalion, 1778. (C-45)
    Signer, Oath of Allegiance to Md., 1778. (A-36, B-21, J-239)

* "Joseph Styles" was compensated by the Harford County Committee for "keeping a mare to forward Express," August, 1776. (E-332)

STONE, JOHN.
    Signer, Oath of Allegiance to Md., 1778. (A-36, B-30, J-247)

STONE, JOSEPH.
    Signer, Association of Freemen, 1776, Susquehanna. (I-319)

STOOKSBERY, WILLIAM JR.
    Signer, Oath of Allegiance to Md., 1778. (A-36, B-28, J-245)

STOOKSBERY, WILLIAM SR.
    Signer, Oath of Allegiance to Md., 1778. (A-36, B-28, J-245)

STRATFORD, VALENTINE.
    Private, Capt. Bussey's Company, July 27, 1776. (E-128, F-60)

STREET, THOMAS.
    Born 1737, in England or Baltimore County, Maryland.
    Died 1822, Streett's Hunting Ground, The Rocks, Harford Co., Md.
    Married: (1) Mary Fox, 1755; (2) Sarah James, 1772. Children:
    John, Thomas, David, Sarah, Elizabeth, Rodgers, William, Mary.
    Signer, Association of Freemen, 1776, Bush River Upper Hundred.
    Signer, Oath of Allegiance and Fidelity to Maryland, 1778.
    (A-36, B-30, J-247, I-320, G-687, G-688, M-173, O-18, O-23, X-656)

STREET, THOMAS JR.
    Signer, Association of Freemen, 1776, Bush River Upper. (I-320)
    Signer, Oath of Allegiance to Md., 1778. (A-36, B-30, J-247)

STRICKLAND, HENRY.
    Signer, Association of Freemen, 1775, Gunpowder Neck. (I-327)

STRODE, THOMAS.
    Signer, Oath of Allegiance to Md., 1778. (A-36, B-28, J-245)

STRONG, NATHAN.
    Militia Substitute, 1781. (E-131, F-400)

STROWD, WILLIAM.
    Private, Capt. Love's Co. No. 10, September 14, 1775. (E-116)
    Signer, Association of Freemen, 1776, Spesutie Upper. (I-319)

STUART, ALEXANDER.
    Signer, Association of Freemen, 1775/1776, Susquehanna. (D-357)
                                                            (I-321)
STUMP, HENRY.
    Signer, Association of Freemen, 1775/1776, Susquehanna. (D-357)
                                                            (I-321)
STUMP, HENRY JR.
    2nd Lieutenant, 23rd Battalion, Militia, 1778.
        "Removed from State." (C-45)

STUMP, JOHN JR.
    Signer, Association of Freemen, 1775/1776, Susquehanna. (D-357)
                                                            (I-321)

STURGEM (STURGEON), ROBERT.
    Signer, Association of Freemen, 1776, Bush River Upper. (I-320)
    Signer, Oath of Allegiance to Md., 1778. (A-36, B-23, J-241)

SULLIVAN (SULLAVIN), JAMES.
    Recruit, New Regiment, August 1, 1780. (E-130, F-343)

SULLIVAN (SWILLIVIN), JOHN.
    Signer, Association of Freemen, 1776, Susquehanna. (I-321)
    Militia Substitute, 1781. (E-132, F-400)

SULLIVAN, LAWRENCE.
    Signer, Association of Freemen, 1776, Harford Upper. (I-325)

SULLIVAN (SULLAVIN), NATHANIEL.
    Recruit, New Regiment, July 28, 1780. (E-130, F-343)

SUOIT, ALEXANDER.
    Signer, Oath of Allegiance to Md., 1778. (A-36, B-10, J-234)

SUTLER, ISAAC.
    Signer, Oath of Allegiance to Md., 1778. (A-36, B-20, J-239)

SUTTON, OZWAIN.
    Private, Capt. Rodgers Co. No. 5, September 15, 1775. (E-111)

SUTTON, REUBEN.
    Private, Capt. Dorsey's Co. No. 8, October 31, 1775. (E-115)
    Signer, Association of Freemen, 1775, Spesutie Lower. (I-317)

SUTTON, SAMUEL.
    Born 1733. Married Ruth Cantwell in 1757. (M-174)
    Signer, Oath of Allegiance to Md., 1778. (A-36, B-17, J-237)

SUTTON, THOMAS.
    Private, Capt. Aquila Hall's Co. No. 4, Sept. 9, 1775. (E-109)
    Private, Capt. Francis Holland's Harford Rifles, 1776. (E-124)
    Signer, Association of Freemen, 1776, Harford Lower. (I-324)
    Signer, Oath of Allegiance to Md., 1778. (A-36, B-21, J-239)

SWAIN, GABRIEL.
    Private, Capt. Dorsey's Co. No. 8, October 31, 1775. (E-114)

SWAIN, NATHAN,
    Married Mary Drew in 1764. (M-174)
    Private, Capt. Holland's Harford Rifles, 1776. (E-124)

SWAIN, NATHANIEL.
    Sergeant, Capt. Dorsey's Co. No. 8, October 31, 1775. (E-114)

SWANN, FREDERICK.
    Signer, Association of Freemen, 1776, Bush River Upper. (I-320)
    Signer, Oath of Allegiance to Md., 1778. (A-36, B-30, J-247)

SWANTON, PETER.
    Private, Capt. Harris' Company Payroll, 1776. (E-130, F-304)

SWART (SWARTS), SAMUEL.
    Private, Capt. Anderson's Co. No. 3, Sept, 23, 1775. (E-108)
    Signer, Association of Freemen, 1776, Susquehanna. (I-321)

SWEENEY, DAVID.
    Signer, Oath of Allegiance to Md., 1778. (A-36, B-14, J-236)

SWEENEY (SWENY, SWEANEY), MATHEW.
    Private, Capt. Love's Co. No. 10, September 14, 1775. (E-116)
    Signer, Association of Freemen, 1776, Spesutie Upper. (I-318)
    Signer, Oath of Allegiance to Md., 1778. (A-36, B-13, J-235)

SWIFT, LUKE.
    Furnished a gun to the Harford County Committee, 1776. (E-330)

T

TAES, ANDREW.
    Signer, Oath of Allegiance to Md., 1778. (A-36, B-13, J-235)

TALBEE, ZEPHANIAH.
    Married Mary Woolling in 1763. (M-175)
    Signer, Association of Freemen, 1775, Gunpowder Neck. (I-327)

TALBOTT, EDMOND.
    "Edmund Talbott" married Dorcas Hall, 1749; Rebecca Robinson, 1752.
    Signer, Association of Freemen, 1776, Gunpowder Upper. (I-325, M-175)

TALBOTT, EDWARD.
    Born 1744. Died c.1783. Married Margaret Slade in 1763.
    Signer, Oath of Allegiance to Maryland, 1778.
    (A-36, B-29, J-246, M-175, X-664)

TALBOTT, JAMES.
    Signer, Association of Freemen, 1775, Gunpowder Neck. (I-327)
    1st Lieutenant, Capt. Stewart's Co. No. 9, 1775. (D-359, E-115)
    Captain, 8th Battalion, Militia, 1778. (C-46)
    Signer, Oath of Allegiance to Md., 1778. (A-36, B-23, J-241)

TALBOTT, MATTHEW.
    Ensign, under Col. Benjamin Rumsey; resigned January 3, 1776. (C-30)
    Signer, Association of Freemen, 1776, Gunpowder Upper. (I-325)
    Signer, Association of Freemen, 1776, Bush River Upper. (I-320)
    1st Lieutenant, 8th Battalion, Militia, 1778. (C-46)
    Signer, Oath of Allegiance to Md., 1778. (A-36, B-23, J-241)

TANNEHILL (TANNAHILL), ADAMSON.
    Lieutenant, 4th Maryland Regiment, 1776-July, 1777. (E-129, F-301)
    2nd Lieutenant of Stephenson's Maryland Virginia Rifle Regiment,
       July 11, 1776; 1st Lieutenant of Rawlings' Continental Regiment,
       January, 1777; Captain, in Maryland part of the Rifle Regiment,
       July 20, 1779, to rank from April 1, 1778. (F-365, L-532)
    Supernumerary, January 1, 1781; retired. (F-365, L-532)
    Maryland Officer's Pay Certificates No. 89437, $116.67; No. 89438,
       $2209.71; No. 89439, $300.40. (P-494)
    Original Member of the Society of the Cincinnati in Maryland, 1783.
       (T-185)
    Captain, Land Warrant 2209 (300 acres) applied June 9, 1789. (N-80)
    Brigadier-General, Pennsylvania Volunteers in 1812. (L-532)
    Died July 7, 1817.

TANNER, JAMES RICHARD.
    Signer, Association of Freemen, 1775, Susquehanna. (D-357)

TANY, JAMES.
    Signer, Oath of Allegiance to Md., 1778. (A-36, B-19, J-238)

TAPLER, JOHN.
    Private, Capt. Bussey's Company, July 27, 1776. (E-128, F-60)

TARE, JAMES.
    Signer, Oath of Allegiance to Md., 1778. (A-36, B-17, J-237)

TATE, TIMOTHY.
    Sergeant, Capt. Baker's Co. No. 15, Jarrettsburg Militia,
       January 27, 1776. (E-120)

TAWLARD, BENJAMIN.
    Signer, Oath of Allegiance to Md., 1778. (A-36, B-29, J-246)

TAYLOR, ABRAHAM.
    Private, Capt. Dorsey's Co. No. 8, October 31, 1775. (E-115)
    Signer, Association of Freemen, 1776, Spesutie Lower. (I-318)

TAYLOR, AMASA.
    Private, Capt. Dorsey's Co. No. 8, October 31, 1775. (E-114)
    Signer, Association of Freemen, 1776, Spesutie Lower. (I-318)

TAYLOR, AMATIO.
    Private, Capt. Paca's Company, July 24, 1776. (E-126, F-59)

TAYLOR, ASA.
    Married Hannah Kimble in 1777. (M-176)
    Private, Capt. Dorsey's Co. No. 8, October 31, 1775. (E-114)
    Signer, Association of Freemen, 1776, Spesutie Lower. (I-318)
    2nd Lieutenant, 23rd Battalion, Militia, 1778. (C-45)

TAYLOR, BENJAMIN.
    Private, Capt. Harris' Company Payroll, 1776. (E-130, F-304)
    Maryland Line, last date March 10, 1781. (F-414)

TAYLOR, CHARLES.
    Married Elizabeth Standeford in 1750. (M-176)
    Signer, Association of Freemen, 1776, Gunpowder Upper. (I-326)
    Signer, Oath of Allegiance to Md., 1778. (A-36, B-23, J-241)
    Harford County Grand Juror, 1779. (E-75)

TAYLOR (TALER), DAVID.
    Signer, Association of Freemen, 1776, Bush River Upper. (I-320)

TAYLOR, ISRAEL.
    Private, CApt. Taylor's Co. No. 7, September 9, 1775. (E-113)
    Signer, Association of Freemen, 1776, Gunpowder Upper. (I-326)

TAYLOR, JAMES.
    Married Sarah Kimball in 1747. (M-176)
    Constable, Susquehannah Hundred, 1774. (E-64)
    Signer, Association of Freemen, 1775, Eden Hundred. (I-324)
    Signer, Association of Freemen, 1776, Gunpowder Upper. (I-326)
    Signer, Oath of Allegiance to Maryland, 1778. (B-24, J-242)

TAYLOR, JAMES JR.
    Clerk, Capt. Dorsey's Co. No. 8, October 31, 1775. (E-114)
    Signer, Association of Freemen, 1775, Spesutie Lower. (I-317)

TAYLOR, JOHN.
    Signer, Bush Declaration, March 22, 1775. (D-355)
    War Committee, Harford County, 1775. (D-358)
    Captain of Company No. 7, September 9, 1775. (D-359, E-113)
    Signer and solicitor, Association of Freemen, 1775, Bush River
    Lower; Signer, 1776; Solicitor, Gunpowder Upper, 1776, and
    referred to as Major. (E-263, I-315, I-319)
    Signer, Oath of Allegiance to Md., 1778. (A-36, B-21, J-239)
    Second Sheriff of Harford County, 1778. (E-357)

TAYLOR, JOHN (Planter).
    (1) Private, Capt. Webb's Co. No. 16, October 14, 1775. (E-121)
        Signer, Association of Freemen, 1776, Deer Creek Upper. (I-323)
        Signer, Oath of Allegiance to Md., 1778. (A-36, B-15, J-236)
    (2) Private, Capt. Harris; Harford Rifles, 1776. (E-124)
        Paid subsistence for 3 weeks, 3 days, Oct. 7, 1776. (K-436)
        Signer, Association of Freemen, 1776, Bush River Lower. (I-319)
        Signer, Oath of Allegiance to Md., 1778. (A-36, B-22, J-240)

TAYLOR, JOHN, of Charles.
    Signer, Association of Freemen, 1776, Gunpowder Upper. (I-326)
    Signer, Oath of Allegiance to Md., 1778. (A-36, B-23, J-241)

TAYLOR, JOHN, of John.
    Signer, Association of Freemen, 1776, Gunpowder Upper. (I-326)
    Signer, Oath of Allegiance to Md., 1778. (A-36, B-15, J-236)

TAYLOR, JOHN HODGES.
    Signer, Association of Freemen, 1775, Gunpowder Neck. (I-327)
    Signer, Oath of Allegiance to Md., 1778. (A-36, B-14, J-236)

TAYLOR, ROBERT.
   Private, Capt. Dorsey's Co. No. 8, October 31, 1775. (E-114, N-80)
   Signer, Association of Freemen, 1776, Spesutie Lower. (I-318)

TAYLOR, ROBERT.
   Private, Capt. Love's Co. No. 10, Sept. 14, 1775. (E-116, N-80)

TAYLOR, STEPHEN.
   Private, Capt. Dorsey's Co. No. 8, October 31, 1775. (E-114)
   Signer, Association of Freemen, 1776, Spesutie Lower. (I-317)

TAYLOR, THOMAS.
   Private, Capt. Rumsey's Co. No. 6, September 16, 1775. (E-112)
   Signer, Association of Freemen, 1775, Gunpowder Neck. (I-327)
   Signer, Oath of Allegiance to Md., 1778. (A-36, B-14, J-235)

TAYLOR, WALTER.
   Private, Capt. Rodgers' Co. No. 5, September 15, 1775. (E-111)
   Signer, Oath of Allegiance to Md., 1778. (A-36, B-26, J-243)

TAYN, JOHN DEALY.
   Signer, Oath of Allegiance to Md., 1778. (A-36, B-29, J-246)

TEATS, C. S.
   Signer, Oath of Allegiance to Md., 1778. (A-36, B-25, J-242)

TENCH, LUSTER.
   Signer, Association of Freemen, 1776, Bush River Upper. (I-320)

TERREY, JOHN.
   Signer, Oath of Allegiance to Md., 1778. (A-36)

TERREY, PATRICK.
   Signer, Oath of Allegiance to Md., 1778. (A-36, B-28, J-245)

THACKER (THAKER), JOHN.
   Signer, Association of Freemen, 1776, Eden Hundred. (I-323)
   Signer, Oath of Allegiance to Md., 1778. (A-36, B-19, J-238)

THOMAS, ANDRA.
   Signer, Association of Freemen, 1776, Bush River Upper. (I-320)

THOMAS, BENJAMIN.
   Private, Capt. Webb's Co. No. 16, October 14, 1775. (E-121)
   Signer, Association of Freemen, 1776, Deer Creek Upper. (I-323)

THOMAS, DANIEL.
   Private, Capt. Taylor's Co. No. 7, September 9, 1775. (E-113)
   Signer, Association of Freemen, 1776, Gunpowder Upper. (I-326)
   Signer, Oath of Allegiance to Md., 1778. (A-36, B-12, J-234)

THOMAS, DAVID.
   Private, Capt. Love's Co. No. 10, September 14, 1775. (E-116)
   Signer, Association of Freemen, 1776, Spesutie Upper, (I-318)

THOMAS, EVAN.
    Militia Substitute, 1781, 3 years. (E-133, F-401)

THOMAS, HENRY.
    Private, Capt. Love's Co. No. 10, September 14, 1775. (E-116)
    Signer, Association of Freemen, 1776, Spesutie Upper. (I-318)
    Signer, Oath of Allegiance to Md., 1778. (A-36, B-13, J-235)

THOMAS, JAMES.
    Private, Capt. Love's Co. No. 10, September 14, 1775. (E-116)
    Private, Capt. Paca's Company, July 24, 1776. (E-126, F-59)
    Signer, Association of Freemen, 1776, Spesutie Upper. (I-318)

THOMAS, JAMES.
    Ensign, Deer Creek Battalion, Militia, March 10, 1776. (E-266)

THOMAS, JOHN.
    Corporal, Capt. Love's Co. No. 10, September 14, 1775. (E-115)
    Signer, Association of Freemen, 1776, Spesutie Upper. (I-318)
    Signer, Oath of Allegiance to Md., 1778. (A-36, B-23, J-241)

THOMAS, JOHN.
    Signer, Association of Freemen, 1776, Harford Lower. (I-324)

THOMAS, JOSEPH.
    Signer, Association of Freemen, 1775/1776, Bush River Upper.
    Signer, Oath of Allegiance, 1778. (A-36, B-29, J-246, I-316, 320)

THOMAS, THOMAS.
    Private, Capt. Baker's Co. No. 15, January 27, 1776. (E-120)
    Signer, Association of Freemen, 1776, Eden Hundred. (I-324)
    Signer, Oath of Allegiance to Md., 1778. (B-24, J-242)
    Land Warrant 11758 (100 acres) applied Jan. 11, 1796. (N-80)

THOMAS, THOMAS.
    Signer, Oath of Allegiance to Md., 1778. (A-36, B-29, J-246)

THOMPSON, ALEXANDER.
    Signer, Association of Freemen, 1776, Spesutie Upper. (I-319)
    Signer, Oath of Allegiance to Md., 1778. (A-36, B-30, J-247)
    Ensign, 8th Battalion, Militia, 1778. (C-47)

THOMPSON, ANDREW.
    Private, Capt. Baker's Co. No. 15, January 27, 1776. (E-120)

THOMPSON, DANIEL.
    Signer, Oath of Allegiance to Md., 1778. (A-36, B-30, J-247)

THOMPSON, DAVID.
    Corporal, Capt. Rodgers' Co. No. 5, September 15, 1775. (E-110)
    Private, Capt. Francis Holland's Harford Rifles, 1776. (E-124)
    Signer, Association of Freemen, 1775, Bush River Upper; listed
       as "D. Thompson." (I-316)

THOMAS, ISAAC.
    Furnished 4 guns and 3 bayonets to the committee, 1776. (E-328)

THOMPSON, EDWARD.
    Private, Capt. Archer's Co. No. 2, September 16, 1775. (E-107)

THOMPSON, JOHN.
    Private, Capt. Rumsey's Co. No. 6, September 16, 1775. (E-112)
    Sergeant, 1st Company of Maryland Riflemen under Colonel Moses Rawlings, 1776. (D-361)
    Sergeant, 4th Maryland Regiment, 1776-July, 1777. Fought at Battle of Fort Washington, Nov. 16, 1776. (E-129, 136, F-301)
    Militia Substitute, 1781 "to 10th December." (E-133, F-401)

THOMPSON, SAMUEL.
    Private, Capt. Dorsey's Co. No. 8, October 31, 1775. (E-114)

THOMPSON, THOMAS.
    Private, Capt. Love's Co. No. 10, September 14, 1775. (E-116)
    Signer, Association of Freemen, 1775, Bush River Upper, and Spesutie Upper, 1776. (I-316, I-318)

THOMSON, ALEXANDER.
    Signer, Association of Freemen, 1775, Bush River Upper. (I-317)
    Private, Capt. Robert Harris' Harford Rifles, 1776. (E-123)
    Paid subsistence for 2 weeks, October 17, 1776. (K-436)

THOMSON, ANDREW.
    Signer, Association of Freemen, 1775, Bush River Upper; listed as "A. Thomson." (I-317)
    Signer, Oath of Allegiance to Md., 1778. (A-36, B-29, J-246)

THOMSON, DANIEL.
    Signer, Association of Freemen, 1776, Bush River Lower. (I-328)

THOMSON, JAMES.
    Signer, Association of Freemen, 1776, Eden Hundred. (I-323)
    Signer, Oath of Allegiance to Md., 1778. (A-36, B-30, J-247)

THORIMAN, WILLIAM.
    Private, Capt. Webb's Co. No. 16, October 14, 1775. (E-121)

THORNTON, GEORGE.
    Signer, Association of Freemen, 1775, Gunpowder Neck. (I-327)

THURSTON (THUSTON), THOMAS.
    Private, Capt. Love's Co. No. 10, September 14, 1775. (E-116)
    Signer, Association of Freemen, 1776, Spesutie Upper. (I-318)
    Signer, Oath of Allegiance to Md., 1778. (A-36, B-15, J-236)

TIARNEY, PATRICK.
    Born 1748, in Ireland. Private, Flying Camp. Lt. John Smith enlisted July 15, 1776, in Colonel Thomas Ewing's Battalion. At time of enlistment he was 5'4½" tall with black hair and a sandy complexion. (E-125, F-56)

TILBROOK, JOHN.
    Signer, Oath of Allegiance to Md., 1778. (A-36, B-26, J-243)

TIMMONS, AMBROSE.
    Private, Capt. Bussey's Company, 1776. (E-127, F-60)

TIMMONS, JOHN.
    Signer, Association of Freemen, 1775, Gunpowder Neck. (I-327)
    Signer, Oath of Allegiance to Md., 1778. (A-36, B-18, J-237)

TINNY, JOHN.
    Private, Capt. Archer's Co. No. 2, September 16, 1775. (E-107)

TODD, ANDREW.
    Signer, Oath of Allegiance to Md., 1778. (A-36, B-12, J-234)

TODD, GEORGE.
    Militia Substitute, 1781. (E-132, F-400)

TODD, PATRICK.
    Signer, Oath of Allegiance to Md., 1778. (A-36, B-12, J-234)

TOLLENGER, GEORGE.
    Private, Capt. Archer's Co. No. 2, September 16, 1775. (E-107)
    Signer, Association of Freemen, 1776, Harford Upper. (I-325)

* TOLLEY, EDWARD CARVEL (1753-1790). Married Cordelia Hall c.1774.
    Private, Capt. Josias Hall's Co. No. 1, Sept. 12, 1775. (E-105)
    Signer, Association of Freemen, 1776, Spesutie Lower. (I-318)
    Signer, Oath of Allegiance to Md., 1778. (A-36, B-21. J-239)

TOLLEY, ZEP.
    Private, Capt. Rumsey's Co. No. 6, September 16, 1775. (E-112)

TOMBY, THOMAS.
    Signer, Oath of Allegiance to Md., 1778. (A-36, B-28, J-245)

TOOLE, JOHN.
    Private, Capt. Bussey's Company, July 20, 1776. (E-127. F-60)

TOPPEY, WILLIAM.
    Signer, Oath of Allegiance to Md., 1778. (A-36, B-10, J-233)

TOSSETT. JONATHAN.
    Signer, Oath of Allegiance to Md., 1778. (A-36, B-10, J-234)

TOULSON, ISAAC.
    Private, Capt. Dorsey's Co. No. 8, October 31, 1775. (E-114)

TOUT (TOUTE, TONTE), ABRAM.
    Signer, Association of Freemen, 1776, Bush River Upper. (I-320)
    Signer, Oath of Allegiance to Md., 1778. (A-36. B-19, J-238)

* Edward Tolley also was commissioned to collect the fines imposed on the non-associators in 1777 in Spesutia and Harford Lower Hundred. (E-338)

TOWNLEY (TOWNSLEY), JOHN.
    Private, Capt. Archer's Co. No. 2, September 16, 1775. (E-107)
    Signer, Association of Freemen, 1776, Harford Upper. (I-325)
    Signer, Oath of Allegiance to Md., 1778. (A-36, B-27, J-244)

TOWNLEY (TOWNSLEY), JOHN.
    Private, Capt. Archer's Co. No. 2, September 16, 1775. (E-107)
    Signer, Association of Freemen, 1776, Harford Upper. (I-325)

TRACEY, JARRET.
    Harford County Pensioner in 1840. (E-262)

TRACEY (TREASY), USHER.
    Private, Capt. Dorsey's Co. No. 8, October 31, 1775. (E-115)
    Signer, Association of Freemen, 1775, Spesutie Lower. (I-317)

TRAVIS, ROBERT.
    Private, Capt. Taylor's Co. No. 7, September 9, 1775. (E-113)
    Signer, Association of Freemen, 1776, Gunpowder Upper. (I-326)

TREADWAY, DANIEL.
    Born 1724. Died 1810/1812, Harford County. Married Sarah Norris in 1744. Son of Thomas and Ann Treadway. Children: Crispin, James, Sarah, Thomas, Edward, Ann Hughes, Hannah Meads, Susanna Reston, Elizabeth Miles (all named in his will). (M-181, and R, Box 2, G5048) Thomas Treadway married Christiana Saunders.
    Signer, Association of Freemen, 1775, Bush River Upper. (I-316) Record indicates two signers with this name. (I-317)

TREADWAY (TREDWAY), EDWARD.
    Born 1730. Son of Thomas and Ann Treadway. (R, Box 2, G5048)
    Signer, Association of Freemen, 1776, Bush River Lower. (I-328)

TREDWELL, DANIEL.
    Private, Capt. Rumsey's Co. No. 6, September 16, 1775. (E-112)
    Signer, Association of Freemen, 1775, Gunpowder Neck. (I-327)

TRENE (TRENO), JAMES.
    Private, Capt. Robert Harris' Harford Rifles, 1776. (E-123)
    Paid subsistence for 6 weeks, 2 days, Sept. 16, 1776. (K-435)

TRICKERT, OBADIAH.
    Signer, Oath of Allegiance to Md., 1778. (A-37, B-17, J-237)

TRONS, JOHN.
    Signer, Oath of Allegiance to Md., 1778. (A-37, B-10, J-234)

TROTTER (TROTER), JAMES.
    Private, Capt. Webb's Co. No. 16, October 14, 1775. (E-121)
    Signer, Association of Freemen, 1776, Deer Creek Upper. (I-323)

TROTTER (TROTER), RICHARD.
    Private, Capt. Webb's Co. No. 16, October 14, 1775. (E-122)
    Signer, Association of Freemen, 1776, Deer Creek Upper. (I-323)

TRUELOCK, ISAAC.
    Signer, Association of Freemen, 1775, Spesutie Lower. (I-317)
    Signer, Association of Freemen, 1776, Gunpowder Neck. (I-327)

TRUELOCK, MOSES.
    Signer, Association of Freemen, 1775, Spesutie Lower. (I-317)
    Signer, Association of Freemen, 1776, Gunpowder Neck. (I-327)

TRUSS, WILLIAM.
    Militia Substitute, 1781. (E-132, F-400)

TRY, PAULTIS.
    Signer, Oath of Allegiance to Md., 1778. (A-37, B-22, J-240)

TUCKER, SEABORN.
    "Seaborn Tuckin" married Elizabeth Hitchcock in 1762. (M-182)
    Private, Capt. Rigdon's Co. No. 12, December 2, 1775. (E-118)
    Signer, Association of Freemen, 1776, Deer Creek Upper. (I-322)

TUDER, JOHN.
    Signer, Oath of Allegiance to Md., 1778. (A-37, B-14, J-236)

TURK, JAMES.
    Private, Capt. Baker's Co. No. 15, January 27, 1776. (E-120)

TURNELL, THOMAS.
    Signer, Oath of Allegiance to Md., 1778. (A-37, B-29, J-246)

TURNER, ALEXANDER.
    Signer, Association of Freemen, 1775, Bush River Upper. (I-316)

TURNER, ANDREW.
    Signer, Association of Freemen, 1775, Bush River Upper. (I-328)
    Signer, Association of Freemen, 1776, Spesutie Upper. (I-319)
    Signer, Oath of Allegiance to Md., 1778. (A-37, B-28, J-245)

TURNER, DANIEL.
    Signer, Association of Freemen, 1776, Spesutie Upper. (I-319)
    Signer, Oath of Allegiance to Md., 1778. (A-37, B-29, J-246)

TURNER, JOHN.
    Married Anne Elizabeth Mariner in 1788, Harford County; marriage proven through Maryland pensions application. (N-124)
    Private, Maryland Line. (N-52) There were 7 pay certificates issued in the name of John Turner in the 1st and 2nd Maryland Regiments (80825, 81830, 84938, 84943, 86178, 86938, 87354). No indication as to which were issued to this John Turner. (P-514)
    Signer, Oath of Allegiance to Md., 1778. (A-37, B-23, J-241)

TURNER, PATRICK.
    Signer, Oath of Allegiance to Md., 1778. (A-37, B-29, J-246)

TURNER, ROBERT.
    Signer, Association of Freemen, 1775, Bush River Upper. (I-316)
    Signer, Association of Freemen, 1776, Bush River Upper. (I-328)
    Signer, Oath of Allegiance to Md., 1778. (A-37, B-19, J-238)

TURNER, SAMUEL.
    Signer, Association of Freemen, 1775, Bush River Upper. (I-316)
    Signer, Association of Freemen, 1776, Bush River Upper. (I-328)

TURNER, THOMAS.
    Signer, Association of Freemen, 1775, Bush River Upper. (I-328)
    Signer, Oath of Allegiance to Md., 1778. (A-37, B-20, J-239)

TUSH, SAMUEL.
    Private, Capt. Dorsey's Co. No. 8, October 31, 1775. (E-114)

TWEEDELL, ALEXANDER.
    Signer, Association of Freemen, 1776, Bush River Upper. (I-320)

TWINING, NATHANIEL.
    Signer, Association of Freemen, 1776, Gunpowder Upper. (I-326)

TYNDALL, SAMUEL.
    Pensioner (maimed soldier), 1778. (F-661)

U

USHER, JOHN.
    Militia Substitute 1781. (E-131, F-400)

V

VAN BIBBER, ABRAHAM.
    Shipped gunpowder supplies, 1776. (K-170, K-171, K-414)

VANCE, DAVID.
    Private, Capt. Bradford's Co. No. 13, September 30, 1775. (E-119)
    Signer, Association of Freemen, 1775, Gunpowder Neck. (I-327)
    Signer, Oath of Allegiance to Md., 1778. (A-37, B-10, J-233)

VANCE, JOHN.
    Private, Capt. Bradford's Co. No. 13, September 30, 1775. (E-119)
    Signer, Association of Freemen, 1776, Bush River Upper. (I-328)
    Signer, Oath of Allegiance to Md., 1778. (A-37, B-29, J-246)

VANCE, SAMUEL.
    Private, Capt. Bradford's Co. No. 13, September 30, 1775. (E-119)
    Signer, Association of Freemen, 1775, Gunpowder Neck. (I-327)
    Signer, Oath of Allegiance to Md., 1778. (A-37, B-10, J-233)

VANCLEAVE (VANCLEANE), JOHN.
    Signer, Oath of Allegiance to Md., 1778. (A-37, B-21, J-239)

VANDERGRIFT (VANDEGRIFT), GEORGE.
    Private, Capt. Archer's Co. No. 2, September 16, 1775. (E-107)
    Signer, Oath of Allegiance to Md., 1778. (A-37, B-16, J-237)

VANGHAN (VAUGHN, VAGHAN), GEORGE.
    Captain, Deer Creek Battalion, Militia, 1778.
    "Left the County." (C-43)

VANHORN, AARON.
    Signer, Oath of Allegiance to Md., 1778. (A-37, B-29, J-246)
    2nd Lieutenant, Deer Creek Battalion, Militia, 1779. (C-43)

VANHORN, EZEKIEL.
    Private, Capt. Archer's Co. No. 2, September 16, 1775. (E-108)
    Signer, Oath of Allegiance to Md., 1778. (A-37, B-25, J-242)

VANHORN, GABRIEL PETERSON.
    Signer and solicitor, Association of Freemen, 1775, Bush River
      Lower Committee. (E-263)
    Signer and solicitor, Association of Freemen, 1776, Eden
      Hundred. (I-315, I-323)
    Signer, Oath of Allegiance to Md., 1778. (A-37, B-29)
    Listed in record as "G. P. Vanhorn."
    Captain, Deer Creek Battalion, Militia, 1778. (C-43)
    Quartermaster, Maryland Service (non-pensioner). (N-105)
    Colonel; married Mary Van Sant; died c.1815. (X-700)

VANHORN, RICHARD.
    Signer, Oath of Allegiance to Md., 1778. (A-37, B-25, J-242)

VANN, EDWARD.
    Signer, Association of Freemen, 1776, Harford Hundred. (I-325)

VANSICKLE (VANSICKLES, VANSUKLER), HENRY.
    Private, Capt. Aquila Hall's Co. No. 4, September 9, 1775. (E-109)
    Signer, Association of Freemen, 1775, Spesutie Lower. (I-317)
    Signer, Oath of Allegiance to Md., 1778. (A-237, B-21)
    Harford County Grand Juror, 1779. (E-75)

VANTWORTH, WILLIAM.
Private, Capt. Rodgers Co. No. 5, September 15, 1775. (E-110)

VANZANT, JOHN.
Pensioner (maimed soldier), 1778. (F-661)
Pay Certificates No. 81847, $80, 2nd Md. Regt.; No. 84958, $43.30, Md. Regt. paid to November 16, 1783; No. 86216, $80, Maryland Regt. paid to January 1, 1782. (P-518)

VARNEY, JAMES.
Signer, Oath of Allegiance to Md., 1778. (A-37, B-29, J-246)

VEACH, GEORGE.
Private, Capt. Rodgers Co. No. 5, September 15, 1775. (E-111)

VERNAY, JAMES.
Signer, Association of Freemen, 1776, Spesutie Upper. (I-318)

VOGAN, GEORGE.
Signer, Association of Freemen, 1776, Bush River Upper. (I-320)

VOGAN, JAMES.
Signer, Association of Freemen, 1775 and 1776, Bush River Upper. (I-317, I-320)

W

WADLOW, JOHN.
Signer, Association of Freemen, 1776, Bush River Lower. (I-319)

WAILEY, BENJAMIN.
Private, Capt. Robert Harris' Harford Rifles, 1776. (E-123)
Paid subsistence for 2 weeks, 4 days, Oct. 18, 1776. (K-436)

WAKELING, JOHN.
Signer, Oath of Allegiance to Md., 1778. (A-37, B-30, J-247)

WALCOTT, JOHN.
Signer, Oath of Allegiance to Md., 1778. (A-37, B-21, J-239)

WALDRON, RICHARD.
Signer, Association of Freemen, 1776, Spesutie Upper. (I-319)
Signer, Oath of Allegiance to Md., 1778. (A-37, B-26, J-243)

WALKER, JAMES.
(1) Private, Capt. Archer's Co. No. 2, Sept. 16, 1775. (E-107)
(2) Private, Capt. Taylor's Co. No. 7, Sept. 9, 1775. (E-113)
(3) 2nd Lieutenant, 23rd Battalion, Militia, 1778. (C-45)
Signer, Association of Freemen, 1776, Gunpowder Upper. (I-326)
Signer, Oath of Allegiance to Md., 1778. (A-37, B-26, J-243)

WALKER, JOHN.
    (1) Private, Capt. Rodgers Co. No. 5, Sept. 15, 1775. (E-111)
    (2) Private, Capt. Dorsey's Co. No. 8, Oct. 31, 1775. (E-115)
    (3) Private, Capt. Paca's Company, August 5, 1776. (E-127, F-59)
    Signer, Association of Freemen, 1775, Bush River Upper. (I-316)
    Signer, Association of Freemen, 1776, Bush River Upper. (I-320)
    Signer, Association of Freemen, 1776, Spesutie Lower. (I-318)
    Signer, Oath of Allegiance to Md., 1778. (A-37, B-10, J-233)

WALKER, JONATHAN.
    Private, Capt. Paca's Company, July 24, 1776. (E-126, F-59)
    Signer, Association of Freemen, 1775, Spesutie Lower. (I-317)
    Signer, Association of Freemen, 1776, Harford Lower. (I-324)

WALKER, SAMUEL.
    Signer, Association of Freemen, 1776, Bush River Upper. (I-320)

WALKER, THOMAS.
    Private, Capt. Rodgers Co. No. 5, September 15, 1775. (E-110)

WALKINS, JOHN.
    Signer, Oath of Allegiance to Md., 1778. (A-37)

WALLACE, THOMAS.
    Signer, Association of Freemen, 1776, Deer Creek Lower. (I-321)

WALLINGSFORD, BENJAMIN.
    Signer, Association of Freemen, 1775, Spesutie Lower. (I-317)

WALSH, NICHOLAS.
    Signer, Association of Freemen, 1776, Deer Creek Upper. (I-322)
    Signer, Association of Freemen, 1776, Gunpowder Upper. (I-326)

WALSH, PATRICK.
    Signer, Association of Freemen, 1776, Gunpowder Upper. (I-326)

WALTHAM, CHARLTON.
    Signer, Association of Freemen, 1775, Gunpowder Neck. (I-327)
    Signer, Oath of Allegiance to Md., 1778. (A-37, B-20, J-239)

WALTHAM, THOMAS.
    Signer, Oath of Allegiance to Md., 1778. (A-37, B-14, J-235)

WALTHAM, WILLIAM.
    Signer, Association of Freemen, 1775, Gunpowder Neck. (I-323)
    Signer, Oath of Allegiance to Md., 1778. (A-37, B-14, J-236)

WAMAGIN, THOMAS.
    Signer, Oath of Allegiance to Md.,1778. (A-37, B-25, J-242)

WANN, JOHN.
    Signer, Association of Freemen, 1776, Gunpowder Upper. (I-325)

WARD, EDWARD SR.
    Signer, Bush Declaration, March 22, 1775. (D-355)
    War Committee, Harford County, 1775. (D-358)
    Signer, Association of Freemen, 1776, Deer Creek Lower. (I-322)

WARD, EDWARD JR.
    Born 1736. Died 1783. Married: Mary Griffith, 1761. (M-186, X-715)
    Private, Capt. Aquila Hall's Co. No. 4, September 9, 1775. (E-110)
    Signer, Oath of Allegiance to Maryland, 1778. (A-37, B-21, J-239)

WARD, JAMES.
    Private, Capt. Rigdon's Co. No. 12, December 2, 1775. (E-118)
    Signer, Association of Freemen, 1776, Deer Creek Upper. (I-322)

WARD, JOSHUA.
    Private, Capt. Rigdon's Co. No. 12, December 2, 1775. (E-118)
    Signer, Association of Freemen, 1776, Deer Creek Upper. (I-322)

WARD, RICHARD.
    Signer, Association of Freemen, 1776, Deer Creek Lower. (I-322)
    Ensign, Capt. Patrick's Co. No. 17, April 1, 1776. (E-122, E-266)
    Ensign, Deer Creek Battalion, 1778; 1st Lieut., 1779. (C-44)

WARE, JOHN.
    2nd Lieutenant, Capt. Stewart's Co. No. 9, 1775. (D-359, E-115)
    Signer, Association of Freemen, 1776, Bush River Upper. (I-320)
    Signer, Oath of Allegiance to Md., 1778. (A-37, B-30, J-247)

WARE, THOMAS.
    Signer, Association of Freemen, 1775, Bush River Upper. (I-316)
    Signer, Oath of Allegiance to Md., 1778. (A-37, B-30, J-247)

WARFIELD, HENRY.
    Signer, Association of Freemen, 1775, Spesutie Lower. (I-317)
    Signer, Association of Freemen, 1776, Harford Lower. (I-324)
    Signer, Oath of Allegiance to Md., 1778. (A-37, B-22, J-240)
    Harford County Grand Juror, 1779. (E-75)

WARMAN, JOSEPH.
    Signer, Association of Freemen, 1776, Deer Creek Upper. (I-323)
    Signer, Oath of Allegiance to Md., 1778. (A-37, B-14, J-236)

WARNOCK, PHILIP.
    Private, Capt. Patrick's Co. No. 17, April 1, 1776. (E-122)
    Signer, Association of Freemen, 1776, Deer Creek Lower. (I-322)

WARWICK, ANDREW.
    Private, Capt. Bond's Co. No. 11, December 9, 1775. (E-117)

WARWICK (WARRICK, WORRICK), JOHN.
    Private, Capt. Baker's Co. No. 15, January 27, 1776. (E-120)
    Signer, Association of Freemen, 1776, Eden Hundred. (I-324)
    Signer, Oath of Allegiance to Md., 1778. (A-37, B-19, J-238)

WARNER, CUTHBERT.
    Furnished 13 musquets to the County, June, 1776. (E-330)

WARWICK (WARRICK), WILLIAM.
    Private, Capt. Baker's Co. No. 15, January 27, 1776. (E-120)
    Signer, Association of Freemen, 1776, Eden Hundred. (I-324)
    Signer, Oath of Allegiance to Md., 1778. (A-37, B-19, J-238)

WATERS (WATTERS), THOMAS.
    Signer, Association of Freemen, 1776, Bush River Upper. (I-328)
    Signer, Oath of Allegiance to Md., 1778. (A-37, B-12, J-234)

WATKINS, JOHN SR.
    Signer, Association of Freemen, 1776, Deer Creek Upper. (I-322)

WATKINS, JOHN.
    Private, Capt. Rigdon's Co. No. 12, December 2, 1775. (E-118)
    Source G-741 states he was born 1755 and died 1826; source X-721
    states he was born 1758 and died 1847. Both sources state that
    he married Ruth Guyton.
    Children: Samuel, John, Isiah, Elizabeth. (G-741)
    Signer, Association of Freemen, 1776, Deer Creek Upper. (I-322)
    Listed as "John Watkins, Jr."
    Signer, Oath of Allegiance to Md., 1778, (B-21, J-239)

WATKINS, SAMUEL.
    2nd Lieutenant, Deer Creek Battalion, Militia, 1778. (C-43)
    Signer, Oath of Allegiance to Md., 1778. (A-37, B-19, J-238)

WATSON, ABRAHAM.
    Private, 4th Maryland Regiment, 1776. Rifleman, Battle of Fort
    Washington, November 16, 1776. On furlough, January, 1778;
    deserted when on furlough. (E-129, E-136, F-301)

WATSON, ARCHIBALD.
    Signer, Association of Freemen, 1776, Harford Upper. (I-325)
    Signer, Oath of Allegiance to Md., 1778. (A-37, B-26, J-243)

WATSON, JAMES.
    Private, Capt. Robert Harris' Harford Rifles, 1776. (E-123)
    Paid subsistence for 4 weeks, 3 days, October 4, 1776. (K-435)
    Signer, Association of Freemen, 1776, Spesutie Upper. (I-318)
    Signer, Oath of Allegiance to Md., 1778. (A-37, B-28, J-245)

WATSON, WILLIAM.
    Signer, Oath of Allegiance to Md., 1778. (B-30, J-247)

WATT (WAT), ROBERT.
    Signer, Oath of Allegiance to Md., 1778. (A-37, B-30, J-247)

WATT, SAMUEL.
    Signer, Association of Freemen, 1776, Deer Creek Upper. (I-322)

WATTS, RICHARD.
    Private, Capt. Rodgers Co. No. 5, September 15, 1775. (E-110)

WAVY (WARY), DAVID.
    Private, Capt. Robert Harris' Harford Rifles, 1776. (E-123)
    Paid subsistence for 4 weeks, 4 days, October 1, 1776. (K-436)

WEAIN (WEARIN), JOHN.
    Signer, Oath of Allegiance to Md., 1778. (A-37, B-31, J-248)

WEAR, JOHN.
    Signer, Association of Freemen, 1775, Bush River Upper. (I-317)

WEBB, JOHN JR.
    Ensign, Capt. Webb's Co. No. 16, October 14, 1775. (E-121)
    Ensign, Militia; widow applied for pension. (N-53)

WEBB, SAMUEL.
    Signer, Association of Freemen, 1776, Deer Creek Upper. (I-323)
    Signer, Oath of Allegiance to Md., 1778. (A-37, B-14, J-235)
    1st Lieutenant, Deer Creek Battalion, Militia, 1778. (C-43)
    Harford County Grand Juror, 1783. (E-77)

WEBB, SAMUEL JR.
    Born 1746. Died 1813. Married: Sarah_____. (X-724)
    Ensign, Capt. Webb's Co. No. 16, October 14, 1775. (E-265, E-267)
    Signer, Association of Freemen, 1776, Deer Creek Upper. (I-323)
    Signer, Oath of Allegiance to Md., 1778. (A-37, B-14, J-235)

WEBB, WILLIAM.
    Signer, Bush Declaration, March 22, 1775. (D-355)
    War Committee, Correspondence, 1775. (D-359, E-96)
    Representative to Maryland Convention, June, 1775. (E-97)
    Captain, Company No. 16, Militia, October 14, 1775. (D-359, E-121)
    Captain, 8th Battalion, Militia, appointed 1776. (E-265, E-267)
    Signer, Association of Freemen, 1776, Deer Creek Upper. (I-323)
    Signer, Oath of Allegiance to Md., 1778. (A-37, B-14, J-235)
    Administered the Oath, 1778 ("Worshipfull William Webb"). (B-14)
    Harford County Court Justice, 1774. (E-63) Furnished a draw bow gun
                                      with bullet moulds, 1776. (E-335)

WEBSTER, ISAAC, of John.
    Married Sarah Robinson in 1761. (S-369) Member of Bush River Company.
    War Committee, Correspondence, 1775. (D-358, E-95)   (E-232)

WEBSTER, JAMES.
    Son of Isaac Webster and Margaret Lee. (S-369)
    Private, Capt. Josias Hall's Co. No. 1, Sept. 12, 1775. (E-105)
    Signer, Association of Freemen, 1776, Deer Creek Lower. (I-321)
    Another James Webster signed in Harford Hundred, 1776. (I-325)

WEBSTER, JOHN LEE.
    Son of Isaac Webster and Margaret Lee. Married: (1) Susanna
        Griffith; (2) Elizabeth (Skinner) Carter. (S-369)
    Private, Capt. Josias Hall's Co. No. 1, Sept. 12, 1775. (E-106)
    Signer, Association of Freemen, 1775, Spesutie Lower. (I-317)

WEBSTER, JOSEPH.
    Signer, Association of Freemen, 1775, Gunpowder Neck. (I-327)

WEBSTER, MICHAEL.
    Signer, Association of Freemen, 1776, Harford Upper. (I-325)

WEBSTER, SAMUEL, son of Isaac.
    Signer, Association of Freemen, 1776, Harford Upper. (I-325)

WEBSTER, SAMUEL JR.
    Signer, Association of Freemen, 1776, Harford Upper. (I-325)

WEBSTER, SAMUEL SR.
    Signer, Association of Freemen, 1776, Harford Upper. (I-325)
    Signer, Oath of Allegiance to Md., 1778. (A-37, B-10, J-234)

WEBSTER, THOMAS.
    Private, Capt. Francis Holland's Harford Rifles, 1776. (E-124)

WEDONEY, PETER.
    Militia Substitute, 1781 "to 10th December." (E-133, F-401)

WEEKS, JOHN.
    Signer, Association of Freemen, 1776, Bush River Lower. (I-319)

WELCH, JOHN.
    Private, Capt. Archer's Co. No. 2, September 16, 1775. (E-107)
    Signer, Association of Freemen, 1776, Spesutie Upper. (I-319)

WELLS, JAMES.
    Signer, Oath of Allegiance, 1778. (A-37, B-26, J-243)

WELLS, RICHARD JR.
    Harford County War Committee, 1775. (D-358)

WELLS, WILLIAM.
    Signer, Oath of Allegiance, 1778. (A-37, B-14, J-235)

WELSH, JAMES.
    Signer, Association of Freemen, 1776, Spesutie Upper. (I-319)
    Another James Welsh signed in Harford Upper, 1776. (I-325)

WELSH, JOHN.
    Private, Capt. Love's Co. No. 10, September 14, 1775. (E-116)
    Signer, Association of Freemen, 1776, Harford Upper. (I-325)

WELSH, THOMAS.
    Private, Capt. Paca's Company, July 24, 1776. (E-126, F-59)

WELSH, WILLIAM.
    Sergeant, Capt. Rodgers Co No. 5, September 15, 1775. (E-110)
    Signer, Association of Freemen, 1776, Harford Upper. (I-325)

WEST, DAVID.
    Signer, Association of Freemen, 1776, Bush River Upper. (I-320)
    Signer, Oath of Allegiance to Md., 1778. (A-37, B-30, J-247)

WEST, ENOS.
    Married Jane Robinson in Harford County. Marriage proven through Maryland pension application; nothing given on service. (N-125)

WEST, JOHN.
    Private, Capt. Patrick's Co. No. 17, April 1, 1776. (E-122)

WEST, JONA.
    Drafted, Militia, 1781; "poor; a wife and children to support." (E-132, F-400)

WEST, JONATHAN.
    Private, Capt. Love's Co. No. 10, September 14, 1775. (E-116)
    Signer, Association of Freemen, 1776, Spesutie Upper. (I-318)
    Signer, Oath of Allegiance to Md., 1778. (A-37, B-28, J-245)

WEST, JONATHAN JR.
    Married Sophia Kimball in 1758. (M-191)
    Signer, Association of Freemen, 1776, Spesutie Upper. (I-318)
    Signer, Oath of Allegiance to Md., 1778. (A-37, B-28, J-245)

WEST, MICHAEL.
    Private, Capt. Rodgers Co. No. 5, September 15, 1775. (E-111)

WEST, NATHANIEL SR.
    Ensign, Capt. Love's Company No. 10, September 14, 1775. (E-115)
    Ensign, Deer Creek Battalion, Militia, 1778. (C-43)
    Signer, Oath of Allegiance to Md., 1778. (A-37, B-28, J-245)

WEST, NATHANIEL JR.
    Signer, Association of Freemen, 1776, Bush River Upper. (I-320)
    Signer, Oath of Allegiance to Md., 1778. (A-37, B-28, J-245)

WEST, ROBERT.
    Private, Capt. Anderson's Co. No. 3, September 23, 1775. (E-108)
    Signer, Association of Freemen, 1775/6, Susquehanna. (D-357, I-321)

WEST, THOMAS.
    Private, Capt. Rodgers Co. No. 5, September 15, 1775. (E-110)

WEST, WILLIAM.
    Private, Capt. Love's Co. No. 10, September 14, 1775. (E-116)
    "Rev. William West" on Committee of Correspondence, 1775. (E-95)
    Siger, Association of Freemen, 1776, Spesutie Upper. (I-318)
    Signer, Oath of Allegiance to Md., 1778. (A-37, B-21, J-239)

WETHERALL (WETHERELL), HENRY.
    Harford County War Committee, 1775. (D-358)
    Signer, Association of Freemen, 1775, Gunpowder Neck, and Solicitor, Gunpowder Lower Committee, 1776. (E-263, I-327)
    Signer, Oath of Allegiance to Md., 1778. (A-37, B-14, J-236)

WHALER, JACOB.
    Signer, Oath of Allegiance to Maryland, 1778. (A-37, B-30, J-247)

WHEELER, BENJAMIN.
    Signer, Association of Freemen, 1776, Spesutie Upper. (I-319)

WHEELER, BENNETT.
    Private, Capt. Hall's Company No. 1, September 12, 1775. (E-106)
    Signer, Association of Freemen, 1776, Spesutie Upper. (I-319)
    Signer, Oath of Allegiance to Maryland, 1778. (A-37, B-28, J-245)

WHEELER, IGNATIUS, JR.
    Born 1744. Died 1793. Married Henrietta (Neale) Smith. Children:
    Monica Wheeler married Jacob Rutledge; Theresa (Treacy) Wheeler
    married Capt. Henry McAtee; Henrietta Maria Wheeler; Mary Ann
    (Polly) Wheeler married Samuel Brown; Elizabeth Wheeler married
    Samuel Brown after Mary's death; Bennett Wheeler; Ignatius
    Wheeler, never married; Francis Ignatius (Frank) Wheeler. Source
    E-224 states Col. Wheeler died in 1793, not 1786, and is buried
    in St. Ignatius Church in Hickory, MD. (E-224, E-226, G-752)
    Signer, Association of Freemen, 1776, Spesutie Upper. (I-318)
    Colonel, Deer Creek Battalion, Militia, April 9, 1778. (C-43, C-46)
    Harford County Court Justice, March 23, 1779. (E-75)
    1781-1783: Intendants Ledger A No. 9, ff. 22, 38; Army Accounts
        No. 1, p. 130; 1782: Intendants Ledger A No. 10, ff. 29, 37;
    1782-1786: Intendants Ledger Book 11, p.282; Intendants Orders No.1,
        f.56; No.2, f.15; Intendants Day Book 2, pp. 57, 103. (HR-50)
    1st Lieutenant, Capt. Webb's Co. No. 16, October 14, 1775. (D-359)
    1st Lieutenant, 8th Battalion, 1776. (E-121, E-265, E-267).
    Representative to Maryland Convention, June 26, 1775. (E-97)

WHEELER, IGNATIUS SR.
    Born c1714. Died 1786. Married Elizabeth Rosier; had 6 children.
    Signer, Association of Freemen, Deer Creek Upper Hundred, 1776. (I-323)

WHEELER, ISAAC.
    Private, Capt. Bradford's Co. No. 13, September 30, 1775. (E-119)
    Signer, Association of Freemen, 1776, Bush River Lower. (I-319)

WHEELER, JACOB.
    Born 1740. Died 1799. Married: Ann_____. Children: Thomas,
        Francis, Harriett, John, Sally, Benjamin, Healan, Jacob. (G-752)
    Signer, Oath of Allegiance to Maryland, 1778. (X-733, G-752)
    Signer, Association of Freemen, 1776, Eden Hundred. (I-323)

WHEELER, JAMES.
    Signer, Oath of Allegiance to Maryland, 1778. (A-37, B-10, J-234)

WHEELER, JOSEPH.
    Private, Capt. Hall's Co. No. 1, September 12, 1775. (E-106)
    Private, Capt. Francis Holland's Harford Rifles, 1776. (E-124)
    Signer, Association of Freemen, 1776, Spesutie Upper. (I-319)
    Captain, 23rd Battalion, Harford County Militia, 1778. (C-45)

WHEELER, JOSIAS.
    Private, Capt. Hall's Co. No. 1, September 12, 1775. (E-106)
    Private, Capt. Francis Holland's Harford Rifles, 1776. (E-124)
    Signer, Association of Freemen, 1776, Spesutie Upper. (I-319)

WHEELER, JOSIAS.
    Private, Capt. Love's Co. No. 10, September 14, 1775. (E-116)

WHEELER, THOMAS.
    Born 1755. Died 1809. Married:_____. Children: Ann Maria,
    Ellen, Sylvester, Ann. Juliet, Charles, Angus, James, Elizabeth.
    (G-753, X-733)
    Private, Capt. Love's Co. No. 10, September 14, 1775. (E-116)
    Private, Capt. Francis Holland's Co., Harford Rifles, 1776. (E-124)
    Signer, Association of Freemen, 1775/1776, Bush River Upper. (I-316)
    Signer, Oath of Allegiance, 1778. (A-37, B-20, J-247)   (I-320)

WHEELER, THOMAS, son of Benjamin.
    Signer, Association of Freemen, 1776, Spesutie Upper. (I-318)

WHELAN, RICHARD.
    Signer, Association of Freemen, 1775/1776, Bush River Upper. (I-317)
                                                                  (I-320)
WHITAKER (WHITACRE), ABRAHAM.
    Born 1737. Died 1784. Married Elizabeth Wheeler in 1771. (M-193)
    Children: Susanna, Abraham, Thomas, George, Josias. (W-177)
    Served with his brother Isaac in Capt. Christopher Gist's Company
    in the French and Indian War, enlisting in Baltimore County in
    1756 (5'8" tall, and a hunter by trade). Active in politics
    after the formation of Harford County in 1773. (W-177)
    Signer, Bush Declaration, March 22, 1775. (D-355, W-177)
    War Committee, Correspondence, June 11, 1775. (D-358, E-96, W-177)
    Listed as "Abram Whitaker."
    Signer, Association of Freemen, 1775/1776, Bush River Upper.
    Listed as "A. Whitaker."
    Signer, Oath of Allegiance to Md., 1778. (A-37, B-29, B-31)
    Administered the Oath ("Worshipfull Abraham Whitaker"), 1778.
    (J-245, J-246, J-247, J-248)
    Harford County Court Justice, 1783 ("Abraham Whitacre"). (E-77)

WHITAKER (WHITACRE), HEZEKIAH.
    Son of Peter Whitaker and Emele Hitchcock.
    Born c.1754. Married Mary Taylor in 1784. (W-173)
    Private, Capt. Aquila Hall's Co. No. 4, Sept. 9, 1775. (E-109)
    Signer, Association of Freemen, 1776, Harford Lower. (I-324)

WHITAKER (WHITEAKER, WHITACRE), ISAAC.
    Born c.1735. Died c.1800. Married Elizabeth Hill in 1759. (M-193)
    Son of Charles Whitaker and Mary Kemball. (W-173)
    Served with his brother Abraham in Capt. Christopher Gist's Co.
    in the French and Indian War (listed as 5'6" tall, and hunter
    by trade). (W-176)
    Children: John, Joshua, Samuel, Elizabeth, Benjamin, Martha.
    Private, Capt. Bond's Co. No. 11, December 9, 1775. (E-117)
    Signer, Oath of Allegiance, 1778. (A-37, B-10, J-233)

WHITAKER, ISAAC.
    Son of Peter Whitaker and Emele Hitchcock. Born c.1758.
    Died c.1806. Widow married William Cronin. (W-173)
    Signer, Oath of Allegiance, 1778. (A-37, B-21, J-240)
    Signer, Association of Freemen, 1776, Bush River Lower. (I-319)

WHITAKER, JAMES.
    Born 1726. Died 1789. Married: (1) Mary Sanders in 1749;
    (2) Catherine Potee in 1763. Children: Aaron, Isaac, Charlotte,
    Elizabeth, Abraham, James, Daniel. (M-193, W-176, X-734)
    Private, Capt. Love's Co. No. 10, September 14, 1775. (E-116)

WHITAKER (WHITEAKER, WHITACRE), JOHN.
    Son of Peter Whitaker and Emele Hitchcock. Born 1753. Died 1833.
    Married Ann Dunn in 1776. Lived in Harford Co., Md. until 1784;
    York Co., Pa. until 1789; Washington Co., Md. until 1793;
    Bourbon Co., Ky. until 1812; and Harrison Co., Ky. until 1833.
    (W-172, and National Archives Revolutionary War Pension W9001)
    Private, Capt. Aquila Hall's Co. No. 4, Sept. 9, 1775. (E-109, W-172)
    Private, Capt. Francis Holland's Co. Harford Rifles, 1776. (E-124)
    Signer, Association of Freemen, Bush River Upper, 1776. (I-328)
    Another John Whitaker signed in Susquehanna, 1776. (I-321)
    Signer, Oath of Allegiance to Md., 1778. (A-37, B-22, J-240, W-172)
    Private, Militia; widow applied for pension. (N-54, W-172)
                           (O-6, O-15, O-17, O-20)

WHITE, CHARLES.
    Private, Capt. Dorsey's Co. No. 8, October 31, 1775. (E-115)
    Signer, Association of Freemen, 1776, Spesutie Lower. (I-318)

WHITE, GRAFTON.
    Signer, Oath of Allegiance to Md., 1778. (A-37, B-10, J-234)

WHITE, GREGORY.
    Private, Capt. Robert Harris' Harford Rifles, 1776. (E-123)
    Paid subsistence for 6 weeks, 2 days, Sept. 16, 1776. (K-435)

WHITE, JAMES.
    Signer, Oath of Allegiance to Md., 1778. (A-37, B-20, J-239)

WHITE, JOHN OLDHAM.
    Militia Substitute, 1781; "a very great imposter." (E-133, F-401)

WHITE, JONATHAN.
    Private, Capt. Archer's Co. No. 2, September 16, 1775. (E-107)

WHITE, JOSEPH WOOD.
    Private, Capt. Bussey's Company, July 25, 1776. (E-128, F-60)
    Signer, Association of Freemen, 1776, Deer Creek Lower. (I-322)

WHITE, RICHARD.
    Private, Capt. Anderson's Co. No. 3, September 23, 1775. (E-108)
    Signer, Oath of Allegiance to Md., 1778. (A-37, B-21, J-239)

WHITE, STEPHEN.
    Private, Capt. Taylor's Co. No. 7, September 9, 1775. (E-113)
    Signer, Association of Freemen, 1776, Gunpowder Upper. (I-326)

WHITE, STEPHEN.
    Private, Capt. Bradford's Co. No. 13, Sept. 30, 1775. (E-119)
    Signer, Association of Freemen, 1775, Gunpowder Neck. (I-327)
    Signer, Oath of Allegiance to Md., 1778. (A-37, B-10, J-233)

WHITE, THOMAS.
"Colonel Thomas White (1708-1779) was born in London and sailed for America in 1720. A colonial planter and vestryman at St. George's Parish, Harford County, Md. Married Sophia Hall, daughter of Capt. John Hall and Martha Gouldsmith. After Sophia's death, Col. White moved to Philadelphia and married Esther Newman. He died at Sophia's Dairy (Harford County) where he was buried. His remains were moved to Spesutia Cemetery (St. George's Parish) in 1877." (A Walking Tour of Spesutia Cemetery) (E-202, 203, 204, 205)
Signer, Oath of Allegiance to Md., 1778. (A-37, B-21, J-239)
(An historic roadside marker in Abingdon, Maryland, indicates that Colonel White was the largest colonial landowner in Harford County. His son William became Chaplain for the Continental Congress, and his daughter Sophia married Colonel Aquila Hall.)

WHITEFLATT (WHITEFEATT), JOSEPH.
Born 1726 in England. Private, Flying Camp. Lt. John Smith enlisted July 15, 1776, in Col. Ewing's Battalion. At time of enlistment he was 5'4" tall with curled hair. (E-126, F-56)

WHITEFORD, DAVID.
Signer, Association of Freemen, 1776, Gunpowder Upper. (I-325)

WHITEFORD, HUGH.
Born c.1754. Died c.1812. Married: (1) Mary Sample; (2) Elizabeth Ross. (Y-224)
Private, Capt. Webb's Co. No. 16, October 14, 1775. (E-121)
Harford County War Committee, 1775. (D-359)
Signer, Association of Freemen, 1776, Deer Creek Upper. (I-323)
Signer, Oath of Allegiance to Md., 1778. (A-37, B-23, J-241)

WHITEFORD, JOHN.
Private, Capt. Rigdon's Co. No. 12, December 2, 1775. (E-118)
Harford County War Committee, 1775. (D-359)
Signer, Association of Freemen, 1776, Deer Creek Upper. (I-322)
Signer, Oath of Allegiance to Md., 1778. (A-37, B-29, J-246)

WHITEFORD, WILLIAM.
Private, Capt. Webb's Co. No. 16, October 14, 1775. (E-121)
Signer, Association of Freemen, 1776, Deer Creek Upper. (I-323)
Harford County Petit Juror, 1783. (E-77)

WHITERKER, _____.
Signer, Oath of Allegiance to Md., 1778. (B-30, J-247)

WHITING, THOMAS.
Signer, Association of Freemen, 1776, Bush River Lower. (I-328)

WHITLATCH, CHARLES.
Signer, Association of Freemen, 1776, Deer Creek Upper. (I-322)

WIGGINS (WIGINGS), SAMUEL.
Private, Capt. Bradford's Co. No. 13, Sept. 30, 1775. (E-119)
Signer, Association of Freemen, 1776, Harford Upper. (I-325)
Signer, Oath of Allegiance to Md., 1778. (A-37, B-10, J-233)

WILD, JOHN.
    Private, Capt. Love's Company No. 10, September 14, 1775. (E-116)
    Signer, Oath of Allegiance to Maryland, 1778. (A-37, B-10, J-234)

WILEY, MATTHEW.
    Born 1751. Died 1840. Son of David Wiley of Chester County, PA.
    Ground at his three grist mills in Harford County, Maryland during
    Revolution. Owned Amos Mill, Wiley Mill and Ivory Mill. (D-187, 188)

WILGERS (WILGUS), JAMES.
    "James Wilgus" was Private, Capt. Harris' Harford Rifles. (E-123)
    "James Witgurs" paid subsistence for 2 weeks, 5 days, 1776. (K-436)
    "James Wilgus" signed Association of Freemen, Bush River, 1775. (I-316)
    "James Wilgers" signed Association of Freemen, Bush River, 1776. (I-328)

WILKINSON, RICHARD.
    Pensioner (maimed soldier), 1778. (F-661)

WILLARD, JOHN.
    Militia substitute, 1781. (E-132, F-400)

WILLIAMS, ABRAHAM.
    Elected 2nd Lieutenant, Upper Cross Roads, November 30, 1776. (K-496)

WILLIAMS, CHARLES.
    Private, Capt. Paca's Company, August 5, 1776. (E-127, F-59)
    Signer, Association of Freemen, Deer Creek Lower Hundred, 1776. (I-322)

WILLIAMS, DANIEL.
    Private, Capt. Rodgers' Company No. 5, September 15, 1775. (E-111)

WILLIAMS, DAVID.
    Signer, Oath of Allegiance to Maryland, 1778. (A-37, B-23, J-241)

WILLIAMS, FRANCIS.
    Born in Pennsylvania in January, 1752 and moved to Maryland in infancy with
    his mother (father having died). In Harford County he volunteered early in
    the Revolution and was a Private in Capt. Bennett Bussey's Company of troops.
    They marched from Baltimore to Annapolis and back, and then by way of Phila-
    delphia to Fort Washington. His company was not actually engaged in Battle
    of White Plains but three members of his company were killed. Following the
    war he moved to Tennessee and died March 1, 1833 in White County. Children:
    Mary, James and Francis. (Zella Armstrong's Some Tennessee Heroes of the
    Revolution, 1933, page 79). He also served in Capt. Bond's Company No. 11,
    December 9, 1775 (E-117). He signed the Association of Freemen, Bush River
    Lower Hundred, 1776 (I-319) and Oath of Allegiance, 1778 (A-37, B-12, J-234).

WILLIAMS, JAMES.
    Signer, Association of Freemen, Susquehanna Hundred, 1775/1776. (D-357, I-321)

WILLIAMS, JOHN.
    (1) Private, Capt. Anderson's Company No. 3, September 23, 1775. (E-108)
    (2) Private, Capt. Rodgers' Company No. 5, September 15, 1775. (E-111)

WILLIAMS, MOSES.
    Recruit, New Regiment, July 17, 1780. (E-130, F-343)

WILLIAMS, WILLIAM.
    (1) Private, Capt. Archer's Company No. 2, September 16, 1775. (E-108)
    (2) Sergeant, Capt. Rodgers' Company No. 5, September 15, 1775. (E-110)
    Signer, Association of Freemen, Spesutie Upper Hundred, 1776. (I-319)

WILLIAMSON, GEORGE.
    Private, Capt. Dorsey's Company No. 8, October 31, 1775. (E-115)
    Signer, Association of Freemen, Spesutie Lower Hundred, 1775. (I-317)

WILLIAMSON, JEREMIAH.
    Militia Substitute, 1781. (E-132, F-400)

WILLIAMSON, ROBERT.
    Private, Capt. Webb's Co. No. 16, October 14, 1775. (E-122)
    Signer, Association of Freemen, 1776, Deer Creek Upper. (I-323)

WILLNOTH, GODFRAY.
    Signer, Oath of Allegiance to Md., 1778. (A-37, B-30, J-247)

WILMER (WILMERE, WILMORE), LAMBERT.
    Married Hannah Ricketts in 1767. (M-197)
    War Committee, Harford County, 1775. (D-358)
    Signer, Association of Freemen, 1775, Gunpowder Neck. (I-327)
    Ensign, 8th Battalion, 1776; 1st Lieutenant, 1778. (E-267, C-47)

WILMOTT, RICHARD.
    Married Mary Gittings in 1741. (M-197)
    Private, Capt. Holland's Harford Rifles, 1776. (E-124)
    Signer, Association of Freemen, 1776, Harford Upper. (I-325)
    Signer, Oath of Allegiance to Md., 1778. (A-37, B-26, J-243)

WILMOTT, RICHARD JR.
    Private, Capt. Josias Hall's Co. No. 1, Sept. 12, 1775. (E-105)
    Signer and solicitor, Association of Freemen, 1776, Harford
      Upper Committee. (I-315, I-325)

WILMOTT (WILMOTH), SAMUEL.
    Private, Capt. Bond's Co. No. 11, December 9, 1775. (E-117)
    Signer, Association of Freemen, 1776, Bush River Lower. (I-319)

WILSON, ANDREW.
    Private, Capt. Archer's Co. No. 2, September 16, 1775. (E-107)
    Signer, Oath of Allegiance to Md., 1778. (A-37, B-26, J-243)

WILSON, ARCHIBALD.
    Private, Capt. Webb's Co. No. 16, October 14, 1775. (E-121)
    Signer, Association of Freemen, 1776, Deer Creek Upper. (I-323)

WILSON, ARSBEL.
    Signer, Oath of Allegiance to Md., 1778. (A-37, B-14, J-236)

WILSON, BENJAMIN.
    Private, Capt. Rumsey's Co. No. 6, September 16, 1775. (E-112)
    Signer, Association of Freemen, 1775, Gunpowder Neck. Record
      indicates there were two signers with this name. (I-327)

WILSON, HENRY (Quaker).
    Signer, Oath of Allegiance to Md., 1778. (A-37, B-28, J-245, E-217)

WILSON, HENRY JR.
    Married Margaret Wilson in 1771. (M-198)
    Signer and solicitor, Association of Freemen, 1776, Bush River
      Lower Committee. (E-263) Another one in Spesutie Upper. (I-319)
    Captain, 23rd Battalion, Militia, May 16, 1776. (C-44)   (E-218)
    Signer, Oath of Allegiance to Md., 1778. (A-37, B-13, J-235)

WILSON, JAMES.
  2nd Lieutenant, Deer Creek Battalion, March 10, 1776. (E-266)

WILSON (WILLSON), JAMES.
  Private, Capt. Paca's Company, July 24, 1776. (E-126, F-59)

* WILSON (WILLSON), JOHN.
    (1) "Dr. John Wilson" was Private, Capt. Rumsey's Co. No. 6,
        September 16, 1775. (E-112)
    (2) "John Wilson" was Private, Capt. Taylor's Co. No. 7,
        September 9, 1775. (E-113)
    (3) "John Wilson, Sr." signed Association of Freemen, 1776,
        Deer Creek Lower, 1776. (I-322)
    (4) "John Willson" signed Association of Freemen, 1776,
        Gunpowder Upper. (I-326)
    (5) "John Wilson, Scot'n" signed Association of Freemen, 1776,
        Deer Creek Upper. (I-322)
    (6) "John Wilson" was Private, 4th Maryland Regiment, enlisted
        March 20, 1778; Brunswick Hospital, July 6, 1778-February,
        1779. (E-129, F-302)
    (7) Militia Substitute, 1781, 3 years. (E-133, F-401)
    (8) Signer, Oath of Allegiance to Md., 1778. (A-37, B-14, J-236)

WILSON, JOSEPH.
  Private, Capt. Webb's Co. No. 16, October 14, 1775. (E-121)

WILSON, JOSEPH.
  Sergeant, Capt. Rigdon's Co. No. 12, December 2, 1775. (E-118)

WILSON, JOSEPH, of John.
  Signer and solicitor, Association of Freemen, 1775 and 1776,
  Deer Creek Upper. (I-315, I-322)

WILSON, ROBERT.
  Private, Capt. Taylor's Co. No. 7, September 9, 1775. (E-113)

WILSON, SAMUEL, of William.
  Sergeant; pensioner (maimed soldier), 1778. (F-661)
  Signer, Oath of Allegiance to Md., 1778. (A-37, B-16, J-237)

WILSON, WILLIAM.
  Signer, Oath of Allegiance to Md., 1778. (A-37, J-237)
  Administered the Oath ("Worshipfull William Wilson"). (B-16)

WILSON, WILLIAM.
  Recruit, New Regiment, July 24, 1780.
  "Deserted since enlistment." (E-130, F-343)

WILSON, WILLIAM JR.
  Harford County War Committee, 1775. (D-358)

WINFRED, AARON.
  Recruit, 1st Maryland Regiment, 1780. (E-130, F-343)

* One of these John Wilsons rendered material aid and was paid for two
    casks of brimstone by the Harford County Committee, 1776. (E-334)

WISE, EDWARD.
    Signer, Association of Freemen, 1776, Bush River Lower. (I-328)

WISE, WILLIAM.
    Private, Capt. Rodgers Co. No. 5, September 15, 1775. (E-110)

WOOD, HENRY.
    Signer, Oath of Allegiance to Md., 1778. (A-37, B-29, J-246)

WOOD, JAMES.
    Private, Capt. Anderson's Co. No. 3, September 23, 1775. (E-109)

WOOD, JOHN.
    Signer, Association of Freemen, 1775, Spesutie Lower. (I-317)
      Another John Wood signed in Bush River Upper, 1775. (I-320)
      Another John Wood signed in Gunpowder Upper in 1775.(I-327)
    1st Lieutenant, Capt. Dorsey's Co. No. 8, October 31, 1775. (D-359)
    Captain, 23rd Battalion, April 9, 1778. (C-45, C-46)   (E-114)
    Signer, Oath of Allegiance to Md., 1778. (A-37, B-22, J-240)

WOOD, JOSHUA.
    Private,Capt. Anderson's Co. No. 3, September 23, 1775. (E-108)

WOODARD, JOHN.
    Signer, Association of Freemen, 1776, Deer Creek Upper. (I-323)

WOODARD, THOMAS.
    Signer, Association of Freemen, 1775, Spesutie Lower. (I-317)

WOODDOGY, ANDER (?)
    Signer, Association of Freemen, 1776, Gunpowder Upper. (I-326)

WOODEN, RICHARD.
    Private, Capt. Rumsey's Co. No. 6, September 16, 1775. (E-112)

WOODLAND, JONATHAN.
    Signer, Association of Freemen, 1775, Gunpowder Neck. (I-327)
    Signer, Oath of Allegiance to Md., 1778. (A-37, B-14, J-236)

WOODS, JOSEPH.
    Private, Capt. Harris' Company Payroll, 1776. (E-130, F-304)

WOODWARD, THOMAS.
    Private, Capt. Aquila Hall's Co. No. 4, September 9, 1775. (E-109)

WOODWARD, JOHN.
    (1) Private, Capt. Love's Co. No. 10, September 14, 1775. (E-116)
    (2) Private, Capt. Webb's Co. No. 16, October 14, 1775. (E-121)

WOOLEN, JOHN.
    Private, Capt. Rumsey's Co. No. 6, September 16, 1775. (E-112)

WOOLLIN, MAJOR.
    "Major Woolling" married Frances Johnson in 1756. (M-200)
    "Major Woollin" was Private, Capt. Rumsey's Co. No. 6,
        September 16, 1775. (E-112)
    Signer, Oath of Allegiance to Md., 1778. (A-37, B-14, J-236)

WOOLLIN (WOOLEN), RICHARD.
    Born 1700. Died 1784. Married Elizabeth Buchanan in 1758,
        name being spelled "Richard Woolling." (M-200, X-762)
    "Richard Woolen" signed Association of Freemen, 1775,
        Gunpowder Neck. (I-327)
    "Richard Woollin" signed Oath of Allegiance to Md., 1778.
        (A-37, B-14, J-236)

WOOLMORE, GODFREY.
    Private, Capt. Bussey's Company, July 20, 1776. (E-127, F-60)

WOOLSEY, JOSEPH.
    Signer, Association of Freemen, 1776, Harford Upper. (I-325)
    Signer, Oath of Allegiance to Md., 1778. (A-37, B-22, J-240)

WORRELL, RICHARD.
    Signer, Oath of Allegiance to Md., 1778. (A-37, B-28, J-245)

WORSBY, GEORGE H.
    Signer, Oath of Allegiance to Md., 1778. (A-37, B-29, J-246)

WORSTER, RICHARD.
    Signer, Oath of Allegiance to Md., 1778. (A-37, B-27, J-244)

WORTHINGTON, CHARLES.
    Private, Capt. Patrick's Co. No. 17, April 1, 1776. (E-122)
    Signer, Association of Freemen, 1776, Deer Creek Lower. (I-321)

WORTHINGTON, SAMUEL.
    Born 1733. Died 1815. Married: (1) Mary Tolley in 1759;
        (2) Martha Garrettson. (M-201, X-763)
    Private, Capt. Patrick's Co. No. 17, April 1, 1776. (E-122)
    Signer, Association of Freemen, 1776, Deer Creek Lower. (I-321)

WRAINE (WRAIN), WILLIAM.
    Private, Capt. Dorsey's Co. No. 8, October 31, 1775. (E-115)
    Signer, Association of Freemen, 1776, Spesutie Lower. (I-318)

WRIGHT, JOHN.
    Born 1738. Died c.1813. Married: Jemima Hendon in 1762.
        Quartermaster, Maryland Service. (X-765, M-201)
    Private, Capt. Webb's Co. No. 16, October 14, 1775. (E-122)
    Signer, Association of Freemen, 1776, Deer Creek Upper. (I-323)

WRIGHT, WILLIAM.
    Private, Capt. Bussey's Co., July 25, 1776. (E-128, F-60)
    Signer, Oath of Allegiance to Md., 1778. (A-37, B-19, J-238)
    Militia Substitute, 1781. (E-132, F-400)

WRIGHT, WILLMAN.
  Signer, Association of Freemen, 1776, Eden Hundred. (I-324)

YARDLEY, NATHANIEL.
  Private, Capt. Taylor's Co. No. 7, September 9, 1775. (E-113)

YATES, GEORGE GILBERT.
  Signer, Association of Freemen, 1776, Harford Upper. (I-325)

YEAMAN, THOMAS.
  Private, Capt. Bradford's Co. No. 13, September 30, 1775. (E-119)

YOE, WILLIAM.
  Private, Capt. Bradford's Co. No. 13, September 30, 1775. (E-119)
  Signer, Association of Freemen, 1775, Gunpowder Neck. (I-327)

YOUNG, GEORGE.
  Private, Capt. Josias Hall's Co. No. 1, September 12, 1775. (E-106)
  Private, Capt. Francis Holland's Harford Rifles, 1776. (E-124)
  Signer, Association of Freemen, 1776, Harford Upper. (I-325)
  Appointed to guard a wagon to South Carolina, 1777. (E-343)

YOUNG, JAMES.
  Captain, 2nd Maryland Battalion of the Flying Camp, July, 1776 to
    December, 1776. (L-610)

YOUNG, ROBERT.
  Siger, Association of Freemen, 1776, Harford Upper. (I-325)

YOUNG, SAMUEL.
  Signer, Oath of Allegiance to Md., 1778. (A-37, B-21. J-239)

YOUNG, WILLIAM.
  Private, Capt. Josias Hall's Co. No. 1, September 12, 1775.
  1st Lieutenant, Capt. Hall's Co. No. 1, 1775. (D-359, E-105, E-106)

YOUNG, WILLIAM.
  2nd Lieutenant, Capt. Archer's Co. No. 2, October 15, 1776,
    Flying Camp. Harford Rifles. (D-359, E-124, H-153, K-350)

YOUNGE, WILLIAM.
  Harford County Committee on Correspondence, June 11, 1775. (E-96)

YOUNGER, THOMAS.
  Private, Capt. Paca's Company, July 24, 1776. (E-126, F-59)

YORK, GEORGE.
  Furnished a gun to the county committee, June, 1776. (E-330)

HARFORD COUNTY MILITIA COMPANIES

1775 - 1776

Company No. 1	Capt. Josias Carvil Hall
Company No. 2	Capt. John Archer
Company No. 3	Capt. Charles Anderson
Company No. 4	Capt. Aquila Hall
Company No. 5	Capt. John Rodgers
Company No. 6	Capt. Benjamin Rumsey
Company No. 7	Capt. John Taylor
Company No. 8	Capt. Greenberry Dorsey
Company No. 9	Capt. James Stewart
Company No. 10	Capt. John Love
Company No. 11	Capt. Jacob Bond
Company No. 12	Capt. Alexander Rigdon
Company No. 13	Capt. William Bradford
Company No. 15	Capt. Charles Baker
Company No. 16	Capt. William Webb
Company No. 17	Capt. John Patrick

HARFORD RIFLES

Company No. 1	Capt. Robert Harris
Company No. 2	Capt. Francis Holland

OTHER COMPANIES ENROLLED BY THE FOLLOWING:

Capt. Aquila Paca	Capt. Bennett Bussey
Lt. John B. Hall	Lt. Joshua Miles
Lt. Asael Hitchcock	Lt. Aquila Amos

Capt. Alexander Lawson Smith

THE BUSH DECLARATION

In 1775, the feeling of discontent intensified rapidly and kindled a determination to be free from the rule of Great Britain.

On March 22, 1775, a committee of thirty-four Harford County men, duly elected, met at the Bush Tavern and signed the Bush Declaration. It is the first Declaration of Independence made by a representative body in America.

"We the Committee of Harford County, having most seriously and maturely considered the Resolves and Association of the Continental Congress, and the Resolves of the Provincial Convention, do most heartily approve of the same, and as we esteem ourselves in a more particular manner intrusted by our constituents to see them carried into execution, we do most solemnly pledge ourselves to each other, and to our Country, and engage ourselves by every tie held sacred among mankind to perform the same at the risque of our lives and fortunes."

Aquila Hall	Thomas Johnson
Josias Carvil Hall	Alexander Rigdon
George Patterson	Edward Ward
William Morgan	Abraham Whitaker
Francis Holland	Charles Anderson
Samuel Caldwell	William Fisher, Jr.
Aquila Paca	Richard Dallam
James Lytle	John Durham
Aquila Hall, Jr.	James McComas
Robert Morgan	William Bradford
Robert Lemmon	William Smithson
Thomas Brice	John Donahuy
John Patrick	Greenberry Dorsey
Daniel Scott	John Archer
Benjamin Bradford Norris	W. Smithe
James Harris	William Webb
Edward Prall	John Taylor

DECLARATION OF THE ASSOCIATION

OF THE FREEMEN OF MARYLAND

JULY 26, 1775

"THE long premeditated and now avowed design of the British government to raise a revenue from the property of the colonists without their consent on the gift, grant and disposition of the commons of Great Britain; the arbitrary and vindictive statues passed under colour of punishing a riot, to subdue by military force and famine the Massachusetts Bay; the unlimited power assumed by parliament to alter the charter of that province and the constitution of all the colonies, thereby destroying the essential securities of the lives, liberties and properties of the colonists; the commencement of hostilities by the ministerial force and the cruel prosecution of the war against the people of Massachusetts Bay, followed by General Gage's proclamation, declaring almost the whole of the inhabitants of the united colonies, by name or description, rebels and traitors, are sufficent causes to arm a free people in defence of their liberty, and to justify resistance, no longer dictated by prudence merely, but by necessity, and leave no alternative but base submission or manly opposition to uncontrollable tyranny. The Congress chose the latter, and for the express purpose of securing and defending the united colonies, and preserving them in safety against all attempts to carry the abovementioned acts into execution by force of arms, RESOLVED, THAT the said colonies be immediately put in a state of defence, and now supports, at the joint expence, an army to restrain the further violence and repel the future attacks of a disappointed and exasperated enemy.

"WE, therefore, inhabitants of the province of Maryland, firmly persuaded that it is necessary and justifiable to repel force by force, do approve of the opposition by arms to the British troops employed to enforce obedience to the late acts and statutes of the British parliament for raising a revenue in America, and altering and changing the charter and constitution of the Massachusetts Bay, and for destroying the essential securities for the lives, liberties and properties of the subjects in the united colonies. And WE, do unite and associate as one hand, and firmly and solemnly engage and pledge ourselves to each other and to America, that we will, to the utmost of our power, promote and support the present opposition, carrying it on, as well by arms, as the continental association, restraining our commerce.

"AND as in these times of public danger, and until a reconciliation with Great Britain on constitutional principles is effected (an event we most ardently wish may soon take place) the energy of government may be greatly impaired, so that even zeal unrestrained may be productive of anarchy and confusion, WE do in like manner unite, associate and solemnly engage in maintenance of good order and the public peace, to support the civil power in the due execution of the laws so far as may be consistent with the present plan of opposition, and to defend with our utmost power all persons from every species of outrage to themselves or their property and to prevent any punishment from being inflicted on any offenders, other than such as shall be adjudged by the civil magistrate, the continental congress, our convention, council of safety, or committees of observation."

This declaration was pledged by Harford Countians in 1775 and 1776.

OATH OF ALLEGIANCE AND FIDELITY

TO THE STATE OF MARYLAND

(PATRIOTS OATH 1778)

On February 5, 1777, the General Assembly of Maryland enacted a law which made it necessary to sign an Oath of Allegiance and Fidelity to the State of Maryland and the cause of freedom.

These oaths were taken before a magistrate of the court. They included every free male, eighteen years and over, every civil officer, senator, delegate to congress or assembly, members of council electors of the senate, attorneys at law, every voter for delegates, sheriffs, electors of the senate, and all persons holding any office of trust or profit in the state.

Residents of Harford County were administered the oath in 1778, and lists were prepared by the different magistrates and returned by them to the Harford County Court.

"I do sware I do not hold myself bound to yield any Allegiance or obediance to the King of Great Britain his heirs or Successors and that I will be true and faithful to the State of Maryland and will to the utmost of my power Support maintain and defend the Freedom and Independence thereof and the Government as now established against all open enemies and secret and traterous Conspiraces and will use my utmost endeavours to disclose and make known to the Governor or some one of the judges or Justices thereof all Treasons or Treaterous Consperaces, attemps or Combinations against this State or the Government thereof which may come to my Knowledge so help me God."

ADDENDUM

AMOS, MORDECAI (p. 5).
Pensioned in 1832, age 81. Private, Maryland Militia (AA-49).

AMOS, NICHOLAS (p. 5).
Nicholas Day Amoss, only son of Thomas Amos and Elizabeth Day, was born in Baltimore County on September 19, 1742 and married Christiana Ditto in 1761. He took the Oath of Allegiance in 1778 and was an Ensign in the 8th Battalion of Harford County. The family of Nicholas Day Amos moved to Washington County, Maryland prior to 1792 and they migrated to Hinkston Creek near Ruddle's Mill in Bourbon County, Kentucky circa 1795. Descendants later moved to Rush County, Indiana (CC-3, CC-4).

BAILEY, GROOMBRIGHT (p. 10).
Son of Thomas "Baley" who died in Baltimore County in 1771. Near Marshall's Ferry in White County, Illinois is his grave marker: "Sacred to the memory of Groombright Bailey, born in Baltimore, Maryland, May 1 A.D. 1732, Died 1817." (Information from Lillian Bayly Marks and Maxine Bayley Hughes, published in the Maryland Genealogical Society Bulletin, Volume 24, No. 2, Spring, 1983, pp. 114-115).

BOULDERSON, ISAIAH. Paid for making and furnishing guns in 1775 (E-317).

BRIERLY, GEORGE (p. 25).
Served under Capt. Benjamin Amos. Married Mary Garrison in 1793. In 1832 George produced the depositions of Abraham Williams, Thomas Mountjoy and George Mefford in Mason County, Kentucky, to prove his military war service. His wife was still living in 1856 (CC-17).

BULL, WILLIAM (p. 30).
He made a deposition on September 20, 1790 in Harford County, age 56, that about the year 1782 he and Lemuel Howard were preparing to travel to New York City where they believed their sons Walter Bull and Aquila Howard were prisoners of war. Thomas Smithson also requested that they bring his son Archibald Smithson home as he was also a prisoner (Land records of Harford County, Maryland, Liber JLG, No. G, folio 407).

CAIN, EDWARD (p. 33).
In April, 1790 he appeared before the Harford County Court and stated he was wounded in the arm while serving in the 4th Maryland Regiment under Colonel Hall (BB-22, BB-26, BB-38, BB-40) and received payment.

CHALMERS, GEORGE (p. 39). State's Attorney in 1774 and 1775 (E-358).

CHRISITE, ALEX. (p. 41). His correct name spelling is "Christie" (E-132).

COINS (COYNS), DOMINICK (p. 51).
Private in the Maryland Line. Pensioned in 1819, age 81. Died on September 10, 1822 (AA-37).

COOP, BARACHIUS (p. 48)
Moved to Orange County, North Carolina in 1788 and Blount County, Tennessee in 1798. Pension #1193 filed in Blount County, Tennessee. He was a brother of Horatio Coop. (Information from Phillip G. Coop of Cordova, Tennessee in 1986).

COOP, HORATIO (p. 48).
Moved to North Carolina in the 1790's and Tennessee in 1810. Pension #14457 filed in Bedford County, Tennessee. Brother of Barachius Coop. (Information from Phillip G. Coop of Cordova, Tennessee in 1986).

CRAIG, JOHN.
In his will written on August 25, 1793 he devised to his wife Ann "all right, title and claim I have to five years service in the Continental Army under Gen. Moses Hasel, being the Congress Own Regiment" (Harford County Will Book No. 2, page 118).

CRAVEN, ANDREW (p. 51).
Pensioned in 1819, age 82. Private in Maryland Line (AA-37).

CRESWELL, SAMUEL.
Commissioner of Harford County on June 8, 1775 (E-304).

DEAVER, AQUILA (p. 60).
Private in the 3rd Maryland Line in 1780 (DD-65).
Pensioned in 1818, age 80 (according to source AA-37).

DEAVER, WILLIAM.
Born in Harford County in 1756/7 and enlisted in 1778 in the 3rd Maryland Line. In 1820 he applied for a pension in Mason County, Kentucky, having applied in 1818 in Scioto County, Ohio and then transferring to Kentucky. He received pension S12754. Was a prisoner during the war (CC-38).

DEBRULER, WILLIAM (p. 62).
Sarah Watters was not the wife of William DeBruler. "I believe she was this man's step-mother, as her husband, William DeBruler, Sr., had died in 1772, leaving a will which named William Jr. and othrs. I expect your signer was this William DeBruler, Jr. Sarah Watters and her first husband, Godfrey Watters, were my ancestors." (Information from Elbert Vowell of Palatine, Illinois in 1988).

ELLIOTT, ROBERT (p. 73).
Pensioned in 1819, age 92. Private in the Maryland Line (AA-37).

ELLIS, THOMAS.
Pensioned in 1819, age 72. Private in the Maryland Line.
Died on August 11, 1821 (AA-37).

EWING, JAMES.
There are no significant records on James Ewing to be found in Harford County. However, in the land records of Allegany County is a deed in Liber 28, folio 435, dated December 21, 1868, naming the heirs at law of James Ewing, late officer in the Maryland Line of the Continental Army. Names of heirs: James Ewing, Nancy Wiles, Edwin Ewing, James J. Ewing (of William), Elizabeth Riley, William Ewing, John Hawkins, John Ewing, William E. Carroll, Margaret Hawkins, Alexander Ewing, James W. Ewing, John A. Ewing, Richard Sheridan, Luther Sheridan, George Sheridan, Mary E. Sheridan, Tabitha M. Sheridan, and William S. Sheridan. (Data by Jon H. Livezey in Maryland Gen. Soc. Bulletin, Vol. 30, No. 1, page 19).

GARREGUIES, JOHN (p. 84). 8th Maryland Regiment, 1780 (DD-330).

GILES, JACOB (p. 90). Furnished supplies to militia in 1779 (DD-368).

HALL, JOSIAS (p. 100).
3rd Lieutenant in Capt. Alexander Smith's Company in 1776 (E-331).

HEAPS, ARCHIBALD (p. 109). Pensioned in 1834, age 75 (AA-49).

HEAPS, JOHN (p. 109). Pensioned in 1832, age 82 (AA-49).

HOLLAND, JOHN F.
Pensioned in 1819, age 73. Private in the Maryland Line (AA-37).

HORNER, NATHAN.
Furnished a gun for the militia and was paid in 1776 (E-330).

HOWARD, JOHN (p. 110).
A maimed soldier of Col. Nicola's Corps of Invalids, he was paid in Harford County in 1786 (BB-26).

HOWE, JOHN (p. 116).
Born in 1755 and enlisted in Harford County on July 22, 1776, serving in Capt. Alexander Smith's Company in Col. Rawlings' Regiment. In 1818 he applied for and received a pension as a Sergeant in Hardin County, Kentucky. His widow, Rachel Pindell, received pension W10113. She moved to Harrison County, Indiana circa 1831 and died there in 1844 (CC-76).

LAURENTZ, WENDLE.
Pensioned in 1818, age 64. Private in the Maryland Line.
Died on March 15, 1823 (AA-37).

LEE, SAMUEL (p. 137).
Paid for horses and supplies in August, 1780 (DD-246).

LEWIS, CLEMENT (p. 138).
Appointed Harford County Coroner on December 30, 1779 (DD-45).

LONEY, AMOS (p. 139).
Son of John and Mary Loney. Born in 1752 and married Polly Donellan in 1782. Died in 1832. (Information from the Dielman-Hayward File in the Maryland Historical Society and The Hall Family of West River and Kindred Families, by Thomas J. Hall 3rd (Denton, MD: Rue Publishing Company, 1941).

LONEY, WILLIAM (p. 140).
Son of John and Mary Loney, and twin of Amos Loney. Married the widow Mary Frisby. Died in 1807. (Maryland Historical Magazine 31:350, and Thomas J. Hall 3rd's The Hall Family of West River & Kindred Families).

LOWERY (LOWRY), JOHN (p. 142).
Born in Scotland. Married Hannah Finney. Served in the 7th Maryland Regiment from Harford County. Died in Baltimore (National Society DAR Lineage Books, Vol. 113, p. 260, and BB-23, BB-38, BB-39).

McADOW (McADON), ANDREW (p. 143).
Pensioned in 1833, age 73. Private in the Maryland Line (AA-49).

McADOW, JOHN (p. 143).
Born in 1745 in Harford County, he enlisted in 1777 for 4 years at Pittsburgh for the Maryland Line under Capt. Richard Brown. Became a Sergeant, and after the war moved to Kentucky. Died in 1838 (CC-96).

McCOMAS, ALEXANDER (p. 146).
Appointed Tobacco Inspector at Otter Point on August 30, 1780 (DD-271).

McCRACKEN, JOHN.
Pensioned in 1818, age 82. Private in the Maryland Line. Dropped from the pension rolls in 1820, but reinstated in 1827 (AA-37).

McCULLOUGH, WILLIAM (p. 148).
Enlisted in August, 1776 in Col. Rawlings' Regiment, Maryland Line. In Fleming County, Kentucky he applied for and received pension S36085 in 1818, stating he was age 65. He died in 1832 and his children moved to Indiana (CC-98, CC-99).

McILHANEY (McELHANEY), MATHEW (p. 150).
Born circa 1755 in Ireland and emigrated to Baltimore (date unknown). Married Margaret Cope in 1778 and lived in Harford County. Children: James, Eleanor, Patrick, Richard, Mathew and Catherine (Information from Leann Steele of Hastings, Nebraska in 1989).

MAKEMSON (p. 154). Additional data on this family is in Reference CC-94.

MATTHEWS, JAMES (p. 156).
Appointed Harford County Coroner on December 30, 1779 (DD-45).

MILLER, JAMES (p. 159).
Name was originally "Milles." In 1781 he married Mary Martin and between 1783 and 1828 they lived in Pennsylvania, Maryland, Virginia, Kentucky, Ohio and Indiana, where he died in 1828 (CC-102, CC-103).

NABB, ELISHA.
Born circa 1755 and served in the Kent County Militia. He married Mary -----, and was in Harford County by 1803 when he purchased land. He died in March, 1811. Chidlren: Mary Nabb married (1) Thomas Spencer and (2) Richard Shekell; William Nabb married Phebe M.-----; Avarilla Nabb married Waldon Gilbert Middleton; John Nabb married Elizabeth Onion; and, Elisha Nabb married Elizabeth -----; and possibly Rebecca Nabb who married James Maxwell Day (Research by Henry C. Peden, Jr., a descendant of William and Phebe Nabb, in 1990: 707 Bedford Rd., Bel Air, MD 21014).

O'CONNER, MiCHAEL.
Pensioned in 1819, age 67. Private in the Pennsylvania Line. Died in April, 1822 (AA-37).

OLIVER, JAMES (p. 171).
Charged and then apologized for unpatriotic remarks in 1776 (E-323).

REED, JOHN 2nd.
Pensioned in 1819, age 86. Private in the Maryland Line (AA-37).

RICKETTS, SAMUEL (p. 190). Furnished muskets for militia in 1776 (E-330).

RUTLEDGE, JOSHUA (p. 197). Pensioned in 1819, age 76 (according to AA-37).

SMITH, VALENTINE (p. 209).
A maimed soldier, he was ordered to appear before the Harford County Court in 1790 to explain where and how he was wounded, but he never appeared (BB-22, BB-26, BB-38, BB-40). He was paid previously.

SMITHSON (p. 210). See additional information under William Bull, q.v.

TALBOTT, EDMOND (p. 217).
Harford County Commissioner in 1780 (DD-133).

TAYLOR, THOMAS (p. 220).
Governor Lee to Alexander Clagett, Esq., of Washington County, on February 24, 1780: "Sir, the enclosed is a pardon for Thomas Taylor a prisoner in your custody. When you discharge him over to a recruiting officer and desire the officer to pay the pecuniary bounty that Taylor may be entitled to to his wife who lives in Harford County and who with several children are in extreme indigent circumstances: In this instance I think it not amiss to direct the application of the Continental and State Bounty of 450 dollars, however improper it might be in any other. Communicate this letter to the Recruiting Officer and inform me of his name." (DD-96). On April 28, 1780, John Stull, Washington County, to His Excellency Thomas Sim Lee: "Sir, I take the liberty to inform you that Thomas Taylor, agreeable to your reprive, did enlist in the service of the United States, has since deserted with two others, stole three horses. They are again apprehended and now in gaol. I would be glad, your Excellency, would take order with said Taylor as he is an extraordinary fellow and perhaps get a way." (DD-483).

THOMAS, ISAAC.
Paid for making and furnishing guns in 1776 (E-319).

WANN, JOHN (p. 229).
Pensioned in 1819, age 71. Private in the Pennsylvania Line. Died on August 14, 1824 (AA-37).

WHITAKER, JOHN (p. 237). Additional information is in Reference CC-153.

WILMOT, JOHN.
Paid for unspecified service on Ocober 6, 1780 (DD-315).

FURTHER ADDENDUM

LOWREY, JOHN (p. 142).
In January, 1790 he appeared before the Harford County Court and stated he served in the 1st Maryland Line under Colonel Smallwood and received a wound through the groin at the Battle of Long Island on August 27, 1776 (BB-38).

SURNAME INDEX

Able 1
Adams 1
Admiston 1
Ady 1
Affurly 1
Aikens 1
Akeright 1
Akerite 1
Akins 2
Albert 2
Alexander 2
Allen 2, 179
Allender 2, 3
Allin 3
Allinder 3
Allison 3
Almon 178
Almony 3, 9
Alton 3
Amby 3
Ames 3
Ammott 3
Amos 4, 5, 6, 168, 179, 190, 245, 249.
Amoss 3, 4, 5, 6
Anderson 6, 10, 12, 15, 17, 22, 25, 32, 37, 39, 44, 45, 47, 55, 65, 70, 77, 79, 81, 83, 84, 87, 88, 89, 90, 93, 102, 105, 124, 126, 150, 166, 176, 183, 186, 192, 197, 202, 204, 205, 206, 207, 217, 234, 237, 239, 242, 245, 246.
Andrew 31
Andrews 6
Angelly 59
Annin 7
Antill 7
Aooistock 7
Archer 3, 7, 12, 20, 21, 28, 32, 33, 43, 52, 53, 56, 58, 61, 64, 65, 97, 105, 106, 107, 108, 110, 111, 123, 124, 126, 132, 136, 144, 145, 151, 152, 155, 156, 157, 159, 161, 162, 171, 178, 180, 182, 195, 202, 203, 205, 207, 208, 213, 222, 223, 224, 227, 228, 233, 237, 240, 244, 245, 246.
Arkwright 7
Armott 3, 7
Armstrong 8

Arnold 8
Ashley 9
Ashman 9
Ashmead 9
Ashmore 9
Ashton 9
Ask 9
Atkinson 9
Austin 15
Ayers 9
Ayres 9

Baggot 10
Bailess 15
Bailey 10, 249
Baker 5, 10, 11, 14, 23, 35, 37, 38, 41, 42, 46, 49, 51, 55, 56, 58, 59, 66, 72, 74, 75, 76, 81, 85, 97, 112, 113, 119, 120, 123, 127, 129, 136, 158, 159, 176, 178, 179, 188, 189, 192, 193, 196, 197, 200, 201, 203, 205, 218, 221, 225, 230, 231, 245.
Baldwin 11
Baley 10
Balf 12
Balys 15
Bamhill 13
Bankhead 12
Banks 12
Barclay 12
Barnard 12
Barns 12
Barnes 12, 13
Barnett 13
Barnhill 13
Barnhouse 13
Barrett 13
Barry 14
Bartly 14
Barton 14, 42, 169, 179
Base 14
Bassett 14
Baxley 14
Baxter 154
Bay 14, 109
Bayd 15
Bayles 15
Bayless 16, 102
Bayley 200
Bemis 9

Baylis 15, 16
Beach 16
Beall 16
Beard 16
Beatty 16
Beaty 16
Beaven 16
Beaver 16, 168
Beck 17
Bek 17
Bell 17, 26, 77
Benfield 17
Beninton 18
Bennet 18
Bennett 17, 18
Bennington 18
Benson 18
Bently 18
Benton 18
Berry 18
Beshang 18
Bets 19
Betts 19
Bevard 19
Bezerly 26
Bibb 19
Biddle 19, 197
Biggs 19
Billingslea 19, 20
Billingsley 19, 20, 170
Birckhead 20
Bishop 20, 187
Biven 194
Black 20
Blackburn 20
Blacklear 20
Blackston 20
Blackiston 20
Blaney 20, 21
Bleany 21
Blunder 21
Boadsman 21
Boardsman 21
Bolton 21
Bonar 21
Bond 2, 4, 6, 13, 21, 22, 25,
27, 28, 30, 31, 35, 37,
43, 56, 60, 68, 71, 82,
94, 96, 102, 111, 118,
124, 127, 128, 130, 131,
134, 135, 138, 146, 151,
152, 162, 163, 169, 173,
178, 180, 181, 182, 187,

Bond (continued)
194, 195, 196, 198, 200,
201, 209, 210, 212, 213,
230, 236, 239, 240, 245.
Boner 22, 23
Bonfield 24
Booner 152
Booth 23
Bork 23
Bose 23
Bosley 23, 124
Botton 21
Botts 23   Boulderson 249
Bowden 23
Bowen 28
Boyce 23, 50
Boyer 23, 94
Boyle 24
Bradford 6, 23, 24, 25, 26, 30,
33, 37, 51, 55, 56, 65,
72, 73, 82, 83, 92, 103,
129, 131, 134, 142, 146,
147, 156, 157, 164, 167,
168, 169, 170, 180, 190,
194, 195, 199, 206, 210,
212, 214, 226, 227, 235,
237, 238, 244, 245, 246.
Brady 24
Brager 24
Brakenridge 24, 25
Branan 25
Brandrick 25
Brannon 25
Braser 25
Brasher 25
Breckenridge 24, 25
Breden 25
Brewer 25
Brice 25, 246
Bridge 25
Brierley 25, 26, 249
Britchard 26
Brittain 26
Britten 26
Britton 26
Bromley 26
Bronnley 26
Bronnwood 26
Brook 26
Brooks 26
Brown 26, 27, 28, 154, 235, 251
Browne 28
Brownley 28

Brownly 28, 29, 37
Browley 29
Bruce 29
Brucebanks 29
Brusebanks 29
Bryerly 25, 26
Buchanan 29, 243
Buck 29
Buckley 29
Buckman 29
Bull 5, 29, 30, 31, 41, 249
Bulling 31
Bullock 31
Bunting 31
Burgess 31, 175
Burk 31, 100
Burke 31
Burns 31
Burr 31
Burton 31
Bush 31
Buskirk 40
Bussey 1, 3, 4, 5, 14, 30, 31,
        32, 36, 37, 38, 41, 43,
        46, 48, 51, 55, 56, 58,
        62, 63, 66, 68, 78, 81,
        83, 84, 85, 86, 92, 96,
        101, 111, 112, 113, 116,
        117, 120, 122, 123, 126,
        135, 140, 142, 152, 153,
        157, 158, 159, 162, 166,
        170, 171, 177, 180, 181,
        182, 187, 188, 191, 193,
        197, 200, 202, 205, 207,
        208, 210, 211, 212, 215,
        218, 223, 237, 243, 245.
Butcher 32
Butersbo 32   Butters 32
Butler 32, 87
Byard 32
Byfoot 33

Cahill 33
Cain 33, 46, 249
Caine 33
Cairnes 33
Cairns 33
Calder 34
Caldwell 34, 246
Calgrove 34
Calhoun 160
Callahan 34
Callendar 34
Callender 34
Callindar 34

Calmer 34
Calwell 34
Cambel 35
Cambess 46
Cameron 35
Cammel 35
Camp 35
Campbell 35
Canclear 35
Candean 35
Cantler 35
Cantlin 35
Capbell 35
Capeland 49
Capen 36
Caple 36
Car 37
Carey 36
Carlan 36
Carlen 36
Carlile 36, 99
Carlisle 36
Carman 36, 37
Carnan 36, 37
Carr 37
Carroll 37, 250
Carson 37
Carter 38, 232
Cartherwood 38
Cartin 38
Carvil 100
Casedy 38
Casseldine 38
Caswell 38
Catherwood 38
Catman 38
Cattrell 38
Cattrill 38
Cave 56
Cavenaugh 38
Chalk 38
Chalmers 39, 249
Chambers 39
Chance 39
Chancey 39
Chandley 40
Chaney 39
Chapman 40
Chauncey 39
Cheney 39
Chenowith 40
Chesny 40
Chew 40, 115, 163, 175
Childs 40
Chineth 40

Chinneth 40
Chiswell 40
Chock 40
Chocke 40
Chrisholm 41
Christie 41, 249
Chriswell 52
Cilison 202
Clancey 41
Clar 41
Clark 41, 42, 43, 66, 188
Clarke 20, 43
Clayton 43
Clemens 43
Clements 43
Clemmons 43
Clendenen 43
Clendenin 43, 91
Close 171
Cluver 44
Clyton 44
Coale 44, 45
Coaleman 44
Cochean 44
Cochran 44
Cockerton 44
Coe 44
Coen 44
Cole 44, 45, 87
Coleman 45
Collings 45
Collins 45, 46
Colter 46
Colthough 54
Coltman 50
Combess 46
Combest 46
Comene 46
Comeve 46
Concking 46
Condron 46
Conhoway 46
Conley 46
Conn 46
Connaway 46
Connelly 46
Conner 46
Conney 47
Connis 47
Connolly 47
Connor 46
Connoway 46
Conor 46
Coob 211
Cook 47

Cooley 47
Cooly 47
Coop 48, 249, 250
Cooper 48, 49
Coops 48
Cope 48, 252
Copeland 49, 66
Corbet 49
Corbett 49
Corbit 49
Corbitt 49
Cord 50
Cornelius 170
Corsby 50
Corsley 50
Corvin 50
Costlet 50
Cotman 50
Coupland 50
Courson 53
Courtney 50
Cowan 50, 51
Cowen 50, 51
Cowley 51
Cox 51, 107, 135
Coyn 51, 249
Coyne 51
Crabtree 180
Crail 51   Craig 250
Craton 52
Craven 51, 250
Crawford 51
Creaton 52
Creeter 51
Creighton 51
Creswell 51, 52, 73, 250
Cretin 52
Criswell 51, 52
Crockett 53
Croesen 53
Cromwell 23, 53
Cronin 236
Crook 53, 212
Crooke 53
Crooker 53
Crooks 54
Crop 54
Crosby 54
Cross 54
Crouch 54
Cuddy 54
Culough 54
Cultraugh 54
Culver 54
Cummings 54, 176

Cummins 55
Cunning 55
Cunningham 55, 56
Curey 56
Curl 56
Curry 56
Curtis 56
Cussack 56
Cusick 56
Cussick 56
Cutchin 190
Cuthbert 56

Dailey 57
Dale 57
Dallam 33, 57, 58, 90,
    105, 137, 246.
Daly 58
Darby 58
Darley 58
Dars 58
Daugharty 67
Daugherty 58, 67, 68, 134
Davidson 58
Davis 58, 59, 143, 169
Dawes 59
Day 59, 60, 157, 249, 252
Dazan 68
Deacon 60
Deal 60
Deale 60
Dealy 60
Dean 199
Dearmon 60
Dearson 197
Dearmott 60
Deaver 60, 61, 250
Deavour 61
Debrular 61
Debruler 61, 62, 250
Debueler 62
Deimer 64
Deingan 62
Deiver 63
Delaney 62
Delaney 62
Deleney 62
Delong 62
Deney 62
Denison 62
Dennis 62
Dennison 62
Denney 62, 63
Dent 63
Dereale 63

Dermott 60
Derrow 63
Dever 60
Devier 63
Devin 63
Devine 63
Dew 64
Dick 64
Dickson 64
Dickson 64
Diemer 64
Dignan 64
Dillion 64
Dines 64
Dinham 64
Dinse 64
Disney 101
Ditto 5, 249
Divan 63
Divers 64
Dixon 64
Dobbins 65
Doherty 65
Dome 65
Donahay 65
Donahey 65
Donahuy 65, 246
Donavin 65
Donel 65   Donellan 251
Donham 70
Donnavan 65
Donohoe 66
Donohoo 66, 70
Donnaly 66
Donnelly 66
Donoley 66
Donovan 65
Dooley 66, 208
Dooly 66
Doran 66
Dorney 66
Dorrah 66
Dorsey 9, 13, 18, 29, 35, 36, 40,
    41, 42, 45, 46, 47, 50,
    61, 62, 66, 67, 68, 69,
    74, 75, 76, 77, 78, 79,
    80, 83, 85, 86, 93, 101,
    106, 111, 117, 125, 131,
    133, 134, 135, 137, 141,
    144, 146, 148, 156, 158,
    164, 172, 173, 177, 183,
    184, 203, 204, 216, 218,
    219, 220, 222, 223, 224,
    226, 229, 237, 239, 242,
    245, 246.

Dougherty 67, 68
Downes 68
Downey 68
Downs 68
Dozens 68, 72
Drennen 68
Drew 69, 84, 132, 216
Driver 69
Drummond 69
Dublin 69
Dueberry 69
Duff 69
Dufft 69
Duffy 69
Dugan 68
Dulany 69
Duley 70
Dulin 186
Duly 70
Dunahoo 70
Duncan 70, 138
Dungan 70
Dunham 70
Dunlap 54
Dunn 237
Dunnahoe 70
Dunnavin 65
Dunny 63
Dunsheath 70
Durbin 70, 71, 107, 198
Durham 71, 72, 246
Durner 72
Dutton 167, 202
Duvall 169
Duzan 68, 72
Duzart 72
Duzent 68
Dyre 72

Eadin 72
Eagle 72
Eager 72
Eagon 72
Eavs 72
Ecksen 72
Eckson 72
Eckston 72
Eddy 73
Edmonston 73
Edwards 73
Eken 73
Elder 73
Ellett 73
Elliott 73, 250
Ellis 73, 74, 138, 250

Ellison 74
Ely 74
Enlows 74
Ensor 74
Eratt 74
Erwin 74
Eseldein 74
Esther 74
Evans 74, 75
Evens 213
Evins 74
Everett 75, 76, 113, 118
Everest 76
Everist 76
Evitt 76
Ewing 2, 27, 31, 45, 46, 63, 65,
    67, 76, 81, 94, 98, 103,
    110, 134, 158, 165, 172,
    173, 182, 188, 197, 206,
    207, 214, 222, 238, 250.
Eyre 76

Farish 77
Farmer 77
Faulkner 77
Faust 77
Fawcett 77
Feat 77
Feely 77
Fell 77
Ferguson 77
Fie 77, 78
Fields 78
Fincham 78
Fing 78
Finley 78
Finleyson 78
Finliston 78
Finn 78
Finnagon 78
Finnch 78
Finney 13, 79, 251
Firm 78
Fisher 79, 246
Fitzgerald 79
Flanigan 79
Flannagan 79
Flat 79
Flatt 79
Flenn 79
Flynn 79
Ford 79, 80
Forestdale 80
Forrisdale 80

Fort 80
Forwood 80
Foster 81
Fowler 81
Fox 81, 215
Fraley 81
France 81
Fraulkner 81
Frazier 81
Freeman 81, 82
Fremble 82
French 82
Frew 82
Frier 82
Frisbey 82, 251
Frost 82
Fryer 82
Fulfet 82
Fulfit 82
Fullerton 43
Fulton 83
Furrey 83

Gaddis 83
Gage 247
Gail 83
Gaile 83
Gale 83
Gallion 83, 84, 88, 114, 168
Galloway 84
Gamery 84
Ganetson 85
Garder 84
Gardner 84
Gardners 84
Garland 84, 112
Garlon 84
Garreguies 84, 250
Garrett 84, 85
Garrettson 85, 97, 206, 243
Garrigues 84, 250
Garrison 85, 86, 249
Garson 86
Gash 86
Gatheridge 86
Gavett 86
Gelley 86
Giant 86
Gibb 86
Gibbens 86
Gibbons 86
Gibs 86
Gibson 87, 186
Giffen 87
Giffin 87

Gilbert 87, 88, 89, 90
Gilchrist 90
Giles 90, 91, 250
Gillaspey 91
Gillespay 91
Gillespie 91
Gillis 91
Gilmore 91
Gist 148, 236
Gittings 240
Givdon 91
Gladden 91
Gleen 91
Glen 91
Glenn 91
Glory 92
Gloury 92
Glyn 92
Goddin 92
Godfrey 92
Godsgrace 92
Goffey 92
Goldsmith 92
Goodwin 45, 92
Gordon 93
Gormilley 93
Gorrel 93
Gorrell 93
Gott 93
Gough 94
Gouldsmith 94
Gover 58, 94, 115
Grace 94
Grafton 94, 181, 182
Grant 95
Grates 42
Gray 95
Grayson 99
Greedland 96
Green 31, 95, 96
Greene 90
Greenhill 96
Greenland 96
Greenlee 96
Greer 96
Greme 96
Grene 96
Griffin 96, 97
Griffith 97, 118, 206, 230, 232
Grimes 97
Guff 97
Gunby 197
Guyon 97
Guyton 97, 231

Hackett 98
Hagen 98
Haig 98
Haily 98
Haley 98
Halfpenny 98
Hall 1, 7, 13, 14, 17, 18, 19, 20, 24, 27, 28, 29, 32, 36, 39, 41, 43, 46, 49, 50, 51, 54, 64, 66, 69, 77, 78, 80, 82, 83, 84, 85, 89, 91, 94, 97, 98, 99, 100, 101, 102, 103, 104, 109, 113, 114, 116, 118, 126, 127, 129, 130, 132, 133, 137, 139, 140, 141, 143, 144, 150, 154, 155, 156, 157, 162, 163, 165, 166, 171, 172, 173, 174, 177, 178, 179, 181, 186, 187, 188, 189, 193, 195, 196, 206, 208, 209, 213, 214, 216, 217, 223, 227, 230, 232, 235, 237, 238, 240, 242, 244, 245, 246, 249, 251.
Hallsall 79
Hambleton 102
Hamilton 28, 102, 198
Hamlin 102
Hammond 91, 101, 102
Hamon 102
Hampton 102
Handersides 109
Hanesey 102
Haney 102
Hanna 102, 103
Hannah 103
Hanson 45, 103, 104
Hardesty 96
Hardgrove 104
Hargrass 104
Harmer 104
Harpan 104
Harper 104
Harrington 105
Harriott 105
Harris 1, 6, 7, 8, 9, 11, 20, 24, 25, 30, 31, 35, 36, 39, 44, 46, 47, 48, 51, 52, 53, 54, 56, 58, 62, 66, 67, 68, 69, 70, 72, 73, 77, 80, 87, 93, 95, 98, 103, 105, 106, 108, 110, 113, 114, 115, 119,

Harris (continued)
120, 122, 127, 130, 131, 134, 136, 139, 141, 148, 150, 159, 161, 163, 165, 170, 172, 175, 176, 182, 186, 187, 190, 191, 198, 201, 205, 207, 212, 213, 217, 218, 219, 222, 224, 228, 231, 232, 237, 239, 242, 245, 246.
Harrison 106, 175
Harrod 106
Harry 106
Hart 106, 107
Harthey 107
Hartley 107
Haslet 107
Haslett 107
Hasset 107
Hassett 107
Hathorn 108
Hawey 107
Hawey 107
Hawkins 87, 88, 107, 108, 250
Hawley 108
Hawthorn 108
Hay 108
Hays 108
Hazel 108, 250
Hazen 36, 88
Hazle 108
Healy 108
Heany 108
Heap 108
Heaps 109, 251
Hearn 109
Heartt 106
Heaton 109
Helly 86
Hendersides 109
Henderson 66, 109
Hendon 243
Henion 110
Henley 110, 123
Henlon 110
Henry 110
Herbert 110
Herd 110
Herriott 105
Hewett 110
Hews 110
Hick 137
Hicks 110
Hill 110, 111, 236
Hillen 105

Hilliday 111
Hilton 111
Hinds 111
Hines 111, 120, 204.
Hinks 111
Hipkins 111
Hitchcock 112, 113, 225, 236, 237, 245.
Hodges 113
Hodgkins 113
Hodgskins 113
Holland 12, 13, 15, 27, 30, 34, 36, 44, 46, 47, 49, 57, 59, 66, 69, 73, 77, 82, 88, 90, 91, 94, 99, 100, 101, 102, 104, 113, 116, 121, 127, 140, 151, 156, 157, 160, 163, 166, 170, 172, 174, 179, 184, 186, 188, 189, 193, 195, 200, 204, 206, 208, 214, 216, 221, 233, 235, 236, 237, 240, 244, 245, 246, 251.
Hollingsworth 113
Hollis 113, 114
Holloway 114
Holmes 114
Home 67
Honnoll 114
Hooper 114
Hope 114, 154
Hopkins 115, 163
Hormott 115
Hormott 115
Horner 115, 251
Horton 115
Hoshal 116
Hoskins 116
Howard 101, 116, 249, 251
Howe 117, 251
Howell 19, 117
Howlett 117
Hudson 117
Huff 117
Hugeston 117
Hugg 117
Huggins 117
Hughes 100, 117, 118, 213
Hughston 118, 119
Hugins 117
Hunt 119
Hurley 119
Hurst 119
Husband 119
Huskins 119

Huston 119
Hutcheson 119
Hutchings 120
Hutchins 120
Huton 120
Hutson 120
Hynds 120

Ingram 121
Ire 121
Irons 121
Isaacs 121
Islander 121

Jackson 97, 121, 122
James 122, 123, 215
Jameson 123
Jamison 123
Jarman 123
Jarrett 123. 124
Jarves 124
Jarvis 124
Jay 124
Jebb 126
Jeffers 124
Jefferys 124
Jeffrey 124
Jeffries 125
Jenkins 125
Jerves 125
Jervis 125
Jessup 80
Jewett 125, 126
Jibb 126
Jinkins 124
Jivdon 126
Johns 70, 172
Johnson 81, 126, 127, 128, 144, 190, 243, 246
Johnston 128
Joice 130
Jolley 128
Jolly 128
Jones 57, 122, 128, 129, 130, 179
Jordan 130
Jordin 130
Jordon 130
Jourdan 130
joyce 130
Jrudir 130
Judd 130
Jyb 126

Kaiger 131
Kain 33

Kant 132
Kean 131
Kearns 131
Keeps 131
Keer 131
Keith 131, 133
Kelley 131
Kelly 131
Kemball 236
Kemble 133
Kembol 133
Kenley 131
Kenly 131
Kennard 132
Kennedy 132
Kent 132
Kerne 132
Kerns 132
Kerr 17, 40, 132
Key 132, 133
Keys 133
Kidd 133
Kimbal 133
Kimball 219, 234
Kimble 133, 134, 218
King 134
Kinnard 132
Kinneer 134
Kirby 162
Kirk 134
Kirkpatrick 134
Kirkwood 134
Kitely 134, 167
Knight 135
Knott 135
Knowlman 135
Kroesen 53, 135
Kyle 135

Lacy 135
Lafayette 60, 96, 190
Lancaster 135
Landon 135
Lane 136
Langhin 136
Larramore 136
Lary 136
Latimore 136
Latomore 136
Lattamore 136
Lattimore 136
Latomore 136
Laughlin 136
Laverty 136
Lawrence 136
Laurentz 251

Leaekin 136
Leaquer 136
Lee 136, 137, 163, 232, 251
Leecans 137
Legoe 121, 123, 137
Legs 137
Lemmon 137, 246
Lenagin 137
Leonard 137
Lerter 137
Lester 42, 137
Lettemore 136
Leviston 137
Lewes 41, 137
Lewin 128, 138
Lewis 47, 138, 251
Leyde 194
Liang 138
Lightbody 24
Ligon 138
Lilly 138
Linam 138
Lindsay 138, 139
Lindsey 138
Linsey 139
Linton 139
Little 139
Litton 139
Lively 139
Lockhart 139
Lockheard 139
Logan 139
Logne 139
Logue 139
Loney 139, 140, 251
Long 33, 140, 152, 169
Loran 140
Lorden 140
Lordon 140
Lott 140
Lovatt 141
Love 1, 2, 7, 10, 29, 30, 32, 34,
    35, 37, 41, 41, 43, 48, 52,
    60, 81, 83, 92, 95, 96, 110,
    111, 116, 126, 128, 132, 140,
    141, 151, 152, 159, 165, 175,
    179, 181, 182, 184, 188, 190,
    195, 197, 199, 201, 203, 215,
    217, 220, 221, 222, 234, 236,
    237, 239, 242, 245.
Lovell 141
Lovely 141
Lovett 141
Low 141
Lowery 142, 251, 253

Lowry 142, 251, 253
Loyd 142
Lucas 142
Lurk 142
Lushody 142
Lynch 142
Lyon 29, 142
Lytle 142, 143, 246

McAdon 143, 251
McAdoo 143
McAdow 143, 251
McArty 143   McAtee 235
McAway 143
McBride 143
McCall 143
McCandley 143
McCann 143, 144
McCanny 144
McCarty 144
McCaskey 144
McChan 144
McClain 144
McClane 144
McClelan 144
McClintock 145
McClmong 145
McCloskey 145
McClong 145
McClung 145
McClure 145
McCluse 145
McColough 145, 146
McComas 5, 146, 147, 167, 168,
    180, 204, 246, 252.
McConal 147
McConner 147
McCord 147
McCormick 27, 147
McCourtie 147
McCracken 148, 252
McCradey 148
McCreary 148
McCrery 148
McCroady 148
McCulah 148
McCulloch 148
McCullough 148, 252
McCune 148
McCurdy 148
McCure 148
McCurty 149
McDaniel 149
McDonal 149
McDonald 149

McDonnell 149
McDowns 149
McEhnen 149
McElhaney 150, 252
McElmarey 150
McFadden 150
McFaddin 150
McFaden 150
McGaw 150
McGay 150
McGeaugh 150
McGee 150
McGettegan 150
McGill 150
McGlaughlin 151, 152
McGough 150
McGrill 151
McGruigen 151
McGuire 151
McIlhinny 150, 252
McIntire 151
McIntosh 151
McKeem 158
McKalheny 150
McKell 151
McKenney 151
McKenzie 151
McKill 151
McKinley 151
McKinney 151
McKinsey 151
McKinzie 151
McKnight 151
McLaney 151, 152
McLaughlin 152
McLees 152
McMath 152
McMillan 152
McMillen 152
McMullen 152
McMurphy 152
McMurray 152
McNabb 152
McNair 152
McNamara 152
McNear 152
McNeare 153
McNeile 153
McNely 153
McNutt 153
McOwen 153
McPhail 153
McQueland 153
McSwain 153

Macamson 154
Maccubbin 101
Macken 153
Macken 153
Mackey 153
Maddin 153
Maddon 153
Madford 153
Magee 150
Mahan 153, 154
Major 154
Majors 154
Makemson 154, 252
Makimson 154
Makson 154
Manen 191
Manley 155
Manly 154, 155
Mansel 27
Marford 155
Marierty 163
Mariner 225
Markham 155
Marmold 155
Marret 155
Marsh 155, 156
Marshall 155
Martin 155
Mash 156
Mason 156
Mather 156
Mathews 156, 157, 213
Matthews 156, 157, 252
Mattocks 157
Mattox 157
Maulden 5
Maxwell 59, 67, 157, 190
May 157
Mays 157
Mead 157, 158, 190
Meads 157, 158
Meegaa 158
Meek 158
Meekmoor 158 Mefford 249
Mekeem 158
Mekemson 154
Mekmoor 158
Melanhy 158
Meloy 158
Merrarter 158
Mical 158
Michael 158
Middleton 158, 252
Miles 158, 159, 205, 245
Miller 159, 252

Millien 159
Mills 159 Milles 252
Mires 159
Mitchell 44, 159, 160, 174
Mobsler 161
Modin 161
Moffet 161
Mogan 161
Moland 161
Monahan 161
Monk 161
Monohan 161
Monroe 161
Montgomery 161
Mooberry 162
Moobry 162
Moor 162, 163
Moore 162, 167
Moores 162
Moorn 162
More 163
Morfey 165
Morford 155
Morgan 59, 90, 99, 163, 183, 246
Moriarity 163
Morris 163, 164
Morrison 164
Morrow 164
Morsell 164 Mountjoy 252
Mubery 164
Mullen 164
Multon 164
Munday 165
Mundey 165
Munroe 165
Murdock 165
Murdough 165
Murfey 165
Murphy 165
Murray 165
Nabb 252
Neal 166
Neill 166
Nelson 113, 114, 166
Newberry 166
Newman 170, 238
Night 113, 166
Ninon 166
Nixon 166
Noble 195
Noland 166
Nolstone 166
Nora 166
Norrington 167, 170
Norrinton 167

Norris 112, 167, 168, 169, 170, 189, 224, 246.
Norton 170
Norwood 101
Novinton 167
Nower 170
Nowland 170
Nutterwell 170

O'Bed 171
O'Brian 171
O'Close 171   O'Conner 252
O'Dannell 171
O'Dillen 171
Odle 171
O'Donald 171
O'Donel 171
O'Donnell 171
Offield 171
Ogle 171
O'Hara 171
O'Keil 171
Oldham 171
Oliver 171, 172, 252
O'Mullan 172
O'Neal 172
O'Neale 172   Onion 252
O'Queen 172
Ore 172
O'Reilly 172
Orr 172
Osborn 158, 172, 173
Osborne 160, 172, 173
Osbourn 173
Overman 174
Overstock 7, 174
Owens 174

Paca 1, 2, 14, 18, 24, 29, 43, 45, 46, 54, 57, 67, 68, 69, 70, 72, 73, 86, 88, 92, 100, 101, 102, 106, 107, 119, 126, 128, 129, 139, 141, 149, 151, 163, 164, 165, 166, 172, 174, 175, 177, 178, 192, 197, 199, 210, 214, 218, 221, 229, 233, 239, 241, 244, 245, 246.
Pain 175
Paine 175
Palmer 95
Pant 175
Paris 175
Park 175

Parke 175
Parker 175, 176
Parks 182
Parris 175
Parsons 169, 176
Partridge 21
Patrick 3, 4, 7, 8, 12, 13, 16, 19, 25, 37, 52, 57, 58, 61, 67, 79, 94, 108, 111, 115, 122, 129, 135, 141, 151, 152, 153, 163, 164, 165, 170, 176, 186, 187, 199, 200, 204, 211, 212, 213, 230, 234, 243, 245, 246.
Patterson 176, 177, 246
Paul 177
Payne 177
Peach 177
Pearce 177
Pearis 177
Pearson 177
Peden 177
Peiken 178
Penchieff 178
Pendall 178
Pendegast 178
Pendergrass 178
Pennick 178
Pennith 178
Pentenney 178
Perkins 178
Perry 178
Peteel 178
Peverlye 195
Phillips 178, 179
Phinney 142
Phipps 179
Phips 179
Picturn 178
Pike 179
Pillet 179   Pindell 251
Pinnick 179
Pitt 179
Plant 175
Platt 179
Poak 179
Poceer 179
Pocock 179
Pogue 211
Polson 179
Pool 180
Pope 11, 180
Porter 180
Posey 135

Potee 180, 237
Poteet 180, 181
Potter 180
Poulson 179
Pound 180
Powar 180
Power 180
Prall 180, 246
Preble 180
Presbury 59, 85, 97, 181
Preston 88, 89, 99, 160,
        181, 182, 195
Prible 180
Price 182
Prigg 183
Prim 183
Pritchard 61, 183, 184
Pritchett 184
Pryne 184
Pugh 184
Punteney 184
Putteets 181
Pyle 184

Queen 185
Quindin 185
Quinn 185
Quinnlin 185

Rain 186
Rampley 186
Ramsay 186
Ramsey 162, 186
Ranshar 186
Ranson 186
Ratagan 186
Rattican 186
Ravin 105
Rawlings 2, 24, 116, 139, 194,
         198, 206, 218, 222
Reaven 187
Reaves 187
Redding 187
Redman 187
Ree 187
Reed 187, 252
Reese 187
Reeves 187
Reid 187
Reiley 174
Reilly 187, 197
Renshaw 187, 188
Reves 188
Reynol 188
Reynolds 193

Rhoads 188
Rhodes 188
Rice 188
Richards 189
Richardson 73, 145, 167, 169, 189,
           24, 34.
Richman 190
Rickets 190
Ricketts 88, 190, 240, 252
Riddle 190
Rider 162
Riely 190
Rigbie 190
Rigdon 18, 19, 24, 25, 31, 38,
       42, 43, 51, 60, 61, 62,
       63, 65, 73, 79, 80, 82,
       86, 87, 107, 108, 111,
       117, 125, 126, 127, 128,
       129, 130, 131, 132, 136,
       138, 144, 148, 150, 159,
       163, 170, 177, 185, 190,
       191, 194, 208, 209, 225,
       230, 231, 238, 246.
Riggs 191
Riley 191, 252
Roads 191
Robbards 191
Roberts 191
Robertson 191
Robins 192
Robinson 85, 192, 193, 232, 234
Robison 113
Robson 193
Rockhold 193
Rockwell 193
Rodgers 2, 16, 24, 31, 34, 35,
        44, 45, 60, 61, 71, 73,
        76, 77, 80, 81, 86, 90,
        92, 95, 104, 111, 117,
        119, 135, 136, 141, 148,
        149, 151, 153, 155, 158,
        159, 160, 161, 165, 172,
        173, 179, 180, 184, 189,
        193, 201, 204, 212, 216,
        221, 228, 229, 231, 233,
        234, 239, 242, 245.
Roe 193
Rogers 193, 194
Rolston 194
Roney 194
Root 194
Rose 194
Rosier 235
Ross 194, 195, 238
Rowe 193
Rowland 195

Rowntree 195
Ruckman 195
Ruff 89, 181, 195
Rumage 195
Rumsey 1, 3, 8, 10, 23, 25, 29,
 41, 50, 53, 59, 63, 67,
 72, 78, 81, 82, 84, 92,
 95, 100, 105, 107, 108,
 110, 114, 116, 119, 121,
 138, 139, 157, 160, 173,
 179, 181, 182, 183, 187,
 196, 200, 202, 208, 214,
 217, 220, 222, 223, 224,
 240, 241, 242, 243, 245.
Russ 196
Russell 196
Ruth 196
Rutledge 196, 197, 252
Rutter 197
Ryan 197
Rydon 197
Rylie 197
Ryon 197

Sadler 198
Sain 198
St. Clair 198
St. Goodman 198
Sample 238
Sanders 198, 237
Sappington 198
Sargent 198
Saunders 198, 199, 224
Savage 199
Scantlin 199
Scarborough 199, 200
Scarff 200
Schivington 200
Schrife 200
Scofield 200   Scoat 200
Scott 6, 116, 140, 167, 169, 170,
 197, 200, 201, 210, 246.
Seale 201
Sears 202
Sedgwick 202
Seemer 202
Seemore 202
Selby 202
Seney 202
Sewell 202
Shagnassey 202
Shane 202
Sharp 91
Sharswood 202
Shaw 202

Shean 202
Sheanes 202
Shearer 202
Sheedy 203
Sheels 203
Shell 203   Shekell 252
Shepherd 203   Sheridan 250
Sheredin 203
Sheredine 203
Sherwood 203
Shidle 19
Shields 203
Shinton 203
Shipley 203
Short 203
Shy 204
Sicklemore 177
Silas 204
Silk 204
Silver 204
Silvers 204
Simpers 204
Simpson 192, 204
Sims 204
Sinckler 204
Sinclar 204
Singleton 204
Sinkcleare 204
Sinkler 204
Sivers 204
Sivest 204
Sivkins 204
Skell 205
Skemmett 205
Skinner 232
Skwington 205
Slack 205
Slade 31, 205, 217
Slaid 205
Slator 205
Slatry 205
Sloan 205
Small 205
Smith 46, 57, 63, 65, 81, 103,
 109, 110, 122, 134, 148,
 158, 172, 175, 188, 204,
 206, 207, 208, 209, 210,
 214, 222, 238, 245, 251, 252.
Smithe 210, 246
Smithson 71, 210, 246, 253
Smyth 210
Snoddy 210
Snodey 210
Snodgrass 211
Soward 211

Spark 211
Sparks 211
Spear 211
Speir 211
Spence 211
Spencer 211, 252
Spenser 211
Stack 211
Stafford 211
Stallings 212
Stallins 211
Standeford 120, 122, 127, 219
Standerford 212
Standiford 120, 189, 212
Standley 212
Staniford 1
Stanley 212
Stansberry 100
Stansbury 22, 205
Stapleton 212
Starr 212
Steel 212
Steele 212
Steet 213
Stenson 213
Stephens 213
Stephenson 213, 218
Sterrett 213
Steuart 213
Stevenson 213, 214
Steward 214
Stewart 179, 183, 213, 214, 217, 230, 245
Stiles 214   Styles 214
Stipleton 212
Stocksdale 214
Stokes 210, 214
Stone 215
Stooksbery 215
Stratford 215
Street 215
Strickland 215
Strode 215
Strong 215
Strowd 215
Stuart 215
Stump 215
Sturgem 216
Sturgeon 216
Sullavin 216
Sullivan 216
Suoit 216
Sutler 216
Sutton 216
Swain 216

Swann 216
Swanton 217
Swart 217
Swarts 217
Sweeney 217
Sweny 217
Swift 217
Taes 217
Talbee 217
Talbott 74, 183, 217, 253
Tannehill 218
Tanner 218
Tany 218
Tapler 218
Tare 218
Tate 218
Tavish 218
Tawlard 218
Taylor 1, 2, 8, 14, 15, 22, 27, 29, 33, 34, 35, 37, 39, 46, 48, 49, 51, 76, 77, 79, 80, 81, 82, 85, 87, 88, 89, 91, 95, 106, 109, 110, 117, 118, 120, 125, 128, 132, 136, 147, 149, 151, 155, 161, 162, 166, 168, 169, 170, 171, 177, 185, 189, 190, 191, 192, 198, 210, 212, 219, 220, 224, 228, 237, 241, 244, 245, 246, 253.
Tayn 220
Teats 220
Tench 220
Terrey 220
Thacker 220
Thomas 95, 103, 220, 221, 253
Thompson 71, 221, 222
Thomson 222
Thoriman 222
Thornton 222
Thurston 222
Tiarney 222
Tilbrook 223
Timmons 223
Tinny 223
Todd 223
Tolby 72
Tollenger 223
Tolley 99, 181, 223, 243
Tomby 223
Tonte 223
Toole 223
Tootle 174
Toppey 223

Tossett 223
Toulson 223
Tout 223
Toute 223
Tower 166
Townley 224
Townsley 224
Tracey 224
Travis 224
Treadway 224
Tredwell 224
Trene 224
Treno 224
Trickert 224
Trons 224
Troter 224
Trotter 224
Truelock 225
Truss 225
Try 225
Tucker 225
Tuckin 225
Tuder 225
Turk 225
Turner 225, 226
Tush 226
Tweedell 226
Twining 226
Tyndall 226

Usher 226

Vaghan 49, 227
VanBibber 226
Vance 226
Vancleave 227
VanCleve 207
Vandegrift 227
Vandergrift 227
Vanghan 227
Vanhorn 154, 212, 227
Vanhorne 140
Vann 227
Vansickle 227
Vansukler 227
Vantworth 228
Vanzant 228
Varney 228
Vaughn 227
Veach 228
Verney 228
Vogan 139, 228

Wadlow 228
Wailey 228
Wakeling 228

Walcott 228
Waldron 228
Walker 228, 229
Walkins 229
Wallace 57, 229
Wallingsford 229
Walsh 229
Waltham 119, 229
Wamagin 229
Wann 229, 253
Ward 131, 142, 230, 246
Ware 230
Warfield 230
Warman 230   Warner 230
Warnock 230
Warrick 230, 231
Warwick 230, 231
Wary 232
Washington 167, 168, 175
Waters 230
Watters 62, 250
Watkins 231
Watson 231
Watt 231
Watts 231
Wavy 232
Wayne 7
Wear 232
Webb 2, 6, 13, 16, 18, 28, 34,
      42, 53, 54, 67, 69, 73, 74,
      78, 79, 84, 85, 88, 90, 96,
      98, 107, 119, 121, 122, 125,
      130, 134, 138, 139, 141,
      143, 148, 149, 150, 153,
      155, 162, 164, 165, 176,
      178, 190, 193, 199, 204,
      207, 208, 209, 211, 219,
      220, 222, 224, 232, 235,
      238, 240, 241, 242, 243,
      245, 246.
Webster 19, 44, 88, 90, 91, 126,
      191, 208, 232, 233, 22.
Wedoney 233
Weeks 233
Welch 233
Wells 183, 187, 233
Welsh 233
West 136, 234
Wetherall 234
Whaler 235
Wheeler 10, 16, 17, 105, 235, 236
Whelan 236
Whitacre 236, 237
Whitaker 97, 205, 236, 237, 246,
White 98, 175, 237, 238   253.
Whiteaker 236, 237

Whitefeatt 238
Whiteflatt 238
Whiteford 238
Whiterker 238
Whiting 238
Whitlatch 238
Whitney 171
Wiggins 238
Wigings 238
Wild 239   Wiles 250
Wilgers 239
Wilgus 239
Wilkinson 239
Willard 239
Williams 109, 159, 160, 239, 249
Williamson 239
Willnoth 240
Willson 241
Wilmer 240
Wilmere 240
Wilmoth 240
Wilmott 240, 253
Wilson 19, 240, 241
Winfred 241
Wise 242
Wood 242
Woodard 242
Wooddogy 242

Wooden 242
Woodland 242
Woods 242
Woodward 242
Woolen 242, 243
Woollin 243
Woolling 217, 243
Woolmere 243
Woolsey 243
Worrell 243
Worrick 230
Worsby 243
Worster 243
Worthington 115, 243
Wrain 243
Wraine 243
Wright 136, 243, 244

Yardley 244
Yates 101, 244
Yeaman 244
Yoe 244
Yorke 1
Young 45, 67, 98, 99, 165, 182, 197, 244
Younge 244
Younger 244

Other books by the author:

A Closer Look at St. John's Parish Registers [Baltimore County, Maryland], 1701-1801
A Collection of Maryland Church Records
A Guide to Genealogical Research in Maryland: 5th Edition, Revised and Enlarged
Abstracts of the Ledgers and Accounts of the Bush Store and Rock Run Store, 1759-1771
Abstracts of the Orphans Court Proceedings of Harford County, 1778-1800
Abstracts of Wills, Harford County, Maryland, 1800-1805
Baltimore City [Maryland] Deaths and Burials, 1834-1840
Baltimore County, Maryland, Overseers of Roads, 1693-1793
Bastardy Cases in Baltimore County, Maryland, 1673-1783
Bastardy Cases in Harford County, Maryland, 1774-1844
Bible and Family Records of Harford County, Maryland Families: Volume V
Children of Harford County: Indentures and Guardianships, 1801-1830
Colonial Delaware Soldiers and Sailors, 1638-1776
*Colonial Families of the Eastern Shore of Maryland
Volumes 5, 6, 7, 8, 9, 11, 12, 13, 14, and 16*
Colonial Maryland Soldiers and Sailors, 1634-1734
Dr. John Archer's First Medical Ledger, 1767-1769, Annotated Abstracts
Early Anglican Records of Cecil County
*Early Harford Countians, Individuals Living in Harford County, Maryland in Its Formative Years
Volume 1: A to K, Volume 2: L to Z, and Volume 3: Supplement*
Harford County Taxpayers in 1870, 1872 and 1883
Harford County, Maryland Divorce Cases, 1827-1912: An Annotated Index
Heirs and Legatees of Harford County, Maryland, 1774-1802
Heirs and Legatees of Harford County, Maryland, 1802-1846
Inhabitants of Baltimore County, Maryland, 1763-1774
Inhabitants of Cecil County, Maryland, 1649-1774
Inhabitants of Harford County, Maryland, 1791-1800
Inhabitants of Kent County, Maryland, 1637-1787
*Joseph A. Pennington & Co., Havre De Grace, Maryland Funeral Home Records:
Volume II, 1877-1882, 1893-1900*
Maryland Bible Records, Volume 1: Baltimore and Harford Counties
Maryland Bible Records, Volume 2: Baltimore and Harford Counties
Maryland Bible Records, Volume 3: Carroll County
Maryland Bible Records, Volume 4: Eastern Shore
Maryland Deponents, 1634-1799
Maryland Deponents: Volume 3, 1634-1776
*Maryland Public Service Records, 1775-1783: A Compendium of Men and Women of
Maryland Who Rendered Aid in Support of the American Cause against
Great Britain during the Revolutionary War*
*Marylanders to Carolina: Migration of Marylanders to
North Carolina and South Carolina prior to 1800*

Marylanders to Kentucky, 1775-1825

Methodist Records of Baltimore City, Maryland: Volume 1, 1799-1829

Methodist Records of Baltimore City, Maryland: Volume 2, 1830-1839

Methodist Records of Baltimore City, Maryland: Volume 3, 1840-1850 (East City Station)

More Maryland Deponents, 1716-1799

More Marylanders to Carolina: Migration of Marylanders to North Carolina and South Carolina prior to 1800

More Marylanders to Kentucky, 1778-1828

Outpensioners of Harford County, Maryland, 1856-1896

Presbyterian Records of Baltimore City, Maryland, 1765-1840

Quaker Records of Baltimore and Harford Counties, Maryland, 1801-1825

Quaker Records of Northern Maryland, 1716-1800

Quaker Records of Southern Maryland, 1658-1800

Revolutionary Patriots of Anne Arundel County, Maryland

Revolutionary Patriots of Baltimore Town and Baltimore County, 1775-1783

Revolutionary Patriots of Calvert and St. Mary's Counties, Maryland, 1775-1783

Revolutionary Patriots of Caroline County, Maryland, 1775-1783

Revolutionary Patriots of Cecil County, Maryland

Revolutionary Patriots of Charles County, Maryland, 1775-1783

Revolutionary Patriots of Delaware, 1775-1783

Revolutionary Patriots of Dorchester County, Maryland, 1775-1783

Revolutionary Patriots of Frederick County, Maryland, 1775-1783

Revolutionary Patriots of Harford County, Maryland, 1775-1783

Revolutionary Patriots of Kent and Queen Anne's Counties

Revolutionary Patriots of Lancaster County, Pennsylvania

Revolutionary Patriots of Maryland, 1775-1783: A Supplement

Revolutionary Patriots of Maryland, 1775-1783: Second Supplement

Revolutionary Patriots of Montgomery County, Maryland, 1776-1783

Revolutionary Patriots of Prince George's County, Maryland, 1775-1783

Revolutionary Patriots of Talbot County, Maryland, 1775-1783

Revolutionary Patriots of Worcester and Somerset Counties, Maryland, 1775-1783

Revolutionary Patriots of Washington County, Maryland, 1776-1783

St. George's (Old Spesutia) Parish, Harford County, Maryland: Church and Cemetery Records, 1820-1920

St. John's and St. George's Parish Registers, 1696-1851

Survey Field Book of David and William Clark in Harford County, Maryland, 1770-1812

The Crenshaws of Kentucky, 1800-1995

The Delaware Militia in the War of 1812

Union Chapel United Methodist Church Cemetery Tombstone Inscriptions, Wilna, Harford County, Maryland

www.ingramcontent.com/pod-product-compliance
Lightning Source LLC
Chambersburg PA
CBHW071659160426
43195CB00012B/1520